CLASS IN AMERICA

CLASS IN AMERICA
AN ENCYCLOPEDIA

Volume 1: A–G

EDITED BY
ROBERT E. WEIR

GREENWOOD PRESS
Westport, Connecticut • London

Library of Congress Cataloging-in-Publication Data

Class in America : an encyclopedia / edited by Robert E. Weir.
   p. cm.
  Includes bibliographical references and index.
  ISBN-13: 978-0-313-33719-2 (set : alk. paper)
  ISBN-13: 978-0-313-33720-8 (v. 1 : alk. paper)
  ISBN-13: 978-0-313-33721-5 (v. 2 : alk. paper)
  ISBN-13: 978-0-313-34245-5 (v. 3 : alk. paper)
  1. Social classes—United States—Encyclopedias. 2. Social classes—United States—
History—Encyclopedias. 3. United States—Social conditions—Encyclopedias. I. Weir,
Robert E., 1952-
  HN90.S6C564 2007
  305.50973'03—dc22   2007008193

British Library Cataloguing in Publication Data is available.

Library of Congress Catalog Card Number: 2007008193

ISBN-10: 0–313–33719–5 (set)   ISBN-13: 978–0–313–33719–2 (set)
       0–313–33720–9 (vol 1)   978–0–313–33720–8 (vol 1)
       0–313–33721–7 (vol 2)   978–0–313–33721–5 (vol 2)
       0–313–34245–8 (vol 3)   978–0–313–34245–5 (vol 3)

First published in 2007

Greenwood Press, 88 Post Road West, Westport, CT 06881
An imprint of Greenwood Publishing Group, Inc.
www.greenwood.com

Printed in the United States of America

The paper used in this book complies with the
Permanent Paper Standard issued by the National
Information Standards Organization (Z39.48–1984).

10 9 8 7 6 5 4 3 2 1

CONTENTS

Alphabetical List of Entries

TOPICAL LIST OF ENTRIES

Books/Journals/Media

Appeal to Reason
Fortune magazine
The Grapes of Wrath
The Great Gatsby
The Hidden Injuries of Class
Invisible Man
The Jungle
literature
The Man in the Gray Flannel Suit
Middletown
media

muckraking
newspaper mergers
The Other America
proletarian literature
The Rise of Silas Lapham
Stiffed
Tally's Corner
The Undeserving Poor
Wall Street Journal
Wealth against Commonwealth

Classes

business aristocracy
bourgeoisie
caste
corporate class
lower class
managerial class
masses
middling sorts
middle class

natural aristocracy
petite/petty bourgeoisie
race, racism, and racial stratification
robber barons
ruling class
servant class
underclass
upper class
working class

Cultural Practices/Debates/Values

accents
American dream
anti-Semitism

art
begging and busking
bilingualism

Irish Americans
Ivy League
Jewish Americans
Ku Klux Klan
labor movement
Latinos and Hispanics
lobbyists
men's clubs
migrant labor
Mormons
NAACP
Native Americans
New Deal coalition

New Left
new middle class
New York Yankees
nonprofits
organization man
pawnbrokers
Reagan Democrats
Skull & Bones
Social Register
Socialist Party
socialite
special interests
women's clubs

Groups (Historical)

American Federation of Labor
American Revolution
Bacon's Rebellion
Boston Brahmins
Bill of Rights
Bracero Program
cattle kingdom
Civil War
Congress of Industrial Organizations
    (CIO)
Dorr Rebellion
factory system
Federalist Party
founding fathers
Gilded Age
Great Depression
Great Society
immigration
indentured servitude
Industrial Revolution
Industrial Workers of the
    World
Jacksonian democracy
Katrina
Knights of Labor
Lowell millworkers
McCarthyism
Molly Maguires
municipal socialism
New Deal

New Deal coalition
New Left
new social history
Okies
populists
Poor People's March
Progressive Era
Prohibition
Puritans
Reconstruction
Red Diaper Babies
Red Scare
rent strikes
robber barons
Seneca Falls convention
settlement houses
sharecroppers and tenant
    farmers
Shays's rebellion
single-tax
sit-down strikes/sit-ins
slavery
slavocracy
Social Darwinism
Social Gospel
Southern Baptists
Southern Tenant Farmers Union
    (STFU)
Students for a Democratic
    Society (SDS)

Victorianism
Wagner Act
War on Poverty

westward expansion
Whiskey Rebellion

People

Abbott, Edith and Grace
Adams family
Addams, Jane
Alger, Horatio
Althusser, Louis
Aronowitz, Stanley
Astor, John Jacob
Auchincloss, Louis
Baltzell, E. Digby
Bellamy, Edward
Berger, Victor
Bernstein, Jared
Blau, Peter Michael
Bluestone, Barry
Bourdieu, Pierre
Brace, Charles Loring
Buchanan, Pat
Bush family
Carnegie, Andrew
Chomsky, Noam
Cloward, Richard Andrew
Coles, Robert
Commons, John R.
Dahrendorf, Ralf
Day, Dorothy
Domhoff, G. William, Jr.
Dreiser, Theodore
Drury, Victor
Du Bois, W. E. B.
Dye, Thomas
Ehrenreich, Barbara
Farrell, James
Flynn, Elizabeth Gurley
Galbraith, John Kenneth
Gates, Bill
George, Henry
Giddens, Anthony
Gilman, Charlotte Perkins
Gold, Mike
Goldman, Emma

Goldthorpe, John
Gompers, Samuel
Grant, Madison
Guthrie, Woody
Harrington, Michael
Haywood, "Big" Bill
Hearst family
Howe, Irving
Hutchinson, Anne
James, Henry
James, Jesse
Kennedy family
Kerbo, Harold
Keynes, John Maynard
King, Martin Luther, Jr.
Kozol, Jonathan
Lathrop, Julia
Lenski, Gerhard
Lewis, John L.
Lewis, Sinclair
Lipset, Seymour Martin
London, Jack
Long, Huey P.
Lowell, Josephine Shaw
Lowell family
Lynd, Robert and Helen
Marcantonio, Vito
Meany, George
Mellon family
Mill, John Stuart
Mills, C. Wright
Moore, Wilbert
Morgan, J. P.
Myers, Gustavus
Myrdal, Gunnar
Nader, Ralph
Norris, Frank
O'Hare, Kate Richards
Parsons, Albert R. and Lucy
Parsons, Talcott

Pesotta, Rose
Piven, Frances Fox
Polanyi, Karl
Poulantzas, Nicos
Powderly, Terence
Presley, Elvis
Reagan, Ronald
Reuther, Walter
Rifkin, Jeremy
Riis, Jacob
Robertson, Pat
Rockefeller family
Roosevelt, Eleanor
Roosevelt, Franklin D.
Roosevelt, Theodore
Rustin, Bayard
Sanders, Bernard
Sanger, Margaret
Schor, Juliet
Seeger, Pete
Sennett, Richard
Sinclair, Upton
Simmel, Georg

Sombart, Werner
Springsteen, Bruce
Steffens, Lincoln
Stokes, Rose Pastor
Stone, I. F.
Terkel, Studs
Thernstrom, Abigail and Stephan
Thomas, Norman
Thurow, Lester
Trump, Donald
Vanderbilt family
Veblen, Thorstein
Wald, Lillian
Wallerstein, Immanuel
Warner, W. Lloyd
Weber, Max
Wharton, Edith
Wilson, William Julius
Winfrey, Oprah
Winthrop, John
Wright, Richard
Zinn, Howard

Places

Appalachia
Armories
Beacon Hill
community colleges
company town
country clubs
edge cities
ethnic enclaves
Fifth Avenue
gated communities
ghetto
Hamptons
Harlem

inner cities
Ivy League
Levittown
Newport
Nob Hill
parochial schools
regionalism
Seven Sisters
Silicon Valley
slums
suburbia
Tuxedo Park
zones of transition

Political Ideologies

anarchism
democracy

legitimation
Leninism

Maoism

Reagan Democrats

socialism

Trotskyists

Public Policy and Debate

antitrust laws

bilingualism

Bill of Rights

campaign financing

casinos

child labor

children and poverty

comparable worth

competitiveness

crime

deindustrialization

disenfranchisement

drug policy

Economic Opportunity
    Act of 1964 (EOA)

education

entitlements

environmentalism

equity pay

ethnic stratification

feminization of poverty

flat tax

free trade

gender stratification

gentrification

gold

guaranteed annual income

Head Start

home ownership

homelessness

housing policies

immigration

inheritance taxes

institutionalized discrimination

Job Corps

job training

justice (civil)

Katrina

law of the jungle

legitimation

life expectancy

living wage

literacy

lotteries

medical care

minimum wage

monopoly

municipal socialism

one-parent families

outsourcing

ownership society

pluralism

poverty calculations

poverty line

progressive/regressive
    taxation

race, racism, and racial stratification

school tracking

school vouchers

segregation

slums

small business/farms

Social Security

special interests

strikes

taxation

think tanks

trickle-down theory

Two Americas

underclass

urban renewal

voluntarism

voting rights

Wagner Act

War on Poverty

wealth

welfare

white-collar work

working poor

zoning

Social Institutions/Practices

academia

advertising

agrarianism

capitalism

civil service

community colleges

country clubs

democracy

education

faith-based charities

family trust

foreign policy establishment

foundations

higher education

Job Corps

Planned Parenthood

Seven Sisters

Social Security

stock market

suburbia

vo-tech schools

welfare

zoning

Theories and Concepts

achievement and ascription

alienation

American dream

American exceptionalism

anti-Semitism

assimilation

authority

capitalism

class consciousness

class formation

class struggle

class subcultures

classism

comparable worth

competitiveness

conflict theory

conspicuous consumption

consumerism

continuous/discontinuous views
    of class

contradictory class location

creationism

creative destruction

critical elite theory

cultural capital

cultural tourism

culture of poverty

Davis-Moore thesis

deindustrialization

democracy

ethnic stratification

false consciousness

feminization of poverty

flat tax

free trade

functional elite theory

glass ceiling

globalization

guaranteed annual income

hegemony theory

high culture

income and wealth

individualism

inequality theory

institutional discrimination

maldistribution of wealth

Marxism/Marxists

means of production

meritocracy

military-industrial complex

mudsill theory

new social history

objective method of determining
    class

ownership society

patriotism

PREFACE

Class in America: An Encyclopedia is both a general reference work and an invitation for dialogue. The 525 entries contained herein are aimed not at academic specialists or advanced researchers but rather at the larger reading public, students commencing projects, anyone seeking quick overviews of various subjects, and those who define themselves as curious but uniformed. The tone has been kept objective, and, to the degree possible, entries have been stripped of arcane references, specialist terms, the minutia of academic debate, and overly complex prose. Nor does this work intend to be comprehensive; the entries were chosen more for diversity than for blanket coverage of any single focus. We did not even choose the most "obvious" selections in some cases because we didn't want to get bogged down in conference-like debates over individuals and the "deeper significance" of their work. For example, there are entries on Marxism as an analytical category and on various Marxist organizations but none on Karl Marx himself. Marx has inspired encyclopedias devoted to his work, and there is little point in treading beaten paths. Moreover, we wanted to illumine how history and ideas have played out on American soil rather than engaging in philosophical and ideological debate. The goal, in short, is to paint in broad strokes rather than with a fine-point brush.

Many of the contributors to this volume are distinguished within their fields, and each is an admirable scholar. I thank each of them for sharing their expertise, hard work, and knowledge. The decision to adopt a less formal tone is laid out in more detail in the introduction that follows, but in essence it relates to a desire to have a discourse on social class in America. Many top-notch studies reveal that the United States is deeply stratified by social class, and some of the brightest minds available have wrestled with what that means and what—if anything—should be done about it. The *reality* of social stratification is, however, quite a different matter from *awareness* of class.

Even those who know about class are often quite confused about how to negotiate or discuss it. Is the gap between the rich and poor a social problem, or is it a confirmation that the promise of American opportunity actually works? Is materialism burying us under a mountain of debt, or is it responsible for accessorizing our homes with conveniences and luxuries that would have been the envy of the princes and pashas of the past? Are rich elites robbing us blind, or are they paving the road to mass prosperity? And who, exactly, are those rich people? What do we mean when we toss out terms such as upper class, the power elite, or the business class? Does a corporate class exist and, if so, how does it differ from the managerial class?

Scholars debate the very terms of discourse, but the general public often opts for what I call the Great Denial; that is, it simply embraces the oft-repeated cliché that America is a middle-class society. Although there are some surveys that phrase questions in such a way that respondents will consider calling themselves "working class," that term is not in vogue with most Americans. For better or worse—mostly the latter—tens of millions of Americans are most comfortable labeling themselves middle class regardless of the myriad absurdities this causes. If some look at this work and find popular entries to be idiosyncratic, we can only reply that class is refracted through too many American lenses to allow us to ignore the widely recognized ones.

About This Encyclopedia

In the front matter are two lists to help readers find entries of interest right off: an Alphabetical List of Entries and a Topical List of Entries. The 525 signed entries each end with a Suggested Reading section, for those interested in further research. A Bibliographical Essay can be found at the end of Volume 3.

ACKNOWLEDGMENTS

As editor and principal writer of this work, I owe a great debt to many people and groups. To reiterate an earlier point, my heartfelt appreciation goes out to all who contributed articles. These volumes simply could not exist without them. Gratitude also goes to those tireless editors, proofreaders, photo researchers, accountants, and support staff at Greenwood whose names don't appear in this book but who are nonetheless the adhesive that gave it shape just as surely as the glue that binds the spine. I offer a special thank-you to my chief contact at Greenwood, Wendi Schnaufer, who served as equal part senior editor and chief cheerleader. Gratitude also goes out to Susie Yates and her crackerjack copyediting crew at Publication Services. Thanks also to the history and American studies departments at Smith College and to Commonwealth College at the University of Massachusetts–Amherst, all of whom took me on when I left a tenured job in order to pursue new challenges. Thanks for helping me pay the bills! Thanks also to my engaging colleagues at those schools and to my many undergraduate students who inspired me with their questions, comments, and observations. To those who despair of America's youth I offer some simple advice: you need to get out more! The young women and men I have had the honor of teaching give me great hope for America's future.

Gratitude goes out to Rick Fantasia of the sociology department at Smith College and Dan Czitrom from the history department at Mount Holyoke College, both of whom gave valuable feedback on choosing entry categories. Thanks also to Ron Story of the history department at the University of Massachusetts–Amherst, who early on considered tackling this project. I can only hope that the end result comes close to what Ron might have done.

Finally, love and hugs to my wife Emily, who has endured still another of the endless projects into which I am constantly immersing myself and who has to listen to my digressions, complaints, and questions. She is my touchstone and anchor.

Robert E. Weir,
Northampton, MA

INTRODUCTION

Is the United States of America divided by social class? Ask academics and social reformers such a question and nearly all of them will reply, "of course." Ask the proverbial person on the street, though, and consensus melts. Unlike race and gender—the other two pillars of social history and social science analysis—class lacks many of the visible markers that seep into social awareness. The very title of SUNY economics professor Michael Zweig's *The Working Class Majority: America's Best Kept Secret* (2000) sums up one of the many problems associated with studying class in modern America. Zweig argues that the working class dwarfs the middle class, a revelation that would shock most Americans who presume they are middle class. He also cites a 1998 Roper Poll in which 53 percent of those polled self-identified as members of the working class. That figure raises eyebrows among those who study class, many of whom have not actually heard the term "working class" used in conversation outside of university and organized labor circles in decades!

There is an often-told story about the 2000 presidential election that—like so many accounts of that fiasco—might be apocryphal. It centers on West Virginia, a state where Vice President Al Gore spent little time campaigning. After all, except for Ronald Reagan's landslide in 1984, West Virginia had gone Democratic in every election since 1928, and the party's electoral roll was twice as large as that of the GOP. President Bill Clinton had carried the state easily in both 1992 and 1996, and Gore carried endorsements from powerful West Virginia Senator Harry Byrd and the American Federation of Labor–Congress of Industrial Organizations, which had a large presence in the state. In the end, though, George W. Bush carried West Virginia by 52 percent to 46 percent and thus claimed its five electoral votes. Those five votes were Bush's precise margin of victory in the Electoral College (271–266) after the legal dust settled from Florida's disputed results.

As the story goes, during one of Gore's rare appearances in West Virginia, he spoke of how Clinton-era prosperity was good for the country, but there were still challenges to overcome. In West Virginia he emphasized the need for a higher minimum wage, for government support programs aimed at the less fortunate, and for the need to help all Americans enjoy the American dream. When Gore spoke of helping the underprivileged, his audiences applauded. What they did *not* do was grasp the fact that Gore was talking about them.

The story may well be a latter-day folk tale, but it highlights one of the biggest problems in studying class in America: separating fact from perception. Objectively speaking, Al Gore *should* have rolled over Bush in such a historically blue-collar and unionized state. Where, one wonders, was class consciousness hiding in West Virginia? The dilemma facing all of us who contributed to this work is a thorny one: millions of Americans either ignore social class altogether or, from the scholar's point of view, horribly misinterpret it. Put directly, most social scientists agree that American society is deeply stratified, but most American citizens deny it. Few would refute the presence of the poor or the ultra-rich, but a key part of the modern American myth is that both poor and rich are small groups, and that most Americans belong to the middle class. From this perspective, the poor exist to warn of the dangers of idleness, substance abuse, and antisocial behavior, while the wealthy locate a place in the popular imagination not unlike the leprechaun's pot of gold. If one follows the rainbow path of hard work, perseverance, and rugged individualism, one will perhaps get lucky and gain fortune. Even many who profess to despise the rich as profligate, arrogant, and uncaring nonetheless aspire to join their ranks in the sincere belief that they would handle wealth better.

These reference groups—one negative, one positive—notwithstanding, most polls—including that of the National Center for Opinion research—disagree with Zweig's figures and reveal that vast sections of the American public believe they are middle class. They cling to such thinking irrespective of the jobs, salaries, and property they hold (or do *not* hold). More than one-third of those who make less than $15,000 per year nonetheless *think* they are members of the middle class, but so too do many of those making more than $200,000, according to a 2005 *New York Times* poll. From the standpoint of self-esteem it is understandable why few of those with low incomes would wish to identify with the lower class, but the reluctance of those in high-income brackets to claim their place in the upper class is more puzzling. It may well be that both groups are confused by the way views on class have been skewed across time. The poor are tainted by suspicions of laziness and low intelligence; the rich by frivolity, profligacy, and corruption. If historian Martin Burke is correct in *The Conundrum of Class* (1995), since the mid-nineteenth century the middle class has been assumed to be the repository of positive values such as hard work, concern for family, morality, civic virtue, charity, common sense, and thrift. Indeed, the middle class is often viewed as the very seedbed from which the American meritocracy is plucked.

But who does determine classes? How many are there? Is there a separate "managerial class"? Does it differ from the "business aristocracy"? Do we subdivide classes to account for obvious differences? Should a real estate developer who makes $150,000 and moguls such as Bill Gates or Donald Trump all be lumped in the upper class? Are Gates and Trump even members of the upper class? (They wouldn't have been considered so in an earlier age; they lack the proper family credentials and breeding.) Does it make sense to assign values to inanimate categories such as class? Defining class has been elusive since the American Revolution. The founders of the new republic jettisoned British class distinctions as well as its government. In theory, the lack of a birth aristocracy or customary gentry made the United States a meritocracy in which all status was achieved rather than ascribed. In practice, however, powerful families have often acted in an imperious fashion and have taken advantage of favorable taxation and inheritance laws. Families such as the Cabots, Lowells, Rockefellers, Kennedys, and Bushes have been de facto aristocracies. The failure (or refusal) of many Americans to recognize this frequently baffles foreign observers and frustrates scholars.

The traditional indicators of class are wealth, power, and prestige, but even these may be social science markers from an earlier era in which the discourse about class was considerably more informed than it is now. How does one classify, for example, police officers and firefighters? In many cities such individuals are now professionals with six-figure salaries. Are they members of the middle class? What about blue-collar auto workers in Michigan who make more than public school teachers? Even more problematic is the fact that many American families sustain material lifestyles consistent with middle-class status by assuming consumer credit debt. Do such examples and trends muddy the definition of the middle class to such a degree that it is meaningless as a social category?

Category dilemmas such as these have led many scholars to conclude that objective measures of class—wealth, power, and prestige—must take into account subjective and reputational factors that locate social class, at least to some extent, in the eyes of the beholder. After all, even Marxists agree that "class consciousness" is central to class formation. But how does one measure subjective factors, and what happens when objectivity is ignored? How can one hope to have a substantive discussion about class if we collapse distinctions and allow self-ranking? (Any teacher who has ever allowed students to grade themselves on an assignment knows the problems associated with self-evaluation.) Moreover, what happens when fashion dictates the terms of discourse? Fewer Americans now proclaim themselves "working class," a distinction that was once a source of pride for many and, according to Zweig, the objective reality of the majority of contemporary Americans. These days, if used at all, the term is often tinged with a note of tragedy. There were, for example, references to the neglected working class in the wake of Hurricane Katrina, but the term was used in such an imprecise manner that it was often a synonym for the poor.

The best one can say is that objective class measurements provide categories that millions of Americans reject, and subjective methods tell us more about perception than reality. There are, additionally, a host of other factors that mediate how class is constructed and perceived, such as age, ideology, race, gender, ethnicity, religion, regional identity, and politics. Some would argue that environmentalists, feminists, teens, suburbanites, the elderly, and others are distinct social classes. This assertion has merit, if one considers a class to be a community of shared interests, concerns, values, and challenges. But this classification too is fraught with analytical difficulty. Radical feminists, for example, blame sexism for the alarming poverty statistics on female-headed households and might posit an overthrow of patriarchy as its solution. Socialist feminists, by contrast, often subsume sexism within a Marxist framework that sees capitalism as the culprit. Which is it? And how does one even begin to negotiate the slippery terrain in which factors such as gender, race, and ethnicity are presumed to be more important than social class? Nor should anyone ignore the ideological constraints on class discourse. Liberals often complain that, the moment they raise issues of inequality, conservatives accuse them of promoting class warfare. Conservatives counter that liberals focus on doom-and-gloom rather than progress. Political candidates, regardless of ideology, depend on the well-heeled to back their campaigns; media outlets, no matter their editorial preferences, depend upon advertisers to keep them afloat.

This encyclopedia will delight some and infuriate others, depending on how one thinks class ought to be approached (or avoided). Because the national dialogue on class is contentious, we have opted to look at class from a variety of traditional perspectives: economic, historical, and sociological. But we have also included references from popular culture and everyday conversations. Thus, we have entries on Pierre Bourdieu and Oprah Winfrey, Fifth Avenue and Wal-Mart, the stock market, and shopping, for example. Given the diversity of opinion, we tried to think of how a people unaccustomed to thinking about class at all might encounter the very concept, hence our decision to survey popular culture as well as academic tomes.

It is not easy to deal with collective amnesia, nor can one consistently rely upon the time-honored methods of studying class. Take education, for example. There used to be a discernible earnings gap between those with a college degree and those without, and the very possession of a degree often conferred middle-class status. There are still income differences, but there is considerably less consistency or predictability about the importance of education. In today's climate of contingency labor, a machine operator lacking a high-school degree earns far more than an adjunct college professor. Once there were predictable educational attainment voting differences; there was a positive correlation between education and liberalism. In the 2000 election, however, those without a high-school diploma preferred Gore by 59 to 39 percent and those with college degrees went for Bush by a 51 to 45 percent margin.

Election 2000 data reflect changes in American society that mediate class analysis. Take for instance, the Marxian notion that manual workers are likely to become alienated from their labor. That group was supposed to develop class consciousness when it realized that the owning classes were exploiting workers. In the 2000 election, however, roughly 55 percent of all blue-collar voters identified themselves as economic conservatives, a rate nearly identical to that of managers. Thus, the very constituency to which Gore pitched his message saw his economic populism as too radical. To put it glibly, the workers of the world were not disposed to unite.

The election also showed that class opinion makers were changing. Predictably, Gore won the organized labor union vote handily, 59 percent to Bush's 37. In past decades that would have carried West Virginia, but given that labor unions now represent just 13 percent of American workers, the bulk of wage earners are subject to other influences. Increasingly the views of conservative ideologues have come into play. In 2000, 56 percent of all blue-collar workers identified themselves as religious and moral conservatives. Bush won the Protestant vote by 56 to 42 percent and lost the Roman Catholic vote by just 50 to 47 percent. (In 2004 Bush won the Catholic vote even though his opponent, John Kerry, was a Catholic.)

Some political observers argue that the Gore campaign based its electoral strategy on antiquated notions of class and ideology. The Gore campaign spent a considerable amount of time addressing what was perceived to be a working-class agenda: jobs, wages, movable capital. By contrast, Bush spent nearly one-third of his time talking about values, and the Republican National Committee spent

35 percent of its budget on advertisements about character and virtue. Gore's campaign workers behaved as if unions were the dominant institution in West Virginia when, in fact, it was churches. They acted from the assumption that blue-collar workers would vote their economic self-interest; instead, many embraced the conservative economic brief that workers were best served by business incentives and tax cuts for the wealthy.

None of this is meant to pass judgment on West Virginia voters, but rather to remind us that social class is complex. It is easy to saddle blue-collar workers with hazy class awareness, but are self-styled intellectuals any more enlightened? In a trenchant 2005 review of authors such as Tom Wolfe and Curtis Sittenfeld, Professor Walter Benn Michaels marvels over the ways in which American writers construct stories set in elite schools and affluent neighborhoods as though these are the norm. But the professoriate has been little better. Social scientists and humanists assert that race, gender, and class are the big three of social analysis. At least, that is what they say. In practice, class is often the poor relative who occasionally comes to visit and must be tolerated.

Since the 1970s, identity politics has had an impact on the intellectual community as thoroughly as on society as a whole. Thus, while scholars *claim* that race, gender, and class are inextricably linked, they *write* as if race and gender matter more. It is exceedingly rare to find black scholars who, following the lead of W. E. B. Du Bois, overtly link economic exploitation to the construction of racism. One will, however, find African American scholars, such as Stephen J. Carter, who seek to decouple economics and race and argue that affirmative action programs and race-based initiatives are a *cause* of modern racism.

Similarly, although many gender studies are quick to point out the economic dislocation of women in American society, most take it as a given that sexism trumps class in explaining it. Only socialist feminists and a handful of popular writers such as Barbara Ehrenreich bother to follow the money trail to see who, exactly, benefits from keeping women in economic thralldom.

Our purpose is not to criticize other scholars, nor is it to topple racial and gender paradigms and reify class in its stead. Rather it is to suggest that, if we are to make sense of social class in modern America, we must look at the roots of how class has been discussed across the political and social spectrum in the past and acknowledge that present-day conceptions, constructions, and awareness of class are multilayered and maddeningly inconsistent.

If one looks to social scientists for help in understanding class, the results are often disappointing. As noted earlier, most agree that social class is important and that American society is stratified. Beyond this there is little agreement. What, for example, is the median income in America? It depends on whether you mean *individual* income, or *family* income, and it depends on which source you consult. Is the poverty rate 13 percent, the official level, or closer to 20 percent, as some researchers assert? There is no consensus on how many classes there are, what they are, how much they earn, what defines them, or how they matter.

In 1966 sociologist Gerhard Lenski outlined the debate over social class. He juxtaposed arguments for dismantling stratification—injustice, inequality, the tendency to elevate ascribed status over merit, the stifling of potential—against those that saw class as natural and positive. Defenders of the class system—a group that includes many contemporary conservatives—often argue that inequality is necessary for innovation, that unequal rewards breed incentive, that stratification ensures that worthy individuals are entrusted with power, and that social stability is preferable to equality. Lenski's 1966 parameters continue to limit the debate—such as it is—over class.

To a great extent, the defenders of inequality have been more in vogue in recent times. Their point of view dovetails nicely with success tales (and myths) of achieving the American dream, especially the assertion that hard work yields rewards. The American dream has, in fact, proved so powerful that it has trumped notions of America as a haven of equality. History records that the United States never has been an equal society, but equality has nonetheless served as a touchstone value for the American republic. Lately, though, many Americans have jettisoned hopes of an equal society for more generalized support of equality of *opportunity*, and even this manifests itself more in rhetoric than in political activity. The same individuals who believe in equal opportunity often reject social programs, school-funding schemes, and progressive taxation reforms that would help level the playing field.

The entries in this encyclopedia are designed with several purposes in mind. First, they exist as historical overviews on the question, practice, and changing perceptions of class in America. As such, this is a reference work on social history. Second, they highlight the ways in which class is made manifest in contemporary society. In this regard, the work is part sociology and part cultural history. Finally, the encyclopedia seeks to provide information that is useful to conceptualize class in today's world. Call it political science with a touch of old-fashioned civics.

As stated in the preface, it is decidedly *not* the be-all and end-all, nor can it hope to be comprehensive. Writers have prepared entries with a general readership in mind, not academic specialists. Our purpose is to offer a reference tool that does what fewer and fewer Americans choose to do: look at social class. We hope to call attention to the very real existence of stratification even though many Americans prefer to think we live in a middle-class society with a few extraordinary poor and rich people on the fringes. It seeks only to be the first word on the subject, not the last.

References

Gerhard Lenski, *Power and Privilege: A Theory of Social Stratification*, New York: McGraw-Hill, 1966; Michael Nelson, ed., *The Elections of 2000*, Washington, DC: CQ Press, 2001; Jack Rakove, ed., *The Unfinished Election of 2000*, New York: Basic Books, 2001; Michael Zweig, *The Working Class Majority: America's Best Kept Secret*, Ithaca, NY: Cornell University Press, 2000.

Robert E. Weir

A

ABBOTT, EDITH (September 26, 1876–July 28, 1957)
AND GRACE (November 17, 1878–June 19, 1939)

ROBERT E. WEIR

Edith and Grace Abbott were sisters who pioneered in social work and child advocacy and improved conditions for immigrants and the poor.

The Abbott sisters were born in Grand Island, Nebraska, during the **Gilded Age**, a time in which many members of the **middle class** adhered to the precepts of **Social Darwinism**. The concept of social problems was still murky, and conditions such as **poverty** were viewed as personal failings linked to inferior intellectual or moral development. The Abbotts, however, grew up in a household that rejected essentialist arguments about character, in part because their mother was an ardent suffragist and pacifist accustomed to challenging assumptions about human nature.

Edith attended Browning Hall, a boarding school in Omaha, and then took up teaching because the family could not afford to send her to college. However, despite these financial limitations, she began taking correspondence and summer school classes at the University of Nebraska, obtaining a bachelor's degree in 1901. She continued teaching until 1903, when she went to the University of Chicago, where she obtained a PhD in economics in 1905. Courtesy of a **Carnegie** fellowship, Abbott attended University College in London and the London School of Economics. At the latter she met Beatrice and Sidney Webb, Fabians whose belief that **socialism** could evolve peacefully was popular among the British middle class. Fabian socialists were committed to the idea that poverty was a social ill, an idea Edith retained when she returned to the United States.

Edith taught at Wellesley College during 1907, but left to join her sister at Chicago's Hull House, the famed **settlement house** experiment begun by **Jane Addams**. Abbott was also active in the suffrage movement and worked as an assistant to Sophonisba Breckinridge at the Chicago School of Civics and Philanthropy, where she learned about juvenile delinquency. In 1924, Abbott became the first female dean of a graduate program when she headed the School of the

Grace Abbott, Chief of the Children's Bureau of the Dept. of Labor, ca. 1929. Courtesy of the Library of Congress.

Social Service Administration at the University of Chicago. The latter is considered the nation's first graduate program in social work.

Abbott held the deanship until 1942. During that time, she helped create the Cook County Bureau of Public Welfare, assisted in drafting the **Social Security** Act, and wrote voluminously to educate the public on topics such as poverty, prison reform, and the need for state and federal governments to take active roles in alleviating social problems. For many years she also edited the influential journal *Social Science Review*, which she and Breckinridge founded in 1927. She retired in 1953, returned to Grand Island, and died of pneumonia four years later.

Grace was equally passionate about helping members of the **lower class** and moved in many of the same circles as her older sister. She graduated from Grand Island Baptist College in 1898, taught high school for several years, and did graduate work at the University of Nebraska and the University of Chicago. In 1907, she moved to Chicago and moved into Hull House. Two years later, she obtained a PhD in political science from the University of Chicago.

From 1908 to 1917, Grace worked with immigrants at Hull House and became the director of the Immigrants Protective League. Abbott also immersed herself in other Chicago reform movements of the **Progressive Era**, and her experiences exemplify both the promise and the limitations of government-directed social reform in the early twentieth century. She was particularly interested in the problem of **child labor** and left Hull House in 1917 to direct the Industrial Division of the Children's Bureau, where she worked closely with **Julia Lathrop** to enforce child labor laws passed by Congress in 1916. When the Keating-Owen Act, which had created those laws, was declared unconstitutional in 1918, Abbott left the Children's Bureau to direct the Illinois State Immigrants Commission, an experience she recounted in her 1917 book *The Immigrant and His Community*.

Abbott's concern for children brought her back to the Children's Bureau in 1921, when she replaced Lathrop as director. Her years of advocating federal aid for infant and maternity care seemed to bear success in 1921, when she published *Maternity and Infant Welfare*, and Congress passed the Sheppard-Towner Act. Alas, the latter was struck down as unconstitutional just one year later. Abbott nonetheless stayed in her post until 1934. During that time she advised the League of Nations on the exploitation of female and child laborers, and she threw herself into the task of compiling solid social statistics to back her assertions. This culminated in numerous books, including the two-volume *The Child and the State*, a work sometimes cited as a model of rigorous collection and interpretation of social science data.

Grace left the Children's Bureau in 1934 to take up a professoriate in social work at the University of Chicago. Like her sister, she also edited the *Social Science Review* (1934–39), and she also joined Edith in helping draft the Social Security Act. Her career and passion were cut short when she died of cancer in 1939.

Both sisters greatly increased public awareness of how poverty and injustice can be embedded in social systems that operate independently of individual character or effort. They did much to legitimize the role of government in addressing social problems.

Suggested Reading

Lela Costin, *Two Sisters for Social Justice: A Biography of Grace and Edith Abbott*, 1983; Richard Edwards, ed., *Encyclopedia of Social Work*, 1995; Patricia Lengermann and Jill Niebrugge-Brantley, *The Women Founders: Sociology and Social Theory*, 1998.

ACADEMIA

MURNEY GERLACH

The concepts of the modern academy and university grew originally out of the Scholasticism movement of twelfth-century Europe, when scholars, students, and religious leaders mingled in places to study universal knowledge, philosophy, and science. By the thirteenth century, such places in Bologna, Paris, Oxford, Cambridge, and several locales in the German and Italian states had evolved into universities.

From the beginning, academia was associated with social **elites**. The church controlled the universities, and students were considered clerics. Under the primogeniture rules that dominated much of Europe, elder sons inherited land; the church was dominated by second and third sons of nobility. Moreover, it took a certain level of **wealth** for most students to indulge in long hours of discipline, study and analysis. Medieval students pored over complex theological texts, Latin and Greek classics, philosophy, and scientific treatises.

Universities and the academia thus became the fundamental living centers for basic research, learning, and the pursuit of knowledge, but they were also largely places of privilege and bastions for the aristocracy. They incorporated the idea that knowledge was its own reward, and also the idea that learning could improve society and improve humankind. After the Reformation, scholars and academics could more freely pursue their research, speculations, and conclusions about science and their age, but it was during the eighteenth-century Enlightenment that expansive views of the individual, reason, and philosophy led to scientific and humanistic revolutions in the academy. Writers and thinkers such as Voltaire, Rousseau, Diderot, and other *philosophes* provided new models that were beneficial for the pursuit of republican and **democratic** experiments that spread around the world in the period between 1760 and 1800, especially in America, France, and Britain. In British North America, the founding of the American Philosophical Society and the philosophical writings of Thomas Jefferson, James Madison, and Benjamin Franklin were instrumental in the decades leading up to the **American Revolution** and the eventual writing of the Constitution.

Even before then, transformational and revolutionary ideas infused the academic halls of Harvard, Yale, Brown, and the rest of the **Ivy League**. Scholars studied the writings of John Locke and Thomas Hobbes as well as Scottish and British philosophers and economists. It is important to note that Adam Smith's *Wealth of Nations*, a book widely regarded as a founding document in the development of **capitalism**, was published in 1776, the same year Jefferson penned the Declaration of Independence.

Seminal to the emergence of academia in the mid-nineteenth century was Cardinal John Henry Newman's classic *The Idea of the University* (1852), a work that discussed learning, research, and the pursuit of knowledge in relationship to liberal education and research in science, technology, archaeology, and medicine. These ideas dovetailed with the reforming zeal of public education advocates such as George Henry Evans and Horace Mann. In 1818 Massachusetts opened the nation's first free public high school, and by the 1840s, it was an accepted idea that there was a responsibility to educate the general public, not just those of wealth and means. The University of North Carolina opened its doors in 1789 as the nation's first public university, but it was the Morrill Land-Grant College Act of 1862 that inspired the evolution of major American public universities.

Still, just 4 percent of the American population entered college in 1900, and most of them came from the **upper class** or upper **middle class**. Numbers increased steadily and, by World War II, about 18 percent of high school graduates attended college, but it was still unusual for children of the **working class** to pursue higher education. That changed with the passage of 1944 Servicemen's Readjustment Act, popularly known as the GI Bill. Also important was the postwar baby boom that led to a population explosion. By 1960 about 40 percent of all high school graduates entered higher education; by 1970 about 50 percent did so. Not all completed a four-year degree, but by 1990, 13.1 percent of Americans had obtained a bachelor's degree, and by 2000, 15.5 percent had done so.

Academia has been democratized to a great extent since World War II and has generally been a leader in advancing multiculturalism and **pluralism**. Mentoring, internships, practical experiences, and active and engaging learning in urban and world centers have made the once-narrow world of academia open to African Americans, **Asian Americans**, **Hispanics**, and the international community.

That said, the academy retains many of its medieval associations with wealth and privilege. Ivy League schools and other elite colleges and universities have made strides in diversifying, but the economic profiles of student families remain far above median income levels, and the schools obtain relatively few students from working-class backgrounds. Many argue that American academia is tiered, with the wealthy attending prestigious private schools, the middle class flagship state universities, and the working class **community colleges** and smaller state colleges. The **legacy** system, though it has eroded, still gives wealthier students a leg up in gaining admission to top schools and is seen as an important aspect of **social reproduction** in America.

Social reproduction patterns are also replicated in hiring practices. In 2003, for example, Ivy League schools hired 433 tenure-track professors. Of these, just 14 were African American, 8 were Hispanic, and 150 were women. Moreover, many of the new hires had degrees from Ivy League schools. There is a tendency across academia for institutions to hire professors who have been educated at similar institutions. Entry into the most prestigious law and medical schools also correlates with a high **socioeconomic status** (SES).

There remains a **wage** premium involved in obtaining a college education. In 2005, an individual with a bachelor's degree earned an average salary of $51,206 per annum, whereas the average for those with just a high school degree was $27,915. Although a college education remains a major contributor to upward **social mobility**, social class continues to set the parameters of how high one can climb.

Suggested Reading

Thomas Bender, ed., *The University and the City. From Medieval Origins to the Present*, 1988; Lawrence A. Cremin, *American Education. The Metropolitan Experience, 1876–1980*, 1988; C. J. Lucas, *American Higher Education: A History*, 1994; Jaroslav Pelikan, *The Idea of the University. A Reexamination*, 1992.

ACCENTS AND LANGUAGE PATTERNS

ROBERT E. WEIR

Accents and language patterns are regional, ethnic, and affected communication variations. Most language patterns are rooted in historical circumstances, and their sociolinguistic implications are of particular interest to social scientists.

There is no particular reason, other than custom, to favor one accent, set of grammatical expressions, or communication pattern over another. Scholarly studies of the history of English, for example, reveal that the language has evolved repeatedly since departing from original Germanic tribal tongues some time around the sixth century. Modern English derives from a particular set of preferences and practices that emerged in London in the fifteenth century, and the idea that there is a "standard" or "proper" form of English is largely the product of British imperialism in the eighteenth and nineteenth centuries. This so-called standard form did not displace regional variations in Britain or North America until free public education became widespread in the late nineteenth century. What came to be known as Standard English is thus a top-down imposition from the British **upper classes**, particularly the aristocracy and **social climbers** in the **middle class**. Even now, an affected upper-class dialect—sometimes called "BBC English" in reference to the fact that broadcasters for the British Broadcasting Corporation once had to master it—remains an external marker of good breeding.

In Colonial America, regional accents and speech patterns established themselves well in advance of standardization efforts and were further creolized by the numerous variations brought by millions of immigrants. In the mid-nineteenth century, however, some members of the upper and upper middle class began to cultivate faux British accents and embrace Standard English to show their sophistication vis-à-vis the masses. Their grammatical and syntactical preferences came to dominate how English was taught in schools, and some educators envisioned a day in which uniform English would eliminate accents, colloquialisms, and alternative grammar usage.

That hope proved naïve, but language became an important class barrier. The American upper classes, motivated in part by **Europhilia**, integrated speech preferences into their class identity. Both **Theodore** and **Franklin D. Roosevelt**, for example, spoke English with hints of an affected British accent, as does contemporary conservative commentator William F. Buckley Jr. For much of the twentieth century, upper-class accents and slavish devotion to precisely defined grammar rules were commonplace in **Ivy League** colleges. The use of "poor" grammar or the use of certain regional dialects marked a person as socially and intellectually inferior.

Southern and Appalachian accents came to connote a lack of sophistication, even stupidity, whereas an accent common in the greater New York metropolitan area was associated with **working-class** bluntness and crudity. Although linguists assert there are at least three dozen distinct dialects spoken in the United States, it has become customary for Americans seeking middle-class **status** to flatten or deemphasize their accents. There are even classes and speech consultants that work with individuals interested in altering speech patterns. This is because multiculturalism has yet to make dominant inroads in matters of verbal communication. Studies indicate that listeners still negatively associate certain accents, particularly those deemed Southern, rural, or ethnic. There is also evidence that candidates who do not use Standard English also face uphill battles during job interviews.

The class distinctiveness of language impacts racial and ethnic minorities in particularly dramatic ways. Immigrants who learn English often find it difficult or impossible to speak it without an accent or to obliterate grammar and syntax patterns of their native languages. Attempts to address language-based discrimination often cause heated arguments within communities. Some **Latinos**, for instance, advocate replacing **bilingual** school programs with intensive English training, including speech therapy. African American leaders and educators arguing that a nonstandard form of English known as Ebonics should be recognized as a distinct language run afoul of black leaders who accuse them of further ghettoizing African American youth.

It remains to be seen whether linguistic class barriers will weaken in the future, but they remain strong at present. Thus far, the only class that has crossed language barriers to its advantage has been the upper class. In some cases, those in power find it advantageous to sound more "common." For example, politicians know that an upper-crust accent and an overly active vocabulary can make them seem aloof and snobbish. During his 1996 bid for the presidency, George H. **Bush**, who grew up on the East Coast, attended Yale, and spent many of his adult years in ambassadorial roles abroad, employed speech consultants to help him sound more Texan and broaden his populist appeal.

Suggested Reading

John Baugh, *Beyond Ebonics: Linguistic Pride and Racial Prejudice*, 2000; Robert MacNeil and William Cran, *Do You Speak American?* 2004; Robert McCrum, Robert MacNeil, and William Cran, *The Story of English: Third Revised Edition*, 2002.

ACHIEVEMENT AND ASCRIPTION

SHANNON J. TELENKO

The terms *achievement* and *ascription* are used by social scientists to describe the means through which someone attains class **status** as well as to describe how an institution or society creates hierarchical structure. Achievement is the attainment of socioeconomic or class status based on individual effort. Although achievement is most often associated with hard work, education, occupation, and motivation, it can be enhanced or reduced through ascribed or assigned class status.

Ascription is the attainment of class status based on who one is and into what social and economic situation one was born. Families who have descended from industrialists and other entrepreneurs enjoy **upper-class** status through ascription, despite their benefactors' achievement of that status. The **Rockefeller** and **Kennedy** families are, at this point, beneficiaries of ascribed status. The children of these families can live off the old money and the recognition that their ancestors established for them long ago.

It is argued that U.S. culture values achievement over ascription. However, some individuals and organizations have grown accustomed to building their personal and professional relationships on ascription. This is often what people mean when they mention "good old boy" clubs or **social networks**. This, in turn, affects how individuals acquire certain positions within society regardless of the official or ideological stances that the government takes on equal opportunity and **individualism**.

Institutions, governments, and organizations within the United Sates usually claim they select members on the basis of their "earned" status and achievements and not because of the status into which members were born. However, many people find their opportunities enhanced by who they are and whom they know. For example, presidents of the United States should be elected based on achievement. Nevertheless, presidential candidates must either have money or be able to raise money through reputation or recognition before they can hope to launch a bid for office. Therefore, some question the assumption that the United States is a **meritocracy**. Many high-level positions in government, business, and other institutions appear to result from ascription rather than achievement.

To cite a hypothetical scenario, a university admits a student because she graduated high school with a high grade-point average. This student then excels and graduates college with honors. Because of her superb study and leadership skills, she is hired shortly after commencement. Despite the fact that this hypothetical woman grew up with **working-class** or **working-poor** status, her dedication to higher education, traditionally a realm for only upper- and middle-income families, has elevated her to **middle-class** status. If her job paid enough, or she went on to receive more education, she could eventually rise to upper-class status. In this way, achievement is also a vehicle for **social mobility**.

Some, however, argue that such a scenario is rare because upper-class status is ascribed and exclusive. There is, moreover, a distinction between "old money" and the **nouveau riche** in the United States. Old-money families have historically looked down on individuals or families who have become newly wealthy through achievement.

Leaders in American society have historically been considered those with ascribed upper-class status. These leaders included government officials (including the **Founding Fathers**), professors, and scientists. Groups who have traditionally been ascribed lower-class status are minorities, **immigrants**, the working classes, single mothers, the mentally ill, and the disabled. Some argue that these assignments still plague American society, despite the increased opportunities for all groups as well as the higher positions to which those historically considered "**lower class**" have been appointed.

Under **capitalism**, people are taught to believe that hard work always pays off and that one can achieve almost anything regardless of socioeconomic background or family name. Some think that this is a myth and that the lower classes exist to permit the upper classes to have what they have. They believe that this idea of achievement serves as a false hope for the lower classes so that they will not complain about their position in society. If a few actually "make it" through individual efforts, this only serves to reinforce the myth of social mobility through achievement.

Therefore, although it is argued that there are two ways to attain status, through achievement and ascription, barriers to the attainment of higher class status still exist in the United States. Some individuals may never be able to enjoy the status that is ascribed to American society's very upper classes. Members of lower classes in American society may have to work even harder to overcome discrimination in achieving higher class status, which can be a difficult and tiresome obligation.

Suggested Reading

Trompenaars Hampden-Turner, The Seven Dimensions of Culture (http://www. 7d-culture.com); Steven L. Nock and Peter H. Rossi, "Ascription versus Achievement in the Attribution of Family Social Status," *The American Journal of Sociology*, 1978 (http://www.jstor.org/); Katherine Stovel, Michael Savage, and Peter Bearman, "Ascription into Achievement: Models of Career Systems at Lloyds Bank, 1890–1970," *The American Journal of Sociology*, 1996 (http://www.jstor.org/).

ADAMS FAMILY

ROBERT E. WEIR

Adams is the family name of one of America's oldest **elite** families. Although many of the family members lived in nearby Quincy, the Adams clan is often numbered among the **Boston Brahmins**, in part because of family wealth and the tendency of prominent members to adopt imperious airs. A few of the more public Adams family members are profiled here.

John Adams (October 30, 1735–July 4, 1826) was the first Adams to immerse himself in public affairs. His father was a church deacon, farmer, and town official in Braintree, Massachusetts. John Adams attended Harvard College, became a lawyer, and gained a reputation for eloquence and a disputative nature. By the 1760s he routinely took cases defending colonists against royal power, though, surprisingly, he successfully defended British troops accused of murder in the 1770 Boston Massacre. In the buildup to the **American Revolution**, however, Adams firmly identified with the Patriot cause. He attended both Continental Congresses, and it was he who nominated George Washington to be commander-in-chief of the Continental Army. He also assisted Thomas Jefferson in writing the Declaration of Independence.

Adams spent most of the war in various diplomatic ventures and helped negotiate the 1783 Treaty of Paris that secured American independence. In 1785 he became the new nation's first ambassador to Great Britain, but was considered so haughty by American detractors that they called him the "Duke of Braintree." Like many of the **Founding Fathers**, Adams was distrustful of the common people and expressed the view that men of breeding and wealth were more worthy of public service. He even suggested the new nation create an upper legislative body analogous

John Adams, second president of the United States. Courtesy of the Library of Congress.

to the British House of Lords. These views derailed any hopes that Adams would become the first president of the United States. Instead, he became Washington's vice president in 1789.

Within what came to be known as the **Federalist Party**, Adams and Alexander Hamilton led a conservative faction that was often criticized for imperial pretensions. Adams is credited with helping maneuver positive American foreign policy toward Britain and away from France; the French Revolution seemed to signal anarchy and the tyranny of the masses. This led to a political squabble between Adams and Jefferson, who at least publicly expressed more faith in democracy. Adams barely defeated Jefferson in 1796 and succeeded Washington as president.

His presidency was also marked by controversy. His open support for Britain in its war against France led to public battles with Jefferson, and Adams was lampooned severely in pro-Jefferson newspapers. The 1798 Alien and Sedition Acts clamped down on pro-French and anti-Adams utterances, but fueled criticisms that Adams was a closet aristocrat. In 1800 Adams lost his reelection bid to Jefferson. He retired to Quincy and, ironically, died the same day as Jefferson in 1826.

Abigail Adams (November 22, 1744–October 28, 1818) was the wife of John Adams and the mother of John Quincy Adams and three other children. She and John enjoyed an affectionate relationship, and the tone of their correspondence is remarkable for its frankness and emotionality. Abigail spent most of her marriage apart from her politically active husband and demonstrated great skill and courage in managing both economic affairs and family safety during the American Revolution. Her admonition to John to "remember the ladies" as he helped draft the new government is often quoted, and some have viewed her as a proto-feminist. Although such an assessment is overly charitable, Abigail Adams was as headstrong and opinionated as her husband. She joined John in England while he was ambassador, but spent most of the twelve years he served in the new government shuttling back and forth between the family home in Quincy and Philadelphia, the temporary capital. In 1800 she became the first presidential spouse to live in the newly built White House.

John Quincy Adams (July 11, 1767–February 23, 1848) was the eldest son of John and Abigail and the sixth president of the United States. His childhood was consumed by war and politics. He accompanied his father to Europe several times before he was thirteen and went to Russia as a private secretary to Ambassador Francis Dana when he was fourteen. Like his father, he graduated from Harvard with a degree in law, though most of his early career was consumed by diplomacy rather than legal matters. He helped draft the Jay Treaty in 1794 that secured peace with Great Britain but angered Jeffersonians. He also secured a treaty with Prussia during his father's presidency.

He served in the Massachusetts legislature and in the U.S. Senate and did so first as a Federalist, but he angered some colleagues by supporting President Jefferson's purchase of Louisiana and his trade embargo of Britain and France. These acts led the Federalists to dump him as a senator in 1808, and J. Q. Adams responded by aligning himself with the Republican (today's Democratic) Party and supporting President James Madison and the War of 1812, which most Federalists opposed. Adams served as an envoy to Russia and then as secretary of state under President James Monroe. In that latter post, he was a key architect of the Monroe Doctrine, which asserted U.S. hegemony in the Western hemisphere, and he was furthermore an ardent booster of what was later dubbed Manifest Destiny, the idea that it was America's fate to expand westward to the Pacific coast. He also negotiated a treaty with Spain that transferred control of Florida to the United States and one with Britain in 1818 that averted war by establishing the border between the United States and Canada.

In 1824 John Quincy Adams, having lost the popular vote to Andrew Jackson, became president in an election decided by Congress. His presidency was marked by as much controversy as his father's, with Jackson as his chief antagonist. Battles over chartering a federal bank and over federal funding for internal improvements and a trade tariff marked his single term. The tariff sparked the Nullification Crisis in which South Carolina threatened secession, and it was a key issue in the 1828 election in which Jackson soundly defeated the incumbent J. Q. Adams.

In 1830 J. Q. Adams returned to national politics via election to the House of Representatives. He became one of the foremost opponents of **slavery** and introduced an unsuccessful amendment to gradually end it. Outraged Southerners accused him of being an aristocratic meddler, and Adams returned their contempt. Ironically, though, he used popular democracy as a pressure tactic by introducing citizen petitions calling for slavery's end. These prompted Jacksonians to institute a gag rule that prohibited antislavery discussions. Adams also angered the South by securing freedom for African mutineers from the ship *Amistad* on the grounds that the ship violated slave-importation laws. He died after suffering a brain hemorrhage during an impassioned speech opposing the Mexican War.

Charles Francis Adams (August 18, 1807–November 21, 1886) was the son of John Quincy and Louisa (Johnson) Adams. His career path followed that of his progenitors: Harvard, a law degree, a well-connected marriage, politics, and diplomatic service. Like his father, he was an ardent opponent of slavery. After a short stint in the Free Soil Party, he joined the newly formed Republican Party and won election to Congress in 1858 to the Massachusetts seat his late father had once held. When Abraham Lincoln won the presidency in 1860, Charles became the latest Adams to serve as ambassador to Great Britain. He played a key role in the Civil War by dissuading the British from their early support for the Confederacy. Also a historian, he edited the memoirs of both his father and his grandfather. His son, Charles Francis Adams Jr. (1835–1915), later wrote Charles Sr.'s biography. Charles Francis Adams III (1866–1954) also went into politics and served as President Herbert Hoover's secretary of the navy.

Two of Charles Francis Adams Sr.'s other sons made their mark during the **Gilded Age**. Brooks Adams (June 24, 1848–February 13, 1927) parlayed his Harvard education into a career as a historian at a time in which said profession was often that of wealthy dilettantes. Like his eldest brother, Charles, one of his favorite subjects was his own family. In keeping with the views of so many Adamses before him, he expressed skepticism about the virtues of democracy. Brooks Adams authored several works of history, the most significant being *America's Economic Supremacy* (1900), in which he accurately predicted that the United States and Russia would become dominant world powers. In his later life, he questioned the Adams family maxim that wealth and worthiness to hold power went hand in hand. Seeing the social turmoil of the late Victorian period, he and others came to suspect that members of the **upper class** had grown soft and irresponsible. His nephew Charles Jr. embraced these same ideas and grew so disgusted with the "low instincts" of business that he abandoned his railroad career to write history.

Brooks Adams's reputation was surpassed by that of his brother Henry Brooks Adams (February 16, 1838–March 27, 1918), also a historian and writer. Henry Brooks Adams worked as a journalist and edited the influential *North American Review* from 1870 to 1876, by which time he was also a history professor at Harvard. He wrote a nine-volume history of the Jefferson and Madison administrations.

Henry Adams's life took a sharp turn in 1885, after his wife, Marian (Hooper) Adams, committed suicide. He began traveling extensively, writing two books that established his reputation. The first, *Mont-Saint-Michel and Chartres* (1904), is still considered a classic for the way in which the author combined philosophy, art history, and religion. He is even better known for his autobiography *The Education of Henry Adams* (1907), the companion piece to *Mont-Saint-Michel and Chartres*. In many ways, this book is a metaphor for the Adams family. He contrasted the unity of the Gothic Age and what he dubbed the "multiplicity" of his own age. With family history lurking in the background, Adams presented himself as a man adrift and one whose "education" left him ill-prepared for modern life.

The Adams family is certainly one of America's most distinguished clans, but decades of public service notwithstanding, many of its offspring struggled to reconcile wealth, *noblesse oblige*, and democracy. In many ways, the Adamses illustrate the limits of top-down leadership patterns.

Suggested Reading

Henry Adams, *The Education of Henry Adams*, 2003; David McCullough, *John Adams*, 2002; Paul Nagel, *John Quincy Adams: A Public Life, A Private Life*, 1999.

ADDAMS, JANE (September 6, 1860–May 21, 1935)

VICTORIA GRIEVE

Jane Addams was a famed reformer, social worker, peace activist, and champion of the **working class**. She is best known for cofounding Hull House, a **settlement house** in Chicago for poor and **immigrant** families. Addams also received the Nobel Prize for Peace in 1931 for her lifetime contributions to social work.

She was the youngest child born to a large, wealthy family in Cedarville, Illinois. After her mother died when Addams was two, Addams developed a close relationship with her father, who encouraged her to pursue her education. After graduating from Rockford Female Seminary in 1881, Addams announced to the dismay of her family that she would pursue a medical degree. However, her father died, and Addams was bedridden for more than a year with spinal problems. In 1883 she traveled to Europe for two years and then returned home to what was a traditional life for a well-off, unmarried woman: living with and caring for her family. In 1885, however, she again traveled to Europe, this time with her friend Ellen Gates Starr, and they visited London's Toynbee Hall, a settlement house.

Both Addams and Starr were greatly influenced by British social reform movements, and shortly after returning to the United States, they moved to Chicago, a center of industry and commerce that required cheap labor supported by massive migrations from Europe. The Halsted Street neighborhood on Chicago's West Side was a poor neighborhood dominated by immigrant slums where overcrowded tenements, crime, disease, inadequate schools, inferior hospitals, and insufficient sanitation were common. Mobilizing the generosity of wealthy donors, Addams and Starr opened Hull House in 1889 to employ the underutilized talents of educated, **middle-class** young people to serve the poor. In response to the need for child care, they opened a kindergarten, and soon they also offered medical care, legal aid, and classes in English, vocational skills, sewing, cooking, music, art, and drama.

Addams's involvement with the **working poor** transformed her from a philanthropist into an activist. Shocked by the poor housing, overcrowding, and **poverty** they witnessed, she and other Hull House workers gradually became more involved in their community and urban politics. Addams was appointed to the Chicago School Board in 1905 and additionally accepted the position as garbage inspector for the Nineteenth Ward. She lobbied for **child labor** laws, a factory inspection system, and improvements in the juvenile justice system. She fought for legislation to limit the working hours of women, mandate schooling for children, recognize labor unions, and provide for industrial safety. Hull House attracted a variety of social reformers, including Florence Kelley, a member of the **Socialist** Labor Party, who introduced the middle-class Hull House residents to political and trade union activity. In 1903 several Hull House residents, including Addams, were involved in establishing the Women's Trade Union League.

Her increasing political activity convinced Addams of the need for women's suffrage. She joined the National American Woman Suffrage Association in 1906 and became its president in 1911. In 1909 Addams was a founding member of the National Association for the Advancement of Colored People (**NAACP**). Hoping to see her work become part of a national political agenda, Addams actively campaigned for Progressive presidential candidate Theodore Roosevelt in 1912. Addams traveled and lectured widely; between

Jane Addams, ca. 1914. Courtesy of the Library of Congress.

1907 and 1930, she wrote hundreds of articles and delivered countless speeches on topics ranging from settlement work to the **labor movement**, prostitution, and women's suffrage. She wrote seven books, including her 1910 autobiography, *Twenty Years at Hull House*.

The outbreak of the Spanish-American War in 1898 and the rising threat of American imperialism led Addams to oppose war. She joined the Anti-Imperialist League and in 1904 spoke at the Universal Peace Conference. In her 1907 *Newer Ideals of Peace*, she argued for a moral substitute for war, and she worked to keep the United States out of World War I. She served as chairman of the Woman's Peace Party and accompanied a delegation to the International Congress of Women to The Hague in 1915. Addams served as president of the Women's International League of Peace and Freedom (WILPF) from 1919 until she resigned in 1929, and she remained honorary president until her death.

Addams's involvement in labor, suffrage, and peace movements, and especially her opposition to American involvement in World War I, stirred public criticism. She was castigated in the press and expelled from the Daughters of the American Revolution, but in 1918 she worked for Herbert Hoover's Department of Food Administration to provide relief supplies to the women and children of enemy nations. Many thought her a traitor for her pacifism, and in the 1920s, she was called the most dangerous woman in America for opposing the mass arrests and deportation of suspected radicals during the **Red Scare**. Shocked by such political persecution, Addams was among the founders of the American Civil Liberties Union (ACLU) in 1920.

Addams's reputation revived with the onset of the **Great Depression**, and she was awarded the Nobel Prize for Peace in 1931. She supported Franklin Roosevelt's **New Deal** and remained active in social issues, but her health steadily declined. She died of cancer on May 21, 1935, and her funeral service was held in the court-yard at Hull House.

Suggested Reading

Victoria Bissell Brown, *The Education of Jane Addams*, 2004; Jean Bethke Elshtain, *Jane Addams and the Dream of American Democracy: A Life*, 2002; James Weber Linn and Anne Furor Scott, *Jane Addams: A Biography*, 2000.

ADVERTISING

JANEAN MOLLET-VAN BECKUM

Advertising is the promotion of goods, services, or ideas through paid announce-ments to the public. Professional ad creators use different advertising techniques to sway the public's view on a product or issue. They have become adept at targeting certain segments of the population, making their ads very effective.

When targeting a particular group of people, advertisers rely on demographic statistics relating to the group, including the group members' age, gender, **income**, race, and education. This allows ads to be placed in areas of a city or during media programming where the promotional messages will most likely reach the target audience. For example, an advertiser selling a clothing line targeted at teenagers may advertise products during television programming popular with teens. Like-wise, a company such as **Wal-Mart** is more likely to advertise in moderate- or low-income areas than in affluent areas.

Recent controversy regarding advertisements has centered on the promotion of alcohol and, particularly, tobacco products to children. For example, the mascot used to promote Camel cigarettes from 1987 to 1997 was a cartoon camel named "Joe Camel." Research showed that the cartoon image appealed to young children, and under pressure from activist groups and the government, R.J. Reynolds removed Joe Camel from its advertising campaigns. Anti-tobacco activists claim that Camel cigarettes were intentionally targeted at young children, causing them to smoke at a younger age as well as encouraging brand loyalty at a young age; the company denies these allegations. This is only one of several examples of compa-nies allegedly marketing to children a product intended for use by adults. The idea was that if children were introduced to the cigarettes as children, they would be more likely to remember them when choosing cigarettes when they turned eight-een or to begin smoking at an even earlier age.

One of the advertising profession's strongest strategies is to create a desire for a product that may not really be needed. To create a need where there is none, advertisers often show an ideal standard of living when the product is used, suggesting social and economic upward mobility. This is one of the most common types of advertising, promising heightened social status by promising acceptance in the higher group. This type of advertising may also suggest the acquisition of everything that is perceived to go along with the higher status, such as wealth, beauty, and leisure, when a particular product is purchased. **Luxury** car ads are particularly adept at this type of persuasion. Drivers are portrayed as successful, wealthy, happy individuals with an abundance of leisure time to enjoy their car. The reality is that those in **lower classes** who buy these cars in an effort to attain a higher status often have less **wealth** and leisure and therefore less happiness because of the increased expense required to pay for the high-end car.

These marketing tools work because material things are connected both to how a person perceives himself or herself and to how others perceive him or her in American society. Goods communicate what we think of ourselves and how we want others to think of us. Therefore, ads focusing on what people want to be, and how they want to be seen, are very successful. They create perceived increases in **status** that are often illusory. Scholars such as **Juliet Schor** argue that targeting luxury goods at various income groups is a new phenomenon in American culture that has led to social shifts. Whereas Americans of earlier generations compared themselves with those in their specific peer groups, modern advertising encourages them to measure their worth vis-à-vis the lifestyles of the affluent Americans.

Another good example of this is the wedding industry. Many couples do not want huge, expensive weddings but still end up with them because of the ideals portrayed in magazines, at bridal shows, and in the media. The fairytale wedding of the high class and popular entertainers becomes the ideal and is expected by guests. Couples want guests to remember their wedding as akin to glamorous media images, and they are therefore driven to buy the accessories and clothing advertised, even though they may not consciously want them or be able to afford them.

Ads also perpetuate or create stereotypes, most obviously in the case of gender roles. Just like fifty years ago, **middle-class** women are still portrayed as the caretakers and nurturers of the family, although their roles may have also expanded to work outside the home. This particular stereotype is rooted in the desire to be all things to all people. It says women can be good mothers and housekeepers, as well as breadwinners to keep their families at a middle or higher social class, as long as they have the proper products on hand.

Advertisers use the ideas and ideals already ingrained in American society to reinforce the desire for upward **social mobility** and attainment of the **American dream**. In the competitive commercial world of the modern day, consumers must be careful that they are buying a product for what it is, and not for what it purports to be.

Suggested Reading
Martin M. Grossack, *Understanding Consumer Behavior*, 1964; William Leiss, Stephen Kline, and Sut Jhally, *Social Communication in Advertising*, 1990; Gerard S. Petorne, MD, *Tobacco Advertising: The Great Seduction*, 1996.

AFFIRMATIVE ACTION

See Institutional Discrimination; Quotas.

AFFLUENT SOCIETY, THE

See Galbraith, John Kenneth.

AFRICAN AMERICANS

See Institutional Discrimination; Race, Racism, and Racial Stratification. (Many entries also discuss African Americans within specific contexts.)

AGRARIANISM

ROBERT E. WEIR

Agrarianism is a set of ideals that posits virtue in agricultural production and rural life. For many years, it was also linked to notions of independence and self-reliance among North Americans of European descent.

When Europeans established their North American colonies, most common people made their living from the land. Landholding was closely connected to **wealth** and vocation, with many Europeans imposing their social and religious views about property and productive labor onto unsuspecting **Native Americans**. Seizures of Native lands were sometimes justified on the grounds that Natives had not made those lands "productive" and hence had abrogated claims to them. Natives likewise found deeded land transactions baffling and often ceded land to colonists under the mistaken impression that they had agreed to mutual use of the land rather than to colonists' exclusive ownership.

By the time of the **American Revolution**, farming and other rural pursuits such as hunting and trapping were the primary occupations of most whites residing in the English colonies. Even intellectuals such as Benjamin Franklin and Thomas Jefferson opined that farming was the best way for most people to gain "independence," a term they interpreted in both political and economic terms. Although **capitalism** had begun to develop, the prevailing view was that working for wages made a person dependent on others, and true mastery came only when one was self-sufficient. In many places, property ownership conferred the status of "freeman," and one could not vote unless one owned land. This pattern persisted in many places until after the War of 1812 and in Rhode Island until the 1841–42 **Dorr Rebellion**. Jefferson even offered the opinion that the United States should remain an agricultural nation and rely upon European imports only for what few manufactured goods Americans might need.

The Jeffersonian ideal of an independent yeomanry was challenged by the antebellum **factory system** and the post–Civil War **Industrial Revolution**, but one can easily exaggerate the overall impact of each. Most Americans were farmers on the eve of the Civil War, and as late as 1890, some 24,771,000 Americans worked on farms—over 42 percent of the nation's total population of 62,947,714. Moreover, not until 1920 did more than half of Americans reside in urban units larger than 5,000 people. As America industrialized, agrarianism remained the ideal for most Americans; even labor organizations such as the **Knights of Labor** called for comprehensive land reforms to make farm ownership easier.

But not all nineteenth-century farmers were Jeffersonian models of rural independence. The bulk of antebellum Southern agricultural workers were **slaves**, not independent yeomen. The failure of **Reconstruction** after the Civil War saw the bulk of African Americans become tenant farmers and sharecroppers rather than farm owners. Farmers and ranchers everywhere felt the sting of economic changes that transformed their products from goods for local consumption into commodities for regional and national markets. Banks, railroads, grain elevators, stockyards, and meatpackers increasingly came to dictate prices and production, often leaving farmers to struggle with high interest rates, exorbitant storage costs, and soaring freight rates. Farmers expressed collective anger by organizing into reform groups such as the Grange, the Farmers' Alliances, the Greenback and "free silver" movements, and the Populist Party.

These groups, especially the Populists in the 1890s and **Progressive Era** movements such as the **Industrial Workers of the World**, the Citizens Non-Partisan League, and Minnesota's Farmer-Labor Party, helped legions of farmers, but several economic trends began to erode agrarian ideals. First, expansion of the industrial and service sectors created a permanent wage-earning **working class** and shifted economic relations to money-based exchanges. Second, the scale of the economy favored large enterprises over small ones, with farming subject to the same consolidation practices as manufacturing. Ranching was the first to give way. By the 1880s much of the meatpacking trade relied on animals from large ranches that employed wage-earners, not the livestock of small ranches.

The decline of family farms is much discussed in contemporary America, but it has been accelerating since the late 1920s. During and after World War I, many farmers expanded production to meet military needs and to feed war-ravaged Europe. As Europe recovered, American farmers faced dropping prices because of overproduction. The **Great Depression** officially began in late 1929, but many rural areas were in decline several years earlier.

The Depression further ravaged rural America. Even **New Deal** programs such as the Agricultural Adjustment Act (AAA), which brought price subsidies for many commodities, favored large operations over small farms. Although the total amount of tilled acreage actually increased slightly between 1930 and 1940, the number of farms and farmers declined. As farms were foreclosed, corporations bought small farms and consolidated them. What came to be called agribusiness emerged in full force in the 1930s.

The post–World War II expansion of the economy was not marked by resurgence in family farming. In 1930 more than 30 million Americans worked in agriculture; by 1950 barely half that number worked in the agrarian sector. Small-scale agriculture began an inexorable decline. In 1950 just 15.3 percent of Americans lived off the land; by 1970 that figure had slipped to 8.7 percent, and by 1990 a mere 1.9 percent made their livelihood by farming. This is because farming has become a corporate activity. The total amount of tilled acreage in 1990 was just slightly down from 1930 levels, but the average farm size was over 300 percent larger. Between 1982 and 1997 alone, some 339,000 small farms ended up in the hands of approximately 2,600 consolidated operations. Today, many producers, wholesalers, and retailers are the same corporate entity. Firms such as Tyson and Perdue operate their own chicken ranches; just four firms control nearly three-quarters of U.S. beef production; and corporate giants such as ConAgra, Cargill/Monsanto, Archer Daniels Midland, and AgriMark own vast amounts of American farm and grazing lands. There are reputedly still about 100,000 family-run dairy operations, but the price farmers get for milk is often dictated by cream-eries and distributors such as AgriMark, Dean Foods, Hood, and Hershey Foods. Recent changes in the AAA favor corporate enterprises even more. The reality is that agrarianism has given way to agribusiness in contemporary America.

Suggested Reading

Jane Adams, *Fighting for the Farm: Rural America Transformed*, 2002; William Conlogue and Jack T. Kirby, eds., *Working the Garden: American Writers and the Industrialization of Agriculture*, 2002; Milton Hallberg and M. C. Hallberg, *Economic Trends in U.S. Agriculture and Food Systems since World War II*, 2001.

AGRIBUSINESS

See Agrarianism.

AID TO FAMILIES WITH DEPENDENT CHILDREN (AFDC)

See Welfare.

ALGER, HORATIO (January 13, 1832–July 18, 1899)

ROBERT E. WEIR

Horatio Alger Jr. was a **Gilded Age** novelist of more than 130 books; his very name is now synonymous with rags-to-riches stories of sudden upward **social mobility**. His books are seldom read today, and only a handful are still in print, though they provide useful documentation of nineteenth-century urban problems.

Alger's own youth was far from ideal, though he was raised in **middle-class** comfort. The senior Alger was an exacting Unitarian minister who tutored his son in math and reading and encouraged him to enter the ministry. But childhood stuttering and his diminutive size—he was just five feet two inches when fully grown—isolated Alger socially. Still, he entered Harvard, graduated Phi Beta Kappa in 1857, and entered Harvard Divinity School. After his ordination in 1860, he left for a seven-month tour of Europe. When he returned, the **Civil War** had begun, but asthma disqualified him from military service; instead, he became a minister of a Unitarian congregation in Brewster, Massachusetts. He began writing during this time, perhaps to supplement his meager ministerial salary.

In 1866 Alger was abruptly fired by his church. It was later revealed that he was suspected of pedophilia with two teenaged boys. Alger fled to New York City, a metropolis being rapidly transformed by mass **immigration**, industry, and an ever-widening gap between **wealth** and **poverty**. Alger witnessed firsthand the crushing effects of life in the **slums**, **child labor**, **homelessness**, and nativism. He befriended numerous street urchins, though the nature of his relationship with these children is unknown. Alger's legions of posthumous defenders claim that he was remorseful for his earlier actions and rescued street children as acts of penitence. This may be the case, but suspicion lingers because his sister destroyed his papers upon his death, perhaps in an attempt to conceal his homosexuality and physical attraction to boys.

Horatio Alger. Courtesy of the Library of Congress.

Alger's interest in rescuing street children coincided with pioneering efforts such as those of **Charles Loring Brace** and the Children's Aid Society. As many as 34,000 children were homeless in New York City alone, and neighborhoods such as the infamous Five Points region were awash in prostitution, violence, political corruption, and despair. Alger made street boys the heroes of most of his novels. The first, *Ragged Dick; or Street Life in New York with the Bootblacks* was serialized in 1867 and appeared in book form the following year. The novel juxtaposes a virtuous but poor bootblack, Dick Hunter, and the wastrel Johnny Nolan. Although Nolan succumbs to vice, Hunter saves a businessman's son from drowning, wins the man's patronage, and begins his rise within the firm.

Achieving salvation through hard work, cheerfulness, luck, determination, and patronage forms the story arc of most of Alger's books. These "dime novels," as the pulp fiction of the day was called, were akin to modern-day romance novels in that they are formulaic and quickly penned, and they resolve positively for their protagonists. Alger's books are essentially **inner-city** fairy tales, with young boys assuming the roles that fairy tales often reserved for princesses-in-the-making. *Ragged Dick* became a series, as did several other Alger fictional franchises, including *Tattered Tom*, *Pluck and Luck*, and *Joe the Hotel Boy*. Alger's novels were famed for the manner in which central characters obtain the **American dream**. They were widely consumed by **working-class** readers in the Gilded Age, a time in which **capitalism** was hotly contested, and they may have played a role in advancing **Social Darwinian** beliefs in **self-reliance**. Some historians dispute Alger's influence, arguing that such ex post facto interpretations of the importance of his work developed after the suppression of working-class radical movements in the early twentieth century. Nonetheless, some 20,000,000 copies of Alger's books were sold before they passed from fashion in the early 1920s. His works were so well-known that Mark Twain penned two Alger parodies in 1875.

Ironically, Alger was not himself a rags-to-riches story. His books sold well, but his various acts of **philanthropy**—the YMCA, the Children's Aid Society, the Newsboys Lodging House, and various missions—quickly depleted his funds, and some of the boys he tried to assist flimflammed him. He also gave money to various political reform causes, including efforts to end contract labor and to enact child labor law reform. In addition to writing, Alger also tutored children of rich New Yorkers; one of his charges was future Supreme Court justice Benjamin Cardozo. Shortly before he died from pneumonia in 1899, Alger left New York and moved in with his sister, Augusta, and her husband in Natick, Massachusetts.

The importance of Alger's writing is hotly contested. In his lifetime he was widely read, and **Theodore Roosevelt** and Ernest Hemingway were among his youthful devotees. His work inspired similar ventures, such as the Hardy Boys and Nancy Drew series, and in death, Alger himself became an icon. To his detractors, Horatio Alger was a spinner of mindless pap and platitudes. His very name is sometimes invoked to convey naivety, simplicity, and unexamined **individualism**. Some damn Alger for contributing to the myth that poverty is attitudinal rather than systemic.

Conservatives sometimes link Alger to American ideals of economic opportunity, the value of hard work, and the openness of the American system of social mobility. The Horatio Alger Association of Distinguished Americans, founded in 1947, awards annual scholarships to high school students who overcome adversity in an Alger-like fashion. The association's members have included an unusual assortment of former **sports** figures (Hank Aaron, Julius Erving, Wayne Gretzky); business leaders (Thomas Watson, T. Boone Pickens); celebrities (Joyce Carol Oates, **Oprah Winfrey**); and political figures. The latter category tends to draw from conservative ranks—**Ronald Reagan**, Clarence Thomas, Robert Dole, John Connally—but it has also included liberals, such as Mario Cuomo. There is a Horatio Alger Society devoted to his literary outpouring, and Alger's personal life also inspired the formation of the North American Man/Boy Love Association, a group that lobbies for the elimination of laws governing consensual homosexual relations between minors and adults.

Suggested Reading

Horatio Alger, *Ragged Dick*, 2005 (1867); Alger, *Bound to Rise*, 2005 (1873); Jack Bales and Gary Scharnhorst, *The Lost Life of Horatio Alger*, 1985; The Horatio Alger Association of Distinguished Americans (http://www.horatioalger.com/index.cfm); Carol Nackenoff, *The Fictional Republic: Horatio Alger and American Political Discourse*, 1994.

ALIENATION

KAREN BETTEZ HALNON

Alienation is a term used in sociology, critical social theory, and more generally among **Marxists** to refer to an activity or a state in which a person, a group, an institution, or a society becomes estranged. For example, an individual might come to perceive himself as outside what he feels is a "natural" (or, for some theorists, "normative") relationship with the self, others, the community, or the world. For most Marxists, the concept of self-alienation is the essence of capitalist oppression, and in turn, de-alienation involves the potential for revolutionary social action. Revolutionary action then lies in political economic education, or in unmasking what some call **false consciousness**—the ideologies or inverted desires that distract from accurately perceiving and rejecting deficient and dehumanizing material realities.

Alienation can assume several different forms, but all are ultimately a form of self-alienation, or estrangement from the potentiality of the achievement and expression of the self. These forms include alienation from one's self; alienation from other human beings, from the humanity of others, and from our natural and interdependent state of community with others; alienation from nature or from the material world in which we are situated; and alienation from one's own life activities.

Religious alienation is one possible form of self-alienation because it subordinates individuals to a non-objective ideology. For Marx (following Ludwig Feuerbach, *The Essence of Christianity*), religious alienation attributes part of the self, the potential for humanity, and ultimately the perfection of the self and humanity to an objective existence as God, or as the cultural imagining of human perfection. Such beliefs are dominant and also oppressive. Marx famously proclaimed religion to be the "opiate of the **masses**." Similarly, economic activity in the forms of money, commodities, and capital remove and abstract one away from direct relation with one's life activities and their products. For example, the surplus value extracted in the labor process (i.e., profit), in particular, has the effect of intensifying economic, social, and cultural domination by the **capitalist** class (or those who own the **means of production**). In fact, Marx felt that capitalist production modes were alienating by nature because they divorced the **working class** from the fruits of their own labor and attempted to substitute money and goods. The state, the law, and social institutions further conspire to trick individuals into identifying themselves and their activities with separate and simplified objects. Such alienation renders the individual slavish, powerless, and dependent. At minimum, a de-alienated individual is an autonomous and creative self-producer of meaning and is in direct conscious relation with the products of her or his life.

Whereas traditional Marxist theory focused on production-related alienation, contemporary social theory focuses on alienation as the deliberate production of unreality. Many see **consumerism** and its attendant **advertising**-based dreams as a dominant, oppressive force colonizing contemporary social life. The focus of critics of consumerism is on the dehumanizing effects of living in a **globalized** world of mass media and advertising, of spectacle and simulation, and of consumption of simulated experiences and homogenized (and branded) lifestyles and identities. A particular emphasis of such work is on the commoditization of dissent or how the modern capitalist state assimilates (and even markets) opposition to its **hegemony**.

Suggested Reading

Erich Fromm, *Marx's Concept of Man*, 1961; Karen Bettez Halnon, "Alienation Incorporated: 'F*** the Mainstream Music' in the Mainstream," *Current Sociology*, 53.4 (May 2005), pp. 441–464; Georg Lukacs, *History & Class Consciousness*, 1920; Herbert Marcuse, *One-Dimensional Man*, 1968; Bertell Ollman, *Alienation: Marx's Conception of Man in Capitalist Society*, 1971.

ALTHUSSER, LOUIS (October 19, 1918–October 23, 1990)

ROBERT E. WEIR

Louis Althusser was an influential French **Marxist** thinker whose interpretations of Marx have influenced numerous social scientists, especially those with leftist political views.

Born in Algeria, Althusser had a troubled childhood but excelled in school. His education at the well-regarded École Normale Supériuere was interrupted by World War II, and he spent much of the war in a German prisoner-of-war camp. His public career began after the war, and he wrote numerous books and articles, many of which are intellectually dense and hard to penetrate, but which have greatly influenced Marxist theory. His later life was marred by tragedy. In 1980 he murdered his wife, was declared mentally incompetent, was treated for three years in a psychiatric hospital, and spent the remainder of his life as a recluse.

His work is important for the way in which he addressed seeming contradictions in Karl Marx's writings. He defended Marx from those who saw his work as a form of crude economic determinism that reduced all human decision-making and social change to one's relation to the **means of production** and to economic shifts. Althusser argued that Marx himself underwent an "epistemological break" that he did not completely understand, but that Marx nonetheless saw complexity in the ways in which the economic substructure of society interacted with social forces and institutions. In other words, people's social needs also condition their political actions, economic decision-making, and ideological development.

Much of Althusser's thought is of interest mainly to political theorists, but his emphasis on what he called "ideological state apparatuses" is an important reminder that **capitalists** often take advantage of their power over social institutions to reinforce values vital to maintaining their dominance as enshrined in the relationship to the means of production. Althusser saw two levels of control: repressive state power embodied in police, the legal system, and the military; and "professionals of ideology," such as schools, popular culture, religion, and the family, that manufacture consent for the capitalist state. Like Antonio Gramsci

(1891–1937), an Italian **communist** whose health was ruined in a fascist prison camp, Althusser understood that ideological consent was a more potent form of social control than coercion and, hence, less likely to induce revolutionary fervor. Although he agreed with Marx and others that this consent was a form of **false consciousness**, he also realized that ideas such as democracy, divine judgment, or patriotism can place individuals in what he dubbed "an imaginary relationship" with the world.

Althusser's explication of this "imaginary relationship" is quite complex, and many aspects of his work are problematic. However, one need not embrace his Marxism or immerse oneself in his writing to appreciate the distinction he makes between repressive and ideological agency or to realize the potency of his explanation for how individuals can come to embrace things that are not necessarily in their self-interest. Gramsci called the ability to make repressive systems appear as common sense "cultural hegemony." Both theorists help explain, for example, social phenomena such as the relative quiescence of those living in **poverty**, why some members of the **working class** refuse to join labor unions, or the ways in which many people admire members of the **upper class** even if they know that their wealth was gained dishonestly or exploitatively. Both also help one see how social-class relations can be reinforced subconsciously; Althusser was a student of psychology—especially Freud and Lacan—and Gramsci noted the power of popular culture to embed and encode ideas about social class.

Suggested Reading

Louis Althusser, *For Marx*, 1969; Perry Anderson, *Considerations on Western Marxism*, 1979; Antonio Gramsci, *Selections from the Prison Notebooks*, 1971.

AMERICAN DREAM

ROBERT E. WEIR

American dream is a vague, but inspiring, term that refers to the belief of many Americans that they will be happy, materially well off, and economically secure. Embedded within it is the expectation that each generation will do better than their parents. Because the term is so unspecific, it has been subject to exploitation by all political persuasions.

The first known use of the term comes from *The Epic of America*, authored by historian James Truslow Adams in 1931. Adams, however, merely coined a phrase to describe an impulse that is as old as European settlement in North America. A key component of the American dream is freedom, loosely construed to embody ideas as diverse as land acquisition, ideals enshrined in the Bill of Rights, and a nonregulatory business environment. In essence, the American dream often corresponds to what groups or individuals believe the promise of America to be, although economic opportunity has often been central to its construction.

By the mid-nineteenth century, the American dream was increasingly linked to notions of acquiring personal wealth. The fortunes made by various entrepreneurs,

robber barons, and industrialists offered hopes of upward **social mobility** to millions, and the **conspicuous consumption** patterns of the wealthy fueled the dream. So too did the rags-to-riches novels of **Horatio Alger**, propaganda from **Social Darwinists**, laissez-faire economic policies, and the aspirations of the millions of immigrants who poured into American society between 1870 and 1920. Although labor unions and radicals tried to convince the masses they were being exploited, the opulent wealth of enclaves such as **Newport** ameliorated potential anger; many looked upon the mansions, gilded carriages, and possessions of the wealthy with envy rather than desire to redesign society. By the turn of the twentieth century, many viewed individuals such as **Andrew Carnegie**, **John Rockefeller**, and Henry Ford as folk heroes, not robber barons.

During the 1930s and 1940s, the American dream was challenged by the **Great Depression** and World War II. By the 1950s, however, postwar prosperity had unleashed a wave of **consumerism** that fed the American dream. Key material components of the American dream included home ownership, access to consumer goods, and economic security. These were reinforced by core beliefs in the superiority of the American political, economic, and social system and the idea that hard work would result in material success. Television and film images also served to promote the American dream, and **advertisers** seized upon the idea to promote their products. Not coincidentally, there was a marked decline in the number of Americans who identified themselves as **working class** and an increase in those claiming middle-class identity. Although membership in labor unions remained high, militancy declined, and labor leaders such as **George Meany** opined that workers were indeed becoming **middle class**. On a less benign level, the American dream was often linked to enforced conformity. The Cold War brought not only a fear of and backlash against **communism**, but also the idea that there was a singular American "way of life" and that all who deviated from it were suspect. The political right labored to equate the American dream with unquestioning patriotism, anticommunism, and support for market capitalism.

In the 1960s, however, awareness rose that not everyone had access to the American dream. African Americans, ethnic minorities, and working women complained that systemic discrimination kept them in subordinate positions both socially and economically. Moreover, **poverty** studies revealed that economic data did not support the idea that America was predominately a middle-class society. Social activists such as Rev. **Martin Luther King Jr**. and **Michael Harrington** co-opted the American dream image to argue in favor of anti-poverty programs, racial justice, and redistribution of wealth. Radical groups such as the **Students for a Democratic Society** issued manifestos challenging the American dream.

Since the 1960s competing versions of the American dream have, to some degree, symbolically framed political debate within American society. In the 1980s, for example, President Ronald Reagan evoked the American dream to solicit support for tax cuts and conservative political views, a tactic renewed by Karl Rove and other conservative political consultants in the early twenty-first century. One of the most notable results of this has been declining public and government support for **welfare** programs, the prevailing critique being that welfare destroys **self-reliance** and works against the American dream. Conservatives have even formed groups, such as the American Dream Coalition, to promote property ownership, low taxes, and the dismantling of business regulations.

By contrast, liberals often use images of a derailed American dream to drum up support for their own views. They point to **homelessness**, large numbers of **working poor**, and widespread discrimination as evidence that the American dream is as much mythic as real. For example, 80 percent of Americans state a goal of owning a single-family home with a stand-alone yard. Nearly three-quarters of all white families own property, but less than half of all African American and Latino families can make this claim. Moreover, liberals charge that conservatives misuse the American dream to draw attention away from racism, gender bias, regressive taxation, sinking wages, and other factors that give the rich unfair advantages.

Suggested Reading

Jeffrey Decker, *Made in America: Self-Styled Success from Horatio Alger to Oprah Winfrey*, 1997; Jason DeParle, *American Dream: Three Women, Ten Kids, and a Nation's Drive to End Welfare*, 2004; Richard Florida, "The New American Dream," *Washington Monthly*, March 2003.

AMERICAN ENTERPRISE INSTITUTE

See Class; Think Tanks.

AMERICAN EXCEPTIONALISM

ROBERT E. WEIR

American exceptionalism is a postulate put forth by some scholars that American society and history departed from that of the Europeans who settled North America because of special advantages that existed in the United States after its revolution against Great Britain. In particular, scholars point to the relative openness of the American social system resulting from its lack of an aristocracy of birth, an abundance of available land for settlers, and a political system that granted many basic liberties and individual freedoms for which Europeans had to struggle for decades to attain. The theory is often evoked to explain the relative lack of class conflict in the United States.

The term originated with Alexis de Tocqueville and appeared in his four-volume *Democracy in America* (1835–40). Tocqueville cited liberty, equality of birth, individualism, popular democracy, and laissez-faire business practices as hallmarks of American exceptionalism. These, he felt, differentiated the United States from the feudalism-scarred past of Europe. Americans, he argued, felt loyalty to their families and to a vaguely constructed notion of their nation, but were not burdened by obligations to social class and hierarchy.

Tocqueville's musings were simply a restatement of ideas that many original settlers had brought with them to the American colonies even before the **American**

Revolution. The Puritan vision of constructing a "city upon a hill" is one expression of making the New World substantively different from Europe, and many other settlers consciously set forth to reject what they perceived to be Old World values.

As an intellectual construct for scholars, American exceptionalism has waxed and waned, the prevailing notion at the present being that it has been overstated. During the nineteenth century, many Americans belonging to the upper **middle class** revived American exceptionalism as a form of class identity masquerading as national pride. Conservatives often evoked some form of it to justify Manifest Destiny designs on the continent in the antebellum period as well as imperialist ventures at the turn of the century. Often, ideals of exceptionalism mingled with those of Americans as a chosen people of biblical proportion. The notion also shows up in Frederick Jackson Turner's famed "frontier thesis," in which he argued that the availability of free land operated as a "safety valve" that softened the development of radicalism in the United States. American exceptionalism also appeared in works from worried **Victorians** such as Charles **Adams**, who feared that immigrants and debased culture were weakening the American character.

Exceptionalism received a big boost from German scholar Werner Sombart, whose 1906 *Why Is There No Socialism in the United States?* touched off an academic debate that continues to roil. Sombart put forth a thesis that American workers were prosperous vis-à-vis those in other industrial nations and hence were less likely to embrace **socialism** or other radical notions. His views were often cited to explain why the United States never developed an independent labor party. Another strain of exceptionalist debate took the position that Sombart was overly optimistic, but socialism held little attraction because it was viewed as a foreign import and could not successfully compete with older, indigenous forms of American radicalism. In the 1920s, however, scholars working at the University of Wisconsin, such as John R. Commons and Selig Perlman, tended to echo Sombart and argue that American workers were more wage-conscious than Europeans and that they also had more outlets within the traditional political system.

American exceptionalism also proved palatable for the sort of nationalist history that dominated much of the twentieth century. Whether overtly or by implication, exceptionalism often emerged in histories that evoked themes such as the glory, genius, and power of the United States. Many of America's most eminent historians—including Charles Beard, Daniel Bell, Daniel Boorstin, Henry Steel Commager, Richard Hofstadter, Horace Kallen, **Seymour Lipset**, Vernon Parrington, Henry Nash Smith, and Arthur Schlesinger—have played off exceptionalist themes.

In the 1960s, however, scholars practicing what was dubbed the **new social history** began to call into question the underlying assumptions of American exceptionalism. First, they argued that exceptionalist scholars confused form and essence. Each nation has practices, laws, and events that are outwardly different, but often these are only surface manifestations of trends, problems, and issues that arise elsewhere; in other words, most things are not as unique as they might appear to be. Scholars also charged that exceptionalism was such a diffuse concept that it was used to explain everything when, in fact, it was too imprecise to explain much of anything. More significantly, critics charged that American exceptionalism assumed a social consensus on values and ignored the role of

power. It was not that American workers rejected radicalism so much as the fact that organized **capitalism**, court systems, and politicians crushed radical movements. Nor could one sustain a prosperity thesis if one looked at the social data pertaining to the **working class**. Whereas defenders of American exceptionalism tended to embrace consensus theory, most of its critics were **conflict theorists** who charged defenders with historical distortion, reductionism, amnesia, or a combination of these.

Despite attacks on exceptionalism from the 1960s on, the theory remains very much alive. More recent scholarship has tinkered with the thesis to locate exceptionalism in more recent history. In other words, America wasn't born exceptional; it became so after the defeat of radical movements that might have brought America's history more in line with Europe's. This scholarship stands as an attempt at finding middle ground between consensus and conflict schools.

American exceptionalism has remained very attractive to the political right, especially since the collapse of the Cold War. From their viewpoint, America's triumph is testament to the resiliency of its political, social, and cultural institutions, and America's status as the dominant superpower is proof of uniqueness. Quite often, the **Founding Fathers** are evoked in defense of such positions. Exceptionalism also meshes well with social views that celebrate the opportunities conservatives believe are inherent within American capitalism.

Among scholars, the prevailing view is that American exceptionalism has been overstated. Much of what once appeared to be exceptional has largely been a matter of the dearth of comparative studies. Many scholars do believe, however, that a belief in exceptionalism is useful in explaining the tendency of some Americans toward xenophobia and the nation's awkwardness in international relations. It also retains a devoted core of intellectuals who feel the concept retains merit.

Suggested Reading
Rick Fantasia and Kim Voss, *Hard Work: Remaking American Labor*, 2004; Martin Seymour Lipset and John Laslet, eds., *Failure of a Dream? Essays in the History of American Socialism*, 1974; Kim Voss, *The Making of American Exceptionalism: The Knights of Labor and Class Formation in the Nineteenth Century*, 1993.

AMERICAN FEDERATION OF LABOR (AFL)

SARAH CROSSLEY

The American Federation of Labor (AFL), a labor federation organized in 1886 by cigar maker **Samuel Gompers**, was a reorganization of a previous federation: the Federation of Organized Trades and Labor Unions. Initially, the AFL was organized as a response to dissatisfaction with the **Knights of Labor**, which developed a centralized structure and fostered a workers' culture under which anyone from the "producing classes" could be a member.

The AFL sought to distinguish itself from the inclusiveness of the Knights of Labor through various means. Rather than fighting what they saw as the inevitability

American Federation of Labor building, ca. 1920–50. Courtesy of the Library of Congress.

of wage labor, the AFL was determined to work within the established **capitalist** system through two fundamental principles: (1) pure and simple unionism and (2) voluntarism. Pure and simple unionism simply referred to bread-and-butter issues such as wages, hours, and working conditions.

Voluntarism meant that constituent unions would rely only on themselves and their members. This was a far cry from the Knights of Labor's ideology, which insisted that "an injury to one is an injury to all." In fact, the only real similarity between the two organizations was the campaign for the eight-hour day. After that, the AFL promoted autonomy of the unions and limited its membership to workers only. Member unions were encouraged to set up high initiation fees and dues to support workers themselves if they went on **strike**.

Initially, the AFL promoted a platform of egalitarianism and industrial unionism. However, as craft unionism came to dominate the landscape of the AFL, both the principle of egalitarianism and the practice of industrial unionism were hard-pressed to find a place. The AFL did not actively exclude workers based on **race** or nationality, but many of its affiliates did, and the skilled workers' craft unions in the AFL rarely included workers of color or **immigrant** workers. Initiation fees and high dues made it impossible for unskilled workers, most of whom were women, immigrants, and people of color, to join an affiliate union.

By the mid-1890s, both egalitarianism and industrial unionism had become less of an issue as industries such as construction and railroads actively sought to exclude immigrant and African American workers. The AFL sought to work around the racist policies of affiliate unions by organizing segregated locals. By the early 1900s segregated locals had become the norm. The AFL followed the lead of its affiliate unions and soon began to support anti-immigration legislation, including the reaffirmation of the 1882 Chinese Exclusion Act.

Although the AFL was formed by members of the **Socialist Party**, this leftist approach was almost immediately discarded for a more conservative approach to unionism. The experiences of the Knights of Labor had convinced AFL founders that such an all-encompassing union of workers with a political agenda was no way to create a stable **labor movement**. For AFL members, immediate issues pertaining to a skilled workforce of craft unionists offered more possibility for stability than working on a political agenda. Thus, from its inception, the AFL refused to align itself with any political party, including any labor party.

For AFL president Samuel Gompers, party affiliations did not dictate who may or may not be a friend to labor. Gompers's disillusionment with the political process in regard to labor led him to dismiss even legislation beneficial to workers because it would hurt collective bargaining processes that sought the same protections.

At the turn of the twentieth century, the AFL stayed with its method of pure and simple unionism while other organizations such as the Socialist Party and the **Industrial Workers of the World** took more radical stances regarding the transformation of the American labor movement. Collective bargaining remained the centerpiece for AFL organizing, and despite the influx of unskilled labor into the labor market, craft unions remained the focus of AFL organizing. When AFL leaders did try to organize unskilled workers, it was into "federal labor unions (FLU)." FLUs were separate unions that existed within the federation for unskilled laborers whose work did not fit into the structure of craft unions. The exclusivity of the federation prohibited large numbers of women, African Americans, and immigrants from unionizing within the AFL.

Despite its shortcomings, in the early twentieth century, the AFL proved a powerful and vital influence on the labor movement and the creation of an expanded **middle class**. Although union membership often followed the ebbs and flows of the larger political economy, it remained the **working classes'** most powerful ally, claiming anywhere from approximately 1.7 million members in 1904 to almost 4 million in 1920.

By 1935 the AFL was struggling with internal dissension over how to organize the industrial workforce. The AFL's tried-and-true method of organizing along craft lines was proving an inadequate way of organizing larger industries such as rubber and steel. Led by **John L. Lewis**, several union leaders formed the **Committee for Industrial Organization** (CIO) to promote the unionization of a rapidly growing unskilled workforce. Fearful that such large numbers of unskilled workers, many of whom spoke little or no English, would hurt the bargaining power of skilled workers, the AFL resisted. By 1937 the federation had expelled the ten member unions that made up the increasingly powerful CIO. The two groups remained rival federations, vying for new members until their merger in 1955 under then-president of the AFL **George Meany**.

Although the AFL and its successor, the **AFL–CIO**, have been plagued with many shortcomings in their history, the labor federation has also proved itself a resilient force in the American labor movement. Its focus on the creation and protection of a new middle class has successfully remained the heart of its motivation. Its failure to address adequately the concerns of women, minorities, and immigrants (the vast majority of the unskilled workforce) is an ongoing challenge for the modern labor movement as it struggles to remain vital in an increasingly diverse and rapidly changing workforce.

Suggested Reading

Paul Buhle, *Taking Care of Business: Samuel Gompers, George Meany, Lane Kirkland, and the Tragedy of American Labor*, 1999; Samuel Gompers, *Seventy Years of Life and Labor: An Autobiography*, Reprint, 1984; Julie Green, *Pure and Simple Politics: The American Federation of Labor and Political Activism, 1881–1917*, 1998.

AMERICAN FEDERATION OF LABOR–CONGRESS OF INDUSTRIAL ORGANIZATIONS (AFL–CIO)

SARAH CROSSLEY

The AFL–CIO is a voluntary federation of labor unions. Initially, the **American Federation of Labor** (AFL) and the **Congress of Industrial Organizations** (CIO) were two separate federations. Formed in 1886, the AFL originally opened itself up to skilled tradesmen within their particular trade. The CIO initially formed in 1935 within the AFL to organize previously ignored unskilled workers. Members of the CIO felt that with the onset of industrialization and mass production, all workers within a given sector should be organized, regardless of their skill level. Expelled from the AFL in 1937, the CIO remained a rival federation until the two merged in 1955, under the leadership of AFL president **George Meany**. Part of the impetus for merger was the passage of the anti-labor Taft-Hartley Act in 1947, which the AFL–CIO vowed to have repealed.

Under Meany's leadership, the AFL–CIO reached its apex as the **labor movement** readied itself to "organize the unorganized." In the 1950s, unions represented approximately one-third of all private enterprise workers. Historians credit a strong post–World War II economy, demobilization, and Meany's ambitious leadership with labor's rise in the 1950s. It did not, however, succeed in overturning Taft-Hartley, nor did it make major inroads in the South, where right-to-work laws and Red-baiting tactics sidetracked AFL–CIO efforts.

By the 1970s divisions over the Vietnam War were causing significant rifts within the federation. The AFL–CIO leadership, with Meany at the helm, was mostly pro-war, supporting the corrupt anticommunist Vietnamese Confederation of Labor (VCL) through its Asian American Free Labor Institute. Unhappy with the VCL, with Meany's steadfast support for the war, and with the AFL–CIO's perceived slowness in embracing the Civil Rights Movement, several unions formed the Alliance for Labor Action, an alternative organization to the AFL–CIO spearheaded by Meany critic **Walter Reuther**. The alliance proved short-lived and unsuccessful.

When Meany retired in 1979, labor was in deep decline. Postwar unionism bolstered a new **middle class** that included well-paid **blue-collar** workers who gave labor temporary respectability but decreased its militancy. The changing face of labor hampered incoming AFL–CIO president Lane Kirkland. The administration of President **Ronald Reagan** in the 1980s continually challenged pro-labor legislation, while the growth of international corporations, increasing uses of outsourcing, **deindustrialization**, and a general decline in labor organizing all contributed to sinking union membership levels. Labor leaders were caught off guard by the creation of new jobs in the booming service sector and were ill-prepared for the aggressive anti-union environment of the late 1970s and beyond.

Conservatives—many of whom were angered by the AFL–CIO's electoral support for the Democratic Party—attacked labor unions as relics of a past era and obstacles to making American business competitive in a global economy. Many businesses overtly smashed unions, while others forced them to make significant concessions on wages, benefits, and workforce strength. Conservatives also turned Meany-era logic against labor and argued that because most Americans were now members of the middle class, there was no need for labor unions. By the mid-1980s, labor unions were viewed as obstructionist and antiquated by a substantial number of Americans.

Traditional methods of organizing grew obsolete in this anti-labor climate, and large and virulently anti-union employers such as **Wal-Mart** became typical. Between 1979 and 1983, for instance, service jobs such as domestic or janitorial jobs increased by about 38 percent, while production jobs such as those in the automotive industry decreased by 12 percent. Many union activists accused the AFL–CIO of being overly bureaucratic, of caving in to concessionary demands, and of squandering federation resources in political campaigns. The AFL–CIO's relationship with the Democratic Party was particularly scrutinized, with some activists arguing that the federation had received poor return on its large campaign expenditures.

Pressure to reverse the downward trend in union membership resulted in the 1995 election of current president John Sweeney. Sweeney stressed the need for renewed militancy, but organizing in the new economy has proved a daunting task. Rhetoric of a "new" middle class aside, since the 1980s, the gap between **wealth** and **poverty** has widened. The AFL–CIO sought to make changes. It recognized that the number of women and minorities in the workforce has grown steadily and that **immigrants** continue to make up sizable percentages of the labor force, especially in the service sector. The Sweeney-led AFL–CIO attempted to revitalize union activism through programs designed to train new organizers—especially women and minorities—and to recruit younger members. The new tactics may have slowed union decline, but they have yet to stimulate resurgence.

As unionism has stagnated, detractors have turned against Sweeney. His supporters argue that labor must remain united in this time of crisis in order to secure strong union membership. They point to the success of the labor movement in mobilizing union voters during the 2004 election and the AFL–CIO's aggressive push to organize as symbols of strong leadership and signs that the movement is headed in the right direction.

Critics assert that a single federation fosters complacency among the AFL–CIO hierarchy and that a second rival federation would push labor leaders to act more aggressively in defense of their constituency. They cite the strength of labor in the pre–World War II era as an example of the efficacy of multiple federations. On July 25, 2005, five unions split from the AFL–CIO to form the Change to Win Coalition. By 2006, this coalition had grown to include seven constituent unions, but labor continued to struggle, with just 8 percent of private-sector workers belonging to unions.

Whether competing federations will aid or harm the labor movement remains an open question. What is clear is that as the face of labor continues to change, the labor movement must be willing change with it.

Suggested Reading

AFL–CIO Media Center (http://www.aflcio.org/mediacenter); Paul Buhle, *Taking Care of Business: Samuel Gompers, George Meany, Lane Kirkland, and the Tragedy of American Labor*, 1999; Jo-Ann Mort, *Not Your Father's Union Movement: Inside the AFL–CIO*, 1998.

AMERICAN INDIANS

See Native Americans.

AMERICAN REVOLUTION

ROBERT E. WEIR

Between 1775 and 1783, colonists in thirteen of England's fifteen North American colonies waged a war for independence that ultimately resulted in the formation of the United States of America. The American Revolution is so thoroughly engrained in the American psyche that it exists in popular memory as much as a myth as an actual event. This is especially true of the so-called **Founding Fathers**, such as George Washington, Thomas Jefferson, and Benjamin Franklin. For many years, the story of the American Revolution was told mostly through the deeds and words of **elites**, with commoners mentioned mostly for their roles as soldiers and local militiamen.

This oversight went largely unaddressed until the emergence of the **new social history** during the 1960s, when historians began to pay more attention to pre-Revolutionary protest that established protest traditions. Long before the clash with Britain became apparent, commoners were expressing their discontent. Numerous **slave** rebellions took place, as did individual acts of rebellion ranging from running away from masters to resisting the lash. **Indentured servants** engaged in similar protests, a few of which became violent. In 1676, for instance, indentured servants and runaway slaves in the Chesapeake region joined backcountry farmers in **Bacon's Rebellion**, which briefly overthrew the royal government of Virginia.

Colonial artisans also resisted arbitrary authority, especially after 1720, when new waves of Scots-Irish and German immigrants altered the social landscape of the colonies. Many of these individuals came from humble backgrounds and were already distrustful of aristocrats and elites. In the cities, many of them joined journeymen's associations and friendly societies that became the basis for trade unions, with the 1724 Philadelphia Carpenter's Company often credited as the first to regulate prices, apprenticeship, and wages.

Likewise, there were periodic bread riots in the colonies during periods of shortage, several of which took on class dimensions when desperate artisans and wives directed their anger at wealthy merchants, tax collectors, or royal officials. In the countryside, rising land prices and taxes also led to upheaval. As social historians now note, much of the pietism and religious experimentation associated with the Great Awakening revivals from the 1720s on had as much to do with popular discontent as with religious fervor. In New England, the revivals often saw land-poor youths strike out against their elders, while in the Mid-Atlantic region and the South, new converts openly challenged existing elites.

By the 1740s Colonial society was under stress. Religious fervor split numerous communities into opposing camps of "New Lights" embracing revivalism and the "Old Lights" who opposed them, the latter group disproportionately representing elites. There was also an emergent land crisis in which most of the best land and that closest to settled areas was already claimed. As settlers ventured deeper into the backcountry, they often encountered **Native Americans**, whom they saw as obstacles in need of removal, though colonial officials were often loath to do so. Religion, land, and Native policy often yielded anger toward established authority, which spilled out in events such as rent protests in New York during the 1740s, the Regulators' rebellion of South Carolina planters from 1767 to 1771, and the Paxton Boys' march on Philadelphia in 1763.

The aftermath of the French and Indian War (1754–63) further heightened tension, especially in Colonial cities. Although originally hailed as a great victory for "Mother England," the cost of conducting the war—which was part of a greater European struggle known as the Seven Years' War—bankrupted the English treasury and necessitated raising taxes. The colonial tax burden was actually light in comparison with rates within Britain, but new taxes coincided with a general dullness of trade, sinking wages, and increasing impoverishment of the urban poor. Colonial cities saw increases in debt imprisonment and almshouse applications, and it was exceedingly difficult for a man to support his family solely on his own wages. Many artisans, especially hard-hit shoemakers, braziers, coopers, and sailors, took note of the fact that in cities such as Philadelphia, the wealthiest 10 percent controlled two-thirds of the total wealth.

By the late 1760s an odd alliance had crystallized between merchants and intellectuals resisting British authority and the farmers and urban workers whose discontent was more generalized. Many commoners took part in protests against the Stamp Act, though they seldom needed to buy one; against the Townshend duties, though most of the taxed goods were luxury items they did not consume; and against the Tea Act, though many had never drunk a cup of tea. Popular protests such as hangings-in-effigy or attacks on royal officials broke out in the colonies, and commoners joined groups such as the Sons of Liberty and various corresponding societies. The 1770 Boston Massacre also stoked the flames of discontent because all five victims were laborers. Women began to weave homespun cloth as colonists boycotted English goods and also tended farms and shops once hostilities broke out in 1775.

It is difficult to determine how many colonists actually took part in the American Revolution; several estimates claim that only about 40 percent of males old enough to fight actually did so and that they were divided rather evenly between Patriots and Tories. Moreover, in an agrarian economy, few farmers could be away from their fields for long, and thus, they were more likely to be part of a temporary militia—such as the famed "Minutemen"—which saw only brief, local action. What is known is that the bulk of fighters came from the ranks of commoners, with artisans and sailors disproportionately represented. Soldiers in the Continental Army suffered an array of hardships ranging from lack of supplies, disease outbreaks, and inadequate housing to missed pay. Commoners made up the bulk of casualties.

Historians now believe that those commoners went to war for different reasons than their leaders. Men such as Jefferson, Franklin, and Patrick Henry were inflamed by new ideas of governance emanating from the Enlightenment, whereas merchants such as John Hancock favored the removal of British trade restraints. Although many commoners were idealists, most farmers and artisans probably cast their lot with colonial leaders in hopes of bettering their economic lot in a new republic. Alas, this was not immediately in the offing. Inflation, a postwar recession, the devaluation of the Continental dollar, the contraction of available credit, and newly enacted taxes left some war veterans in worse shape than before the American Revolution, which precipitated such popular revolts as **Shays's Rebellion** and the **Whiskey Rebellion**. Whatever else the American Revolution accomplished, it did not address inequality, impoverishment, or social privilege.

Suggested Reading

Billy Smith, *The "Lower Sort": Philadelphia's Laboring People, 1750–1800*, 1990; Gordon Wood, *The Radicalism of the American Revolution*, 1992; Alfred Young, *Beyond the American Revolution: Studies in the History of American Radicalism*, 1993.

ANARCHY

DAVID V. HEALY

Anarchy is a political theory developed by numerous political philosophers since the mid-1800s. The word *anarchy* is derived from the Greek αναρχία, which translates to "without rulers." Anarchy, a political theory also known as anarchism, proposes a system without hierarchy. In anarchist thought, class is not defined solely by social or economic class, but rather by the relationships of **power** present in society. Anarchists criticize any system where a person is subservient to or dependent on another because such constructions place individuals and groups in supposedly unnatural relationships. These unbalanced interactions, according to anarchists, are the root cause of most of society's ills, for the **elites**' exploitation of government, business, and religion is responsible for the destitution of the masses.

Important late nineteenth- and early twentieth-century anarchist theorists such as Pierre-Joseph Proudhon, Mikhail Bakunin, and **Emma Goldman** helped shape the discourse of their times and the course of history. Early anarchists were major competition to **communist** revolutionaries and thinkers, Marx included. Perhaps the most notable institution of anarchist theory was Catalonia in the 1930s, before Franco's victory in the Spanish Civil War. Catalonian anarchy eventually collapsed, along with the 1871 Paris Commune and many other anarchist societies. Christiania, Denmark, is hailed as the current anarchist model society, though it is threatened by numerous actions on the part of the Danish national government. Once considered a major threat to the power structures of Western society—anarchists were even accused of involvement in the assassination of President William McKinley—anarchism since has waned in society at large.

Anarchist thought today is divided into several specialized fields, each tailored to the beliefs and priorities of various anarchists. Though "pure" anarchy still exists, anarcho-communism, anarcho-syndicalism, and anarcho-primitivism are all common "modified" anarchist theories. Anarcho-communism blends the theories of anarchism and communism, whereas anarcho-syndicalism takes a different course for workers' liberation, positing that workers' organizations (syndicates) hold the ideal for social organization. Anarcho-primitivists believe that the best world possible requires a rejection of technology, on the assumption that it is technology that destroys the inherent humanity of social interaction and drives us to form hierarchies that inevitably exploit the weak. This strain of anarchism has surfaced in recent protests against **globalization**, particularly at meetings associated with the World Trade Organization. Anarcho-communists have also been active in these protests.

In the course of anarchist development, numerous actions have come to the fore. Perhaps most well-known of anarchist institutions in the United States is the **Industrial Workers of the World**, a union based on the principles of anarcho-syndicalism. Also prevalent are Food Not Bombs, a charity supported by anarchists that provides free vegan meals for homeless people worldwide, and Earth First!, a radical environmental group loosely based on anarchist precepts. The Anarchist Black Cross, formed as the anarchist answer to the Red Cross, is involved with assisting prisoners trapped in jails worldwide as well as educating them. Domestically, many cities are home to Infoshops, which are essentially anarchist community centers; inside, gatherings, workshops, and other events take place, while the infoshops themselves also function as libraries, soup kitchens, and bicycle shops.

Today, the biggest challenge facing anarchists is their exclusion from mainstream social discourse. Whereas once their views were common and well-known, few modern North Americans are cognizant of anarchist political theory. Anarchists constantly struggle against a mass public misconception that anarchy is chaos and strife, all the while attempting to have their voice heard. Aside from **Noam Chomsky** and a few others, few anarchists are taken seriously at all, and in the mass media they are essentially voiceless. Some anarchists argue that globalization will re-energize movements, but merely being considered remains elusive at present.

Suggested Reading
Hakim Bey, *The Temporary Autonomous Zone, Ontological Anarchy, Poetic Terrorism*, 1985; Noam Chomsky, *A New Generation Draws the Line*, 2000; Emma Goldman, *Anarchism and Other Essays*, 1911; Peter Kropotkin, *Kropotkin's Revolutionary Pamphlets*, 1927.

ANGLOPHILIA

See Europhilia.

ANTI-SEMITISM

MAXINE LEVAREN

Anti-Semitism, prejudice against Jews, has crossed all class lines, not only in the United States, but all over the world. However, the reasons have been different, depending on the times as well as on the economic and social class of the population. Historically, anti-Semitism among Christians was associated with the mistaken belief that the Jews were responsible for Jesus' crucifixion. However, the reasons ranged from economic and religious to the desire for racial purity and national identity, as well as the need to find a scapegoat when times were perilous.

In medieval Europe, when the church prohibited money lending, Jews were the only ones who were able to lend money to the rulers and nobility. Therefore, they were often targets when debtors were unable to repay their loans. By expelling, terrorizing, or exterminating the Jews, debtors not only were "forgiven" their loans, but also had the opportunity to confiscate Jewish property. By appealing to the fears of the lower class, the nobility were often supported by the uneducated classes.

Because Jews had different customs and were kept in **ghettos** separate from the majority population (not always by their choice), they were often feared and therefore blamed for any catastrophe that occurred. One of the greatest incidents of this was during the Black Plague in the fourteenth century, when the Jews were systematically blamed for the outbreak and were exterminated from several communities as a result. There were also other events and periods of widespread anti-Semitism, such as the Crusades and the Spanish Inquisition, and as late as the mid-twentieth century, the Jews were blamed for the dire economic conditions in Germany, which gave rise to the Nazi Holocaust. These incidents of anti-Semitism also crossed class lines.

For the most part, American anti-Semitism has had less to do with religion than with the concept that Jews were not "white" or that they often supported the "wrong" end of the political spectrum. During Colonial times, the Jewish population, though very small, fully participated in the economic and social life of the community and fought on both sides during the American Revolutionary War. They populated all the colonies and also supported both North and South during the **Civil War**, which caused outbreaks of anti-Semitism when the Jews were blamed by each side for aiding the other side. In the early twentieth century, Henry Ford, one of the most famous American anti-Semites, was at least partially influenced by an anti-intellectual and politically conservative viewpoint; Jews, as a whole, tended to emphasize education and embrace liberal politics, such as support for organized labor, which certainly was against Ford's political and economic advantage.

Although American anti-Semitism has been less extreme than in many other countries, Jews were often persecuted and were not allowed to vote in some states until the late nineteenth century, and anti-immigration laws enacted in 1924 restricted the number of Jewish immigrants. These laws in the 1930s and 1940s prevented Jews fleeing the Holocaust from entering the United States.

More often, American anti-Semitism was subtle, taking the form of negative stereotypes and discrimination in housing and employment and exclusion from universities, professional organizations, and social clubs. This had the effect of keeping Jews out of the institutions that would allow them to rise to the highest rungs of the social and economic ladder.

The racist **Ku Klux Klan** was also anti-Semitic, based on the desire to maintain American racial purity, because they didn't consider the Jews as Caucasian (note that Roman Catholics were a close third in the groups that the Klan vilified). During the years between World War I and the end of World War II, American anti-Semitism underwent several changes. In the period between the two world wars, several Americans, including aviator Charles Lindbergh and radio demagogue Father Charles E. Coughlin, accused the Jews of pushing American entry into war against Germany. However, in the postwar years, as Americans learned more about the Holocaust, most people adopted a more sympathetic attitude toward Jews. However, that did not prevent a white-supremacist minority from denying that the Holocaust even occurred.

This attitude was particularly emphasized during the Civil Rights Movement of the 1960s, when young Jews openly and visibly supported the breakdown of racial barriers in the South and throughout the nation. Jews were also active in the movement against the Vietnam War and supported many liberal causes, which in some people's minds made them anti-American. Despite heavy Jewish involvement in the Civil Rights Movement of the 1960s, some of the more militant black organizations claimed that Jews were responsible for exploiting blacks.

Some of the white and black racist attitudes toward Jews still remain. However, another dimension of this problem has emerged because of the conflicts in the Middle East. Jewish interest groups are sometimes accused of using their lobbying might to create a pro-Israel bias in U.S. foreign policy toward the Israeli-Palestinian conflict. For the first time, anti-Semitism has gained a foothold in the American liberal community and on university campuses. Many liberals counter that anti-Zionism (opposition to support of Israel), which is a political stand, should not be equated with anti-Semitism, which is more of a prejudice against a particular group, but their intellectual parsing does little to explain away the overtly anti-Semitic graffiti and hate speech that are on the rise on American campuses.

Modern anti-Semitism is not as closely linked to social class as the religious and economic anti-Semitism of the last two centuries, nor is it as thoroughly institutionalized. It remains, however, a distressing aspect of modern American society.

Suggested Reading
Karen Brodkin, *How Jews Became White Folks and What That Says about Race in America*, 1999; Leonard Dinnerstein, *Antisemitism in America*, 1994.

ANTITRUST LAWS

ROBERT E. WEIR

Antitrust laws are regulations that, in theory, ensure business competition by setting guidelines about how much of the market any one manufacturer or service provider can control. Those guidelines are artificial standards determined by legislative and judicial action; hence, they tend to be controversial. Some entrepreneurs argue that economic forces, not politics, ought to govern business activity and that most antitrust laws are inefficient and unwarranted regulations that complicate rather than enhance business. The debate over antitrust laws thus overlaps with larger economic and social questions about how best to provide profits for investors and job opportunities for workers.

American antitrust laws developed out of the historical antipathy toward monopolies, which were viewed as aristocratic. Early presidents, especially Thomas Jefferson and Andrew Jackson, saw monopolies as activities that government itself created. This was part of the reasoning behind Jackson's famed veto of the Second

Bank of the United States (B.U.S.). Jackson was anti-monopoly, not anti-bank, and he quickly dispersed government funds from the defunct B.U.S. among various state and private banks.

The **Founding Fathers** did not foresee the rise of large corporations, and thus, the control over enterprises emerging during the **Industrial Revolution** was left to legislators and the courts. According to critics of monopolies, ruinous and predatory competition threatened **capitalism**, though such arguments took some time to gain support, given that laissez-faire business attitudes were strong among the **upper** and **middle classes**. In 1886 the Supreme Court case of *Santa Clara County v. Southern Pacific Railroad* granted legal corporations many of the same constitutional guarantees as citizens, though it stopped short of calling corporations "persons." Nonetheless, the horizontal integration of firms such as American Tobacco, the rise of vertical monopolies such as Standard Oil, and a rash of state laws led Congress to pass the 1890 Sherman Antitrust Act, which outlawed restraint of trade, backroom price-fixing, trade pools, sweetheart deals, and predatory pricing.

The vagueness of the Sherman Act created as many problems as it solved. The **labor movement** was victimized by it, with some courts ruling that labor unions were illegal restraints of trade. By the **Progressive Era**, many reformers were demanding changes to the Sherman Act on the grounds that it had accomplished little. **Muckraking** studies from writers such as Ida Tarbell, **Upton Sinclair**, **Lincoln Steffens**, and others primed public outrage over corporate abuses, and President **Theodore Roosevelt** led the government charge to break up trusts such as Standard Oil and the Northern Securities Company (contrary to myth, Roosevelt was not opposed to all trusts, only to those he felt abused the public).

Several court decisions affirmed Roosevelt's assault on "bad" trusts and gave greater leeway to applying the Sherman Act. This paved the way for the 1914 Clayton Act, which tightened definitions of illegal business practices and exempted labor unions from restraint of trade charges. That same year, Congress created the Federal Trade Commission and empowered it to define unfair business practices. (FTC powers were expanded by the 1938 Wheeler-Lea amendment.) The 1936 Robinson-Patman Act required sellers to offer the same price to all buyers, thus ending pricing practices that favored large retailers (some critics charge that **Wal-Mart** currently violates the act). In 1950 the Celler-Kefauver Antimerger Act ended the practice of hidden monopolies by forbidding businesses from buying the assets of their competitors to create the illusion of competition.

Antitrust attitudes prevailed in Congress for much of the post–World War II era. In 1980, however, **Ronald Reagan** was elected president. Reagan took power in the midst of a recession, and he and his advisors argued that slashing taxes and unleashing American business were the best ways to stimulate economic growth. In cooperation with the business community, the Reagan administration attacked "needless" business regulations and argued that it was acceptable for large corporations and the upper classes to reap the bulk of tax cuts because they would reinvest their savings and create new jobs for the middle and **lower classes**. In truth, **trickle-down** economics created very few new jobs, and most of these were low-wage positions.

Reagan's defense of big business was given an unintentional boost when, in 1984, courts ruled that AT&T controlled too much of the nation's Bell System telephone and communications network. The chaos that initially ensued when smaller "Baby Bells" were spun off from AT&T seemed to signal that some monopolies benefited the public. This is much the approach taken by Microsoft, which was deemed to have violated the Sherman Act in a 2002 ruling. In addition, Microsoft contends that misuse of antitrust laws stifles creativity and invention.

Since the 1980s Congress and the White House have been less likely to stop corporate mergers, though the Clinton administration introduced mild standards that required consideration of the impact on consumers and prices before approving mergers. The Clinton standards, though weak, were largely ignored after George W. **Bush** assumed the presidency in 2001. Moreover, **globalization** complicates the antitrust debate because international cooperation is needed to apply U.S. regulations outside the United States' borders.

Most antitrust debates hinge on business efficiency and profitability rather than class or social-justice implications. Although many theorists in the **Chicago School of Economics** and their conservative allies continue to tout the virtues of unregulated big business, the track record for job creation is poor when one looks at large corporations. In the 1990s small businesses of twenty or fewer employees accounted for about 75 percent of all new jobs. As late as 2003, about 60 percent of all American workers were employed by such firms.

Suggested Reading

Donald Dewey, *The Antitrust Experiment 1890–1990*, 1990; Rudolph Peritz, *Competition Policy in America: History, Rhetoric, Law, 1888–1992*, 2000; Wyatt C. Wells and Wyatt Wells, *Antitrust and the Formation of the Postwar World*, 2001.

APPALACHIA

BRENDA K. BRETZ

Appalachia is defined as a geographic region within the United States that roughly matches the eponymous mountain range in the eastern United States. Over the years, the exact definition of which states are included has changed depending on federal definition and legislative need. Currently, the federal definition includes 410 mountainous counties in twelve states from New York to Mississippi. Appalachia has consistently appeared on various lists as an area of widespread rural **poverty**, with 15.4 percent of its 23 million people officially defined as impoverished. As federal legislation has been proposed to deal with the economic, environmental, and social problems of the region, the boundaries have shifted and expanded. Most attempts to create agencies or organizing entities focusing on the Appalachian region have failed because these require joint ventures that cross state borders and that often conflict or compete with legislative jurisdiction and power held only by the federal government.

The area was the first to be identified as a unique subculture within the United States that has its own folkways encompassing distinctive cultural, religious, and social practices. The region was "discovered" during the last third of the nineteenth century, when railroad companies, mining operations, and people who were not born within the region began moving into the area to exploit natural resources such as minerals and timber. During this time, the United States was in the middle of an **Industrial Revolution**, and those who came in contact with the natives of this region were cognizant of the way in which the peoples in this area held firm to a slower pace and differing values, ideals, and lifestyles. The region as a separate entity within the United States was attractive to those who had a nostalgic viewpoint and who idealized a simplistic culture of the past, and it proved a trove for early folklorists. In the view of others, the region represented the dangers of isolationism and bred provincialism that fostered backwardness and poverty.

The region became known and defined in particular ways, many of which are romanticized myths. As the setting for novels such as *The Trial of the Lonesome Pine* and *The Little Shepherd of Kingdom Come* in the early twentieth century by Kentucky writer John Fox Jr., the region was described and popularized as different from the rest of the United States. These popular novels created the belief that the region was distinctive and beyond the American mainstream. Such stereotypes and the deliberate creation of Appalachian culture persisted throughout the twentieth century; some parts of this culture—such as handicrafts and "hillbilly" music—were aggressively displayed and marketed. It was also a destination for agents of the **New Deal** Federal Writers' Project seeking to record "fading" traditions.

Debate rages as to whether the Appalachian region is or ever was truly a distinct culture within the United States. Those from outside the region created images of Appalachia dwellers that vacillated between romanticism and primitivism, both of which were rooted in stereotype. The creation of culture by those from within the borders, such as John Fox at the beginning of the twentieth century and Harriet Arnow at the end, perpetuated and legitimized stereotypes of the folk crafts, music, and behaviors of the people who lived there. Numerous Appalachian musicians have traded on romantic stereotypes to sell records and concert tickets.

Detractors viewed the culture and the people living there as deviant and created images of them as savage, vicious, crude, and cruel. This belief became so successful that by the twentieth century, everyone "knew" that mountain folk carried on a tradition of feuding—in the vein of the Hatfield–McCoy clashes of the late nineteenth century—and that they engaged in illegal smuggling and moonshine brewing. Other deviant behaviors included backwoods religious practices and the brutal way in which the men treated each other, their wives, and their children. Comic strips such as *L'il Abner* carried these messages to the masses.

Ironically, when individuals from the Appalachian region migrated to northern U.S. cities to escape the poverty and high **unemployment** of the region, they had to be taught their own "culture." Many did not know how to make the crafts that were "known" to be native and ubiquitous to the region, calling into question whether such activities were really distinctive to Appalachian culture. Still, Appalachians migrating to cities such as Detroit to work in the auto industry found that their **accents** and carriage marked them as exotic.

By the 1950s romantic images of Appalachia had largely given way to deprivation and isolation theories. The region was the site of numerous bloody and vicious miner **strikes** in the nineteenth and twentieth centuries, and urban newspapers reporting these conflicts tended to emphasize the remoteness of coal-patch hamlets and the backwardness of residents. (The journalists also conveniently ignored things such as the sophistication of United Mine Workers unionization campaigns or the stellar academic qualifications of instructors at institutions such as the Highlander Folklife Center.) To optimists caught up in the rampant consumerism and economic expansion of the post–World War II era, Appalachia represented a rare repository of American poverty that was quickly being eradicated elsewhere. Those illusions were shattered by writers such as **Michael Harrington**, but **Great Society** programs during the 1960s often treated Appalachia as if it was distinctive, and numerous programs were earmarked at alleviating its special brand of poverty.

There remains a tendency to consider Appalachia as a unique cultural and social region or as the poster child for rural poverty. The latter view has, perhaps, more merit than the first, given the area's persistent high unemployment levels.

Suggested Reading

Margaret Bender, ed., *Linguistic Diversity in the South: Changing Codes, Practices, and Ideology*, 2004; Robert Hendrickson, *Mountain Range: A Dictionary of Expressions from Appalachia to the Ozarks*, 1997; James Still, *The Wolfpen Notebooks: A Record of Appalachian Life*, 1991; Altina Waller, *Feud: Hatfields, McCoys and Social Change in Appalachia, 1860–1900*, 1988.

APPEAL TO REASON

JOHN A. GRONBECK-TEDESCO

Appeal to Reason was a weekly **socialist** periodical in publication from 1895 to 1922. Founded by J. A. Wayland, *Appeal* began in 1895 in Kansas City, Missouri, and in 1897 moved to Girard, Kansas. Wayland enlisted help from a journalist from Missouri, Fred Warren, who became the paper's managing editor. *Appeal* was the most successful radical serial in its day; by 1913 it had reached a peak circulation of 760,000 weekly subscriptions. Often a target for governmental censorship, *Appeal* solicited the help of thousands of men and women—the "salesmen army"—to distribute the publication around the nation.

As an organ of the Socialist Party of America, *Appeal* addressed issues related to industrialization, agriculture, the **labor movement**, and social activism from a left-wing perspective. It often advocated equal distribution of wealth, supported workers' rights, and opposed **capitalism**. The paper flourished in a rapidly changing culture in which the transition from an agricultural to industrial economy and the influx of millions of **immigrants** caused a new social awareness of economic inequality and poor working conditions. The ills of America were deemed the dire by-products of capitalism, with big business the leading scapegoat for social problems. Here the political woes of a new Midwestern radicalism morphed from populism to socialism, which produced an audience of agrarians and urbanites alike. Covered in *Appeal*'s pages were **muckraking** articles that discussed **strikes**, **poverty**, and urban unrest. These invectives took the form of cartoons, columns, poetry, and opinions. *Appeal* was also a venue for women's rights. With women making up a significant portion of its staff, *Appeal* formed a "woman's department" that published news and editorials on suffrage, employment, and home life.

Appeal was an influential magnet for left-wing politics. It was central to campaigns for socialist candidates, including the five-time presidential contender on the Socialist ticket, **Eugene Debs**. The paper published a host of writers, well-known and anonymous, who shared their radical views on current political and social problems of the day. Contributors included **Jack London**, **Upton Sinclair**, and Helen Keller. Also appearing in the publication's pages were the works of **Edward Bellamy**, Karl **Marx**, and **Charlotte Perkins Gilman**.

The political climate surrounding World War I finally caused the paper's demise. Like many radical publications, *Appeal* was federally censored and lost credibility in the new postwar culture.

Suggested Reading

John Graham, ed., *"Yours for the Revolution:" The* Appeal to Reason, *1895–1922*, 1990; James R. Green, *Grass-Roots Socialism: Radical Movements in the Southwest, 1895–1943*, 1978; Elliott Shore, *Talkin' Socialism: J. A. Wayland and the Role of the Press in American Radicalism, 1890–1912*, 1988.

ARMORIES

ROBERT E. WEIR

Armories are sites where military ordnance are stored and troops such as state and National Guard soldiers drill. They are common throughout the United States and evoke little comment today, though in the past, they were often symbols of **class struggle**.

Because weapons and ordnance were stored in armories, rebel groups sometimes targeted them. During the **Shays's Rebellion** of 1786–87, the attempt to capture the Springfield, Massachusetts, armory was the pivotal battle of the conflict. Likewise, John Brown's brief capture of the federal armory at Harpers Ferry, Virginia (now West Virginia), in 1859 is widely regarded as a precipitating event of the American Civil War.

The heyday of armory building occurred in the latter half of the nineteenth century. Most Americans are surprised to learn that many armories were built not to train troops protecting America from invasion, but to offer protection to the **upper** and **middle classes** from perceived threats of a **working-class** revolution. For example, wealthy families such as the **Astors** and **Vanderbilts** donated money to build some of New York City's twenty-nine armories because they were alarmed by the civic unrest of the Civil War anti-draft riots that convulsed the city in 1863.

The upper and middle classes also grew frightened by other events, both home and abroad. When French radicals seized control of the city of Paris and declared the Paris Commune in 1871, it engendered fear in the United States. So too did sensationalized press coverage of alleged **Molly Maguires** activity in northeast Pennsylvania. But it was the nationwide 1877 rail strikes that truly struck terror into the hearts of many **elites**. Numerous state militias were turned against workers, and President Rutherford B. Hayes used federal troops to quash the strikes. The strikes were blamed on **anarchists**, **communists**, and immigrant radicals, though said groups played a very small role overall. In the wake of 1877, a spate of fortress-like red brick armories were built.

Cranston Street Armory, Providence, Rhode Island. Courtesy of the Library of Congress.

Joint state and federal control of a professional National Guard was not finalized until the Militia Act of 1903. Prior to this, the federal standing military was small, states usually raised their own militias, and governors could call out the Guard on their own initiative (although governors retain the right to do so today, the Guard can be activated by federal fiat as well). Armories were often the site of class conflict. Troops that were activated to quell labor disputes, such as the lockouts at Homestead Steel in 1892 and Pullman in 1894, were housed and drilled at local armories. Many workers came to associate armories with repression, an association that lingered into the twentieth century. Boston armories were used to train impromptu militias recruited from Harvard and the city's criminal element during the 1919 Boston police strike, just as Seattle armories were used by militias that crushed a citywide **general strike** that same year. Members of the radical **Industrial Workers of the World** regarded armories and American Legion halls as physical manifestations of worker repression. Well into the 1930s, many members of the working class held negative opinions of armories, having grown accustomed to viewing armories as the site at which anti-union forces gathered.

One can largely credit **New Deal** labor legislation and World War II with changing the way working-class Americans came to view armories. Today, most modern armories are patriotic symbols, and many of their nineteenth-century predecessors have been torn down or gentrified.

Suggested Reading
Jerry Cooper, *The Rise of the National Guard: The Evolution of the American Militia, 1865–1920*, 2002; Robert Fogelson, *America's Armories: Architecture, Society, and Public Order*, 1989; James Whisker, *The Rise and Decline of the American Militia System*, 1999.

ARONOWITZ, STANLEY (1933–)

MICHAEL A. VASTOLA

Stanley Aronowitz is professor of sociology and urban education at the City University of New York Graduate Center, where he has taught since 1983. He is the author of over twenty books on class, culture, sociology of science, and politics, and he has published more than two hundred articles and reviews in publications such as *The Nation* and *The American Journal of Sociology*. Aronowitz earned a BA from the New School for Social Research in 1968 and a PhD from the Union Graduate School in 1975.

Aside from his influential academic contributions to the topic of labor history, institutional critiques of the university systems in the United States, and a pioneering analysis of the production of knowledge in the hard sciences—what is typically called "science studies"—Aronowitz has also worked in factories in New York and New Jersey and has organized for the clothing, oil, and chemical workers' unions. Additionally, he served as associate director of the group Mobilization for Youth on New York's Lower East Side and was director of the first experimental public high school in New York, the Park East High School in East Harlem. In 2002 he led the fight to maintain the official ballot status of the Green Party in New York State and ran for governor on that ticket the same year. He is also a member of the executive council of his university's union, the Professional Staff Congress.

Aronowitz's reasoned critiques of the **capitalist** political economy include influential works on labor history such as *False Promises* (1973) and *The Jobless Future* (1994). *Science as Power* (1988) is an examination and criticism of the relationship between ideology and the institutionalization of scientific practices, and *The Knowledge Factory* (2000) takes a similar approach to the general corporate university structure. His recent *Just Around the Corner: The Paradox of the Jobless Economy* (2005) is an analysis of the changing relationship between job creation and economic growth in the global economy. Though no single book can be called his magnum opus, and they cover an array of distinct topics, each contains a substantial critique of class domination and illegitimate hierarchies within the capitalist economy. Consequently, Aronowitz's greatest strength as an intellectual lies in the exemplary range of his ideas and in his ability to effectively link topics as seemingly disparate as pedagogy or institutional critique to broader issues of class inequality.

Unfortunately, Aronowitz's more recent fame has come at the expense of the reputation of *Social Text*, a journal he founded with Fredric Jameson and John Brenkman. *Social Text*, which took as its initial subtitle "Theory, Culture, Ideology," was intended to do the work of interrogating the critical intersections between those notions, but in a distinctly post-Marxist manner. For instance, the concept of culture was seen as central in its own right, rather than being determined by and subordinate to the economy. Ideology was also treated as something more complex than the orthodox **Marxist** conception of the term as simply **false consciousness**. Recuperating those concepts for new radical theories was something Aronowitz had been doing for some time in his own work. But the political focus of the journal was assailed by a remarkably successful hoax perpetuated by Alan Sokal, a physicist and self-described "Old Leftist" who doubted the political efficacy of such seemingly abstract theorizing.

Sokal's deep belief in scientific objectivity compelled him to write an article that elaborately caricatured what he perceived as the abuses of scholars like Aronowitz, who had pioneered the critique of how scientific knowledge is produced. In fact, after being published in a 1996 issue of the journal, Sokal revealed that his article was manufactured, obscure, jargon-filled nonsense, and he cited

Aronowitz's association with the journal as a main reason for his choosing to publish the article in *Social Text*. Aronowitz exposed Sokal's fallacies in the radical political journal *Dissent*, but despite his persuasive rebuttal, the hoax continues to unjustly tarnish the reputations of many of its targets.

Suggested Reading

Stanley Aronowitz, *False Promises*, 1973; Aronowitz, *Science as Power*, 1988; Aronowitz, *Just Around the Corner: The Paradox of the Jobless Economy*, 2005.

ART

ROBERT E. WEIR

Although few people give it much thought, social class often determines the content of art, the type of art consumed, and how art is valued.

Art made by common people has traditionally been labeled "folk art" rather than "fine art," especially if it is an object whose purpose is functional as well as decorative, such as a weather vane, animal decoy, cane, or quilt. Untrained painters are commonly dubbed "primitivists" and their efforts little appreciated until members of the **middle** and **upper classes** decide that the works of painters such as Erastus Salisbury Field (1805–1900) or Anna Mary Robertson "Grandma" Moses (1860–1961) or of a carver such as Wilhelm Schimmel (1817–90) are worthy of collection. Even when the products of common people show up in museums or fetch large prices at art auctions, they are usually viewed as whimsical rather than fine art or **high culture**.

In the eighteenth and nineteenth centuries, farmers and laborers occasionally appeared as the subjects of professionally trained painters and sculptors, though their depictions were likely to be romanticized or allegorical. Winslow Homer's *Morning Bell* (1873) is typical of the way nineteenth-century painters set their work in idyllic rural settings. It stands in marked contrast to the way a handful of painters such as Thomas Anshultz, Robert Kohler, and John Ferguson Weir depicted labor as gritty and capital-labor relations as contested. In works such as *Gun Foundry* (1866) and *Ironworkers-Noontime* (1881), Weir and Anshultz showed industrial work as dirty and dangerous, and Kohler presented labor conflict in works such as *The Strike* (1886) and *The Socialist* (1885).

More notable than any of these images, however, is the relative absence of the **working classes** in art. Trained artists were more likely to render landscapes, portraits of the middle and upper classes, allegorical works, and high-society life. Industrial workers and farmers were most likely to be seen on items such as fraternal-order certificates, on trade-union posters, and in graphic images appearing in non-mainstream newspapers and journals.

The advent of practical photography in the late nineteenth century played a big role in diversifying the subjective gaze of artists. **Jacob Riis**'s photos in *How the Other Half Lives* (1890) depicted shocking views of New York City **poverty**, particularly in immigrant neighborhoods. His work paved the way for Lewis Hine

(1874–1930), whose photos of arriving immigrants, **child laborers**, and industrial laborers shocked many Americans, though they were rendered with great humanity.

In the early twentieth century, a small group of painters such as Stuart Davis, George Luks, William Glackens, Everett Shinn, and John Sloan also began to show tenement life, work, and capital–labor relations in a less-than-flattering light. Their work so unsettled some members of the pre–World War I middle class that the work was derisively deemed "ashcan" quality, a term the artists came to embrace in describing their approach. Some of them were members of the **Socialist Party**, the **Industrial Workers of the World**, and other radical organizations and found outlets for their artistic expression in journals such as *The Masses* and *The Industrial Worker*.

The **Great Depression** was largely responsible for making common people the center of artistic expression to a far greater degree than ever before (or since). **New Deal** programs such as the Public Works of Art Program, the Works Progress Administration, and the Farm Security Administration subsidized muralists, photographers, painters, and sculptors, and the overall unsettledness of the 1930s stimulated scores of others to express themselves artistically. Many commentators say that a **proletarian** art ethos dominated the 1930s and that a documentary impulse held sway among photographers. Among the many artists whose work dealt with common people were muralists Thomas Hart Benton and Diego Rivera; photographers Margaret Bourke-White, Walker Evans, Dorothea Lange, Russell Lee, Arthur Rothstein, Ben Shahn, and John Vachon; and painters Philip Evergood, William Gropper, Alexandre Hogue, Rockwell Kent, Jacob Lawrence, Alice Neel, and Ben Shahn. Numerous sculptures, some of which were unsigned, appeared in public plazas and parks and in the details of skyscrapers.

As during the Civil War, the Spanish-American War, and World War I, photographers, graphic artists, and painters also depicted common people during World War II. Perhaps the most notable image to come from the 1940s was J. Howard Miller's "Rosie the Riveter" poster, which became iconic and led to spin-offs by many others, most notably Norman Rockwell. Photographers also captured some of the postwar strikes, and photo magazines such as *Life* and *Look* printed numerous images of everyday life. In addition, African American artists built upon traditions established during the Harlem Renaissance (ca. 1920–30) and portrayed the black experience in paintings and photographs.

To a large extent, however, American art of the 1950s was becoming less representational, more personal, and less likely to tackle social issues. Outside of documentary photography, common people were once again sentimentalized—as in the graphic works of Rockwell—or largely ignored. This became particularly obvious in the 1960s and 1970s, when photographers including Earl Dotter, John Kouns, Eliott Landy, Jerome Liebling, Charles Moore, and Milton Rogovin captured the Civil Rights Movement, antiwar protests, and debased labor conditions in ways almost entirely ignored by the painters who were favored by collectors, museums, and the avant-garde.

The current disconnect between art trends and the shared experiences of most Americans has, in the past several decades, exacerbated long-simmering tensions over defining art, portraying it in public, and allocating museum funds to purchase new art. Artist-patron relations date from ancient times, and collecting what is dubbed fine art is nearly always the pursuit of the rich. These private relations seldom trouble most people, but when artists and others who seek to dictate taste place their work before the public, class tensions can emerge.

There have been numerous community struggles over what some view as obscene content. From the 1980s on, the National Endowment of the Arts has been under conservative pressure to deny funding to artists whose work is deemed incendiary, pornographic, or unpatriotic. This reached fever pitch in 1987, when Andres Serrano displayed *Piss Christ*, a crucifix immersed in urine. In 1990 an exhibit that included several homoerotic photographs by Robert Mapplethorpe led to the arrest of Dennis Barrie, the director of Cincinnati's Museum of Contemporary Art. Such high-profile figures as former New York City mayor Rudolph Giuliani joined the chorus of those demanding more public accountability in funding and displaying controversial art.

Critics of unsettling art are often cavalierly dismissed as puritanical or unlettered by **elites** and the avant-garde, many of whom take refuge behind the **Bill of Rights** and assert the right to freedom of expression. One need not take a position on censorship, however, to realize that other issues are at stake. Many Americans simply dislike the art favored by elites. According to a well-publicized 1995 survey of tastes and preferences conducted by artists Vitaly Komar and Alex Melamid, a vast majority—64 percent—of Americans prefer "traditional" art, and just 25 percent preferred anything they deemed "modern." They were especially dismissive of abstract and nonrepresentational art. When pressed further, the American public expressed preference for content that included landscape, wild animals, historical figures, and the color blue.

Cutting-edge artists—including the French Impressionists, who now score high in public-preference polls—are often out of synch with mass society in their own lifetimes. Artists and art critics assert that artists must be free to express themselves independently of public taste. Again, such assertions become problematic when museums and curators cross the private–public boundaries. In recent years, the public reacted negatively to the New York Public Library's secret sale of Asher Durand's nineteenth-century masterpiece *Kindred Spirits*, and the Boston Museum of Fine Arts has taken heat for plans to sell Americans paintings and rent some of its Monets in order to buy more contemporary art. When many Bostonians voiced their dislike for pieces the museum planned to purchase, controversy grew so intense that directors were forced to seek a compromise that saved (some) works by Gilbert Stuart and other American genre painters.

Social class also expresses itself in purchases of art. Aside from high-ticket art auctions whose works are bought by foundations, museums, and wealthy collectors, the majority of the public (60 percent) tend to buy art they like rather than what they feel is collectable or important. In the Komar and Melamid poll, another 34 percent chose art that matched their decor. This, plus the penchant for indulging public preference, helps explain the popularity of Thomas Kinkade, whose production-line works are sold in nearly 300 retail outlets, mostly in malls. Again, critics may scoff, but in 1999, Kinkade sold over $126 million worth of paintings, mostly to members of the lower middle class and upper **lower class**. Even members of the upper middle class, who often pride themselves on refined taste, are more likely to purchase the works of regional and local artists whose works they enjoy than the works of those who are pushing art's boundaries. Across the nation, the word "art" is more often associated with graffiti, favored pieces of jewelry, mass-produced posters of works from established artists, bric-a-brac, porcelain collectables, or even bright paint on a velvet background than with work by those viewed as "serious" artists.

In summary, the link between wealth and so-called fine art is widespread and timeless, and art frequently mirrors the class dynamics of its society. Students of social class can thus look to art to gain insight into the consumption patterns, cultural battles, and political concerns of any given period.

Suggested Reading

Philip Foner and Reinhard Schultz, *The Other America: Art and the Labour Movement in the United States*, 1985; David Halle, *Inside Culture: Art and Class in the American Home*, 1993; Vitaly Komar and Alex Melamid, "The Most Wanted Paintings" (http://www.diacenter.org/index.html).

ASCRIPTION

See Achievement and ascription.

ASIAN AMERICANS

ROBERT E. WEIR

"Asian Americans" is an imprecise term applied largely to immigrants from southeastern Asia, especially those from China, Indochina, Japan, Korea, the Philippines, and Taiwan. It is generally not applied to those from the Indian subcontinent, as there were relatively few immigrants from India, Pakistan, and Bangladesh until the 1970s. Like many terms that treat ethnicity in a collective fashion, the label *Asian American* oversimplifies and makes specious assumptions. Asian Americans come from a variety of backgrounds, represent numerous cultural and religious traditions, and can be found across all lines of social **stratification**.

Americans originally viewed Asians as exotic when contact was limited largely to trade and cultural exchanges. In the late eighteenth and early nineteenth century, thriving trade with China often led the **upper classes** to consume Chinese silk, porcelain, lacquerware, furniture, and artifacts. In 1854 Commodore Matthew Perry negotiated a treaty with Japan that had a similar impact for Japanese goods. Fascination soon gave way to revulsion when Chinese and Japanese immigrants began to arrive on American shores, lured by the post-1849 Gold Rush and opportunities to work on railroads. By the time of the Civil War, there was growing discrimination against Asians, especially the Chinese. This discrimination intensified in the 1870s with vicious verbal and physical attacks on Asian immigrants in ethnic enclaves in cities such as Denver, San Francisco, and Seattle. Many white Americans began to demand an end to Asian immigration. The **working class** was especially susceptible to anti-Asian outbursts because it believed that Asian gang labor was undercutting wages. In 1882 Congress passed the Chinese Exclusion Act, which dramatically curtailed immigration. In 1908 the so-called Gentleman's Agreement with Japan placed similar restrictions on Japanese immigration. The animus against the groups lasted into the 1930s for Chinese and into the 1950s for Japanese. Thousands of the latter had their property seized and were placed in internment camps during World War II as a response to the bombing of Pearl Harbor. Japanese Americans were seen as potential spies, even though earlier immigration restrictions meant that most were second- or third-generation Americans who had little contact with Japan. (The Chinese fared better during these years because China was invaded by Japan and was a putative U.S. ally during the war.)

Filipinos make up the largest group of Americans of Asian descent. The United States acquired the Philippines as a result of the 1898 Spanish-American War. Attempts to assert direct imperialist control over the islands failed because of the opposition of nationalist groups who battled U.S. forces between 1901 and 1913. The United States granted the islands increasing degrees of autonomy until the Philippines obtained full independence in 1946, though it retains deep economic ties to the United States. This troubled history contributed to the discrimination that Filipino immigrants to the United States experienced, though its intensity did not match that directed toward the Chinese or Japanese, and intermarriage with Caucasians took place in greater numbers. Nonetheless, although many Filipinos assimilated, there were also large numbers clustered in low-wage agricultural work. They did not receive the attention given to **Hispanics**, but a large number of Filipino migrant workers were involved in Cesar Chavez's United Farm Workers union movement in the 1960s.

Koreans began arriving in the United States in large numbers because of the Korean War (1950–53), just as large numbers of Cambodians, Laotians, and Vietnamese immigrated to the United States during the Vietnam War, whose active phase for America was between 1965 and 1975. Victories by communist forces in all three places also led many to flee from the late 1970s on. The media dubbed many of these refugees "boat people" in reference to the makeshift vessels on which many ventured toward sanctuary (untold numbers died in such efforts). Smaller numbers of Thais and Burmese have come to the United States in the past three decades, the former mostly for economic and educational opportunity, the latter to escape a repressive military junta. Malaysians and Indonesians have also come, though in smaller numbers than those from the former French Indochina. Indonesian immigration tends to wax and wane according to cycles of political turmoil.

By the 1960s Asian Americans were often touted as "model minorities" because of their high levels of educational attainment, occupational successes, stable family patterns, and propensity for becoming U.S. citizens. By 1990 the average Asian American family income surpassed that of Caucasians, a situation often attributed to the high value Asian Americans place on education. According to 1997 data, 66 percent of all Asian American workers held **white-collar** jobs as opposed to 61 percent of all white workers. By 2000 half of all Asian Americans over the age of twenty-five held at least a bachelor's degree, and about 19 percent had advanced degrees, versus 29 percent of whites with a four-year degree and just 9 percent with graduate degrees.

Figures such as these often obscure other issues. Although it is true that many Asian Americans have excelled, their **poverty** rate is two and a half times higher than that of whites. The data also harm certain groups by treating Asian Americans as a unified whole. Family income, for example, is skewed by the fact that those of Japanese, Taiwanese, and Filipino ancestry have, on the average, extraordinarily high incomes. By contrast, those of Chinese and Southeast Asian backgrounds have incomes roughly half of that of the average Caucasian family. Likewise, though about 58 percent of all Asian Americans will attend at least some college, high school dropout rates for Cambodians, Laotians, and Hmong are higher than that of the general population. In general, Asian Americans who came to America before 1980 have done much better than those arriving after. This improvement is due to pronounced differences in social class and occupation, with the pre-1980 group being better-educated, whereas post-1980 arrivals are more likely to come from a rural peasant background.

Treating Asian Americans as model minorities also serves to obscure nativist discrimination directed at them. Asian Americans tend to live in areas with high concentrations of others of Asian background, partly in response to the cultural distance many feel in their relationships with other ethnic groups. Even high achievement sometimes leads to discrimination. In California, for instance, the high number of Asian American college graduates has led some to call for graduate school **quotas**, especially for competitive medical and law schools whose slots have gone to high-achieving Asian Americans rather than whites. Some Asian Americans also charge that **Ivy League** schools discriminate against them. Whereas Asian Americans make up 41 percent of all University of California–Berkeley undergraduates and over 50 percent at other UCal universities, they average just 15 to 19 percent in most Ivy League schools because of in-place target quotas. Discrimination against Asian Americans often receives little public attention, in part because their diversity tends to mitigate against the formation of high-profile civil rights groups such as those formed by African Americans or **Native Americans**.

According to the 2000 census, there are about 13.5 million Asian Americans in the United States, about 4.2 percent of the total population. Western states have the highest concentrations of Asian Americans, with California leading the way. New York City, however, has more Asian Americans than any other metropolitan area. The overall future of Asian Americans looks promising. Recent figures reveal that an equal percentage of Asian Americans and Caucasians view themselves as **middle class**. Some Asian Americans, particularly those of Vietnamese, Cambodian, and Laotian ancestry, argue that the model minority stereotype is harmful because it blinds policymakers and other Americans to deep social problems within their ranks.

Suggested Reading

Stacey Lee, *Unraveling the "Model Minority" Stereotype*, 1996; Ronald Takaki, *Strangers from a Distant Shore: A History of Asian Americans*, 1998; Meyer Weinberg, *Asian American Education*, 1997.

ASSIMILATION

MAXINE LEVAREN

Assimilation is the absorption of a minority group into a majority population. It has always been an important way for **immigrants** and other disenfranchised groups to improve their position and social class, but it does not come unencumbered.

New immigrants, with minor exceptions, have generally been on the bottom rungs of society for several reasons. Often, those immigrants who come to the United States to improve their economic position or to escape political or religious oppression in their native countries leave their homes with few material or economic resources. These economic hardships and the fact that their customs are incompatible with American culture make it difficult to integrate with the majority population and rise in society. Notable exceptions are cases in which highly educated or economically advantaged people have arrived. Often, these groups have been welcomed into society and have been able to maintain the social class that they had in their native countries. However, in immigrant groups that stay cohesive into subsequent generations, there is less assimilation, even when people rise economically.

Besides class, an important factor that influences assimilation is **race**. When people are racially distinguishable, as in the case of **Asian Americans**, African Americans, and **Hispanics**, assimilation is considerably more difficult. Even as people enter the professions, become entrepreneurs, and acquire wealth, prejudice from the majority population can inhibit assimilation. This consequently enforces the separatism of these groups once they leave the workplace, where they are forced to integrate into the majority population in order to be successful.

Many new European immigrants in the late nineteenth and early twentieth centuries did not easily assimilate into American culture. Adults who arrived often had difficulty learning a new language and adapting to a culture. In addition, the new culture was strange and sometimes viewed as immoral, especially regarding the relationship between parents and children. Therefore, these new arrivals tended to stay in **ethnic enclaves** with other immigrants from their original country, where they could speak their own language, follow their own customs, and establish their own houses of worship. Within these enclaves, they often formed their own social structures, where immigrants with more money or education rose to the top of the social structure. Since many did not have professions, they earned their living through manual labor. For example, in New York, many Italian immigrants were active in the construction trades, and Jewish immigrants gravitated toward the garment industry. Consequently, these immigrants were also active in labor unions, which further alienated them from the upper classes.

Assimilation and the consequent rise in class usually happen in later generations, as children of first-generation immigrants go to American schools, speak English without a foreign accent, and readily absorb American customs. This sometimes leads to conflicts between children and their parents, who don't understand each other. Unlike their parents, second- and third-generation Americans have friends and associates of many different backgrounds, live in mixed neighborhoods, and are open to marrying people of different national backgrounds, religions, and races. The cost, however, is that fully assimilated individuals often reject their cultures of origin, a factor that intensifies intergenerational conflict and makes it difficult for subsequent generations to recover their heritages.

Despite generational conflicts, most immigrants take great pride in watching their children assimilate. By learning the language and becoming educated, they become qualified for **white-collar** jobs; civil service professions such as policing and firefighting; and professional vocations, such as law, medicine, and education. These children often act as interpreters for their parents, helping them navigate through the linguistic and cultural roadblocks they encounter.

Among second- and third-generation immigrants, assimilation is only sometimes a melting pot, where newcomers are completely absorbed in the prevailing culture and social structure. Often, it is more like a tossed salad, where individual ethnic groups maintain features of their own ethnic identities and social structures, such as food, festivals, and faith, while at the same time operating within the majority culture.

Suggested Reading

Nathan Glazer and Daniel P. Moynihan, *Beyond the Melting Pot: The Negroes, Puerto Ricans, Jews, Italians, and Irish of New York City*, 1970; Tamar Jacoby, ed., *Reinventing the Melting Pot: The New Immigrants and What It Means to Be American*, 2004.

ASTOR, JOHN JACOB (July 17, 1763–March 29, 1848)

ROBERT E. WEIR

John Jacob Astor was an early American capitalist and the patriarch of one of the new nation's richest families. The Astors are a prime example of a family that some label an American patrician class.

Astor was born in Waldorf, Baden, Germany, the fourth son of a butcher. An elder brother, George, moved to London, where he manufactured musical instruments. John Jacob joined him in London and learned English there. In 1784, just one year after the Treaty of Paris ended the American Revolution, John Jacob Astor immigrated to New York City. Legend holds that he learned the fur trade that soon enriched him from a fellow German immigrant while in passage to New York, though this story may be apocryphal. Astor initially worked as the New York agent for his brother's musical instrument business before working for a Quaker furrier. Sometime around 1785, he opened his own shop. He also married the former Sarah Todd, who was said to possess equally sound business sense.

It was a propitious time to get into the fur trade. Not only was demand for beaver and other pelts high, but the 1794 Jay Treaty between the United States and Britain had eased tensions between the two nations and had opened sections of the Ohio Valley, Great Lakes region, and Canada to trappers. His major competitor was the Hudson Bay Company, but Astor entered into direct negotiations with Native tribes to supply pelts. Soon, Astor had a string of trading forts stretching from the upper Great Lakes to the Pacific. Historians studying Native Americans have demonstrated that Astor trading posts greatly disrupted traditional Native American life, often turning erstwhile allies into competitive enemies and creating exchange networks that reduced the tribes' self-sufficiency. Astor, however, prospered. By 1800 his net worth had surpassed $250,000 (more than $2.7 million in today's dollars), and he began shipping furs to China in exchange for tea, sandalwood, and luxury items that he sold to the fashionable set back in the United States. Between 1800 and 1817 he was able to trade in ports controlled by the British East India Company, despite mounting tensions between the United States and Britain.

Astor's American Fur Company suffered when President Thomas Jefferson enacted the Embargo Act of 1807, which curtailed trade between the two nations, and the War of 1812 placed further restraints on Astor's burgeoning fur monopoly. By then, however, he had begun to diversify, with holdings in real estate and securities purchases. The war's end in 1817 led to renewed trade when the government enacted protectionist policies that essentially granted Astor the monopoly he had long sought. He also realized a huge profit from his securities purchases and from real estate transactions. His second son, William Blackhouse Astor, built more than 700 stores and buildings in New York, greatly adding to a growing family fortune.

By the 1830s John Jacob Astor was a semiretired philanthropist who patronized libraries, cultural institutions, the scholarly pursuits of John James Audubon, and the literary endeavors of Edgar Allen Poe. Before his death in 1848, Astor's personal fortune of $20,000,000 had made him the richest man in America.

Astor's offspring further enriched the family coffers, and the Astor family was as well-known in England as in America. Several Astor family members obtained aristocratic titles in England, including Baron Waldorf Astor (1879–1952), a member of Parliament; Viscountess Nancy Witcher Astor (1879–1964), the first woman to sit in Parliament; and Baron John Jacob Astor IV (1886–1971), who owned *The Times* of London. Like many rich Americans of the nineteenth century, the American-born Astors often adopted English mannerisms, cultivated an air of sophistication, and maintained an exclusive lifestyle isolated from fellow citizens. Scholars seeking to refute the notion that America escaped aristocratic trappings often point to families like the Astors to bolster their argument, although critics counter that inherited wealth and affected lifestyles make families such as the Astors de facto nobility. The Astors remain a rich and philanthropic family, though in 2006, allegations circulated that 104-year-old Brooke Astor, who once headed the Astor Foundation, has been reduced to living in squalor.

Suggested Reading

John D. Haeger, *John Jacob Astor: Business and Finance in the Early Republic*, 1991; Axel Madsen, *John Jacob Astor: America's First Multimillionaire*, 2001; Jack Weatherford, *Native Roots: How the Indians Enriched America*, 1991.

LOUIS AUCHINCLOSS (September 27, 1917–)

ROBERT E. WEIR

Louis Stanton Auchincloss is a novelist, short-story writer, essayist, and retired lawyer. His fiction is often compared with that of **Henry James** and **Edith Wharton** because of its emphasis on the urban patriciate, **WASP** families, and the manners and social conventions of **socialites**.

Auchincloss writes extensively about the world of which he has been a part. He was born into a wealthy family and received **private schooling** at Groton Academy and Yale University, before obtaining a law degree at the University of Virginia in 1941. He served in World War II and then settled in New York City, where he joined the prestigious law firm of Hawkins, Delafield, and Wood. He specialized in estate law until his retirement in 1986, but was deeply involved in **philanthropy**, support for cultural institutions, and writing even as he practiced law. His first novel, *The Indifferent Children*, was published in 1947, and his 1964 novel, *The Rector of Justin*, was a best seller. In all, Auchincloss has published more than sixty books.

Like James and Wharton, Auchincloss deals extensively with the inner life and tensions of the **upper classes**. Some of his works are set in the late nineteenth and early twentieth centuries, a time in which the lines between the lower upper class and the upper **middle class** had begun to blur. His books deal with what one might call the **ruling class**, rather than with sociological distinctions between groups; that is, his books deal with people who have access to upper-crust education, money, and **power**. The settings often parallel those of his own life: prep schools, the **Hamptons**, law firms, and **country clubs**. Auchincloss is sometimes labeled a novelist of manners. There is indeed a moralistic theme to many of his books, though he is often as critical of the stodginess and hollow conventions of the rich as he is of the declining morals of the masses.

Since the 1960s few serious novelists have situated their stories among the ruling class. Older Auchincloss books such as *Portrait in Brownstone* (1962) and *The Great World of Timothy Colt* (1956) are sometimes consulted for the glimpses of genteel life they provide, whereas newer works such as *The Atonement and Other Stories* (1997) and *Manhattan Monologues* (2002) are viewed as reflections on a passing way of life. Auchincloss disagrees with the latter assessment and asserts that the WASP ruling class simply has more competition in the modern world, but retains much of its social and political power.

His nonfiction also deals with the ruling classes, social convention, and wealth. Among his works are studies of the **Vanderbilts**, Queen Victoria, Woodrow Wilson, the **Gilded Age**, and canonical literary figures such as Proust, James, Wharton, and F. Scott Fitzgerald.

Suggested Reading

Louis Auchincloss, *The Rector of Justin*, 1964; Auchincloss, *A Writer's Capital*, 1974; Carol Gelderman, *Louis Auchincloss: A Writer's Life*, 1993.

AUTHORITY

ROBERT E. WEIR

In sociological terms, "authority" refers to the socially sanctioned and legitimate use of power. With authority comes the ability to make decisions that affect other people, as well as the possibility of shaping social, cultural, and economic institutions in ways that benefit those who command authority. The amount of authority that groups possess tends to mirror the American class structure; that is, the **upper classes** shape decision-making processes to the greatest degree, the **middle classes** possess mid-level power, and the **working** and **lower classes** routinely adjust to conditions dictated by those above them.

Most modern sociological analyses of authority derive from classic work done by **Max Weber** in the early twentieth century. Weber noted that there were three types of authority: traditional, charismatic, and legal. Traditional authority is based in custom and precedent, charismatic in the dynamics of personality, and legal in powers that are rooted in rules and procedures. Weber also called legal authority "rational," to note the ways in which it served modern bureaucratic institutions. It should be noted that Weber did not see these categories as mutually exclusive; leaders often wield authority based on whichever justification best serves them.

Once authority is established, it can hold powerful sway over those compelled to obey it. In a famed 1964 experiment that, among other things, sought to explain why ordinary people succumbed to the lure of fascism, Stanley Milgram demonstrated that authority figures can sometimes compel individuals to act contrary to their moral codes. Some of Milgram's subjects carried out orders to administer an electric shock that appeared to harm other people (in fact, Milgram's "victims" were actors). Others have argued that authority figures can likewise convince people to act against their self-interest. Some have evoked Milgram as a partial explanation as to why many low-paid workers come to reject labor unions or vote for conservative office-seekers.

Authority usually shapes society in subtler ways than those suggested by Milgram. Gender studies indicate, for example, that because men dominate governmental and corporate ranks, an unstated male norm determines everything from agenda items to work-station designs. Organized religion also embodies male bias; male clerics outnumber women by about four to one and determine policy, even though women frequently make up the bulk of congregations.

In more specific class terms, decision making in most occupations filters downward. **CEO**s in distant offices make decisions that impact the jobs and livelihoods of thousands in far-off locations. On the local level, mid-level (and middle-class) managers dictate job routines, the pace of work, and the procedures by which tasks are accomplished, even if workers on the job possess greater knowledge and are capable of increased efficiency.

Authority, when exercised, is seldom cooperative or democratic. Thus, although the intent may be covert or even unconscious, the very use of authority tends to maintain the social status quo.

Suggested Reading

Stanley Milgram, *Obedience to Authority*, 1974; George Ritzer and Douglas Goodman, *Sociological Theory*, 2003; Max Weber, *Economy and Society*, 1920.

B

Bacon's Rebellion

Thomas A. Wing

Bacon's Rebellion was an upheaval in the Chesapeake region in 1675–76. Class distinction and struggle permeated life during the Colonial period. Occurring 100 years before the Declaration of Independence, this event is described as the "first **American Revolution**" and is a case study in **class struggle**: years of distrust and animosity between Virginia **elites** and freemen erupted into violence and lawlessness.

At the center of the rebellion was the effort by wealthy elites to keep the colony's best lands and privileges out of the hands of the freemen. The freemen, formerly **indentured servants**, had worked a specified amount of time for the cost of travel to the colonies. Once released from servitude, the freemen sought land and a new start. Virginia elites felt threatened by the large numbers of freemen and feared grievances would spill over to servants and **slaves** and lead to open rebellion. The fear was somewhat unwarranted, however, as Indian relations on the frontier actually provided the main cause for the revolution. White settlers pushed into the western back country because most of the best coastal lands were in the hands of elites. Left unprotected by inadequate militia, these settlers, many of them freemen and their families, suffered raids by hostile Indian groups living in the same remote regions.

Declining tobacco prices due to England's war with the Dutch had forced many planters to seek favorable trade with friendly Indians, and officials were reluctant to upset relations because of isolated incidents on the frontier. Along the James River a group of freemen of humble means, led by disgruntled wealthy planter Nathaniel Bacon, Jr., took reprisal by carrying out a campaign that made little distinction between friendly and hostile Indian groups. Invited to Jamestown by Governor William Berkeley, Bacon demanded a militia commission. Berkeley, fearing Bacon more than hostile Indians, accused the freemen of treason and declared

Scene from Bacon's Rebellion. Courtesy of the Library of Congress.

their leader a traitor. Bacon was arrested but later released. Bacon persisted in his quest for power, eventually winning a seat in the colonial legislature. Berkeley failed to prevent Bacon from taking his seat, and, faced with violence, he fled Virginia. With Berkeley gone, Bacon increased his forces and plundered the estates of pro-Berkeley elites. The class struggle escalated as Berkeley offered freedom to servants who joined his militia, while Bacon offered freedom to slaves and servants of Berkeley supporters. Troops from England were on the way to suppress the rebellion as Bacon descended into random plunder and theft. Bacon became ill—most sources credit dysentery—and died on October 26, 1676, leaving his men without a leader. The British troops arrived and arrested all but eighty of Bacon's followers in November.

On his return to Virginia, Berkeley carried out the hanging of about twenty-four wealthy men who had supported Bacon. Their estates were taken to compensate pro-Berkeley victims who were plundered by Bacon's forces. King Charles II of England was displeased with Berkeley's response and called him back to England, where he died in 1677. Subsequent legislation loosened Virginia's social system for whites, but made it even more difficult for slaves. Some scholars feel that slavery took a decidedly more cruel turn in the wake of Bacon's Rebellion, with officials there determined to draw rigid color lines to preclude future alliances among poor whites, indentures, and slaves.

Today, Nathaniel Bacon, Jr. is viewed by some as a champion of liberty who fought a cruel tyrant, hence a precursor of the American Revolution. Some scholars think this assessment too charitable and that Bacon was a selfish, power-hungry criminal.

Suggested Reading

Michael Oberg, ed., *Samuel Wiseman's Book of Record: The Official Account of Bacon's Rebellion in Virginia, 1676–1677*, 2005; Wilcomb E. Washburn, *The Governor and the Rebel*, 1957; Stephen S. Webb, *1676—The End of American Independence*, 1984.

BALTZELL, E. DIGBY (November 14, 1915–August 17, 1996)

ROBERT E. WEIR

Edward Digby Baltzell was among the foremost sociologists and historians studying the inner workings of the **upper class**. He is widely credited with having popularized the term **WASP** to describe the privileged white, Anglo-Saxon, Protestant elites who hold and exercise **authority** and **power** in America. Baltzell defended the upper class and viewed their might as proof of an American **meritocracy**.

Nathaniel Bacon. Courtesy of the Library of Congress.

Baltzell was born into an upper-**middle-class** home in Philadelphia, the city where he spent most of his life and which was the focal point for much of his social class research. He obtained his bachelor's degree from the University of Pennsylvania (Penn) in 1940, served in the Navy during World War II, then obtained a PhD from Columbia. He then returned to Penn, where he taught for his entire career. Baltzell's reputation was established upon publication of *Philadelphia Gentlemen: The Making of a National Upper Class* (1958) and *Protestant Establishment: Aristocracy and Caste in America* (1964). The latter book was particularly well received and did much to popularize the term WASP.

Baltzell, unlike many sociologists, distinguished between elites, whom he identified as those at the top of a functional hierarchy, and the **upper class**, which consisted of families several generations removed from their original elite status. A true upper class, he argued, topped a social hierarchy, not just a functional one. The upper class world revolved around preparatory schools, **Ivy League** education, family ties, endogamous marriage patterns, membership in exclusive (and private) social clubs, and adherence to a Protestant religion, especially **Episcopalianism**. Its members were listed in the **Social Register** and came from such occupations as banking, architecture, law, medicine, and museum administration. Those who went into politics or other forms of public service did so out of a sense of *noblesse oblige*.

Baltzell also articulated upper class values, including a greater awareness of the past, a stress on character rather than occupation, and the formation of lineal relationships rather than emphasis on **individualism**. He also saw the upper class as performing valuable social functions, arguing that their control over national and cultural life brought stability, that it served as a hedge against totalitarianism, and that it created folkways and mores that guarded against social chaos. He even defended the exclusivity of private clubs, stating that privacy was necessary to build the **social networks** that made society more efficient and functional. Baltzell fretted over the potential extremism inherent in democracy and praised upper-class traditions as a social safeguard against excess. Like the novelist **Louis Auchincloss**, Baltzell lamented the declining power of the upper class.

Although not as often appreciated, Baltzell was also a fine historian. His work on Philadelphia traced the very construction and evolution of social class within the city, and his works on religion showed important distinctions within American religious practices, including views on business, morality, and war. Among other things, Baltzell argued that the Puritan pessimism toward individuals coincided with optimism toward human institutions, an uneasy compromise embodied in the **Protestant work ethic**.

Suggested Reading

E. Digby Baltzell, *Philadelphia Gentlemen: The Making of a National Upper Class*, 1958; Baltzell, *Protestant Establishment: Aristocracy and Caste in America*, 1964; Baltzell, *Puritan Boston and Quaker Philadelphia*, 1996.

BEACON HILL

RONALD DALE KARR

Located in Boston, Beacon Hill is the oldest, continuous, **upper-class**, residential district in the United States, as well as the site of the Massachusetts State House (state capitol).

In the Colonial period, the Trimountain (or Tremont) was on the northwest fringe of the town of Boston, with its three peaks—Mount Vernon, Beacon Hill, and Pemberton (or Cotton) Hill—looming over the settlement. Until it blew down in 1789, a beacon topped the center peak for over 150 years. Eighteen acres on the southern slope of Mount Vernon constituted the cow pasture of noted artist John Singleton Copley, who left his house here for England in 1774.

The remoteness and unsavory reputation of the area attracted little interest until the 1790s, when the State House was moved from the town center to John Hancock's pasture on Beacon Hill, just east of Copley's lands. In 1795 a group of wealthy Bostonians, the Mount Vernon Proprietors, made a deal with Copley's agent to purchase his lands for $18,450. (Copley vainly sought to nullify his agent's action.) The proprietors laid out streets, sold lots, and scraped away the top fifty to sixty feet of Mount Vernon. Construction began in 1799 with the help of one of the nation's earliest railroads. In 1800 Harrison Gray Otis became the first of many aristocrats to locate there. High demand for building sites prevented wide replication of Otis's detached mansion, and blocks of elegant townhouses became the norm. The most celebrated location on Beacon Hill (as the development soon became known) was Louisburg Square, which was planned in 1826 and constructed in the 1830s and 1840s. This private park soon became Boston's most prestigious address.

Old Boston: Beacon Hill from the site of the reservoir between Hancock and Temple Streets, ca. 1858. Courtesy of the Library of Congress.

By 1850 the Copley lands had largely been developed, and to this day **Boston Brahmins** regard Beacon Hill proper as those original lands, running from the Common at Beacon Street north to Pickney Street, and from Joy Street on the east to the Charles River on the west. The expansion of the downtown commercial district into what had once been quiet streets drove most of the city's antebellum elite to Beacon Hill. After the **Civil War**, the construction of the Back Bay district on filled land provided an attractive alternative to Beacon Hill, and later the burgeoning suburbs of Chestnut Hill, Brookline, and elsewhere drew affluent residents; but the hill never lost its appeal to Brahmins and other well-heeled home-seekers. By the beginning of the twenty-first century, houses here fetched millions of dollars. U.S. senator and presidential nominee John Forbes Kerry maintains a home on Louisburg Square.

The northern half of Beacon Hill experienced a very different history. In fact, Bostonians have long regarded it as part of the West End, the sprawling neighborhood north of Beacon Hill across Cambridge Street. Known in the eighteenth century as "Mount Whoredom," early in the nineteenth it became the center of Boston's small black community and the site of four black churches. Hostile whites called it "Nigger Hill," although blacks never made up a majority of the residents. In 1900 less than a quarter of Boston's African Americans lived there, and by World War I, most inhabitants of the northern slope were Jewish **immigrants**. Today it is a **middle-class** apartment district, the only surviving remnant of the West End, which was destroyed by overzealous urban renewal in the 1950s.

Suggested Reading

Cleveland Amory, *The Proper Bostonians*, 1947; Walter Firey, *Land Use in Central Boston*, 1947; James Oliver Horton and Lois E. Horton, *Black Bostonians: Family Life and Community Struggle in the Antebellum North*, 1999; Walter Muir Whitehill and Lawrence W. Kennedy, *Boston: A Topographic History*, 2000.

Begging and Busking

Robert E. Weir

Begging and busking are forms of soliciting money, food, shelter, or other favors from the public, generally by those living in **poverty**. Other terms include sponging, panhandling, hoboing, tramping, or spanging, the latter a slang term for "spare change." Busking is a more specialized form of begging in which the beggar engages in some sort of performance in order to attract donations. Musical performances are the most common form of busking; others include juggling, mime, recitations, and street theater. Busking is often viewed as a rite of passage for many performers. Even Bob Dylan once busked on street corners for spare change. Busking by student musicians and the later success of former buskers who are now professionals often obscures the fact that the vast majority of buskers do not become famous and that a significant number of them depend on donations in order to live.

Begging is an ancient human endeavor, though the number of beggars in an affluent society like that of the United States is so troubling that some Americans choose to view begging and busking as a lifestyle choice or as a con to avoid work and taxes. This may be true in some cases, but the vast majority of beggars live in **poverty**. The U.S. Census Bureau estimated there were nearly 36 million poor Americans in 2004. There are currently an estimated 750,000 **homeless** people in the United States, and as many as 12 million people in the United States have experienced homelessness in their lifetimes. Many homeless and poor people rely on begging for sustenance as well as indulgences. The forms of begging vary; beggars may make direct appeals to passersby, sit on sidewalks holding signs asking for handouts, or peddle goods for money. Some engage in more desperate acts, such as prostitution, running cons, or otherwise debasing themselves for money.

The exact number of beggars in the United States in unknown, and their numbers fluctuate according to the state of the economy, the season, local ordinances, and other external factors. Historians routinely link the viability and expansion of begging with the rise of urbanization. In agrarian-based economies, begging more often takes the form of casual labor, with those in need offering to work for handouts. Urban societies generally have more formal rules for employment, making it more difficult to barter labor for food or money, though a thriving unofficial employment network does exist in many cities, with illegal immigrants particularly susceptible to being recruited by temporary employment agents who pay them off the books and at substandard rates.

The number of beggars goes up during recessions and depressions. There was a huge rise in the number of beggars and hoboes during the Panic of 1893, for example. Their numbers were so large that the Ohio reformer Jacob S. Coxey led a march on Washington, D.C., consisting of beggars and unemployed workers. This protest, which included **Jack London**, is often cited as the prototype for future marches on the nation's capitol. The **Industrial Workers of the World** attempted to organize migrant workers during the early twentieth century, but for the most part, beggars, hoboes, and buskers have had little political clout. The measure of their desperation was evident during the **Great Depression**. With unemployment rates of over 20 percent for much of the 1930s, untold numbers of Americans survived by acts such as peddling apples on street corners, bartering day labor for food, panhandling, and tramping. Many displaced **Okies** made their way to California, where the lack of sufficient employment opportunities reduced many to beggary.

The post–World War II economic recovery reduced the overall number of beggars, but 1970s stagflation and deep cuts to social programs beginning in the 1980s swelled their ranks once again. The latter point is crucial. The United States, vis-à-vis many other affluent nations, has fewer assistance programs for the poor. **Welfare** reforms since the 1990s weakened those programs available by severely limiting the time that one can draw public assistance benefits. Likewise, the deinstitutionalization of mental facilities beginning in the 1970s also left many marginally proficient individuals to their own devices. Begging is sometimes one of the few options available to those who cannot find steady employment at a rate that pays them enough to survive.

Beggars, street peddlers, and buskers are now a standard feature of American towns and cities. Those with year-round temperate climates, such as San Francisco, Los Angeles, and Miami often have large numbers of beggars, but there is no region that is immune. Even in the dead of winter, for example, one can find rows of tables on streets in Boston or New York City on which peddlers offer their wares or door-ways in which huddled individuals beg for spare change. Many locales have responded to the social problem of begging by enacting tough ordinances against soliciting, busking, or living on the street. Some cities, like Denver, encourage citizens to contribute to social programs rather than give money to beggars. Indeed, one critique against beggars argues that many donations end up fueling drug and alcohol abuse rather than helping the needy. There is little disputing the fact that beggars often have health and addiction problems, but the notion that begging is self-induced or a lifestyle choice is simply not supported by social data.

Suggested Reading
Mitchell Duneier and Ovie Carter, *Sidewalk*, 2000; Jay MacLeod, *Ain't No Makin' It: Aspirations of Attainment in a Low-Income Neighborhood*, 2004; Peter Rossi, *Down and Out in America: The Origins of Homelessness*, 1991.

BELLAMY, EDWARD (March 26, 1850–May 22, 1898)

ROBERT E. WEIR

Edward Bellamy was a journalist and writer whose 1888 novel *Looking Backward* created a sensation and caused many readers to question some of the materialist assumptions of the late **Gilded Age**.

Bellamy was born in Chicopee Falls, Massachusetts, and spent most of his life there. He was the son of a Baptist minister, an upbringing that perhaps instilled in Bellamy the missionary zeal with which he later attacked social injustice. Although he could have observed inequality in Chicopee—a small industrial city crisscrossed with paper and textile mills—he credited study in Germany with awakening his awareness of poverty.

Edward Bellamy. Courtesy of the Library of Congress.

Bellamy attended Union College, studied law, and passed the bar in 1871, but he was not satisfied with a legal career. Instead, he became a journalist for the *New York Evening Post* and continued to write for that paper even after returning to Chicopee Falls in 1872 to become editor for the *Springfield Union*, the metropolitan daily published in an adjoining city. Many of Bellamy's editorials dealt with social issues, but Bellamy also dabbled in fiction. He published his first short story in *Scribner's* in 1875 and his first novel, *Six to One: A Nantucket Idyll*, in 1878. In all, Bellamy published twenty-two short stories and six novels, though only *Looking Backward* was a huge success.

Looking Backward, however, ranks among the most influential books in American literary history; in the nineteenth century, only *Uncle Tom's Cabin* and *Ben Hur* outsold it. Bellamy had previously tried his hand at science fiction and utopian themes, both of which came into play in *Looking Backward*. The book's protagonist, Julian West, is a typical nineteenth-century **social climber**, an upper-middle-class professional about to marry into a **Brahmin** family. Like many members of his class, he is troubled by the violent labor strikes, poverty, and class conflict of his day; in fact, a strike delays work on the very home West is building. Despite his economic and social prospects, West is an insomniac. He employs a hypnotist to help him fall asleep and builds a special subterranean chamber to dampen the constant construction and street noise of his Boston neighborhood. When a devastating fire breaks out and consumes West's home while he is under hypnosis, he is presumed lost in the fire.

In fact, the underground chamber protected West from the flames and smoke, but he remained asleep until he was unearthed during renovations of a house on the site 113 years later. West is gently awakened by Dr. Leete, the man who will become his mentor and guide for the twenty-first century world. The Boston of 2000 could not be more different than that of 1887; in short, Julian West awoke to a utopia.

Nearly all social ills had been corrected by a government-directed **socialist** program in which **individualism** had been supplanted by a collectivist society designed to achieve equality, rationalism, and efficiency. Class conflict has been overcome through the creation of an Industrial Army in which all citizens must serve from ages twenty-one through forty-five, the latter being the retirement age at which one was free to pursue whatever activities he or she wished. Money had been eliminated in favor of a credit system in which all members received equal shares. The nation had also become the sole employer, producer, and supplier; one could redeem credits for goods and services at national stores, restaurants, laundries, and nurseries. Housework, childcare, and cooking were similarly provided by the state, and women were considered the equals of men (although they had a separate government and Industrial Army).

Leete explained to West that this state of domestic harmony prevailed as a result of peaceful evolution; in essence, the strife of West's own day so exhausted Americans that they decided to vote for an end to **capitalism**. By eliminating competition, private enterprise, hierarchy, and power, society was able to banish inequality, slums, labor conflict, slavery, crime, and most other social evils. Much of the book reads as an extended lecture from Leete on how nineteenth-century problems were solved.

Although Bellamy's fictive socialist utopia was fanciful and many readers responded more to the book's conventional **Victorian** romance than to its politics, *Looking Backward* spawned a reform movement. Much to Bellamy's own surprise, many readers came to view his imaginative novel as a literal blueprint from which society could be rebuilt. In 1889 Bostonians created a Bellamy Club devoted to advancing the novel's principles. From this emerged the Nationalist movement, so named because the nation in the form of a centralized bureaucracy directed all economic, social, and political activities. By the mid-1890s, there were about 165 Nationalist clubs in the United States. Clubs also emerged in Europe (especially in The Netherlands), Australia, and New Zealand. Bellamy's ideas also had profound influence on the **Populist** movement of the 1890s, and many scholars credit *Looking Backward* for reforms that emerged in the Progressive Era and under Franklin Roosevelt's New Deal.

The latter claims are given credence when one considers who read the book. Predictably, members of progressive groups like the **Knights of Labor** embraced the book, as did radicals and reformers like **Eugene Debs, Elizabeth Gurley Flynn**, Clarence Darrow, and **Upton Sinclair.** Yet it was members of the **middle class** who devoured the novel and joined Nationalist Clubs with the greatest gusto. Bellamy had indeed struck a responsive chord when describing the many problems of the Gilded Age; during what historians have dubbed the "crisis of the 1890s," a horrible four-year economic slump (1893–97), renewed outbreaks of labor violence, **anarchist** attacks, and other problems convinced many middle-class members that reform was needed. Many within the middle class were comforted by Bellamy's assertion that transition could take place rationally and peacefully. Neither Progressive Era (c. 1901–17) nor New Deal (1933–40) reforms went as far as Bellamy envisioned, but it is credible to attribute Bellamy with partially inspiring both movements.

Looking Backward is at once a hopeful and naïve book. It did not lack critics. For many conservatives, Bellamy was a dangerous anarchist bent on destroying individualism and the American republic; many on the political left saw him as a deluded dreamer with little understanding of the power of **robber barons**, corrupt governmental officials, and greedy stock traders. There are also gaping logical holes in the book. Bellamy himself became caught up in the Bellamy movement. His book was intended to be a work of imagination, but he too came to see it as a blueprint; in 1897 he wrote a sequel titled *Equality*, which addressed some of the critics' charges. The book did not sell well, though Charles Kerr published one chapter as a stand-alone pamphlet titled *The Parable*.

Whatever one might think of Bellamy from a modern perspective, in his own day he stimulated healthy and productive discussions of the American class system.

Suggested Reading

Edward Bellamy, *Looking Backward: 2000–1887*, 1960; John Hope Franklin, "Edward Bellamy and the Nationalist Movement," *The New England Quarterly*, 11 (December 1938), pp. 739–772; Franklin Rosemont, *Apparitions of Things to Come*, 1990.

BERGER, VICTOR (February 28, 1860–August 7, 1929)

ROBERT E. WEIR

Victor Luitpol Berger was a prominent **socialist** politician of the early twentieth century, an antiwar activist, and a defender of the working class.

Berger was born in Nieder-Rehbach in the now-defunct Austro-Hungarian Empire. He attended universities in Budapest and Vienna before immigrating to Bridgeport, Connecticut, in 1878 with his parents, who were innkeepers. In 1880 he moved to Milwaukee and became a teacher, a newspaper editor, and an activist in the city's German-speaking community. The move to Milwaukee also focused Berger's attention on Midwestern agrarian radicalism, and he joined the **Populist** movement during the 1890s. Increasingly, however, Berger was attracted to ballot-box socialism. He helped organize the Social Democracy of America Party in 1897 and the Social Democratic Party (SDP) the following year. In 1901 the SDP became the Socialist Party (SP) after Berger, **Eugene Debs**, and Morris Hillquit reorganized it, in part to differentiate SP efforts from those of radical factions in Daniel DeLeon's Socialist Labor Party (SLP), which they viewed as disruptive, divisive, and nonpragmatic. Not coincidentally, Berger hoped the SP could bring unity to the fragmented socialist movement.

Rather than adhere to strict Marxist views like DeLeon, Berger sought influence in the political realm and felt that elected socialists could help the working class. Berger was defeated in his bid for Congress in 1904 but was successful in several city elections over the next six years. In 1910, Berger was elected to the U.S. House of Representatives on the SP ticket, becoming the first socialist to serve in Congress. Berger lost his reelection bid in 1912 but remained active in Milwaukee politics. He was returned to Congress in 1918, in part because of his outspoken opposition to U.S. involvement in World War I.

In that year, however, Berger was convicted of violating the Espionage Act, a bill passed during the war that made it a felony to impede the war effort. Like many socialists, Berger viewed the conflict as a capitalist war in which laborers had no stake and should not participate. In early 1919, Judge Kenesaw Mountain Landis, who became the commissioner of major league baseball after the 1919 Black Sox scandal, sentenced Berger to twenty years in jail despite his election to Congress.

Berger appealed his conviction, posted bail, and went to Washington. Congress, however, debated whether Berger's credentials should be accepted and, in November of 1919, declared Berger's seat vacant. In a December special election Berger won an even larger majority. Congress once again refused his credentials, and the seat remained unfilled until 1921. In that year the Supreme Court overturned Berger's conviction; Berger stood again for Congress and was again victorious. He was reelected in 1922, 1924, and 1926. Berger was finally defeated in 1928 and returned to Milwaukee to edit the *Milwaukee Leader*, a socialist paper sympathetic to the **labor movement**. In 1929 he died from injuries sustained in a street car accident.

Although Victor Berger is seldom accorded the acclaim of his colleague and contemporary Eugene Debs, he was a more successful political campaigner than Debs. Despite commitment to social programs and the labor movement, animus

Victor Berger. Courtesy of the Library of Congress.

against socialism runs deep in the United States, in part because of negative associations with foreign radicalism and in part because the winner-take-all electoral policy of the United States favors the entrenched two-party system. Berger, Meyer London of New York (1915–21), and **Bernard Sanders** are three of just a handful of socialists who have ever won Congressional seats.

Suggested Reading
Victor Berger, *Voice and Pen*, 1929; Sally Miller, *Victor Berger and the Promise of Constructive Socialism 1910–1920*, 1973; David Shannon, *The Socialist Party of America: A History*, 1955.

BERNSTEIN, JARED (December 26, 1955–)

ROBERT E. WEIR

Jared Bernstein is an economist whose work concentrates on the links between **poverty**, labor markets, and social policy.

He was born in Philadelphia, the son of Fabian and Evelyn Bernstein, a physician and a teacher, respectively. He attended Hunter College of City University of New York and obtained a masters of social work from Hunter in 1982. Subsequent work as a New York City social worker sharpened his interest in how the working class fares in America. In 1992 he joined the Economic Policy Institute (EPI), a **think tank** that seeks to integrate sectors of the American economy. Bernstein is now a senior policy analyst for EPI and the director of the Living Standards program. He has also worked for the Department of Labor. In 1994 he obtained a PhD in economics from Columbia University. Bernstein is a prolific writer and commentator but is perhaps best known for his contributions to the biennial series *The State of Working America*, for which he began writing in 1992.

The State of Working America, which has appeared since 1988 and has been anchored by EPI director Lawrence Mishel, is an important analytical work that crunches data to separate economic reality from political rhetoric. Early editions of the work revealed 1980s prosperity to be illusory for most working class families and highlighted the growing gap between rich and poor. This has been a theme of subsequent editions as well.

Bernstein has focused much of his work on inequality in the American economy, and he points to ways in which American society has grown more unequal since 1979. He blames some of this on balance of trade deficits, some on **deindustrialization**, and some on technological changes, but he does not feel that these alone explain rising poverty rates. Bernstein places much of the blame on labor market imbalances. Put simply, **wages** have not kept pace with inflation. In 2004, for example, adjusted real income fell for 70 percent of female and 80 percent of male workers and was mostly flat even for highly educated workers. The problem is especially acute at the bottom of the social ladder; when adjusted for inflation, a janitor in 1965 earned far more than one in 2004. He also notes that in 1979 the top 5 percent of American wage earners made 11 times as much as the bottom 20 percent; by 2000, they made 19 times more. He argues that though cuts in the social safety net may be politically popular policy, they have exacerbated inequality. This is especially the case for minorities, who are disproportionately placed in low-wage positions, and anyone seeking to survive on the **minimum wage**.

Bernstein observes that many highly publicized economic trends—the introduction of new technology, the development of new products, up-ticks in the gross domestic product, expansions of payrolls—often have virtually no impact on closing the gap between rich and poor. Nor does he feel that the economy is producing new jobs fast enough. This is due in large part to weak labor markets; that is, there is very little pressure on employers to add jobs, raise wages significantly, or to provide more benefits for existing workers. The weakening of the **labor movement** is, hence, bad news for wage earners, especially those in low-paying service sector jobs. Ultimately, Bernstein feels that current trends are also bad for the overall economy as inequality, high **unemployment**, and stagnant wages are incompatible with sustained economic growth. He takes some solace in the burgeoning **living wage** movement.

Although Bernstein's views are dismissed by some as liberal bias, he is seldom shrill in his political remarks and generally garners respect for his statistical prowess and keen analytical skills. Some claim that the Economic Policy Institute generates better data than the Department of Labor, which has been politicized in recent decades. Bernstein also attracts notice as one of the few working economists to focus on the working class.

Suggested Reading

Jared Bernstein, *The State of Working America*, 2004; Bernstein, "Crunching Numbers," *The American Prospect Online*, February 4, 2005; Bernstein, Heather Bousey, Chauna Brocht, and Bethney Gundersen, *The Real Story of Working Families*, 2001.

BIG GAME HUNTING

See Sports.

BILINGUALISM

CHERRY LEI HUNSAKER

Bilingualism refers to the ability to communicate in two languages. To assess language proficiency, several tests have been developed. These tests include rating scales, fluency, flexibility, and dominance. Critics assert that these tests are problematic, arguing that assessing bilingualism is very difficult since there are at least twenty elements of language to consider and many more ways of evaluating each element. Each of the four general language areas—reading, writing, speaking, and listening—include terms given to clusters of smaller, more specific language elements. For example, one's speaking proficiency is a culmination of vocabulary, grammar, and pronunciation.

Bilingualism can be broken down into three dichotomies. The first dichotomy is between receptive and productive bilingual competence. Receptive, or passive, bilingual competence refers to one who is able to understand a second language, spoken or written, but not able to reciprocate the giving of the information. On the other hand, with productive bilingual competence, information is both given and received two ways. This is also sometimes called active bilingual competence. Someone is considered to have productive bilingual competence if they are able to both give and receive information well in a second language.

The second dichotomy of bilingualism is between additive and subtractive. For bilingualism to be additive, the development of the new language must add to and expand one's linguistic repertoire. Subtractive bilingualism has the opposite effect. In this case, the new language being learned is actually replacing existing linguistic ability. Additive bilingualism usually occurs when both languages are useful and serve particular purposes. For example, business leaders often learn a second language to help them in their professional ventures. Additionally, children of **immigrant** families often speak their native language at home and English at school. In these situations both languages serve specific purposes. In contrast, subtractive bilingualism occurs when one language becomes used in all domains of life. For example, a small child adopted from China into an English-speaking family in America will quickly lose his or her ability to speak Chinese if this language is not reinforced.

The third dichotomy of bilingualism is between primary and secondary bilingualism. Primary bilingualism shows that the attainment of dual proficiency has come about naturally, such as through a family context, or developed due to social-contextual demands. In America, for example, an immigrant child may speak his or her native tongue at home and English at school. In this manner, both languages are learned and developed naturally. Secondary bilingualism refers to a more conscientious way of learning language, such as through formal schooling. However cleverly these programs are structured, differences remain between primary bilinguals and secondary bilinguals. For example, if a person learns Korean at home through speaking to family members and English while out and about in the city and at school, he or she will have command over both languages, especially in social settings. However, they may not be able to write Korean well or will perhaps struggle with proper grammar usage. In contrast, if a person learned English at home and school and studies Korean for several hours a week as part of an intensive language program, he or she may know Korean grammar well, but in social contexts he or she may be unable to grasp informal language cues.

An area in which we see these three dichotomies play out is in the social debate around bilingual **education**. In the United States, there is an ongoing debate over the role, effectiveness, and future of bilingual education. The debate centers on the Bilingual Education Act (BEA) signed by President Lyndon B. Johnson in 1968. Education analysts argue whether this act was put into place as an antipoverty initiative, antidiscrimination measure, or an experiment in multicultural education. Since 1968 supporters and critics of the BEA have debated its effects.

Supporters claim that while some bilingual programs have been more successful than others, investing in a child's native language development is still valuable. Evidence supports the conclusion that cleverly structured bilingual programs can generate high levels of long-term academic success without losing English acquisition among minority language-speaking groups. Essentially, encouraging fluent bilingualism and cultivating educational merit is evidenced as complementary. In fact, approaches that stress native language instruction can help overcome other obstacles such as **poverty**, family illiteracy, and social stigmas that have been associated with minority **status**.

Critics, on the other hand, assert the BEA has failed to meet expectations. Despite positive intellectual outcomes, some research suggests bilingual education is counterproductive. Many policymakers have considered dismantling the program, an action that is endorsed by some within the **Latino** community who argue that continuing to use Spanish places Latino students at a competitive disadvantage. Still other critics oppose bilingualism programs because they privilege Spanish, even when it makes little sense to do so. In northern New England, for example, non-English speakers often use French rather than Spanish, and some California schools have become such a polyglot as to render native language instruction impractical. In 1998 the California electorate voted to end native language teaching programs. Furthermore, some Americans have reacted defensively against the diversity brought about by rising levels of immigration in the United States, generating a nation-wide campaign to protect the English language. As a result, several states have passed laws establishing English as the only official language used in the government. Additionally, bills have been proposed in various states, as well as Congress, to limit the amount of time a child can be enrolled in programs that address limited English proficiency.

Suggested Reading
Colin Baker and Sylvia P. Jones, *Encyclopedia of Bilingualism and Bilingual Education*, 1998; Carlos J. Ovando and Peter McLaren, *The Politics of Multiculturalism and Bilingual Education: Students and Teachers Caught in the Cross Fire*, 2000; Christina B. Paulston, *International Handbook of Bilingualism and Bilingual Education*, 1988; Suzanne Romaine, *Bilingualism*, 1995.

BILL OF RIGHTS

ROBERT E. WEIR

The Bill of Rights is the name given to the first ten amendments to the United States Constitution, which were enacted on December 15, 1791. Although most Americans cherish the individual freedoms enshrined in the Bill of Rights, fewer are aware of the battle that took place to secure them, the social class dimensions inherent in those debates, or the struggle that took place to convince many citizens of the very need for a Constitution.

The 1783 Treaty of Paris recognized the United States of America as independent of Great Britain, but it did not establish the structure by which the new nation would be governed. The Articles of Confederation provided for a structure, but they granted the central government few powers beyond those the thirteen former colonies had unanimously granted. Day-to-day life for most citizens was regulated by their individual state constitutions, with those states coining their own currency, defining extradition laws, and proscribing individual liberties. Events like **Shays's Rebellion** and Rhode Island's veto of a tariff bill agreed upon by twelve other states caused some of the same men who led the American Revolution to lobby for a revision of the Articles of Confederation in order to strengthen the federal government. Their efforts led to the calling of a constitutional convention.

Constitutional framers like James Madison and George Washington were motivated in part by what they perceived to be sound governmental theory, but there is little doubt that social class also shaped constitutional debate. A significant number of the **Founding Fathers** were distrustful of mass **democracy**, which they equated with chaos and **anarchy**. Embedded within the United States Constitution are numerous safeguards designed in part to protect minority **elites**. The decision to enact a *representative* (rather than direct) democracy was one measure of this; the decision to create a bicameral legislature and independent, non-elected judiciary are others. In addition, U.S. senators, who hold six-year terms, originally were appointed by state legislatures rather than by popular vote. Unlike many of the state constitutions, whose authority was superseded, the federal Constitution did not impose term limits on office holders, and many who gathered in Philadelphia to draft the document simply assumed that federal offices would and should be the provenance of "worthy" men such as themselves. Alexander Hamilton was among those who thought the masses excitable and prone to the lures of demagogues. The Electoral College was still another proviso that allowed popular will to be undone. It could, if necessary, allow Congress to determine the fate of an election. Hamilton

The original of the U.S. Bill of Rights, the first ten amendments to the U.S. Constitution. Courtesy of Eon Images.

spoke for many when he argued that a Bill of Rights could prove undesirable; he mused, for instance, that an unfettered press might be dangerous.

As the U.S. Constitution took shape, some ex-Revolutionary War patriots grew alarmed at the power invested in the federal government, the curtailment of states' rights, and absence of guarantees of individual liberty. Two factions emerged: Federalists, who supported the new document, and Anti-Federalists, who opposed it. Among the Anti-Federalists were many individuals who had been most active in supporting independence, including Samuel Adams, Elbridge Gerry, George Clinton, Patrick Henry, Richard Henry Lee, George Mason, and James Monroe. Opposition to the Constitution was particularly strong in Virginia, from whence the latter four hailed.

As noted, motives for opposing the Constitution varied, but the Anti-Federalist argument that the document lacked a Bill of Rights, and hence tended to foster oligarchy, resonated with many Americans. Federalists initially countered that there was no need for a separate Bill of Rights as such liberties were automatically granted to American citizens and/or stipulated in state constitutions, but the Anti-Federalist charges clearly placed Federalists on the defensive. In New York, opposition grew so large that Hamilton, John Jay, and James Madison wrote a series of political tracts collectively known as *The Federalist Papers* to defend the need for the Constitution, and less famous tracts appeared elsewhere. Even then, several state legislatures initially rejected the Constitution, and its final passage was slim in Massachusetts (187 to 168), New York (30 to 27), and Virginia (89 to 79).

Ultimate passage of the Constitution was due not to the persuasiveness of pamphleteers, but rather to the decision to write and pass a Bill of Rights. Thomas Jefferson was among those who argued that a Constitution devoid of a Bill of Rights was defective, and he exerted influence on James Madison, the Constitution's chief writer, to include one. Seventeen amendments were proposed, which were whittled to twelve, then ten. Of these, the first eight can be viewed as compromises to popular democracy, including now-cherished rights such as freedom of religion, a free press, freedom of speech, the right to bear arms, and various legal protections.

The Bill of Rights ensured the passage of the Constitution and effectively quashed the Anti-Federalists as a political movement; only eight of its members were elected to Congress in 1789, and they soon aligned themselves with Jeffersonian Republicans. Nonetheless, the Anti-Federalists were more responsible than any other group in securing basic liberties that Americans now take for granted. Although the U.S. Constitution remained a document that favored elites, the democratic impulses of the Anti-Federalists derailed the elitism of those who distrusted the masses.

Suggested Reading

Bernard Bailyn, ed. *The Debate on the Constitution, Federalist and Antifederalist Speeches, Articles, and Letters During the Struggle Over Ratification*, 1993; Charles Beard, *An Economic Interpretation of the Constitution*, 1913; Stanley Elkins and Eric McKitrick, *The Age of Federalism, 1788–1800*, 1993.

BIRTH CONTROL

STACEY INGRUM RANDALL

The struggle for women to control their own reproductive futures predates the founding of the American republic, though the organized movement for birth control rights first emerged in full force in the twentieth century.

Colonial women and those of the early republic engaged in a variety of strategies to delay or avoid unwanted pregnancies, including prolonging the periods they breastfed children, practicing coitus interruptus with their partners, and attempting to confine sexual intercourse to less-fertile times between menstrual cycles. There were also a host of folk practices of varying efficacy, including the use of douches, pessaries, and herbal abortifacients. Abortions, if conducted early in a pregnancy, were also an option well into the nineteenth century, as prevailing wisdom held that a fetus did not develop a soul until several months into development. Although **poverty** was a factor in those seeking to end pregnancies, women of all classes sought either chemical or surgical abortions as the dangers of childbirth far exceeded those of abortion well into the twentieth century. It is estimated that antebellum New York City had several hundred doctors who performed abortions. All manner of improvised prophylactics were in use long before condoms were brought to the United States in 1840.

Birth control restrictions were largely the product of **Gilded Age** moralists, though some states had outlawed abortion before the Civil War. In 1869 the Catholic Church first took the official position that abortion is murder, and Protestant ministers quickly followed suit. The condemnation of abortion led to generalized assaults on all forms of birth control, many of which were led by Victorian moralist Anthony Comstock, who in 1873 convinced Congress to outlaw the dissemination of birth control information on the grounds that it was obscene.

The Comstock laws precipitated a long battle for women to regain reproductive control, a battle that remained in doubt into the 1960s. In the interim, numerous birth control advocates suffered persecution. The list includes Victoria Woodhull, Tennessee Claflin, **Emma Goldman**, Benjamin Reitman, and **Margaret Sanger**. Sanger's birth control campaign, which began in 1912, is often credited with giving rise to the modern birth control movement. Sanger, though, was dogged by controversy. She was originally a **socialist** who saw birth control as a way for working-class women to liberate themselves but later allied herself with the **eugenics** movement and **middle-class** groups.

During the twentieth century, discussions of birth control increased in all areas and among all social classes of the country, though attempts to overturn Comstock laws failed from 1912 on. Nonetheless, as more women began to move into the working world, particularly after World War II, many argued for the necessity of regulating pregnancy. However, mainstream opinion continued to urge women to reject birth control in favor of the natural process of pregnancy and childbirth. Sex surveys by Alfred Kinsey in 1943 and 1948 and several by William Masters and Virginia Johnson after 1957 revealed that American sexual practices were far different than the expectations of moralists. In 1960 the first birth control pills became available, and in 1961 a Connecticut couple set up a birth control clinic in New Haven, which was later raided by Connecticut state police. This led to the 1965 Supreme Court *Griswold v. Connecticut* decision that invalidated the Comstock laws. In 1971 the Boston Women's Health Book Collective published *Our Bodies, Ourselves: A Book By and For Women*, which encouraged women to learn about their bodies and the medical care necessary to maintain their reproductive health.

The authors challenged male-dominated culture and exhorted women to find their own sources of power, particularly with respect to controlling reproduction. This book detailed women's alternatives, including birth control and abortion. Linda Gordon, author of *Woman's Body, Woman's Right*, contends that the lengthy debate over birth control was based on politics rather than technology. Women knew how to terminate unwanted pregnancies and stop them from occurring for hundreds of years, yet these practices were forced out in the modern world. Once the medical profession specialized and moved medical treatment into the hospital setting, women's roles as healers, midwives, and herbalists were quashed by the medical profession, which encouraged women to embrace motherhood as their specific and valuable social role.

While *Our Bodies, Ourselves* revolutionized women's health and birth control awareness, it was lacking in several ways. The members of the Collective were all white, middle- and **upper-class**, educated women. While some of the stories within the book came from women of other backgrounds, the members of the collective had similar experiences that were very different from their readers. Women of different racial, ethnic, and economic backgrounds faced different problems and had different concerns when deciding about birth control.

In *Wake Up Little Susie*, Rickie Solinger discusses single pregnancy prior to the 1973 Supreme Court decision legalizing abortion. Solinger argues that the pressures of class and race radically altered both society's perception of single mothers as well as the choices those women could make with regard to birth control. The state and federal government had a vested interest in promoting conservative values about the family and women's roles rather than supporting women's right to have access to birth control.

Young, white women who became pregnant faced a social crisis both at home and within their community. Many people viewed women who asserted their sexual independence before marriage as "subverting" the idea of the strong family as well as the traditional image of the demure, passive female. A young, pregnant, white girl faced alienation from her family and her home. In most cases, the young girl went to live in a maternity home for the duration of her pregnancy so that it could be hidden from the community. Then, the baby would be put up for adoption by a respectable family. Before World War II, women who had illegitimate children were considered "fallen" women and cast out of society, and their babies bore the same stigma. However, after the war, social workers decided that if the young women put their children up for adoption, they could be socially redeemed and later pursue traditional, acceptable paths of marriage and a family. In addition, their white babies would allow childless couples to gain access to the **American dream** of the nuclear family.

Young women of color, however, experienced a very different path. Young minority women, particularly African American and Latina women, were blamed not only for "getting themselves" pregnant, but also for abusing the federal **welfare** system. These young women's pregnancies were viewed as a product of uncontrollable biology. In effect, pregnancy was seen through the racist lens that nonwhite women could not control their sexuality. In addition to racial issues, many of these young women were also very poor and had to rely on the federal government to support them and their babies, a condition that bred resentment on the part of white tax-payers. Solinger argues that this racially constructed image gave birth to the stereotype of "welfare mothers" as social parasites whose promiscuity leads to unwanted children or who give birth for the purpose of living on the dole.

Unwed mothers, particularly those who are young, poor, and nonwhite, have always lived with racial, social, and class conflict. Single pregnancy threatened the protected status of the American family as well as the image of female sexuality that social reformers fought so hard to preserve. This problem of unmarried mothers allowed different classes and types of women to enter public debate for the first time throughout the twentieth century. Therefore, the women debating single motherhood were actually challenging their position in defining women's roles and sexuality as well as issues of race and class.

Birth control, however, remains contentious on many levels. The 1973 Supreme Court decision *Roe v. Wade*, which once again made medical abortion legal, has never been accepted by many within American society. Since 1973 numerous attempts have been made to limit the scope of *Roe* or overturn it altogether. As in the nineteenth century, abortion battles have also extended to matters of sexuality in general. This has been seen in numerous rancorous state, local, and federal battles on issues such as teaching sex education in public schools, distributing free condoms in schools and colleges, attempts to censor sexual content in the media, and the crusade to keep RU-486—popularly known as the "morning after pill"— unavailable in the United States. Contemporary moralists, like their Victorian counterparts, see birth control as a key component of stemming America's social and cultural decay, while their detractors condemn them as classist, racist, Puritanical, and unrealistic.

Suggested Reading

Boston Women's Health Book Collective, *Our Bodies, Ourselves,* 1973; Linda Gordon, *Woman's Body, Woman's Right: A Social History of Birth Control in America,* 1976; Leslie J. Reagan, *When Abortion Was A Crime,* 1997; Rickie Solinger, *Wake Up Little Susie: Single Pregnancy and Race before Roe v. Wade,* 1992.

Black Conservatism

Carmelita N. Pickett

Black Conservatism is the term used to describe the political beliefs of African Americans who endorse modern Republican values such as **individualism**, materialism, and limited government intervention.

Historically, African Americans favored the Republican Party because of the party's role in abolishing **slavery**. During the 1850s, when the party was founded, it was known as an antislavery party. This was evident when the first Republican president, Abraham Lincoln, signed the Emancipation Proclamation on January 1, 1863, ending slavery in all areas under rebellion. During **Reconstruction**, African Americans registered to vote in large numbers, and most enrolled in the Republican Party. Many even obtained elected office.

The end of Reconstruction and the rise of Jim Crow **segregation** systems led to the wholesale disenfranchisement of African Americans. By the early twentieth century, few African Americans could vote, but for those who could, the Republican Party was the only option considering that the Democratic Party had established all-white primaries throughout the South. Democrats supported poll taxes, grandfather clauses, and other restrictive practices that prohibited African Americans from voting.

During the 1930s, however, African Americans began shifting their support toward the Democratic Party, primarily because of the **New Deal** created by President **Franklin Roosevelt**. The New Deal provided jobs and aid for American families during the **Great Depression**. In 1954 the U.S. Supreme Court's *Brown v. the Board of Education of Topeka* decision ended legal segregation in public schools. Many historians purport that the *Brown* decision gave birth to the modern Civil Rights Movement, which eventually dismantled all vestiges of the Jim Crow systems relegating African Americans to second-class citizenship. Most African Americans became loyal constituents of the Democratic Party after the Civil Rights Act of 1964 and the **Voting Rights** Act of 1965, which were passed during Lyndon Johnson's administration. These were integral to **Great Society** initiatives designed to help underprivileged Americans.

Black conservatives strongly oppose programs like affirmative action (a legal policy designed to end discrimination based on race, national origin, sex, religion, or sexual orientation), minority scholarships, public education, and **minimum wage** laws. They insist that African American communities must embrace the self-help mantra "pulling oneself up by his or her bootstraps." This ideology supports individualism, which black conservatives believe will lead to **wealth** and economic security. Black conservatives receive criticism from many within the African American community because they seldom acknowledge the unique history of African Americans and the historical policies and practices that prohibited the advancement of African Americans in the United States. Black conservatism supports a **Protestant work ethic**, which asserts that a person's hard work, talents, and self-discipline will lead to wealth.

One early twentieth-century black conservative, Booker T. Washington, founder of Tuskegee Institute and author of *Up from Slavery* (1901), was well liked by white Southerners because his belief in **self-reliance** seemed to support segregation. Washington became famous in 1895 after his opening speech at the Atlanta Cotton States and International Exposition held in Atlanta, Georgia. Another well-known black conservative, George Schuyler, wrote *Black and Conservative* (1966). He vehemently criticized the New Deal and the Civil Rights Movement. Other well-known black conservatives include Harlem Renaissance writer Zora Neale Hurston, Supreme Court Justice Clarence Thomas, political commentator Armstrong Williams, scholar Thomas Sowell, former congressman J. C. Watts, U.S. Secretary of State Condoleezza Rice, and former U.S. Secretary of State Colin L. Powell.

Suggested Reading

Peter Eisenstadt, *Black Conservatism Essays in Intellectual and Political History*, 1999; Matthew Rees, *From the Deck to the Sea: Blacks and the Republican Party*, 1991; Gayle T. Tate, *Dimensions of Black Conservatism in the United States: Made in America*, 2002.

BLACK POWER

CARMELITA N. PICKETT

Black power is an ideology that gained prominence during the mid-1960s and supports the political, social, and economic empowerment of African American communities.

Black power embraced African Americans defending themselves against violence and intimidation and abandoned the nonviolent tactics practiced during the Civil Rights Movement. Black power was a response to the increasing race riots that erupted during the 1960s in Detroit, Newark, and Los Angeles (Watts). Many African Americans in these urban communities felt a sense of hopelessness with continued high **unemployment**, substandard housing conditions, and police brutality. In 1965 African Americans witnessed the assassination of Malcolm X, leader of the Organization of Afro-American Unity and former Black Muslim leader. Young African Americans soon became disillusioned with the nonviolent approach to opposing racism espoused by leaders such as the **Rev. Martin Luther King Jr.**, since it seemed as if no traditional civil rights organization spoke to the ills and frustration of young African Americans in urban **ghetto**es.

In 1966, when Stokely Carmichael became chairman of the Student Nonviolent Coordinating Committee (SNCC), he began promoting self-identity, racial pride, and the establishment of African American economic and political power. Carmichael popularized the term "black power" by chanting publicly, "We want black power." Under his leadership, white members were driven out of the SNCC. The SNCC soon lost its white liberal financial base along with large numbers of African Americans who believed in the integration efforts of the SNCC. Ella J. Baker, a civil rights organizer, founded the SNCC in 1960 as a student organization committed to nonviolent protest as a means of ending discrimination. One of

Stokely Carmichael standing at rostrum, speaking at the University of California's Greek Theater. Courtesy of the Library of Congress.

their most noted actions was a sit-in at a Woolworth's lunch counter in Greensboro, North Carolina. Nonviolent demonstrations by SNCC and other civil rights organizations were often met with brutal violence.

On July 20, 1967, the National Conference on Black Power legitimized the black power movement. Over 200 organizations and institutions participated, including the A. Philip Randolph Institute, Black Muslims, Mississippi Freedom Democratic Party, the **NAACP** (National Association for the Advancement of Colored People), the National Council of Negro Women, and the Southern Christian Leadership Conference (SCLC). During the workshops, delegates worked toward creating resolutions requiring specific action plans. The resolutions included establishing a black economic power fund, a black power lobby in Washington, D.C., and the National Black Education Board, and creating international employment services to serve and train the African diaspora. Black power called for the unification of African Americans and created a community that would address community needs through economics, politics, education and building an international black community.

The Black Panther Party (BPP), a black militant group founded by Huey P. Newton and Bobby Seale, gained prominence during the black power movement by promoting black nationalism, along with **communist** ideologies of Karl Marx and Vladimir Lenin. The BPP focused on creating better environments for urban African Americans by establishing social programs, such as kindergartens for African American children and free breakfast and health care programs. The Black Panther Party was the largest black organization during the mid-1960s that advocated for black power.

Black power faded after the 1970s because of the continued condemnation of the concept as an anti-white movement and the organized ruination of Black Panther members. Although the radical politics of black power was discredited, the quest for African American empowerment survived.

Suggested Reading

Bettye Collier-Thomas, *Sisters in the Struggle: African American Women in the Civil Rights-Black Power Movement*, 2001; Jeffrey Ogbonna Green Ogbar, *Black Power: Radical Politics and African American Identity*, 2004; Tommie Shelby, *We Who Are Dark: The Philosophical Foundations of Black Solidarity*, 2005.

BLAU, PETER MICHAEL (February 7, 1918–March 12, 2002)

ROBERT E. WEIR

Peter Michael Blau was a sociologist whose theories on **social mobility** and **status attainment** remain influential in social stratification studies.

Blau was born in Vienna, Austria, the son of secular Jews. He dabbled in radical Socialist Workers' Party politics as a youth and received a ten-year jail sentence for treason when he was only seventeen. Ironically, he was released from prison by the Nazis who, upon assuming power, rescinded the ban on political activity that sent Blau to jail. When Hitler invaded Austria in 1938, however, Blau attempted to escape to Czechoslovakia, but was captured, tortured, and confined to Prague. He made his way back to Austria, where a friend secured permission for him to immigrate to the United States. He entered France under a German passport, surrendered to Allied troops, and was briefly in a French labor camp before sailing to America in 1939.

Blau attended Elmhurst College as an undergraduate and, in 1942, learned that his family had been killed at Auschwitz. After World War II he entered graduate school at Columbia, where he studied under Robert K. Merton, rigorously examined theorists such as Karl Marx, **Robert Lynd**, and **Talcott Parsons**, and met other young scholars also destined to reshape sociology, including Lewis Coser and Martin Seymour Lipset. He obtained his PhD in 1952 and taught at Wayne State and Cornell before going to the University of Chicago in 1953. Blau stayed there until 1970, when he returned to Columbia, where he taught until retiring in 1988. He was also a visiting fellow at Cambridge University, served as the president of the American Sociological Association, and was elected to the National Academy of Sciences.

During his long career, Blau's work traversed many sociological fields, but he is best known for his research in organizational, occupational, and bureaucratic structures. In fact, Blau is often cited as a founder of organizational sociology. Studies of bureaucracy completed in 1955 and 1970 confirmed suspicions that the growing size of any bureaucracy increases its complexity, complicates coordination within it, and can actually decrease efficiency. Later studies anticipated the manner in which **globalization** and corporate **capitalism** would come to define social relations and capital/labor dynamics in the United States.

Blau is famed for a path-breaking study of social mobility that he conducted with Otis Dudley Duncan in 1967. Blau and Duncan looked at the **Horatio Alger** myth of rags-to-riches. Their study confirmed the reality of upward mobility in the United States, but on a much more modest scale than the Alger myth suggests. They used empirical data from the Census Bureau to confirm that upward mobility was generally slight rather than dramatic. Their way of verifying this was novel and compelling. By looking at **status** attainment, the process by which individuals secure a given social position, and situating it within the occupations that confer said status, Blau and Duncan showed that any individual's chosen occupation was only partly dependent on his or her own ability and education, though those factors were important. One also had to look closely at the occupations, educational levels, and status of parents, as well as simple luck. When broken down, rather than seeing a dramatic change in the occupation of children vis-à-vis their parents, one sees the greatest cross-flow between occupations closely related in **prestige** and status. Moreover, children of high-status parents were more likely to inherit that status and improve upon it than children of manual workers. Hence, there has been an historic trend of reproducing existing social stratification rather than a dramatic restructuring of **power** via upward social mobility from the bottom.

The status attainment model has become one of the standard ways through which scholars analyze class. Blau's subsequent work built off this model. He showed that there were other factors that could influence upward mobility, including the role of nonparental significant others. Another factor, often widely refuted by conservatives, is that government policy in forms such as the GI Bill of Rights, educational grants, and low-income initiatives often stimulated greater mobility than ability alone. Still another study confirmed the difficulties that African Americans have in attaining status and asserted that they are far less likely than white families to be able to pass an attained higher status to their children.

Blau also conducted important work on social inequality. He refuted assumptions on the psychology of **poverty** that axiomatically linked high crime rates with being poor. Instead, Blau found a higher correlation between inequality and crime than between poverty and crime. An offshoot of this research verified the existence of "homophily," the tendency of people to associate with others like themselves. In social terms this means that minority or religious out-groups benefit more from inclusion in dominant groups than vice versa, a potentially potent argument in favor of controversial social measures such as school busing, integrated housing projects, and **affirmative action**. Blau was so influential that some scholars use models of what sociologist Miller McPherson dubbed "Blau space" to map the relative status position of individuals within social networks.

Suggested Reading

Peter Blau, *A Formal Theory of Differentiation in Organizations*, 1970; Blau, *Structural Contexts of Opportunities*, 1994; Blau and Oliver Duncan, *The American Occupational Structure*, 1967.

BLUE COLLAR

SUSAN CLEMENS-BRUDER

Blue collar is a term that came into general use after World War II and refers to manual labor, which is usually paid hourly **wages**, might require special uniforms or work clothes, and differs from that of **white-collar** workers, who are usually salaried, do mental labor, and wear clothes not designed to get dirty. The success of the American **labor movement** in the 1930s, accumulated savings from overtime wages and shortages of consumer goods during World War II, and the benefits offered returning veterans after the war encouraged the belief that it was possible to expand the **middle class** to include stable members of the U.S. working class population. Blue collar became useful as a designation in the post-war years that the wages of unionized workers in mass-production industries and building trades would increase to parity with the middle class. By dividing the American workforce into blue-collar and white-collar categories, the middle class could be more easily analyzed by the government, sociologists, economists, and historians.

During the **Cold War**, a policy for increased military capabilities increased government contracts for the research and development of products that could be produced by industry for armed defense. Blue-collar industries benefited unevenly from the policy, which often resulted in slow periods that kept the working class from achieving the hopes of a true middle-class life. In order to keep up with heightened material expectations, blue-collar families often supplemented their income through second jobs for men, or "moonlighting," and/or full- or part-time jobs for women in "pink-collar" clerical and sales positions or in light industry. Critics, including many blue-collar families, argue that their lives were not truly middle class since white-collar families, many of whom had blue-collar roots, raised their own material expectations beyond that of the working class and were more successful in attaining them.

Many blue-collar families found that they could participate in the post-war move to the suburbs, especially to the lower-middle-class tracts such as the Levittowns of Long Island, New York, and Fairless Hills, Pennsylvania. This was made possible in part by Federal Housing Authority Loans and Veterans Administration Loans in the post-war period. Some workers were able to buy a boat or vacation cabin and take **vacations** in places that pre-World War II working class families could not afford. Critics, however, question whether the material success stories of some can speak for an entire group.

Blue-collar families report that there were some good years in industry before 1980, but they hoped that their children would not choose manual, industrial labor since it was physically demanding and often dangerous. Blue-collar families aimed for enough savings to put their children through college with the hope that the next generation could achieve middle-class incomes and white-collar jobs. That dream has been achieved by many second- and third-generation families with blue-collar roots, especially because of Veterans Administration benefits, low-interest government insured loans, and discount rates offered by many colleges and universities.

The heyday of blue-collar life was short-lived. By the 1980s, the concessions won from employers by unions reversed. Concession bargaining of the last twenty years of the twentieth century slowly chipped away at the gains workers had achieved in wages and benefits, and the class bargain of the post-war war years began to fail. Blue-collar workers accused **CEO**s of extravagant spending on entertainment, **country club** memberships, and luxurious business trips. Executives often criticized blue-collar workers of being greedy, lazy, and protected by their unions. They pointed out gains made in benefit packages in health care and extensive paid vacations. Unions continued to make concessions to employers, and although class conflict erupted mostly at the bargaining table and in workplace grumbling, during the 1980s a number of **strikes** erupted, most of which ended in unsuccessful results for workers.

Blue-collar jobs declined as competition from overseas industries increased. American automobile production declined during the two gasoline crises of the 1970s. Consumer electronics products made in America also suffered in the 1970s and 1980s because of Japanese competition. New high-tech industrial jobs required sophisticated training that many older workers saw as unachievable. Job losses in other heavy industries, especially in steel production, helped to complete what has become known as American **deindustrialization**, which ended the so-called heyday of a lucrative blue-collar life.

People employed in the jobs that could be labeled under the original definition of blue collar criticize the current practices of employing illegal **immigrants**, sending jobs overseas, and new technologies such as robotics in production industries and in the building trades as breaking the back-bone of good blue-collar work. Blue-collar jobs from which workers can make a viable living continue to disappear in the United States. Working class jobs are more likely to be found in the service sector, out of temporary employment agencies, or part-time arrangements. **Globalization** has further blurred "collar designations" in the United States.

Suggested Reading

Alfred Lubrano, *Limbo: Blue-Collar Roots, White-Collar Dreams*, 2004; Becky M. Nicolaides, *My Blue Heaven: Life and Politics in the Working-Class Suburbs of Los Angeles, 1920–1965*, 2002; Reg Theriault, *The Unmaking of the American Working Class*, 2003.

BLUE-COLLAR UNIONS

ROBERT E. WEIR

Blue-collar unions refer to craft and industrial unions that emerged during the mature phase of the American **Industrial Revolution**. These unions consist mainly of manual laborers and reached their apex of importance during the period between 1935 and 1965. The decline of American manufacturing has led to an erosion of **blue-collar** work in general and has been a severe blow to the labor union movement. Sources vary on exact percentages, but in the mid-1960s, roughly one-third of all American workers belonged to labor unions; by 2005, union strength had slipped to under 15 percent.

Workers have long sought the right to bargain collectively with employers. The first associations were collections of journeymen trying to wrest concessions from master craftsmen who owned the shops. The first formal unions, often organized despite statutes that declared them illegal, were craft unions—that is, collections of skilled workers performing similar tasks. Scores of craft unions emerged by the 1820s. Only a handful managed to have national strength in the antebellum period, and attempts to organize a larger federation were largely stillborn. Only a few industries, notably textiles, shoes, and iron, could be said to be giant industrial concerns; most American production was still done in small shops manned by skilled craft workers, most of whom were men and most of whom were unorganized.

In the 1880s, the **Knights of Labor** managed to bring hundreds of thousands of workers under its wing, though the Knights organized across skill lines as well as in craft unions. It also pioneered what was later dubbed industrial unionism—that is, organizing workers according to the product they produced or the industry they serviced, not according to the specific task they performed. The **American Federation of Labor** (AFL), organized in 1886, finally brought craft workers into a larger association. By the 1880s, the United States was a major economic power and American manufacturing had moved into a mature phase.

Nonetheless, in the absence of federal laws protecting collective bargaining rights, forming unions of any sort was fraught with difficulty. The 1914 Clayton Act was the first important legislation to give labor the right to organize, but it was not until the passage of the 1935 National Labor Relations Act that collective bargaining was backed by federal protections. After 1935, labor union strength increased. This was due, in part, to the successes of the **Congress of Industrial Organizations** (CIO), which brought industrial workers like automakers, steelworkers, rubber makers, and textile workers into a common federation. Both the AFL and CIO conducted numerous union recognition strikes in the 1930s and early 1940s. By then, blue-collar workers were a staple of American economic life. In 1930 the total U.S. population was under 123 million, of whom roughly onethird worked in blue-collar manufacturing jobs. Powerful blue-collar unions like the United Autoworkers of America, the United Steelworkers, and the United Electrical, Radio, and Machine Workers unions represented millions of laborers in collective bargaining sessions. Despite the lingering effects of the **Great Depression**, by 1940 about 27 percent of all workers were union members.

In the period following World War II, blue-collar unions flexed their collective muscle. When the AFL and CIO merged in 1955, there was hope that "Big Labor," as journalists dubbed it, would serve as a countervailing force to "Big Business" and that industrial and business decisions would need input and acceptance from unions in order to proceed. This did not turn out to be the case. Blue-collar unions were already weakening by the time of the merger, a victim of conservative political legislation, such as the 1948 Taft-Hartley Act, and a furious counter-assault by antiunion forces, which waylaid plans to organize the non-union South. Still, by 1960 labor unions represented over 31 percent of all workers, a figure that climbed as high as 35 percent by 1965.

This seeming rise, however, was due more to post–World War II economic expansion than to AFL–CIO efforts. After 1965 the Vietnam War strained the economy. It was dealt a more serious blow by an embargo launched by oil-producing nations in the 1970s and by recessionary and inflationary pressures. These occurred at an inopportune time; American industries were aging and in need of retooling at precisely the time during which Europe, Japan, and Korea had begun to recover from World War II and build state-of-the-art factories. As American corporations in industries such as electronics, steel, textiles, and rubber lost market share to global competition, their retrenching led millions of blue-collar union jobs to disappear.

Blue-collar unions declined even more in the 1980s as employers demanded wage, hour, and benefit concessions from workers in the name of global competitiveness. Though business won much of what it wanted in the anti-union political climate under **Ronald Reagan**, it did not stem the loss of jobs or the decline of unions. Mergers eliminated more jobs, as did technological changes. For example, hundreds of thousands of telephone operators lost their jobs because of automated answering services. Outsourcing and relocating production to low-wage nations eliminated still more jobs.

In 1995 the AFL–CIO elected John Sweeney as its new president. Sweeney pledged a renewed organizing drive to rebuild labor's strength, but these plans have yielded little, and some have criticized Sweeney for wasting resources trying to rebuild blue-collar unions that they believe are doomed. There are many observers who retain faith in the ability of blue-collar unions to revive, but most observers feel that unions will need to shift their focus to retail and service sector jobs if they are to do so. Traditional blue-collar work is endangered within the United States, and the working class as traditionally understood may need to be reconceptualized. At present, the future of blue-collar work and blue-collar unions is uncertain.

Suggested Reading

Stanley Aronowitz, *From the Ashes of the Old: American Labor and America's Future*, 1998; Sue Doro, *Blue Collar Goodbyes*, 1992; Rick Fantasia and Kim Voss, *Hard Work: Remaking American Labor*, 2004.

BLUES

JAMES PETERSON

The blues are challenging to define because they can refer to a range of feelings or to a multifaceted form of music. The term originates from the phrase "blue devils," which can loosely be defined as a despondent mood. The music known as the blues derives from a rich musical tradition of folk songs, ragtime music, African American spirituals, pre-jazz music, field hollers, and work songs.

The blues must be heard first and only subsequently read about or defined. Blues music exists wholly in oral and aural forms, and most scholars and aficionados of the blues favor live performances over the recorded ones, which by various estimations have been contaminated by **racism** and corporate greed. The blues can be described in a variety of ways: guttural, primitive, primordial, haunting, sad, and lewd. They engender all of these descriptions, yet maintain their status as a complex subject of study for musicologists and historians alike because of their multivalent grass-roots origins. The blues were developing as local forms of musical entertainment and cultural expression in the late nineteenth century simultaneously across the South, including but not limited to Mississippi, Louisiana, Tennessee, and Texas. Most scholars acknowledge that W. C. Handy, sometimes incorrectly referred to as the Father of the Blues, was one of the earliest official blues composers. That is, his encounters with the earliest blues musicians convinced him of the significance and economic import of the blues itself, as well as its commercial potential. Handy encountered the blues as early as 1890, and during one of these encounters he came to terms with the **proletarian** force of this peculiar emerging, moody music. Blues scholar Giles Oakley recounts Handy's experience in Cleveland, where he composed, arranged, and performed conventional nineteenth-century music, which included folk songs, spirituals, and minstrel show tunes, but not the local blues music erupting across the country. In Cleveland, during one such performance, a note was passed to Handy asking him to direct his band in "our native music." He responded by playing "an old time Southern melody," in response to which he received a second note asking if the local band could usurp the stage. He acquiesced and quickly bore witness to the fact that this local band earned more in tips during this impromptu performance than he and his band were being paid for that entire night.

This anecdote about Handy is significant for several reasons. It underscores the economics already at play in any discussions or definitions about the blues and/or those musicians who played them. It also highlights the important tensions between the power of local, nuanced cultural products and the hegemonic force of mass-produced and mass-mediated cultural products. These are the two enduring tensions in the blues and the music industry that tended to exploit the blues and its artisans. Although we cannot pinpoint a single sui generis bluesman or birth-of-the-blues moment, scholars agree that the blues as both emotion and music attempt to capture and express the conditions of bondage in **slavery** and the extent to which these conditions persisted in disguised forms after the collapse of **Reconstruction** and well into the twentieth century.

Historians have documented the horrific conditions of American slavery, the brief respite during Reconstruction, and the awful racial and economic conditions of the Jim Crow era of violent **segregation**. The blues were born in the midst of these conditions. The development of the blues in Southern states in the late nineteenth century can be viewed as a deliberate and willful response to violent racism and severe economic oppression. Alan Lomax argued that for many black working-class individuals, Jim Crow created more bitter feelings than slavery, experiences captured by blues singers. Accordingly, the instruments of the first blues were the most rudimentary: pain-filled human vocals, hand-made banjos, washboards, and other creatively improvised modes of making music. The content of these folk blues was usually love lost and/or severe economic conditions, both of which can be traced directly to the work conditions of the day. Love was usually transitory because individuals had to be mobile in order to defy the stultifying rules of **sharecropping** and other intrinsically unfair labor practices. Well into the twentieth century, African Americans were on the move seeking better opportunities and escape from prejudice.

This constant movement spread the blues even as it contributed directly to both their multifaceted appeal and their ability to develop local potency wherever blues musicians projected their pain into authentic, vernacular art.

This widespread popularity among the folk was an integral component in the development of the record industry. A popular blues record in the first half of the twentieth century could sell hundreds of thousands of copies just among poor African Americans. This economic potential had an adverse affect on America's first popular folk music recorded and performed by African Americans. One of the most dedicated ethnographers of the blues and American folk culture in general, Alan Lomax, complained that record producers cared little for aesthetics and were interested only in what sold well. This, he felt, explained why so many recordings were "slavish and uncreative imitation of others." Notwithstanding this unfortunate damper on the creativity of blues recordings, blues music still thrives not only in its own right as a powerful folk form, but it also continues to influence nearly every other form of popular American music, including **jazz**, rhythm and blues (R&B), rock and roll, and rap music.

Suggested Reading

Alan Lomax, *The Land Where the Blues Began*, 1994; Giles Oakley, *The Devil's Music: A History of the Blues*, 1997; Hazel Rowley, *Richard Wright: The Life and Times*, 2001; Steven Tracy, *Langston Hughes and the Blues*, 2001.

BLUESTONE, BARRY (1944–)

SHANNON J. TELENKO

Barry Bluestone is a political economist, writer, and policy advocate. He currently serves as the Stearns Trustee Professor of Political Economy and Director of the Center for Urban and Regional Policy at Northeastern University. In 1995 he was a member of the senior policy staff for Congressman Dick Gephardt, the Democratic leader of the U.S. House of Representatives and later a United States presidential candidate. Bluestone founded and directed the Public Policy PhD Program at the University of Massachusetts–Boston. From 1971 to 1986 he taught economics at Boston College, where he was also director of the Social Welfare Research Institute. Raised in Detroit, Michigan, a place that has likely influenced and enhanced his scholarship on deindustrialization, Bluestone received his PhD from the University of Michigan in 1974.

There are two main categories for economists in the United States: classical and **Keynesian**. Bluestone would fall more in the second category, making his research and policy work more applicable to Democratic goals for the U.S. economy and federal budget. Fiscal conservatives and corporate leaders often perceive Bluestone's arguments as biased and quasi-**socialist**. His work leans more towards liberal, demand-side economics and encourages public spending and the easing of income inequalities.

In 1982 Bluestone and Bennett Harrison's book *The Deindustrialization of America* was published. Alfred E. Kahn, a former adviser on inflation to President Carter, wrote for the *New York Times* on December 12, 1982, "Even though I found

[Bluestone and Harrison's] analysis distorted, their explanations simplistic and their remedies of dubious efficacy, I commend their message to anyone interested in where America is and where it is going." Bluestone and Harrison also worked together on *The Retail Revolution* (1981), *Corporate Flight* (1981), and *Growing Prosperity* (2000). Bluestone and Harrison's earlier work describes what was going on behind the scenes in the 1980s, when American teachers urged students to surpass their Japanese counterparts in math and science.

Bluestone's early career focused on the changes that American business and industry were undergoing due to increased technology, **globalization**, and the subsequent layoffs of skilled workers. *Deindustrialization in America* highlighted the idea that firms were disinvesting in the United States productive capacity and subsequently in American individuals and communities. Rather than simply focusing on the bottom line, as a political economist Bluestone highlights the political as well as the social aspects of the economy and economic decision making. In 2003, just twenty years after *Deindustrialization in America*, Bluestone noted in the foreword of *Beyond the Ruins* that despite the dismal predictions of economists and other experts in the late 1970s and early 1980s, the mid-1990s were a time of renewed prosperity for many Americans. However, he takes care to note that despite these gains, many workers and communities still bear the brunt of deindustrialization.

Bluestone's career choices continue to highlight his commitment to understanding changes in the economy due to political decision making as well as how those changes affect people's lives and the decisions they make. He has made a deep imprint on young scholars who hope to create a richer understanding of the interactions between government, economy, society, and culture.

Suggested Reading
Barry Bluestone and Bennett Harrison, *The Deindustrialization of America: Plant Closings, Community Abandonment, and the Dismantling of Basic Industry*, 1982; Bluestone, Harrison, and Lawrence Baker, *Corporate Flight: The Causes and Consequences of Economic Dislocation*, 1981; The Center for Urban and Regional Policy at Northeastern University (http://www.curp.neu.edu/).

BOARDING SCHOOLS
See Education; Ivy League.

BOARDS OF DIRECTORS
MURNEY GERLACH

Boards of directors are responsible for the overall fiduciary, policy development, and management review of nonprofit and corporate organizations in modern America. Individuals on a board of directors are either appointed or elected according to law and are authorized to manage and direct the affairs of a corporation, company, or nonprofit entity. They hold powers to review decisions individually but also to form collective policies that are consistent with the overall mission, values, and traditions of the organization.

The duties and responsibilities of a board of directors are set out in either the articles of incorporation, articles of organization, bylaws, or charter agreements. Some agreements date to the eighteenth and nineteenth centuries, and a few go back to Colonial times. Other documents and guidelines for boards of directors are developed in a trustee manual or by various officers, directors, and committees who set rules, regulations, and operating procedures for the board. These set out the basic operating framework and entrust the **CEO** with the responsibility of working with the board to carry out the visions, missions, and day-to-day management of the organization, nonprofit group, or corporation. In all cases, the very best boards value the concepts of "work, wisdom, and wealth," or "time, treasure, and talent," to provide a wide range of fiduciary, strategic planning, and financial and business leadership in what has been recently been called "generative leadership." This later concept, developed by the authors Richard Chait, William Ryan, and Barbara Taylor, places value, community involvement, and forward thinking as critical elements that good boards bring to the management of organizations.

Most board members are passionate about the entity on whose board they serve and are professionals, executives, or community leaders with an understanding of how organizations work. The powers of the board and the CEO are related, integrated, and focused on the ways that decisions may be reached. Duties and responsibilities of directors or trustees include determining the organization's mission and fundamental policies according to its governing documents; setting the organizations long-term and strategic plans; reviewing its yearly progress; establishing fiscal policy by developing budgets and financial controls; fund raising; choosing a chief executive officer and evaluating that person's performance; developing close links and involvements with the community; supporting the CEO; and promoting the work and agendas of the organization.

CEOs are frequently the individuals who receive the most public attention, but their boards act as their superiors and often have the power to dismiss a CEO. Those who serve on boards of large corporations, **Ivy League** and other prestigious universities, and of numerous cultural agencies generally come from the economic **elites**, though less wealthy members of the **middle class** often make up the boards of nonprofit groups and less prestigious entities. There is a remarkable degree of overlap on boards serving the top echelons of society, a reality that leads some scholars to look at the intersections between wealth, **power**, and **prestige** and postulate the existence of a **corporate class** possessing undue influence.

Suggested Reading

John Carver and Miriam Mayhew Carver, *Reinventing Your Board. A Step-by-Step Guide to Implementing Policy Governance*, 1997; Richard P. Chait, William P. Ryan, and Barbara E. Taylor, *Governance as Leadership. Reframing the Work of Nonprofit Boards*, 2005; Lewis D. Solomon and Alan R. Palmiter, *Corporations. Examples and Explanations: A Student's Guide to Understanding Corporations*, 1990; Thomas Wolf, *Managing a Nonprofit Organization in the Twenty-First Century*, 1999

BOBOS

See Neiman Marcus; Status Symbols; Yuppies.

BODY IMAGE

MAXINE LEVAREN

Body image has often been a reflection of the ideals of society and therefore a reflection of social class as well. Throughout history, there have been prevailing body images that were especially favorable among a particular class or ethnic group. This desire to conform to society's concept of beauty is most prevalent among women but is also a concern of some men.

In much of Europe and the United States, the ideal body image has changed throughout history. Up until the twentieth century, when much of society was **agrarian** and abundance was dependent on good crops, thinness indicated **poverty** and hunger, and a plump body image indicated a degree of health, **wealth**, and comfort. In fact, being fat was sometimes cultivated as a way to demonstrate wealth and a higher position in society. This perception of beauty is still held as an indication of a higher social **status** in many parts of the world, particularly in countries where life, dependent on agriculture, is more precarious and a lean figure shows someone who does not have enough to eat. However, as American society became more industrialized and food became more universally available, a lean body indicated access to a more balanced diet rather than a diet that was dependent on more filling and less nutritious foods.

Social class is not the only factor that determines the most desirable or acceptable body image, since different ethnic groups embrace varying ideals of beauty. For example, the African American and **Hispanic** communities tend to value a more full-figured body image, as opposed to the white American and European ideal of leanness. In addition, the ideal body image is most often associated with feminine beauty. In the modern day, men have been relatively immune from these standards.

Until the 1920s, the ideal feminine body image was one that indicated an ability to bear children—full breasts and hips. Fashion reflected this image with corsets and padding designed to emphasize these attributes. In Western Europe and the United States, body image often followed fashion rather than vice versa. For example, the flapper era of the 1920s favored thin women, as did the preference for thinness that started with Twiggy and the fashions of the 1960s.

Films and movies also influenced the ideal body image. During the 1940s and 1950s, the curvaceous images of the screen goddesses such as Rita Hayworth, Marilyn Monroe, and Jayne Mansfield were the epitome of female beauty. In the twentieth century, the media often promoted the ideal body image rather than reflecting it.

Preoccupation with body image is most prevalent among **middle-** and **upper-class** white women, who want to fit in with the ideals of beauty promoted in the media. This has often led to eating disorders, such as anorexia and bulimia, in an effort to be as thin as the most famous models and actresses.

Suggested Reading

Kathy Peiss, *Hope in a Jar: The Making of America's Beauty Culture*, 1999; Teres Riordan, *Inventing Beauty: A History of the Innovations That Have Made Us Beautiful*, 2004; Peter Stearns, *Fat History: Bodies and Beauty in the Modern West*, 2002.

BOSTON BRAHMINS

RONALD DALE KARR

Boston Brahmins are **upper-class** residents of Boston, especially members of a handful of distinguished families. The term "Brahmin" derives from the top echelon of India's **caste** system. Like Indian Brahmins, Boston Brahmins have placed great importance on privilege inherent in being born into particular families.

In 1859 Oliver Wendell Holmes described "the Brahmin caste of New England. . . the harmless, inoffensive, untitled aristocracy" of scholars, nearly always the offspring of old and cultivated families of ministers and intellectuals. In time, however, the term became synonymous with that of the "Proper Bostonian," a man or woman of the city's best families, regardless of level of intellectual activity.

Most of Boston's most celebrated clans were descended from merchants and ship owners who came to prominence following the departure of much of the city's Loyalist mercantile **elite** during the **American Revolution**. Some were already men of means in secondary ports, such as Salem and Newburyport. After the decline of shipping following the Embargo of 1807 and the War of 1812, they invested much of their wealth into manufacturing, banking, and later, railroads, vastly enhancing their fortunes. As the Boston Associates, they owned and managed corporations that controlled a significant proportion of New England's commercial property. Brahmins dominated the cultural and charitable institutions of Boston, founding the Massachusetts General Hospital, the Boston **Symphony Orchestra**, and the Perkins School for the Blind, as well as taking control of existing bodies, such as Harvard College.

Brahmin families, among them surnames such as the **Lowell**, **Adams**, Cabot, Lawrence, Appleton, Coolidge, Forbes, Higginson, Lee, Lyman, Peabody, Sears, and Saltonstall, tended to marry either within their Brahmin circle, with scions of socially-prominent families from other regions—such as New York's Harvard-educated **Theodore Roosevelt**—or with worthy Harvard faculty, such as Henry Wadsworth Longfellow or Louis Agassiz. Throughout most of the nineteenth century Brahmins typically lived on **Beacon Hill** or in the new townhouses of the Back Bay. By the middle of the twentieth century, however, most had moved beyond the Boston city limits to Chestnut Hill, Brookline, Concord, Lincoln, Dover, Beverly Farms, and other elite suburbs, though they often remained employed in the city as business executives, professionals, and brokers.

Boston's Brahmins, unlike their counterparts in New York, Chicago, Los Angeles, and other large cities, managed to fend off challenges from newer **wealth** after the **Civil War** and retain their economic, social, and political power well into the twentieth century. Indeed, one of their own, Senator John Kerry, was the Democratic candidate for President of the United States in 2004. Other notable Brahmins have included numerous members of the Lowell family, the two Senators Henry Cabot Lodge (grandfather and grandson), Senator Leverett Saltonstall, the writer Henry Adams, the two Oliver Wendell Holmes (father and son), historians William Hickling Prescott, Francis Parkman, and Samuel Eliot Morison, and Civil War hero Colonel Robert Gould Shaw.

Suggested Reading

Cleveland Amory, *The Proper Bostonians*, 1947; Robert F. Dalzell Jr., *Enterprising Elite: The Boston Associates and the World They Made*, 1987; Betty G. Farrell, *Elite Families: Class and Power in Nineteenth-Century Boston*, 1993; Frederic Cople Jaher, *The Urban Establishment: Upper Strata in Boston, New York, Charleston, Chicago, and Los Angeles*, 1982.

BOURDIEU, PIERRE (August 1, 1930–January 23, 2002)

DIETER BÖGENHOLD

Pierre Bourdieu was an influential French sociologist whose book *Distinction* (French 1979, English 1984) is considered one of the ten most influential books of the twentieth century according to the International Sociological Association. Most contemporary scholars of social class reference Bourdieu.

Bourdieu was born in Denguin, France, to **sharecropper** parents. He was schooled in Paris and served in the French army during the Algerian War. In 1964 he became director of the School for Advanced Studies on the Social Sciences in Paris and in 1981 became head of the sociology school at the College of France, also in Paris. In 1968 Bourdieu founded the Center of European Sociology. Before his death in 2002, Bourdieu received numerous accolades, honors, and awards.

Bourdieu's sociology is all-encompassing in that he synthesized findings from consumption behavior, education sociology, socialization research, and social **stratification** in a specific form that serves as an interdisciplinary cultural sociology. Bourdieu departed from many of the assumptions of a materialistic class theory. He refined his analysis to highlight social inequalities that exist even within subtle human actions. Differing social class practices can be detected, for example, in the ways in which people furnish their houses, where and how they **vacation**, how they host guests at home, the patterns of their leisure spending, musical preferences, and how they consume food and drink. Bourdieu noted the variations in daily life practices—drinking beer or champagne, for example—and interpreted them as codes that can be translated into a societal practice of differentiation and homogenization. Many such inequalities in differentiated market societies are no longer primarily grounded in conflicts for material resources but rather in practices of symbolic "distinction." Bourdieu's approach combines analysis of social stratification with the analysis of cultural symbols. In essence, Bourdieu sought to analyze objectively those cultural symbols and interactions that were customarily viewed subjectively.

When Bourdieu looked at society, he often employed the metaphor of a multi-dimensional "social space." Contrary to narrow materialistic interpretations, Bourdieu argued in favor of relative autonomous "social fields" covering divergent principles of differences and distributions, which give sources of **power** and **prestige** to individual actors. Individual actors or social groups are defined by their *relative* positions within these fields. One's place within society is, hence, not necessarily defined by social class alone; rather it depends in large part on the amount of social, cultural, and symbolic capital one possesses.

Following the lead of **Max Weber**, Bourdieu analyzed, theoretically and empirically, the relationship between "classes" and "status groups." By doing so he explored the meaning of social inequality relations in advanced consumption societies. Beside the inner workings of social fields, two further analytical pillars of reading Bourdieu's work involve individual capital and habit (Latin, habitus). The category of the field acts as location for the existence of social action and behavior including subfields such as the arts, the economy, law, policy, literature. Social fields are structured by a variety of social figurations and poles with concentrations of different capital. Bourdieu extended an interpretation of capital derived from **Marxism**. He saw it in economic terms and access to material resources, but also as a resource composition that included **social networks**, **education**, and the qualifications of social actors. Bourdieu discussed the financial, social, and **cultural capital** that human beings have at different levels and in different compositions. Cultural capital exists in three different forms; it is incorporated as permanent disposition, it exists objectively, and it becomes institutionalized. Society confers forms such as degrees and titles to express institutional cultural capital.

Social capital is treated within the context of actual and potential resources, all of which are connected to a network of stronger or weaker social contacts. Social capital can be converted to improved **life chances** and/or access to resources. For example, an individual possessing strong social capital has an advantage when seeking credit in financial markets or might land a job to which better qualified individuals simply have no access. In such a fashion, social networks are built and maintained. In this way, habitus becomes a form of cultural and **social reproduction**. The incorporated behavior of human actors and groups is acquired individually over time, but it also serves as permanent dispositions for those with access to those who model and teach those cultural symbols that perpetuate social inequality, including such seemingly insignificant markers of distinction such as **accents**, etiquette, and the carriage of one's body. His work suggests that most Western societies, including the United States, must be viewed through the lens of power relationships, popular rhetoric on **meritocracy** notwithstanding.

Bourdieu's cultural sociology of inequality has become very popular in academic discourse through the last two decades. It serves as a new starting point for research on divergent lifestyle research and mentalities. Apart from the sociological side of Bourdieu's career, he acted as an engaged political citizen and gave many interviews and talks through which he signaled his sympathy for critics of **globalization**.

Suggested Reading

Pierre Bourdieu, *Distinction: A Social Critique of the Judgment of Taste*, 1987; Bourdieu, *Language and Symbolic Power*, 1997; Bourdieu, *Practical Reason: On the Theory of Action*, 1998; Bridget Fowler, *Pierre Bourdieu and Cultural Theory: Critical Investigations*, 1998.

BOURGEOISIE

DAVID V. HEALY

Bourgeoisie is a French word literally referring to a title of nobility, although, iron-ically, it is most often applied to refer to the **middle class**. It is directly related to the English word *burgess*, which has similar usage.

Historically, the word is derived from the class of artisans and craftsmen that emerged in the Middle Ages. It was the bourgeoisie, using the wealth of their new class independence, who found the time to develop much of early European thought on philosophy. Their writings influenced thought for many years, establishing many trends, including those of the Enlightenment and later ages. Most importantly, bourgeoisie thought established concepts of natural and property rights, two ele-ments that would serve as the foundation of Western civilization after the decline of the aristocracy and rise of the middle class that the bourgeoisie became.

In more modern times, the word *bourgeoisie* has become tied to **Marxist** philos-ophy. In many of Karl Marx's works he criticized the middle class as the enemies of the working class, the **proletariat** he endorses in his theories. The reasoning behind this critique cites the relationship between workers and their managers. According to Marx and other **communist** thinkers, the bourgeoisie exploits the labor of the proletariat, expropriating profit at the expense of workers who are beholden to the bourgeoisie for their jobs and livelihood. This is to the detriment of the workers, who are provided less than the worth of their labor on the part of their employers in the bourgeoisie.

Today, as Marxist thought has fallen aside, the word *bourgeoisie* is used less fre-quently. Though understood in academic circles, bourgeoisie is rarely heard in common discussion, although the adjective *bourgeois* is sometimes invoked in a neg-ative way as shorthand for **social climbing**, pretense, excessive conformity, or a lack of imagination. However, while the word is out of fashion, the class conscious-ness that it initially represented and later engendered in common culture remains, as the middle class continues to be a prevalent and influential component of mod-ern society throughout much of the world.

Suggested Reading
Karl Marx, *The Communist Manifesto*, 1998; Michael Mollat and Phillipe Wolff, *The Popular Revolutions of the Late Middle Ages*, 1973; David K. Shipler, *The Working Poor: Invisible in America*, 2004.

BOWLING

ADAM R. HORNBUCKLE

In the United States, bowling usually refers to a game in which a ball is rolled in an attempt to knock down pins. This differentiates American bowling from European games such as lawn bowling or bocce. Ten-pin bowling is the most common form, but thin candle pins and short "duck" pin bowling also enjoy popularity.

The origins of modern bowling are found in the medieval German game of *kegels*, in which participants rolled a wooden ball into a group of wooden pins. Although the Dutch introduced bowling to the American colonies in New York, bowling became increasing widespread as German immigration to the United States intensified in the late 1840s. From the outset of its introduction to America, bowling was closely tied to gambling and the consumption of alcohol, which tarnished its reputation and led to prohibitions against the sport in the late eighteenth and early nineteenth centuries. In 1840, for instance, most of the 200 bowling alleys in New York City were associated with saloons, taverns, and gaming establishments. As such, bowling was mostly associated with the **lower classes** and the lower strata of the working class.

For much of the nineteenth and early twentieth centuries, urban, **immigrant**, working class males constituted the majority of bowlers in the United States. Nearly one-third of the bowling alley proprietors in turn-of-the-century Chicago were German immigrants, who catered to an ethnic, working class clientele. For many German, Italian, Czech, and Polish neighborhoods, the bowling alley was an important nexus of street-corner life, as young working class males would congregate at the establishments, socialize, and demonstrate their skills in an environment considered more respectable than the billiard parlor. For many first-generation Americans, bowling provided cheap entertainment, a source of self-display, and sociability in an environment favorable to sustaining their ethnic identity. In contrast, the cost of bowling was out of reach of most African Americans, few neighborhoods had bowling alleys, and those that did lost them during the **Great Depression**.

In 1895 the American Bowling Congress (ABC) formed to reform the character of the sport, to broaden its appeal beyond the working class, to standardize rules and equipment, and to sanction competition. Reflecting the success of the ABC in reforming bowling, bowling teams representing local businesses and professional organizations formed in the late nineteenth and early twentieth centuries. National prohibition, from 1919 to 1936, had more influence on reforming the character of bowling than the ABC, as many saloon and tavern owners, who maintained bowling alleys, became solely bowling alley proprietors after closing their bars. During the 1920s and 1930s, bowling lost many of its low-life associations and was transformed into an activity for good clean fun, in which both men and women could participate and socialize. In the 1930s, Chicago alone boasted over 500,000 bowlers, who made up nearly 900 leagues, representing various businesses, churches, civic groups, and ethnic societies.

The number of Americans participating in bowling stood at about 12 million after the Depression and increased to about 20 million after World War II. During the postwar era, bowling establishments became increasingly common in suburban shopping malls. Although the sport began to attract a **middle class** clientele after World War II, bowling remained for the most part a working class pastime, in which its participants enjoyed a relatively inexpensive source of entertainment and recreation, besides finding a place for camaraderie, socialization, and cultural identity.

The period between the end of World War II and into the early 1970s is generally held to be the heyday of organized bowling, with industrial leagues flourishing and professional bowlers such as Donna Adamek, Don Carter, Earl Athony, Betty Morris, and Don Weber acquiring sports hero status among the working class.

Some scholars see the popularity of bowling as consumed leisure as a confirmation of the newfound affluence of the working class in the postwar period.

As traditional **blue-collar** work declined during the 1970s and many of the industries that once supported bowling teams began to close, the ABC and other bowling associations made efforts to alter the sport's strong association with the working class. Upscale bowling alleys opened, while special events such as disco bowling nights encouraged cross-class participation. Some observers claim, however, that since the 1980s bowling has lost much of its community association altogether and is now primarily a solitary activity. Such assessments may be overly gloomy in some respects; each year more than 50 million Americans go bowling, about one-third of whom are under the age of twenty-four and bowl in peer groups.

There is little doubt, though, that bowling has never lost its association as a plebeian, low-culture activity. This can be seen in images that appear in such popular TV shows as *The Simpsons* and in films such as *Kingpin* and *The Big Lebowski*. It is also reflected in how professional bowling prize money fares vis-à-vis other sports. In 2005, for example, top-rated professional bowler Mike Scroggins earned over $136,000, a lucrative sum, but one that is just over one-third of the *minimum* salary for professional baseball players. In the same year, American tennis star Andy Roddick made nearly $1.8 million for a sport that attracts more well-heeled followers but in which only 17 million people participate.

Suggested Reading
Andrew Hurley, *Diners, Bowling Alleys, and Trailer Parks: Chasing the American Dream in the Postwar Consumer Culture*, 2001; Robert Putnam, *Bowling Alone: The Collapse and Revival of American Community*, 2000; Benjamin Rader, *American Sports: From the Age of Folk Games to the Age of Televised Sports*, 2004.

BRACE, CHARLES LORING (June 19, 1826–August 11, 1890)

ROBERT E. WEIR

Charles Loring Brace was a pioneering social worker and the founder of the Children's Aid Society, which he directed for thirty-seven years.

Brace was born in Litchfield, Connecticut, and grew up amid upper-**middle-class** comfort in nearby Hartford. He graduated from Yale in 1846 and from Union Theological Seminary three years later. Ordained as a Methodist cleric, Brace ascended the pulpit. Firsthand observance of New York City **poverty** caused Brace to change his focus. By the mid-1850s, New York City teemed with as many as 34,000 **homeless** children and even greater numbers of children living in dysfunctional and/or impoverished families. Some members of Brace's class came to embrace **Social Darwinism**, arguing that the fate of the poor was a product of their own character flaws. Although Brace never entirely shed paternalistic attitudes, he saw the problem of "street Arabs," as bands of street children were often dubbed, as potentially dangerous to social order and argued that the children needed assistance. He also felt that orphanages, soup kitchens, and other benevolent agencies erred in merely offering basic creature comforts; Brace advocated programs that mixed aid with teaching **self-reliance**. In 1853 he founded the Children's Aid Society to provide sustenance, job training, educational opportunities, moral instruction, shelter, and other services for children.

Brace was also an advocate of foster care for troubled or endangered youths. To posterity he is best known for his controversial "Orphan Train" concept that relocated New York City youths and placed them with rural families, many of whom were located in remote Western states and territories. Critics and some later historians charged that many of the children became virtual serfs to farm families looking for free labor, though Brace and his supporters claimed that nearly 90 percent of their placements thrived. Hard data are sparse, however, with even the number of placements in dispute; in the seventy-five years of the program's existence, estimates vary from a low of about 100,000 relocated children to more than 400,000.

Brace was motivated by what he saw as his Christian duty and, hence, is often cited as an early shaper of the **Social Gospel** movement. When he died in 1890, his son, Charles Loring Brace Jr. (1855–1938), assumed control of the Children's Aid Society of New York. This agency continues to deliver services to needy children, and some of its young clients enjoy spectacular success later in life. Brace's life and career serve as a reminder of the complicated face of class relations in the nineteenth century. They illustrate that not all members of the middle class embraced Social Darwinism, but that those who rejected it did not entirely free themselves of its paternalistic, pietistic, and moralistic underpinnings.

Suggested Reading

Charles Loring Brace, *The Dangerous Classes of New York and Twenty Years Work among Them*, 1872; Emma Brace, ed. *Life of Charles Loring Brace, Chiefly Told in His Letters*, 1994; Stephen O'Connor, *Orphan Trains: The Story of Charles Loring Brace and the Children He Saved and Failed*, 2004.

BRACERO PROGRAM

ROBERT E. WEIR

The Bracero Program was an arrangement between the governments of the United States and Mexico in effect between 1942 and 1964 that allowed about 4.5 million Mexicans to cross into the United States and secure temporary employment, especially in agriculture. In many sections of the United States, especially the Southwest and California, controversy rages over the entry of illegal Hispanic immigrants into the country. Stemming the tide of illegal border crossings is often a cause celebre for conservatives. The merits (or lack thereof) of such efforts notwithstanding, contemporary discussions of Mexican immigration often neglect the reality that border crossings have been a long-term historical trend and, on occasion, the United States encourages it, either by official action or benign neglect.

Borders between the new United States and Spanish Latin America were fluid in the eighteenth and nineteenth centuries. Although Mexico obtained independence from Spain in 1810, its northern borders and those of the Louisiana Purchase lands obtained by the United States from France in 1803 were both sparsely populated and imprecisely surveyed. Attempts by Mexico to define her borders and keep Southern slaveholders from illegally settling in the Téjas province were among the tensions that led to the Mexican War. When this conflict was settled by the 1847 Treaty of Guadalupe, Mexico ceded nearly half its territory to the United States, and over 100,000 Mexicans found themselves to be "Americans."

The border between the United States and Mexico remained porous throughout the nineteenth century, but little attention was paid as the United States was under-populated, Mexicans seldom competed with Anglo wage earners, and the special-ized skills of the vaqueros were valued by **cattle kingdom** barons. They were also viewed as preferable alternatives to the Chinese, who were excluded altogether after 1882. To be sure, Mexicans were treated poorly, subject to nativist attacks, dispro-portionately poor, and viewed by many **Victorians** as subhuman, but only isolation-ists and **eugenicists** advocating closing the Mexican border.

Mexican braceros being examined at reception center before being put to work, California, 1959. © Michael Rougier/Time Life Pictures/Getty Images.

During the cataclysmic Mexican Revolution of 1910, nearly two million peas-ants died and others suffered economic deprivation. This led many to cross the U.S. border in search of safety or opportunity. This coincided, however, with heightened rhetoric about Anglo-Saxon racial superiority, which led to a general curtailment of immigration, and a larger number of American officials calling for tightening of border controls. Oddly enough, Mexicans were excluded from a restrictive 1924 immigration act, but the Border Patrol was established in that year.

Sentiment ran for exclusion during the **Great Depression**, but this changed during World War II, when the United States experienced a manpower shortage in agriculture. Under the 1942 bill "For the Temporary Migration of Mexican Agricultural Workers to the United States," Mexican workers were recruited to cross the border to cut sugar beets and harvest crops such as cotton, cucumbers, and tomatoes. This program was popularly called the Bracero Program, for the Spanish slang term meaning, roughly, "strong-arm worker." Before this program ended in 1964, as many as four million Mexican workers came to the United States.

Under the Bracero Treaty signed with Mexico, immigrants were supposed to be over the age of fourteen, have their transportation and living costs paid, and were to receive at least thirty cents an hour in wages. In practice, the thirty-cent guide-line became the default wage, living quarters were routinely substandard, and birth certificates were easily falsified to facilitate hiring children. The bill also provided for repatriation of workers once harvests were completed, but it was quite easy for many to avoid return. Public pressure to end the program did not sit well with **agribusiness**, whose corporate farm structure came to depend on cheap Mexican labor. Lost in the contemporary hue and cry over illegal Mexican immigration is agribusiness's role in perpetuating that immigration and its disingenuous claim that checking green cards and official identification is too difficult a task.

In effect, the Bracero Program never really ended; it simply shifted from official sanction to customary practice. Many **Hispanics** and **Latinos** have been incorporated into business patterns in which they are viewed as a cheap and readily available labor supply. The general exploitation of immigrant and migrant labor led to the formation of the United Farm Workers of America union in 1966, and there have been gains made in wages and working conditions, but the overall status of Hispanic and Latino farm workers is still debased, and many social scientists would use them as negative examples of **ethnic stratification** in the contemporary class system. The future implications of this are profound given that President George **Bush** and Mexican President Vicente Fox have discussed the creation of a new Bracero program. To its defenders, such a program is a realistic way to reduce illegal immigration and provide Mexicans with economic opportunity. To its critics, the Bush-Fox plan simply debases wages and ensures a supply of cheap farm labor for agribusiness, underpaid clerks in urban service sectors, and domestic servants for self-indulgent **yuppies**.

Suggested Reading

Ernesto Galarza, *Merchants of Labor: The Mexican Bracero Story*, 1978; Erasmo Gamboa, *Mexican Labor and World War II: Braceros in the Pacific Northwest 1942–1947*, 2000; Carlos Marentes, Los Braceros 1942–1964 (http://www.farmworkers.org/ benglish.html).

BUCHANAN, PAT (November 1, 1938–)

ROBERT E. WEIR

Patrick Joseph Buchanan is a controversial and enigmatic ultra-conservative. He has served three presidents, has run for the presidency thrice, and is a prolific writer and a ubiquitous commentator on television, radio, and in print.

Buchanan was born in Washington, D.C., one of nine children to William Baldwin and Catherine Elizabeth (Crum) Buchanan. He graduated from Georgetown University in 1961 and obtained a master's degree in journalism from Columbia in 1962. That same year he began writing for the *St. Louis Globe Democrat*. His political activities began when he helped Richard Nixon mastermind a political comeback. When Nixon assumed the presidency in 1969, Buchanan came aboard as a researcher and a speechwriter for Nixon's vitriolic vice president, Spiro Agnew. Some sources credit Buchanan with playing a role in normalizing relations with China and for encouraging Nixon to seek détente with the Soviet Union. He also pressed Nixon to resist allying himself with the civil rights movement and made numerous controversial statements about the slain **Rev. Martin Luther King Jr.**

Buchanan was also involved in some of the activities associated with Watergate, which brought down the Nixon presidency, but he was never indicted.

Buchanan briefly advised Gerald Ford but resigned in 1974 to take up political commentary. Buchanan served as the White House communications director during **Ronald Reagan**'s second term and once again engendered controversy. Buchanan has been a long-time critic of Israel, has asserted that the extent of the Holocaust has been exaggerated, once praised Spanish dictator Francisco Franco, and was the chief architect of an embarrassing scenario in which President Reagan laid a wreath at a German cemetery in Bitburg, where ex-Nazis are interred.

Buchanan again left government in 1987 and resumed his commentator role. He was highly critical of Reagan's successor, George H. W. **Bush**, and fought him for the Republican nomination when Bush sought reelection in 1992. He garnered over three million votes by evoking **culture war** themes, ridiculing Bush's tax increases, and staking out populist turf. When Bill Clinton defeated Bush in the general election, Buchanan turned his ire on the Clinton administration. He tried again in 1996 to secure the Republican presidential nomination; although he did not win, he won the New Hampshire primary.

Buchanan's 1996 campaign highlights why he is such a puzzling figure. Although he was far and away the most conservative figure in the race, he was the only one to address directly the plight of the American working class. Buchanan has been an outspoken opponent of the North American Free Trade Agreement and is a protectionist who feels that high import tariffs are needed to protect American jobs from the pressures of **globalization**. His America-first themes resonate with many American workers, and he enjoys considerable support among imperiled **blue-collar** voters. Although **Ralph Nader** is usually credited with being the "spoiler" in the disputed 2000 election in which the Supreme Court determined that George W. Bush had defeated Al Gore, Buchanan himself played a significant part. He was on the ballot as a Reform Party candidate. In Florida, whose vote determined the final outcome, some voters claimed they accidentally punched Buchanan's name on confusing ballots, thinking they were voting for Gore. This probably did occur in some cases, but in others the populist-sounding Buchanan probably wooed workers who would have otherwise voted for Gore.

Buchanan remains a controversial commentator, whose views can be found in *The American Conservative* and in many other media outlets. His detractors call him racist, sexist, elitist, nativist, homophobic, and bigoted because he has made statements that have outraged abortion rights supporters, immigrants, Jews, African Americans, gays, and women. That said, he remains steadfast in his support for American workers, the need to rebuild American industry, and in his attacks on American economic policy. He also strikes populist chords in his opposition to American interventionism. He opposed both Iraq wars and called upon President George W. Bush to remove American troops from Iraq.

In many ways Buchanan challenges traditional political notions of liberals and conservatives. Although many debate his positions and view him a fringe player, Buchanan has paid more attention to the plight of the working class than most mainstream politicians.

Suggested Reading

Patrick Buchanan, *The Great Betrayal: How American Sovereignty and Social Justice Are Being Sacrificed to the Gods of the Global Economy*, 1998; Buchanan, *Where the Right Went Wrong: How Neoconservatives Subverted the Reagan Revolution and Hijacked* the Bush Presidency, 2004; Joseph Scotchie, *Street Corner Conservative: Patrick Buchanan and His Times*, 2002.

BUSH FAMILY

RICHARD JENSEN

As one of the premier political families in America from the 1950s onward, the Bush family has wrestled with social class. Their **upper-class**, high society, high-income background was obvious to everyone, but has not always been a handicap. In the 1950s, when Prescott Bush (1895–1972) served as Republican senator from Connecticut, men of comparable background held office in the nearby states, including Governor Averill Harriman of New York and Senator John **Kennedy** of Massachusetts. Like the **Rockefeller** and Kennedy families, the Bushes have moved around in search of a geographical base, but always with family support. Prescott Bush's father, Samuel P. Bush (1863–1948), was a manufacturing executive from Ohio, but Prescott moved to Connecticut in 1925 and commuted to a senior position with Brown Brothers Harriman & Co., a Wall Street firm headed by his father-in-law. During the **Great Depression** he maintained a pleasant but not ostentatious home, well staffed with three full-time maids and a chauffeur-bodyguard for the children. Bush became active in local Greenwich town affairs, then in the statewide Republican Party as a moderate similar in views to his friend Dwight Eisenhower. He strongly supported civil rights. His positions also resembled those of Nelson Rockefeller, but the two were estranged. Bush was elected to the Senate in 1952 after defeating celebrity Clare Boothe Luce in the primary. His son, war hero George H. W. Bush (1924–), graduated from Yale in 1948 and went to Texas to start a career in the oil industry, with family encouragement. George's son George W. Bush (1946–) also settled in Texas, while the younger son, Jeb Bush (1953–), relocated to Florida to build a new base. Jeb was defeated for governor in 1994, but won in 1998 and 2002. All the Bushes showed very high levels of commitment to civic duty and activism.

American class tensions in politics peaked around 1948, as the **labor movement** reached its maximum strength. The Bushes avoided this problem in the South, where unions were weak and class conflict did not separate the parties. On the petroleum frontier in West Texas, fortunes were quickly gained and lost. During the 1950s and 1960s the Bushes lived in twenty-eight homes in seventeen different Texas cities. George H. W. Bush realized the state lacked a grassroots Republican Party, and he helped build it from scratch. (Bush even worked with a speech therapist to sound more Texan.) He lost his 1964 Senate race, then was elected to Congress, and subsequently served as ambassador to the United Nations and to China. He also became national chairman of the GOP and Central Intelligence Agency director. In 1980 he challenged **Ronald Reagan** for the party's presidential nomination and lost, but Reagan made him vice president. Bush was elected president in 1988, directed the first Gulf War, and presided over the final collapse of **communism**. He avoided claiming victory in the **Cold War** so as not to destabilize Russia, a new American ally.

Class, however, was an issue in 1992, when Bush lost the presidency to Bill Clinton, a genuine Southerner whose appeal to common people was sharper. Clinton also promised tax relief to the **middle class**. A recession began in July 1990, and **unemployment** surged from 5.3 percent in 1989 to 7.4 percent in 1992. The recession officially ended before Election Day, but voters focused less on economic indicators and more on subtle indicators of character. Once Bush reneged on his pledge never to raise taxes, his moral credibility was shaken. He was also hurt by the populist class- and morals-based challenge of **Patrick Buchanan** in the primaries. That attack was followed immediately by Ross Perot's third party crusade against budget deficits, which he portrayed as a moral failure. Bush also was betrayed by his family's patrician roots at times, most famously during a debate with Clinton in which he was clearly unaware of American **shopping** habits.

For a time, George W. Bush appeared to be a ne'er-do-well, rejecting high society for the bottle and marrying a local librarian, Laura Bush (1946–). She proved a steadying influence, however, and helped Bush reform his character and reemerge as a chastened, born-again Christian. He also polished his public image, evoking a working-class back-to-the land ethic by chopping underbrush and stringing barbed wire on his ranch in Crawford, Texas. Inheriting his father's base and guided by campaign strategist Karl Rove, George W. Bush was elected governor of Texas in 1994 and was reelected in 1998. Republicans rallied around him in the 2000 presidential campaign, though he had to defeat the maverick John McCain to win the nomination. His election as the 43rd president in 2000 turned on 500 ballots in Florida, where Governor Jeb Bush operated a recount strategy that defeated the floundering Al Gore. The defining moments for President Bush were the September 11, 2001 terrorist attacks on the United States and the war in Iraq. In both cases the heroic exemplars of duty and sacrifice were working class Americans: the firemen and police who died saving lives and the volunteer soldiers in Iraq.

That said, both presidents have been more comfortable with business interests than with **blue-collar** America. For example, George W. Bush relied on business and family **social networks** to fund his oil investments and his partial ownership of a major league baseball franchise. He is strongly committed to the idea that federal **income taxes** dampen entrepreneurship and slow long-term economic growth and that high rates are a punitive leftover from the days of **New Deal**-style class conflict politics. An important episode came in 2006, when Bush linked a 40 percent raise in the **minimum wage** to the repeal of the estate tax. To date, Senate Democrats have scuttled the plan because it would be too generous to the rich.

Karl Rove has also helped George W. Bush reframe class as cultural and lifestyle issues. In 2000, Bush appealed to rural working class Democrats in the border states, including opponent Al Gore's Tennessee. Bush made a special appeal to coal miners, truckers, steel workers, and factory workers, many of whom were identified as **Reagan Democrats**. Bush warned that their cultural values were under attack by Hollywood **elites** and that even hunting privileges were threatened by East and West Coast liberals. He swept the South in 2000 and again in 2004 with an anti-elitist appeal that neutralized **income** differences. Indeed, since the 1980s income has not been major determinant of voting behavior. George W. Bush won 41 percent of the poorest fifth of voters in 2004, 55 percent of the richest twenty percent, and 53 percent of those in between. The biggest remaining cleavages break down along **racial** and **educational** lines. Since 1980 African Americans have voted Democratic about 85 percent of the time, regardless of income. In 1988 George H. W. Bush won 52 percent of the total vote, about what his son would win in 2004. But the elder Bush won 62 percent of voters with bachelor's degrees (but no higher), and in 2004 the younger Bush got only 52 percent. Among voters with a master's degree or higher, George H. Bush won 50 percent of their vote in 1988, while in 2004, his son received just 42 percent. Of course, George W. Bush made up the difference by gaining among college dropouts.

The education differential has expressed itself in the Bush family's positions on "**culture war**" issues dividing Americans. The elder Bush attacked the National Endowment for the Arts as unworthy of funding, as interest in the arts correlated with education, but not with income. His son expanded federal spending on science and education, but made a point in attacking projects like stem cell research, which was morally upsetting to the poorly educated, anti-science, religious **fundamentalists** in his base. (In 2004, 70–80 percent of white evangelicals voted for Bush.) In terms of education, Bush's "No Child Left Behind" program reoriented American public schools, demanding that they guarantee basic skills to working class students, while diverting class time away from enrichment programs favored by the well educated. Other fronts on the culture wars included limitations on gay rights, which won support from both fundamentalists and African Americans.

After 2004 much of George W. Bush's support eroded. He was widely criticized for clumsy handling of relief efforts after Hurricane **Katrina**. (In sharp contrast his brother Jeb has dealt better with Florida hurricanes, and his father effectively raised funds for Asian tsunami victims in 2005.) There have also been questions over his handling of the second Gulf War. **Immigration** has also been a hot-button issue, with many Republicans lobbying for a crackdown on illegal aliens. The Bushes, however, have been outspoken supporters of **Latinos**. Jeb Bush married a Mexican woman, became a **Catholic**, and his son, George P. Bush (1976–), is **bilingual** and calls himself Hispanic. George W. Bush's push for more open borders has won backing from the small business owners, such as restaurateurs, hoteliers, farm contractors, and construction company executives, who depend on immigrant labor. It has been criticized by others as coddling illegal activity.

Suggested Reading
Peter B. Levy, *Encyclopedia of the Reagan-Bush Years*, 1996; James Moore and Wayne Slater. *Bush's Brain: How Karl Rove Made George W. Bush Presidential*, 2003; Herbert S Parmet, *George Bush: The Life of a Lone Star Yankee*, 1997.

BUSINESS ARISTOCRACY

KEVIN S. REILLY

Business aristocracy is a frequently pejorative description of business elites that often accompanies debates about class privilege and democracy. In the early nineteenth century, this phrase referred to the potential for politically influential businessmen to act together as a corrupt caste. In the late nineteenth and early twentieth century, it evolved to become a rhetorical disparagement for the wealthiest and most entrenched business leaders. In the post World War II period, sociologists further developed the idea in analyses of the American **upper class**.

In the early republic, American lawmakers were coming to terms with the economic and legal difficulties of democratic **capitalism**. At issue was the development of a legal institution: the corporation. Charters for incorporation granted special rights to the owners. For the generation following the **American Revolution**, such special protections seemed fundamentally at odds with the political philosophy of republicanism. If the government began to endow small groups of investors with privileges, what chance could the typical American individualist have? Writers such as James Fennimore Cooper and others criticized the rising numbers of wealthy "business aristocrats," who seemed to rekindle the decadent corruption of British colonial administrators.

Similar critics emerged in the late nineteenth century when new industrialists, sometimes referred to as "**robber barons**," developed an American aristocratic style—lavish parties, ostentatious mansions, and enormous art collections—to display their vast wealth. Their tendency to build monopolistic businesses and their support of high tariffs to protect domestic industries from competition looked alarmingly like a new kind of feudalism.

The notion of a business aristocracy has been more poetic than descriptive, but in the 1950s, sociologists set about trying to explore the upper class in the United States and give some precision to the term "business aristocracy." Foremost among these scholars was **E. Digby Baltzell**, who argued that the upper class was two groups: one fluid, created by new business wealth, and one less dependent upon wealth than upon family lineages. For Baltzell, the establishment of a European style aristocracy—an exclusive group educated in a few elite schools, practicing **Episcopalian**ism, and exhibiting common Anglo-Saxon backgrounds—was actually a phenomenon that restrained the abuse of power in American society. Unlike **C. Wright Mills**'s self-serving "**power elite**" of business and institutional leaders, Baltzell's aristocracy policed itself against individuals who might violate the group's values and undermine its claims to social authority and privilege.

Suggested Reading

E. Digby Baltzell, *Philadelphia Gentlemen: The Making of a National Upper Class*, 1958; Baltzell, *Protestant Establishment: Aristocracy and Caste in America*, 1964; Seymour Martin Lipset, "The Study of Man—Aristocracy in America," *Commentary*, v. 26, n. 6 (December 1958): 533–37.

BUSINESS CYCLE

GERALD FRIEDMAN

The business cycle refers to the periods of rapid expansion of output and strong employment followed by periods of relative stagnation that are common in capitalist economies. Over the past 100 years, there have been nineteen business cycle downturns in the United States, or about one every five years. Rising output and employment during business cycle expansions are associated with rising wages, especially for low-wage workers; on the other side, declining output and employment are associated with falling wages, rising **unemployment**, and widening inequality.

Economists have long debated whether business cycles are accidents due to unforeseeable natural disasters or bad government policy or whether they are intrinsic to the nature of **capitalism**. The latter was the position of the early nineteenth century English economist Thomas Malthus, who argued that downturns were caused by a "general glut" in which more was produced than could be consumed. He recommended wasteful spending by rich landlords and others to ameliorate the business cycle. Malthus's friend David Ricardo responded by enunciating what has come to be known as "Say's Law" after the French economist Jean-Baptiste Say. Recognizing that individual products may be in excess supply, he denied that there could be a *general* glut. Producers, he argued, never produce except to consume, hence the total volume of production must necessarily be the same as the amount demanded. There can be general business downturns, Ricardo acknowledged, but he attributed them to temporary shocks such as demobilization after wars or else mistakes in governmental or monetary policies. Because they are not due to intrinsic conditions, they are temporary anomalies and should never be the source of general economic policies.

Since the early nineteenth century, most economists have accepted Say's Law and view business cycles as accidents rather than normal parts of capitalist society. One exception was Karl **Marx**, who argued that capitalist economies are inherently unstable because capitalist production is for profit rather than consumption. Capitalists, he argues, hire workers hoping to use their labor to produce goods of greater value than the wages they receive. But once most of the unemployed have been hired, continued expansion drives up wages and squeezes profits. Lower profits then reduce investment until the economy enters a recession or depression in which falling employment restores profits and revitalizes conditions for renewed expansion by driving down wages.

Few orthodox economists have openly embraced Marx, but others agreed that capitalist economies were inherently unstable. In the midst of the **Great Depression** of the 1930s, **John Maynard Keynes** argued that output is unstable because it depends on private investment, which fluctuates with investor confidence. Associating capitalist investment with a gambling casino, Keynes argued that private investment fluctuated with little regard for real need or economic circumstances because investors speculated on how other investors would value these projects in the future, not on the current or future value of their projects. Because private investment is driven by "animal spirits," Keynes argued that society cannot expect that the actions of private capitalists will necessarily produce full employment. Instead, he urged that governments should take an active role in guiding the economy to ensure a high level of output and employment. Only such intervention can limit the prevalence or virulence of business cycles.

Since Keynes, most governments have conducted "countercyclical" policies to increase spending during business recessions and reduce output during inflationary periods. While economists who believe in Say's Law reject such policies, there is evidence that they have lessened the frequency and severity of business cycle downturns.

Suggested Reading
Arthur F. Burns and Wesley C. Mitchell, *Measuring Business Cycles*, 1946; Michal Kalecki, *Essays in the Theory of Economic Fluctuations*, 1972; John Maynard Keynes, *Essays in Biography*, 1951; Keynes, *The General Theory of Employment Interest and Money*, 1936. Michael Perelman, *Marx's Crises Theory: Scarcity, Labor, and Finance*, 1987.

C

CAMPAIGN FINANCING

ROBERT E. WEIR

Many reformers argue that the high cost of political campaigns in America is a class issue. In essence, the capital resources needed to secure election make candidates beholden to either wealthy interests or their overt representatives. Some argue that the connection between money and **power** is so thoroughly entrenched that it imperils the very essence of **democracy**.

Political office has always been more the domain of the wealthy than of those with reduced means. The prevailing ideal among the **Founding Fathers** was that government should be controlled by men of substance; in fact, ideally one engaged in public service only after having retired from a profitable enterprise. Although most Founders felt no one should spend one's entire career in politics, this was precisely the norm that came into being. Regardless, there has been remarkable continuity in the connection between the possession of wealth and the holding of political power. In theory, the United States is a representative democracy; in practice, most that hold high political office come from the upper **middle class** or the **upper class**. This is true even when candidates package themselves as men of "modest" means. Andrew **Jackson**, for example, had substantial land holdings; Abraham Lincoln was a successful railroad lawyer; and William Henry Harrison grew up in middle-class comfort, not the log cabin he used as a campaign symbol. Not a single man holding the presidency in the twentieth or twenty-first century could, in any way, be considered a person of modest means.

U.S. senators were not chosen by the electorate until the passage of the Seventeenth Amendment in 1913; prior to this, they were chosen by state legislatures and were often part of the "spoils system," wherein a winning party doled out rewards to longtime supporters and financial backers.

Mass media have exacerbated the tendency for elections to hinge more on money than on issues. Since the 1960s, television has played a large role in shaping voter behavior. Put simply, name recognition, image, and public perception are as important, if not more so, than issues. Television advertisements are expensive, as are the services of pollsters, public relations firms, and political consultants who craft the images of candidates, help them package their voter appeal, and plot their election strategies. By 1996 it cost an average of $4.7 million to run a campaign for the U.S. Senate, an amount that required winning candidates to spend much of their time in office raising funds for reelection rather than attending to duties. Broken down, a senator needed to raise more than $12,500 each week for an entire six-year term. Races for the House of Representatives soared to an average of over $670,000 for the privilege of serving a two-year term. These numbers have continued to skyrocket. During presidential elections, the amount of money spent is staggering. In 1984 little more than $200 million was spent; just twenty years later it was over $2 billion. Even local and state races feel the impact of money. In 2004 Connecticut studies revealed that winning state senators had spent more than $71,000 on their races.

The amount of money one must raise to get elected means that few candidates can be true "populists" representing "average" people. Corporate interests, labor unions, and political action committees (PACs) are among the few social groups that can command resources of the magnitude needed. Weak campaign finance laws ensure that these interests remain strong. In 1925 Congress passed the toothless Corrupt Practices Act, which failed to curtail influence. Equally ineffective was the 1939 Hatch Act. The Federal Election Campaign Act of 1972 (amended in 1974) set up the Federal Election Commission to oversee elections, partially fund presidential elections, require candidates to disclose the source of contributions, and set limits on the amount that could be given. Under federal law, an individual can contribute $2,000 per candidate and PACs $5,000 per candidate; total contributions are limited to $25,000. These provisos proved wholly inadequate. There were no restrictions on "soft money"—contributions given directly to a political party and then channeled to the candidate indirectly. Nor did laws restrict "issues" advertising, in which advocacy groups run ads that support or attack a candidate's position on specific concerns. Moreover, candidates who come from wealth find very few restrictions placed on how deeply they can tap their own resources. The McCain-Feingold bill of 2002, officially the Bipartisan Reform Act, supposedly banned soft money, restricted "issues" advertising to sixty days before a general election, clamped down on how unions allocated member contributions, and closed several other loopholes.

Evidence suggests that, thus far, the ability to raise money continues to control election results. According to the Center for Responsive Politics, the candidate who raises the most money wins more than 90 percent of the time. Given that incumbents have greater access to potential donors, the current system perpetuates the link between entrenched political power and financial might. As of 2004, 123 of the 435 members of the House of Representatives had personal fortunes of over $1 million; in the Senate, 35 of 100 are millionaires. It should also be noted that Congressional salaries put all members in the top 10 percent of wage earners. A 2003 study also revealed that nearly all members also had assets well above the national average.

Critics of the wealth/elections nexus charge that the high cost of political campaigns makes it difficult for third parties to challenge the Republicans and Democrats.

More serious still is the tendency for ideology and self-interest to drive political giving. Individual donations average just $200. By contrast, in the 2004 election business interests channeled 55 percent of their more than $1.5 billion in donations to Republicans, while organized labor gave 87 percent of its $66.1 million to Democrats. In 2002 Wal-Mart gave eight times more money to Republicans than to Democrats, especially those with conservative leanings. Studies reveal that money is a deciding factor in close races and that it often alters voter perceptions in such a way that many come to support candidates whose positions are antithetical to their own. From the perspective of social class, an obvious problem is that very few groups who advocate for the poor have the resources to buy the sort of influence that corporate interests underwrite. Influence, in fact, is so expensive that even some business groups have called for serious campaign reform. To date, however, substantive reforms, such as setting hard spending caps, limiting the length of the campaign season, banning PACs, and providing free media access, have made little progress.

Suggested Reading

Mark Green, *Selling Out: How Big Corporate Money Buys Elections, Rams Through Legislation, and Betrays Our Democracy*, 2004; OpenSecrets.org, http://www.open secrets.org/; James Thurber and Candice Nelson, *Campaigns and Elections American Style*, 2004.

CAPITALISM

CHUCK BARONE

Capitalism is an economic system in which commodities and services are produced for profit using privately owned goods and wage labor. The owners of capital goods hire wage labor to produce commodities with the goal of making a personal profit. The owners (or their designated managers) make most of the economic decisions and receive profit and other property income, including rent, interest, and dividends. Capitalism generally produces substantial economic growth and inequality.

Capitalism's founding manifesto is often considered to be Adam Smith's 1776 book *Inquiry into the Nature and Causes of the Wealth of Nations*, though Smith based his work on many older ideas. It has in fact been the dominant economic system in parts of Europe since 1600. An inherently expansionary system from its earliest beginnings, capitalism has spread to most places in the world. It has developed very unevenly; in some places it has been a powerful engine of growth and industrialization—as in most of Europe, the United States, and Japan—but has left other parts of the world poor and underdeveloped.

Wherever capitalism has taken root, it has been and continues to be a powerful force for both positive and negative changes. **Globalization**, the result of the accelerated movement of capital around the world, provides opportunities for greatly expanded profits and low-cost consumer goods. Although some businesses and consumers may benefit, **outsourcing** has negative impacts for employees who lose their jobs or must accept lower pay to keep them. The costs and benefits of the changes wrought by capitalism are usually very unequally shared, and those who bear a disproportionate share of the costs are rarely compensated for such losses.

Capitalism features generalized commodity production. Its other distinctive characteristics include private ownership of the **means of production** (capital goods), wage labor, and production for profit. Capitalism is historically the first economic system in which commodity production is generalized and most products are produced for exchange. Exceptions include the household sphere, where the products and services of household labor (performed mostly by women) are not exchanged directly for money in a market. The market is the basic mechanism through which exchanges are facilitated in capitalism. Markets regulate and coordinate commodity exchanges through price movements caused by competitive supply-and-demand conditions in markets for means of production, labor power, and final goods and services.

Although markets are the primary exchange-regulating mechanism, other regulating mechanisms exist in capitalism, such as government regulation and planning. The extent of government intervention is as hotly contested today as it was when Adam Smith argued that markets were self-regulating and needed minimal government regulation. **John Maynard Keynes**, a twentieth-century British economist and financier, was one of the first to make a compelling case for government intervention to stave off depressions and other market failures. Today few question the need for government regulation, yet in practice government intervention varies across countries and depends upon the political balance of power among those who may benefit from regulation and those who do not. Although capitalists may generally favor a loosely or unregulated business environment, this will depend upon whether corporate interests are advanced by government intervention.

Private ownership of the means of production places most of the land, raw materials, tools, equipment, factories, farms, and offices in the hands of privately owned businesses and corporations. Public or government ownership has a very limited place in capitalism, especially in the United States, where private business interests are quite powerful politically. Most production in capitalism takes the form of dependent commodity production, where one group (a distinct minority) owns the means of production and another group (the majority) provides the labor in the form of wage or salaried labor. Those who do not own the means of production must sell their labor power to those who do. Thus wage labor and private ownership of capital goods are closely related in capitalism.

Profits alone determine what will be produced and how it will be produced in a classic capitalist system. Capitalists hire workers to produce output. Out of the total revenue obtained from the sale of the output produced by labor, capitalists pay wages, raw materials, operating costs, and wear and tear on capital goods. The remaining revenue is the capitalist's profit. Capitalists are driven by competition to maximize rates of profits, a goal that is often in conflict with the interests of employees, whose goals are higher wages and salaries and better working conditions.

The hierarchal and authoritative dimension of capitalism is based on an unequal class structure. Capitalists and workers thus constitute separate classes in capitalism, and their competing interests have given rise to conflict and **class struggle**. The working class consists of those who must perform wage labor. Workers produce the total product, but they have little control over the labor of others or the labor process. This internal tension within capitalism has given rise to the **labor movement**, **unions**, and competing socialist movements, the latter rooted in a collective rather than a private ethos.

Karl **Marx** argued that, although capitalism was a powerful force for industrialization, it was a contradictory system that would at some point limit human progress. Marx predicted that antithetical class interests between the capitalist **bourgeoisie** and the wage-earning **proletariat** would precipitate socialist revolution. Advanced capitalism, however, is more complex than Marx envisioned. The **middle classes**, for example, contain many small business owners and those who are self-employed. They own their own means of production but do not rely substantially on the labor of others. Managers and other business professionals are also part of the middle class. They do not own capital goods but often have authority over workers. The growth of these middle classes have tempered to some degree class conflict and struggle.

Suggested Reading

John Bogle, *The Battle for the Soul of Capitalism*, 2005; Samuel Bowles, Richard Edwards, and Frank Roosevelt, *Understanding Capitalism: Competition, Command, and Change*, 2005; Milton and Rose Friedman, *Capitalism and Freedom*, 2002; Adam Smith, *The Wealth of Nations*, 2004 reprint.

CARNEGIE, ANDREW (November 25, 1835–August 11, 1919)

VICTORIA GRIEVE

A business mogul and **philanthropist**, Carnegie is often viewed as the embodiment of the American "rags to riches" dream. He was born in Dunfermline, Scotland, to a working-class weaving family. When steam-powered looms destroyed craft production in Dunfermline, his father, Will Carnegie, was thrown out of work, and in 1848 the family immigrated to the United States. Settling in Pittsburgh, Pennsylvania, the Carnegies relied on an established community of Scottish immigrants for assistance. A fellow Scot offered Andrew his first job as a bobbin boy in a textile mill; he earned $1.20 per week and enrolled in night school to learn bookkeeping.

Carnegie climbed steadily from bobbin boy to clerk to messenger to telegrapher to superintendent of Pennsylvania Railroad's Western Division. In his twelve years with the railroad, Carnegie learned modern systems of management and principles of capital investment that shaped his career. In 1856 Carnegie invested $217.50 in the Woodruff Sleeping Car Company, which provided returns of about $5,000 annually after just two years. His next major investment, in the Columbia Oil Company, produced a profit of more than $6,000 in one year. Carnegie foresaw the need for iron bridges to replace wooden ones and formed the Keystone Bridge Company to make them. By the time he was thirty-three, Carnegie's investment income topped $50,000 per year.

Andrew Carnegie, ca. 1913. Courtesy of the Library of Congress.

Carnegie played a crucial role in shaping the American system of manufacturing in the nineteenth century. Dissatisfaction with iron rails and visits to the Bessemer steel plants in England convinced him that steel would replace iron in manufacturing. Prior to opening his first steel mill, he integrated his Keystone Bridge and Union Iron Mills to reduce costs and streamline production. Carnegie opened the Edgar Thomson Works in 1873 at Braddock, Pennsylvania, twelve miles south of Pittsburgh. In addition to steel rails, Carnegie supplied steel for the Brooklyn Bridge and the new skyscrapers rising in America's cities.

Carnegie's modern manufacturing methods, his relentless drive to reduce costs, his use of the latest equipment, and his emphasis on efficiency allowed him to undersell his competition. His vast Pennsylvania steel mills at Braddock, Duquesne, and Homestead were the most productive in the world and provided thousands of jobs. But steelworkers struggled against falling wages and job security, unsafe conditions, and the end of creative labor. One of the most infamous strikes in American history took place at Carnegie's Homestead plant in 1892. Refusing Carnegie's proposed pay cut, unionized workers were locked out of the factory, and Henry Frick, Carnegie's partner and manager, known for his strident anti-unionism, hired 300 Pinkerton Agency strikebreakers to replace them. Violence throughout the day on July 6 resulted in the deaths of seven workers and three strikebreakers. Henry Frick suffered knife and bullet wounds. Carnegie and Frick won the battle in November, when some workers voted to return to work as non-union employees. The mills remained unorganized for another forty years.

Between 1872 and 1889, Carnegie made his fortune in the steel industry, controlling the most extensively integrated iron and steel operations ever owned by an individual in the United States. In 1900 he sold Carnegie Company to **J. P. Morgan** for $480 million, the largest commercial transaction to that date and one that made Carnegie the richest man in the world. And then, unlike any industrialist of his time, he began to give away his fortune.

Carnegie believed that great wealth conferred social responsibility, a principle he explained in his 1900 essay, *The Gospel of Wealth*. Throughout his life he donated funds for almost 3,000 libraries, hospitals, and universities. By the time he died, Carnegie had given away more than $380 million, almost 90 percent of his fortune. He established the Carnegie Institution in 1902 to provide research for American colleges and universities, endowed his Teachers Pension Fund with $10 million in 1905, and created the Carnegie Endowment for International Peace in 1910. In 1911 Carnegie endowed the Carnegie Corporation with $125 million to aid colleges, universities, technical schools, and scientific research.

Carnegie died at Shadowbrook, his Massachusetts estate, on August 11, 1919.

Suggested Reading

Andrew Carnegie, *The Autobiography of Andrew Carnegie*, 1986; Harold C. Livesay, *Andrew Carnegie and the Rise of Big Business*, 1999; Joseph Frazier Wall, *Andrew Carnegie*, 1989.

CASINOS

ROBERT E. WEIR

Casinos are establishments where legalized **gambling** takes place. They have become a large industry in the United States, with an estimated $68.7 billion having been wagered in casinos and on legal lottery tickets in 2002 alone. Casinos are at the center of intense public debate. Many see casinos as economic incubators that bring jobs and revenue, especially to distressed locales. Critics counter that the social problems associated with casinos far outweigh the advantages.

Although saloon gambling was a staple of nineteenth-century Western lore and large cities have always had a "sporting crowd" that wagered on events and games of chance, the modern casino industry dates from 1931, when the state of Nevada legalized gambling. Las Vegas and Reno became casino centers, with Nevada retaining monopolistic control on legal casinos until 1978, when Atlantic City, New Jersey, banked on casinos to restore its dilapidated Boardwalk and energize an impoverished city. **Native American** tribes, which had operated gaming houses on reservations, also got into the act. In 1979 the Seminoles opened their high-stakes bingo parlor to the public. This prompted legal challenges, but in 1988 Congress passed the Indian Gaming Regulatory Act, which sanctioned Native casinos. In 1992 the Mashantucket Pequot tribe opened its Foxwoods, Connecticut, casino, the first legal casino in New England. There, as elsewhere, other groups petitioned to be granted the same privileges as Natives. Although casinos are often associated with Native Americans, in 2004 just 21 percent of all casino revenue came from Native establishments. There are currently more than 700 casinos operating in thirty-six states, though some are cruise boats that operate outside of state jurisdictions. Massachusetts, for example, currently does not license casinos, but several ships sail three miles off its coast into international waters and run gaming tables.

Many people object to gambling on moral grounds, but another line of criticism argues that casinos exacerbate social problems. The temptation for economically challenged regions to place hope in casinos is great, and it has helped revitalize some regions. Atlantic City's pattern, however, is more typical. There a series of high-rise casinos added glitz and glamour to the oceanfront but failed to generate wealth for the entire city. In essence, the casinos were classic "strip" development—a shiny veneer that extends no more than a few blocks deep. There is also substantial evidence that the same sort of organized crime influence that bedeviled Las Vegas gaming is present in Atlantic City. Racketeering allegations have also surfaced around gaming parlors in California, Michigan, Minnesota, Mississippi, South Carolina, and elsewhere.

The human impact is also controversial. Just as some cities see casinos as a panacea, so do some individuals hope to escape **poverty** through gambling. There are an estimated 15 million gambling addicts in the United States, about one-third of whom are poor. Casino advertising usually features well-dressed patrons gathered around roulette wheels, but casinos are also magnets for those with limited resources who play slot machines or try their luck at blackjack. A 2004 study in Connecticut revealed that the average problem gambler loses $21,542 per year, a staggering sum for most, but not one that would necessarily bankrupt a member of the upper **middle class**. Problem gambling cuts across social classes, but its greatest impact is on those of lower **socioeconomic status (SES)**. Perhaps as many as 6 percent of all bankruptcies within the **working class** result from gambling debt. Other studies reveal high rates of mental health problems and suicides among gambling addicts; these again disproportionately impact lower-income gamers.

Supporters argue that it is unfair to blame casino operators for any individual's lack of self-control and that fewer than 5 percent (some say just 1 percent) of gamblers ever suffer crippling losses. Critics counter that casinos and lotteries thrive on the desperation of poor Americans and are a de facto form of **regressive taxation**. Some casinos in the South even cash welfare checks. The current debate over casinos is complicated by moral and ideological debate, but one can safely assert that the promised economic benefits of gambling have yet to materialize in more than a few cases. Some places, notably Las Vegas itself, have recently begun to deemphasize gambling, with some investors arguing that there is now an overabundance of casinos in America.

Suggested Reading

Kim Isaac Eisler, *Revenge of the Pequots: How a Small Native American Tribe Created the World's Most Profitable Casino*, 2002; Timothy L. O'Brien, *Bad Bet: The Inside Story of the Glamour, Glitz and Danger of America's Gambling Industry*, 1998; John L. Smith, *Sharks in the Desert: The Founding Fathers and Current Kings of Las Vegas*, 2005.

Caste

Robert E. Weir

The term *caste* generally refers to a closed stratification system in which one's **status** is determined by birth and social custom. In traditional caste systems, hierarchy is so rigidly defined as to restrict marriage outside of the caste, either by law or powerful social conventions. In such a system, upward **social mobility** is rare.

Most Americans equate the caste system with Hindu societies, particularly India. In India, caste evolved from Vedic religious practices that predate the articulation of Hinduism and were in place at least as early as 1400 BCE. Indian caste—known as *varna*—was reinforced by religious ideals linked to karma and reincarnation, which dictated that one's social rank was fixed at birth for the course of one's life, though it might change in the next life. There were four main castes in India, plus a group known as "Untouchables," who constituted the majority of Indians but had very low status. In theory, the caste system was abolished after India became independent in 1947; in practice, caste is still very much a part of Indian life, especially in rural areas. It is still exceedingly rare (and socially difficult) for a person from the upper **Brahmin** class to marry an Untouchable.

India's caste system is the most famous, but some African tribes have historically constructed similar systems. Western societies generally frown upon such rigid and closed systems and like to pride themselves on their relative openness. **Max Weber**, for instance, ranked social systems by their relative mobility; he placed caste at the extreme end of the closed scale and market-driven economic systems at the other, open end.

Scholars have come to challenge Weber's optimistic assumptions, as well as the conventional wisdom that American society has no castes. Both **W. Lloyd Warner** and **Gunnar Myrdal** argued that the United States operates a caste system based on **race**. Warner wrote in 1936 and Myrdal in 1944, but other researchers have expanded upon the idea of racial castes. Some have argued that African Americans are akin to modern-day Untouchables in India. In each case, most legal barriers to mobility have fallen, but custom and social taboos remain in place. For example, black/white interracial marriages are still exceedingly rare. About 4 percent of American marriages are considered interracial, but many of these are between **Latinos** or **Asian Americans** and non-Caucasians; fewer than 2 percent of African Americans marry outside their race.

More significant than marriage patterns are ongoing patterns of discrimination in the justice system, hiring and promotion considerations, housing preferences, and a host of other social indicators. Despite decades of affirmative action programs, access to **power**, **prestige**, and status remains elusive for black Americans. In this regard, it makes sense to speak of an American caste system. Some feminist scholars argue that women of all races suffer fates similar to that of African American males. They too find that social mobility is more illusory than real as they bump into the **glass ceiling** and find the overall social system skewed in favor of white males. Moreover, women and African Americans both find themselves the victims of stereotypes that call into question their abilities, intelligence, and emotional stability.

Suggested Reading

Oliver Cox, *Caste, Class and Race*, 1948; Andrew Hacker, *Two Nations: Black and White: Separate, Hostile, Unequal*, 1995; Randall Kennedy, *Interracial Intimacies: Sex, Marriage, Identity, and Adoption*, 2004.

CATHOLICS

MARK NOON

Roman Catholicism has a reputation as a working-class faith, but from the Colonial era to the present American Catholics have demonstrated considerable upward **social mobility**.

In the colonies of the New World through the early Republic, Catholics were largely a minority sect who endured discrimination and harassment, a relic of the religious zeal of the Protestant Reformation. Still, the Catholic faithful remained steadfast, and the church even prospered in some states, particularly Maryland and Pennsylvania. In fact, some Catholic families were wealthy planters active in the gentry class. As late as 1820, however, membership in the American Catholic Church was still low, outside of Maryland, in comparison with other denominations. This would change dramatically over the next few decades. Because Roman Catholicism is a world religion, the Catholic population in the United States ballooned from the thousands to the millions when mass **immigration** ensued in the nineteenth century. Groups such as the **Irish** often suffered discrimination at the hands of nativists and other anti-Catholic zealots.

In the 1850s the recently arrived Catholic immigrants were largely unskilled laborers. They composed the bottom level of Catholic society and were the most numerous. Fewer in number were **middle-class** Catholics—sometimes dubbed the Lace Curtain Irish—who were often native-born Americans who held **white-collar** jobs such as clerks or small businessmen. An even smaller number—usually American-born professionals of German or Irish descent—made it into the **upper class**. As the **Industrial Revolution** moved through the **Gilded Age** and into the **Progressive Era**, an anti-Catholic mindset was still part of American culture, and members of the church were viewed as outsiders. In the 1920s the revived **Ku Klux Klan** added Catholics to their list of undesirables. Still, social mobility moved more and more second- and third-generation Irish and German Catholics into the middle class. Catholics continued to close the gap with the rest of the American population in terms of income as the twentieth century progressed. By the time John F. Kennedy entered the White House in 1961, the immigrant church had faded, replaced by **suburban** Catholics who achieved economic parity with other Americans. By the close of the twentieth century their representation in the upper class even improved. In a reversal of historical trends, a 1970 survey revealed that Catholics were attending college at a higher rate than Protestants.

Initially, the population of Roman Catholics in the United States was centered in the industrial cities and towns of the Northeast. Working-class Catholics were particularly susceptible to the **poverty** and **unemployment** wrought by economic panics and depressions. The Catholic response to social problems was generally conservative, a reflection of the commitment to private property in the Catholic tradition. Catholic clergy placed a high emphasis on charity and the development of philanthropic institutions as the main method of addressing problems in working-class neighborhoods. Many Catholic lay men and women felt other steps were necessary, and, not surprisingly, they were attracted to the developing **labor movement**.

Immigrant Catholic workers joined early labor unions in very large numbers, a development that greatly concerned priests and bishops. They were troubled by the level of violence in many labor struggles, but more problematic was the secret nature of early unions. A key example is found in the clerical response to the **Knights of Labor**. Despite efforts by the Knights' national leader, **Terence V. Powderly**, to remove suspicion, some clergy remained so troubled by the oath-swearing and initiation rituals of the Knights that they denied the sacraments to known members. Eventually, as Catholic participation in the labor movement continued to grow, clerical opposition waned. A major reason for the shift was the publication of Pope Leo XIII's papal encyclical *Rerum Novarum* in 1891. The pontiff decried the excesses of **capitalism** and defended the right of workers to organize, and the social encyclical was initially well received in the United States.

While *Rerum Novarum* failed to ignite a widespread campaign for social justice among American Catholics, the pope's endorsement of labor marked the emergence of the tradition of the labor-priest. There are several examples of priests acting aggressively on behalf of their working-class parishioners, particularly during strikes. The proximity of the priest to the grievances of the workers placed them in a strong position to champion the cause of labor. They often spoke and wrote in support of strikers, planned strike strategy, helped raise strike funds, and worked to negotiate settlements. A significant example is John J. Curren of Wilkes-Barre, Pennsylvania, who provided important assistance to John Mitchell and the United Mine Workers of America during the anthracite coal **strike** of 1902.

On a wider scale, one priest worked particularly hard to blend Catholic social thought with the progressive reform movement in the early twentieth century. John Ryan studied moral theology at Catholic University after his ordination to the priesthood in 1898. His doctoral dissertation, titled "A Living Wage," called for wages for laborers that would allow them "to live in a manner consistent with the dignity of a human being." Later, Ryan wrote another significant book, *Distributive Justice: The Right and Wrong of Our Present Distribution of Wealth*. In his effort to link ethics and economics, Ryan called for a **minimum wage** and helped develop a more public Catholicism.

The Catholic laity was also drawn into social reform movements, particularly by the economic challenges of the **Great Depression**. The major example is the Catholic Worker. This effort to make Catholicism a greater social force began on May Day 1933, when journalist and Catholic convert Dorothy Day began selling a newspaper, *The Catholic Worker*, in New York. The Catholic Worker was a radical movement that put the views expressed in the newspaper into action. Followers across the country established hospitality houses to provide the poor and homeless with food and a place to sleep. Similar reform organizations include Friendship House, established by Catherine de Hueck in **Harlem** in 1938. Friendship House, and such lay reform movements as the Grail and Catholic Action, placed particular emphasis on the role of Catholics in the fight for interracial justice and civil rights.

As noted, by the mid-twentieth century Catholics had largely been assimilated into the American religious mainstream, and most of the discriminatory patterns against Catholics had faded. Today Catholics are distributed across the social class spectrum, a reality that softens potential backlash against church positions on controversial issues such as reproductive rights.

Suggested Reading
Clyde Crews, *American & Catholic: A Popular History of Catholicism in the United States*, 2004; Jay P. Dolan, *American Catholic Experience: A History from Colonial Times to the Present*, 1992; Thomas T. McAvoy, *A History of the Catholic Church in the United States*, 1969.

CATTLE KINGDOM

ROBERT E. WEIR

The term Cattle Kingdom comes from a period in the late nineteenth century that has wended its way into American culture as romance and myth. The cattle kingdom fostered the cowboy, a figure often evoked as the epitome of American **individualism** and **self-reliance**. Relatively few Americans realize that this image is largely false.

The age of cowboy cattle drives was relatively brief, roughly 1875 to 1890, and a substantial number of cowboys were African Americans or Mexican *vaqueros*, not the brooding white men of Hollywood films. The Great Plains were home to the buffalo, millions of which white hunters killed for hides, meat, and sport, and to deny **Native Americans** sustenance. The southern plains were also a grazing ground for sinewy longhorn cattle, which the Spanish introduced in the eighteenth century. Longhorns had little value until the eve of the Civil War, when growing urban areas necessitated expanding the American food supply. This meant that large herds of unclaimed free-range cattle were available for any enterprising person to exploit. The problem was that railroad lines to bring cattle to slaughterhouses and urban markets were located far from grazing grounds. This gave rise to the famed cattle drives, most of which were about 1500 miles in length. Trails such as the Sedalia, the Chisholm, the Western, and the Goodnight-Loving led cattle to railheads in Missouri, Kansas, Colorado, and Wyoming, but only after an arduous journey marked by danger, backbreaking work, and economic risks.

What one received at the end of a drive was determined by the number and weight of the animals delivered and prevailing market prices, minus supplies and wages paid for the crew necessary to keep the herd together. Contrary to popular belief, most cowboys were wage-earning members of the working class, not self-employed entrepreneurs. In fact, it often took large amounts of capital merely to launch a cattle drive; hence a substantial number of cowboys worked for corporate investors, some of whom cheated and exploited cowboys.

The economics of what came to be called the "Long Drive" made little sense, and collapsing beef prices in the 1880s dealt a severe blow to cowboy culture. Moreover, the invention of barbed wire and cross-breeding techniques between longhorns and meatier Hereford and Angus stock led to the cultivation of northern herds on grasslands closer to the railroads. The drives inexorably gave way to ranching, an enterprise fraught with difficulties of its own, such as unpredictable weather in the northern plains, disputed grazing titles, range wars with sheep herders, and fierce competition. The latter was winnowed by the record-cold winter of 1886–87, which largely eliminated small-operation ranchers and left large enterprises and conglomerate cattle associations in its wake. By 1890 corporate interests controlled the beef industry just as surely as they controlled steel and oil.

Given the short duration of the Cattle Kingdom, why did it become such a potent American myth? First, in some cases it was possible for individuals to experience dramatic **social mobility** through cattle, especially in the early days. Several Civil War veterans were able to parlay a few head of cattle into large herds and enrich themselves, though the vast majority of cowboys earned $25 to $40 per month. For the most part, though, the cowboy image was crafted by Hollywood and television. In the 1930s and 1940s, cowboy films were produced mostly for their entertainment value, but in the 1950s and 1960s, the cowboy also had ideological undertones. Cowboys were used as potent symbols of American freedom, self-reliance, and individualism that, during the Cold War, implied a marked contrast to the totalitarian and collectivist image of the Soviet Union. Ironically, only a small number of actual Cattle Kingdom cowboys enjoyed the levels of independence and self-sufficiency embedded in popular culture imagery.

Suggested Reading
Lewis Atherton, *The Cattle Kings*, 1961; David Igler, *Industrial Cowboys: Miller & Lux and the Transformation of the Far West, 1850–1920*, 2005; Richard Slotkin, *The Fatal Environment: The Myth of Frontier in the Age of Industrialization*, 1985.

CEO

ROBERT E. WEIR

CEO is the abbreviation for chief executive officer, the top-ranked official in a corporation or other business enterprise. In recent years CEOs have come under scrutiny for their high salaries, business practices, and relations with employees. To their defenders, CEOs are creative individuals whose business savvy has helped the United States reverse the economic decline of the 1970s. To their detractors, some CEOs are viewed as latter-day pirates who plunder companies for the benefit of a stockholder oligarchy, who have ravaged the American working class, and whose cozy relations with politicians constitute a **power elite** that undermines American **democracy**. Well-publicized financial scandals involving a small number of firms and their CEOs have fueled some of the criticism.

Few would deny that modern business bureaucracy demands strong and active leadership. CEOs generally chair corporate boards. In small firms the CEO is usually also the company president, though these roles tend to be separate in large enterprises. CEOs are charged with working with teams that develop a firm's comprehensive business plan. In consultation with the chief financial officer, a CEO must weigh decisions such as how much to spend on infrastructure, how the company manages its investment portfolios, how to market the firm's products, and a host of issues relating to workers: wages, benefits, pensions, and the like. The various constituencies within a firm often have contradictory demands. For example, long-term growth schemes often run afoul of the demands of some stockholders for immediate return.

Controversy and business procedures are hardly strangers. During the late nineteenth century critics claimed that much American business was dominated by **robber barons**. During the **Progressive Era** and subsequent to it, many regulations were placed on American businesses, some of which curtailed the power of corporate heads. Modern complaints of CEO power date largely from the 1980s, when President **Ronald Reagan** supported the removal of regulations he felt hampered the **competitiveness** of American firms in the global market. Among other things, a wave of **mergers and acquisitions** drew attention to arbitrageurs, investors, and CEOs. The compensation packages of CEOs skyrocketed to levels that struck many as egregious forms of **conspicuous consumption**. According to *BusinessWeek*, the CEOs of America's top 365 companies in 1980 averaged $1.4 million in compensation (adjusted for 2004 dollars); by 2003, they made $8.1 million. By contrast, workers in the same firms saw their average compensation increase from $31,769 to just $31,928. On average, CEOs made 44 times more than their workers in 1980, but by 2003 they made 254 times more. In top corporations, one estimate claims that CEOs make 431 times the average American salary, meaning that they make more each day than their workers do in a year.

The logic of **trickle-down theory** justifies this inequality by arguing that top-notch CEOs create wealth. Statistics do not bear this out, however. Even the successful companies that underwrote the 480 percent increase in CEO compensation saw profits grow by just over one-quarter that rate. In many cases, CEOs commanded fabulous sums though their firms foundered. Apple's Steven Jobs received over $78 million in 2002, though stock returns sank nearly 35 percent; Jeff Barbakow of Tenet Healthcare took in $34.3 million though shares dropped over 58 percent; and Pat Russo of Lucent Technologies saw stocks plummet over 75 percent yet collected $38.2 million. Michael Eisner of Disney averaged over $120 million a year during his six-year tenure though Disney stocks averaged a negative 5 percent return. Compensation packages become especially controversial for CEOs who oversee downsizing campaigns, shift corporate work overseas, slash employee benefits, decertify labor unions, or reduce payroll.

Scandals involving firms such as Enron, Tyco, WorldCom, Adelphia, and other firms that resulted in billions of dollars in lost investment have led many to see the current CEO climate as marked more by arrogance, greed, and corruption than by profit or efficiency. Such a view is unfair to the hundreds of CEOs who do their jobs honestly and well, but there is nonetheless gathering concern that a veritable **business aristocracy** has emerged that exerts undue influence on American politics. In the administration of George W. **Bush**, for example, more than a dozen officials, including Bush himself, Vice President Dick Cheney, and presidential advisor Karl Rove, had deep ties to Halliburton Corporation, a firm often accused of corruption. Many members of Congress from both parties also have ties to lobbyists, maintain friendly relations with CEOs, and have lucrative investments. Critics also question why American CEOs make so much more than their counterparts abroad. British CEOs, for instance, receive about twenty-eight times more in compensation than their employees. They also question why firms spend so much money on such perquisites as CEO apartments, private aircraft, and trips when these individuals are already so handsomely compensated. Some advocates call for nothing less than the re-regulation of American business, an unlikely scenario given the current close links between business and politics. At present, many CEOs stand out as symbols of class inequity.

Suggested Reading

Arianna Huffington, *Pigs at the Trough*, 2003; Greg Palast, *The Best Democracy Money Can Buy*, 2003; Dan Sewell Ward, "CEOs" (http://www.halexandria.org/dward668.htm).

CHAMBER OF COMMERCE

ROBERT E. WEIR

The Chamber of Commerce (C of C) represents the interests of non–government-related business on the local level. The Chamber has a national office in Washington, D.C., that maintains a staff of lobbyists, lawyers, and policy analysts who lobby for policies that benefit business across the nation and abroad. Local and state chambers are loosely affiliated with the national C of C.

Local chambers of commerce have existed at least since 1825, with Daniel Webster often given credit for inspiring the first body in Boston. The national organization came into being in 1912 and was part of the **Progressive Era** impulse to rationalize society, place planning in the hands of supposed experts, and create large associations to coordinate policy. The C of C was one of numerous professional, academic, and business associations formed in the early twentieth century. By 2005 the national body claimed to represent more than 3 million businesses, scattered across more than 2,800 local chambers, 830 separate business associations, and 102 American chambers of commerce operating overseas. The national Chamber of Commerce attempts to create a favorable climate for business. Although much of its activity is mundane, the C of C has been immersed in controversial battles over such things as business tax cuts, deregulation plans, and attempts to blunt the authority of bodies felt to hamper business, such as the Environmental Protection Agency and the Occupational Safety and Health Administration. Many Chamber members have also historically been antithetical to the **labor movement**.

Most Americans encounter the Chamber of Commerce on the local level, where groups are active in promoting economic growth, attracting new business investments, and pressuring local and state government to enact pro-business policies. Many chamber members are also tireless boosters of their municipalities and regions. In many towns, Chamber of Commerce members are major employers and hence enjoy great **prestige**. Most businesses in local chambers are usually small in scale, and their owners, **CEO**s, and managers are likely to be solid members of the **middle class**.

Controversy arises in those areas in which C of C members exert undue influence on local and state politics. Chamber members tend to be active in local affairs and form **social networks** that give them easy access to local officials. Most municipalities have to manage their budgets carefully; hence a decision to allocate funds to improve an access road to a business park might entail cuts to a local school budget or deferring maintenance of residential streets. In some places local citizens charge that the business community receives preferential treatment, while schools, **poverty** programs, and municipal services are shortchanged. There is probably merit to many of these charges. Because municipalities depend heavily on the business community to generate employment and tax revenues, cozy relations between politicians and the local chamber of commerce is commonplace in America. Chamber members are likely to have a greater voice on local issues ranging from issuing bonds to liquor licensing.

Suggested Reading
Marc Benioff and Karen Southwick, *Compassionate Capitalism: How Corporations Can Make Doing Good an Integral Part of Doing Well*, 2004; William DeSoto, *Politics of Business Organizations: Understanding the Role of State Chambers of Commerce*, 1995; U.S. Chamber of Commerce (www.uschamber.com/).

CHARITY BALLS

Laura Tuennerman-Kaplan

Charity balls are formal dinner dances held by nonprofit organizations to raise money. As such they fall into a larger category of fundraisers or charity benefits that mix giving, through the purchase of event tickets or the sponsoring of a table, with opportunities to socialize. Those who attend such events are often part of **social networks** composed of social elites, while others may be **social climbers**. This is especially true of the **nouveau riche**, which hopes to make important social and professional connections. In addition, charity balls are often featured in the society pages of newspapers, thus providing participants with publicity and **prestige**. Reciprocity is also often involved, as members of one organization invite friends to an event and are expected to return the favor by attending their friends' charity events.

Charity balls are usually formal events in which men don evening wear and tuxedos, and women attend in **designer** gowns. As such, they can appear to outsiders to be as much about **conspicuous consumption** as about **philanthropy**. This makes them subject to criticism. Some people question the cost of these lavish events, pointing out that charities could net a larger profit from outright gifts than from hosting events with high overhead. In some cases, charity balls have been replaced by more modest "opening receptions" or "donor dinners," partly to keep down costs and partly to blunt criticism. Other complaints include the charge that charity balls that raise money for the poor smack of paternalism, or conversely that events disproportionately benefit institutions that cater primarily to the **upper class** and upper **middle class**, such as art museums, opera companies, and symphony orchestras.

Charity balls have long been a staple of the privileged classes and, in some ways, are a holdover of aristocratic cultural forms inherited from England. The American form of charity balls, however, also owes much to self-conscious efforts on the part of wealthy **Gilded Age** individuals to cultivate style and taste. Some Gilded Age balls were snapshots of upper class arrogance, excess, and snobbery. Although twentieth-century charity balls retained lavish and sumptuous airs, an overall decline in Victorian social mores muted some of their more exclusive aspects. Moreover, a general loosening of class distinctions that shifted the emphasis more toward wealth and less toward breeding gradually transformed the atmosphere of charity balls. Though most are still formal, they are far less so than those of the late nineteenth century.

In contemporary society, public fundraisers that cut across class lines have usurped many of the functions once filled by charity balls. That said, many organizations continue to rely on charity benefits to raise money. In recent years the Internal Revenue Service has further clarified the rules related to tax deductions taken for these charitable events so that the actual costs of the event are classified as non-deductible.

Suggested Reading

Susan Ostrander, *Women of the Upper Class*, 1984; Francie Ostrower, *Why the Wealthy Give: The Culture of Elite Philanthropy*, 1995.

CHICAGO SCHOOL OF ECONOMICS

JESSICA LIVINGSTON

The Chicago School of Economics is named for the University of Chicago, famed for its free-market economic theorists.

It began to gain attention by the end of the 1950s in large part because of Milton Friedman, who served as a professor of economics at the University of Chicago from 1946 to 1976. Friedman is credited with being the leading proponent of the monetarist school of economic thought, which stresses the importance of money supply on inflation. Chicago School theorists often favored free markets rather than government intervention, a departure from the conventional wisdom of the postwar era. Keynesian economics, based on the ideas of **John Maynard Keynes**, was the dominant economic theory at the time. Keynesianism, which was a response to the **Great Depression**, argues for government-directed policies to fight high **unemployment** and deflation. The inability of Keynesianism in the 1970s to combat stagflation, the combination of high unemployment and inflation, played a significant role in the rising popularity of monetarism.

Friedman had been challenging Keynesianism for several decades preceding the 1970s. In 1947 Friedman and thirty-six other scholars were invited by Friedrich Hayek to form the Mont Pelerin Society. Hayek exerted great influence on the Chicago School. In *The Road to Serfdom* (1944) Hayek argued that **socialism** requires central planning, which leads to totalitarianism. He further claimed that economic freedom is necessary to guarantee political freedom; hence he emphasized the importance of laissez-faire, or free markets, and competition. This economic philosophy is now called neoliberalism for its mixing of neoclassical economics and commitment to personal freedom ideals. Hayek realized that his ideas were not popular at the time, and thus he encouraged those economists who shared them to battle for their acceptance. Friedman, as well as his many loyal students, played a significant role in this mission. Friedman directed his classic *Capitalism and Freedom* (1962) to the general public as well as to economists. In it he argues that the primary role of the government is to foster competitive markets, enforce private contracts, and preserve law and order. The limited role he assigned to government is a defining characteristic of neoliberal doctrine.

The first experiment with implementing neoliberal theory at the national level took place in Chile in 1973, after General Augusto Pinochet's coup against the democratically elected president Salvador Allende. Chilean business elites felt threatened by Allende's move toward socialism, so they—along with U.S. corporations, the Central Intelligence Agency, and Secretary of State Henry Kissinger—backed Pinochet's coup. Pinochet hired the "Chicago boys," a group of economists from the University of Chicago, to reconstruct the Chilean economy along the lines of neoliberal theory. These economists worked with the International Monetary Fund (IMF) to make Chile's economy more hospitable to trade and foreign investment. They reversed the policy of nationalizing assets, and they subjected both natural resources and pension systems to unregulated privatization. The **minimum wage** was abolished, and taxes on **wealth** and profits were lowered.

While Friedman referred to these changes as "The Miracle of Chile," the revival of the economy did not last. Unemployment rose and real wages declined. By the early 1980s Chile was in a recession, and during the 1982 Latin American debt crisis the privatized pensions were lost when the **stock market** collapsed. In addition to challenging the claim that these economic reforms were successful, critics have also pointed to how these reforms were achieved. While the dictatorship in Chile implemented economic reforms, it also tortured and murdered political dissidents. Economic freedom did not lead to political freedom as Friedman had claimed.

While critics of the Chicago School have called it dogmatic and reductionist, by the 1970s it had gained credibility with the award of the Nobel Prize to Hayek in 1974, and to Friedman in 1976. The department also received seven other Nobel Prizes between 1976 and 1995. By the 1990s the ideas of the Chicago School had become mainstream. These ideas were solidified with the articulation of the Washington Consensus, the implementation of the North American Free Trade Agreement, and the formation of the World Trade Organization. Neoliberal policies such as deregulation and privatization have increased income polarization and corporate power while weakening labor unions. The overall effect has been a restoration of elitist class power and increased economic inequality both nationally and internationally.

Suggested Reading

Milton Friedman, *Capitalism and Freedom*, 1962; David Harvey, *A Brief History of Neoliberalism*, 2005; Juan Gabriel Valdes, *Pinochet's Economists: The Chicago School of Economics in Chile*, 1995.

CHILD LABOR

ROBERT E. WEIR

Technically, all employment of individuals under the age of eighteen is child labor, although current federal law places few restrictions on workers over the age of sixteen beyond prohibitions on handling hazardous materials or operating heavy machinery. As of 2005 there were over 5.5 million children between the ages of twelve and seventeen who work for wages. Child labor is often viewed as a rite of passage, with estimates running as high as 80 percent of high school students who have worked while still in school. The forms of child labor that are considered social problems involve illegal employment of children, violations of labor laws, and exposure of children to dangerous conditions.

The definition of child labor has changed through American history as the very concept of childhood evolved. In preindustrial times the period between childhood and adulthood was relatively short. Boys and girls alike were expected to engage in domestic and farm chores as soon as they were able to do so, and the onset of puberty marked entry into adulthood with all its incumbent work expectations. Some religious traditions, especially those of Separatists and **Puritans**, even viewed work as a safeguard against bedeviling idleness.

The development of factory work and the subsequent **Industrial Revolution** altered perceptions of child labor and helped redefine childhood itself. As the American economy expanded in the early nineteenth century, wage labor became a permanent social feature. Urbanization and advances in communications and transportation also transformed the nature of work. Although agriculture remained the dominant production mode throughout the nineteenth century, social reformers saw mining, factory work, and urban manual labor as inherently more dangerous for children than rural labor. By the 1870s the **labor movement** also railed against child labor, in part because unions found it unjust and in part because child labor was often used by unscrupulous employers to undercut adult wages. The call to curb child labor often went hand-in-glove with calls for compulsory public education, which promised the ancillary effects of extending childhood and delaying entry into the labor market.

The lure of wages proved hard to resist for those living in **poverty**, which was the plight of many immigrant families. Even well-established working-class families often needed the supplementary wages of children to survive. By the late nineteenth century child labor was a large social problem, with legions of children employed in sweatshops, mines, textile mills, and elsewhere. Untold numbers hawked newspapers, carried bundles in garment districts, toiled on docks, or engaged in peddling.

Newspaper exposés and photographers such as **Jacob Riis** and Lewis Hine focused attention on abusive child labor to such a degree that it became a source of national shame. In 1904 the National Child Labor Committee began to document the full extent of child labor. States began enacting legislation to curtail child labor in the late nineteenth century, and the federal government followed suit during the **Progressive Era**. Despite heavy opposition from the business community, Congress enacted the Keating-Owen Act in 1916, which set limits on child

Child laborers at a glass works, Indiana, 1908. Courtesy of the Library of Congress.

labor. The law was, however, struck down as unconstitutional in 1918, and a subsequent act, passed in 1919, suffered the same fate in 1922. A proposed constitutional amendment to ban child labor failed in Congress.

It was not until the passage of the Fair Labor Standards Act (FLSA) of 1938 that federal laws finally regulated the age at which children could work and the number of hours they could hold employment. Even then, Congress was forced to enact special exemptions for agricultural work before passage could be secured. An amended FSLA is still the primary federal law governing child labor, although compulsory school attendance laws also play a major role. (In most states one cannot legally leave school until age sixteen.)

Under the current FLSA no child under the age of fourteen can be legally employed, except in agriculture, where the minimum age is ten if the child is employed on a family-owned farm. In theory one has to be twelve to work on any other farm. The FLSA also holds that, until age sixteen, children cannot work during school hours and cannot work more than eighteen hours during a school week or more than three hours on a day school is in session. (During summer vacations they can work up to eight hours daily, not to exceed forty hours per week.) Again, most of these provisions are waived for farm labor. The FLSA also allows employers to pay a sub-**minimum wage** of $4.25 per hour for under-twenty workers for a ninety-day period, at which time it rises to the federal minimum of $5.15. (Farm labor is not subject to these limits.)

In the popular mind abusive child labor is a relic of the American past and a contemporary problem only in developing nations, but that perception is very far from the truth. As in the nineteenth century, modern child labor is strongly correlated with poverty and **immigration**. Harsh conditions are widespread in agriculture, where an estimated 800,000 children work in the fields. More than half of these come from immigrant or imported migrant labor families, many of the latter from families of undocumented illegal aliens. The United Farm Workers of America union has documented cases of children as young as five toiling up to ten hours per day. Abuses also abound among documented aliens and children of citizens, with migrant farm worker children having a school dropout rate of around 45 percent, more than double the national average. Moreover, pesticide exposure and hard labor reduces farm laborer life expectancy to just forty-nine years, twenty-six fewer than the national rate.

Child labor improprieties extend beyond the fields, however. Despite FLSA restrictions on hours, one of six child laborers works more than twenty-five hours per week while school is in session. Each week as many as 148,000 children are illegally employed in the United States, many of whom are under the age of fourteen. In 2003 states collected more than $1.8 million in fines from employers violating federal and state child labor laws. Certain enterprises have been singled out for their cavalier enforcement of the FLSA. The magazine and candy industries, for example, are often accused of exploiting child solicitors to the tune of about $1 billion in yearly revenues, and another 50,000 children routinely work as street peddlers in American cities. In 2005 **Wal-Mart** paid a fine of over $135,000 for allowing youthful employees to operate forklifts and handle hazardous materials. (The size of this fine was denounced by many reformers as a "sweetheart deal" between the government and Wal-Mart.)

Child labor remains a serious problem in America. Studies reveal that whether a child works out of necessity or because of

Two girls wearing banners with slogan "ABOLISH CHILD SLAVERY!!" in English and Yiddish. Probably taken during May 1, 1909, labor parade in New York City. Courtesy of the Library of Congress.

the lure of **consumerism**, the consequences can be costly. Each year approximately sixty-seven workers under eighteen die, and one is injured every thirty seconds (more than 230,000 per year). Students working more than twenty hours also suffer declining academic achievement and higher rates of alcoholism and drug abuse than those who work less.

Suggested Reading

Child Labor Coalition (http://www.stopchildlabor.org/); Sandy Hobbs, Jim McKechnie, and Michael Lavalette, *Child Labor: A World History Companion*, 1999; Laurence Steinberg, Sanford M. Dornbusch, and B. Bradford Brown, *Beyond the Classroom*, 1997.

CHILDREN AND POVERTY

GERALD FRIEDMAN

Entering the twenty-first century, the poorest groups in the United States are children and their caregivers. Children account for over a third of America's poor, and their parents account for another third. One child in six lives in a household with an income below the **poverty line**, a poverty rate nearly twice the rate of **poverty** among the elderly and over twice that of adults between thirty-five and sixty years of age.

Childhood poverty is inevitable in a society that relies on the free-market distribution of income. Following the advice of Adam Smith, **capitalist** societies rely on personal self-interest to produce desired goods and services: "It is not from the benevolence of the butcher, the brewer, or the baker," Smith remarked, "that we can expect our dinner, but from their regard to their own interest." Self-interest does ensure Americans an adequate supply of meat, beer, and bread, but it cannot provide for children who enter the world with great and pressing needs but without access to property or resources. If children are to survive, they must be supported by others—parents, kind strangers, or public agencies.

Because children are a society's future, the entire community wants them to be raised well. Nevertheless, the United States relies on biological and adoptive parents to care for children, often with little community support. For parents, this makes having children an expensive and time-consuming activity. The average American **middle-class** household directly spends over $10,000 per year housing, clothing, feeding, and otherwise caring for each child in addition to opportunity costs, because children require parents' time and attention that could otherwise be devoted to paid work. Altogether, the direct expenses plus lost work time come to over $300,000 per child for the average middle-class American two-parent family. This cost has risen sharply over time because of rising prices for labor-intensive activities, such as child care, and the greater cost of lost work time for mothers now that more women are working for pay outside the home.

For this expenditure, parents can expect virtually no financial return. To use Adam Smith's language, instead of self-interest, we rely on the "benevolence" of parents to provide for the next generation. The financial burden on parents has probably contributed to a declining fertility rate over the past century; the total fertility rate in the United States, the number of births per woman, has fallen sharply since the nineteenth century and is now barely 2.0, below the level needed to maintain the population. More men, especially, have chosen not to raise children. The proportion of children born to two-parent households has fallen sharply in the late twentieth century, down to only 66 percent in 2003. This means that a third of children are born without a father present; because of death, divorce, and parental separation, a majority of children will live in a **one-parent** household at some point in their youth. The poverty rate is especially high for children living with only one parent, because many single parents cannot earn enough to support their children. (This is especially true of single mothers, because women's earnings are significantly less than men's.) Some single mothers (and some single fathers) receive financial support from absentee parents, but 60 percent of all single mothers (and 75 percent of single fathers) manage entirely on their own. The average child support payment received in 2003, only $4,274, was well under the cost of caring for a child. The poverty rate is especially high among single parents; among those receiving child support payments, 22 percent are living below the poverty line, as are 27 percent of those not receiving payments.

By lessening their dependence on often over-tasked parents, community support could reduce poverty among children to ensure care for the next generation of Americans. To ensure that the next generation is educated, for example, the United States spends over $600 billion on public schools. To reduce childhood poverty, a patchwork of social **welfare** programs is in place to provide financial assistance to some categories of children. Those living in very poor households may receive health insurance, either through Medicaid or various state Children's Health Insurance Programs (CHIPs). Others may receive help with food budgets through Food Stamps or, for the very young, Women, Infants, and Children (WIC). The children of disabled workers receive Social Security Disability, and some very poor receive Transitional Assistance to Needy Families (TANF). Children in low-income households may also benefit from the Earned Income Tax Credit provided by the federal government as a supplement to their parent's wages. Compared with more comprehensive programs in other countries, this patchwork approach to poverty amelioration in the United States is relatively ineffective at reducing childhood poverty. Antipoverty programs in the United States raise the income of fewer than half of the non-elderly poor above the poverty line. By contrast, government programs lifted over 80 percent of the poor out of poverty in France and other European countries, and Social Security does the same for over 80 percent of the elderly poor in the United States. One reason that antipoverty programs are relatively ineffective in the United States is that there is such a strong stigma attached to participation that fewer than 60 percent of poor families receive any government assistance.

Suggested Reading

Barbara Bergmann, *Saving Our Children from Poverty: What the United States Can Learn from France*, 1996; Giovanni Andrea Cornia and Sheldon Danziger, eds., *Child Poverty and Deprivation in the Industrialized Countries, 1945–1995*, 1997; Nancy Folbre, *Who Pays for the Kids? Gender and the Structures of Constraint*, 1994; Victor Fuchs, *Women's Quest for Economic Equality*, 1988.

CHOMSKY, NOAM (1928–)

DAVID V. HEALY

A renowned academic and critic of hierarchical systems of government and economics, Chomsky was born on December 7, 1928, in Philadelphia, Pennsylvania. His primary academic background is in philosophy and linguistics, and his first PhD was in linguistics, issued by the University of Pennsylvania in 1955. Starting in the 1960s, Chomsky became heavily involved in politics, using theoretical structures derived from his academic work. Politically, he identifies himself as an anarcho-syndicalist, a type of **anarchist** who subscribes to the theories of Mikhail Bakunin, among others. Though perhaps best known for his linguistic theories, most notably that of generative grammar, Chomsky is also notable for his political activism. He has published dozens of articles and books in several academic fields.

Chomsky has participated in protests for various causes, including anti-Vietnam War protests (as well as both Gulf wars). He has been an outspoken critic of many U.S. foreign policy decisions in the past four decades. However, his most notable contributions to numerous causes are his published works and his many lectures. Many of Chomsky's books are outside his "official" field of linguistics, and they present numerous critiques of political and economic systems.

In line with many of anarchism's tenets, Chomsky considers class and **class struggle** in terms of **power** versus the powerless. This paradigm defines a **power elite** that includes the political, economic, media, and even intellectual leaders. With this structure, Chomsky has repeatedly laid forth arguments against government and **capitalism**, utilizing obscure but public sources to debunk many of the myths and propagandistic structures propagated by the same elites he sets out to

Noam Chomsky (right) during the presentation of his new book at the Book Institute of Havana in October 2003. At left, Cuba's parliamentary president Ricardo Alarcón de Quesada listens to him. © Alejandro Ernesto.

criticize. The common target of Chomsky's critique is America's power elite, though he has dealt with others, including NATO and the global capitalist elite.

Current major targets of Chomsky's critiques include the American War on Terror, **globalization**, and corporations. It is Chomsky's usual method to point out the hypocrisy and falsehoods in elite propaganda systems, and he has done so in dealing with the War on Terror. Though decried for being "anti-American," one of Chomsky's most noted recent theses clearly presents the United States as the largest funder and supporter of terrorism in the world. Highly controversial, this argument has had little coverage in American media, contributing to ongoing criticisms that Chomsky's theories are ignored by the mass media.

Chomsky's supporters, many of them anarchists like him, claim that the leadership class, the elite, conspires to keep Chomsky's ideas out of the common view so that it cannot challenge the status quo. However, Chomsky is well-known on the lecture circuit, especially at universities, where he also confronts the intellectual elite targeted by his criticisms. Chomsky's lectures are as notable as his writings, and many of his lectures have been recorded in published texts or on audio and videotape.

The construction that Chomsky uses—that the elites are all those who rule over society while those beneath have been either fooled or coerced into complying—is more expansive than the definition of class commonly found in discussions on the topic. For Chomsky and other anarchists, there is little difference among those who control vast portions of society and its resources, whether they are found in the fields of government, media, or corporations. This divergence has separated Chomsky from the mainstream class debate in many ways, yet he remains popular for those same divergent positions.

Suggested Reading

Noam Chomsky, *Reasons of State*, 1972; Chomsky, *Manufacturing Consent*, 1988; Chomsky, *A New Generation Draws the Line*, 2000.

CIVIL SERVICE

ROBERT E. WEIR

Civil service jobs are those in which employees perform the various tasks related to carrying out government and public functions. "Civil service" is often synonymous with bureaucracy, but there are many civil service jobs that are not traditional office jobs, including much of the work of the U.S. Postal Service and the diplomatic corps. Since 1883 civil service jobs have been avenues of **social mobility** for many Americans.

Senator William Learned Marcy is often credited with the phrase "to the victor belong the spoils," a phrase he uttered in 1832 to defend President Andrew **Jackson**'s office appointments from attacks by Congressman John Quincy **Adams**. Long before Marcy uttered that phrase, however, the "spoils system" defined the way in which most civil service appointments were made. Adams's own father, President John Adams, made a series of controversial "midnight appointments" the night before he turned over the presidency to Thomas Jefferson. The Supreme Court's validation of those appointments in *Marbury v. Madison* (1803) entrenched the federal spoils system for the next eighty years. This meant that many government posts were filled by cronyism, nepotism, and social class connections. Old New England families came to see the civil service as something of a class perquisite; overall, the civil service was disproportionately staffed by lawyers, professors, and children of wealthy merchants.

The federal civil service remained small until after the **Civil War**, but its expansion thereafter exacerbated the problems of the spoils system and led reformers to equate civil service **meritocracy** with social **democracy**. Cries for reform also came from members of the **middle class**, who had joined the abolitionist cause and had been Republican Party stalwarts but felt locked out of the civil service. Attempted reforms in the Grant, Hayes, and Garfield administrations withered, but when President Garfield was assassinated by a frustrated office seeker, Congress was pressed to act. In 1883 the Pendleton Civil Service Reform Act made approximately half of all appointments subject to merit hiring. This bill, though flawed, led to dramatic changes in the civil service, including the infusion of employees from lower on the socioeconomic scale and an overall professionalizing of many offices.

Changes on the federal level were (and are) slow to filter to the state and municipal level, where the spoils system was often (and still is) viewed as an extension of party politics. The Tweed Ring in New York City was simply the most infamous of dozens of patronage systems controlled by powerful political machines, and the city's Democratic Party continued to dole out patronage long after Tweed himself fell in 1871. Moreover, the Republican Party political machine that dominated much of the rest of New York State also doled out civil service jobs. Attacks on municipal and state manipulation of civil service jobs did not enjoy widespread success until the **Progressive Era**, and even today a large number of local and state jobs across the United States are routinely filled via practices that would not pass muster on the federal level.

During the **New Deal**, President **Franklin Roosevelt** expanded merit-based civil service jobs to include roughly 90 percent of placements, but these restrictions were largely gutted after World War II. Two other significant attempts to reform the civil service came in the Hatch Act of 1939, which restricted federal employees from engaging in political activities, and the Civil Service Reform Act of 1978. The latter dismantled the Civil Service Administration, which had overseen the civil service since the Pendleton Act, and distributed its powers among the Office of Personnel Management, the Labor Relations Authority, and the Merit System Protection

Board. The idea behind this act was to decentralize control to reduce abuses, but it had the opposite effect under President **Ronald Reagan**, who staffed the upper echelons of federal offices with loyalists who often acted on ideological predilections that undermined merit.

All civil service reforms have allowed the possibility of abuse in that most of the highest offices are exempt from merit considerations. Ambassadorships, for example, remain political appointments for which candidates need no special qualifications so long as they can win Congressional approval. One need not even have legal training to be appointed to the U.S. Supreme Court, nor does one need to have specialized expertise to serve on a presidential cabinet or advisory board. **C. Wright Mills** was among the many scholars who argued that the upper levels of the civil service remain the preserve of the **power elite**.

Weaknesses of the civil service aside, entry into it remains a way in which individuals can attain upward mobility. Most administrative, service, and bureaucratic positions have guidelines, exams, and rules on how to advance. It is still possible, for instance, for a police officer to rise through the ranks from a patrol position to a top administrative post, and hence move from the working class to the middle class. Most civil service jobs also reward long service, and it is not unusual for long-time federal employees to draw salaries that would qualify them for upper middle-class **status**. The lure of the civil service is such that there is a thriving market for manuals on how to prepare for civil service examinations.

Suggested Reading

Cindy Aron, *Ladies and Gentlemen of the Civil Service: Middle Class Workers in Victorian America*, 1987; John Donahue and Joseph Nye, eds., *For the People? Can We Fix Civil Service?* 2003; Ari Hoogenbottom, *Outlawing the Spoils: A History of the Civil Service Reform Movement, 1865–1883*, 1961.

CIVIL WAR

THOMAS A. WING

Social class played an important role in the American Civil War (1861–65). Both sides experienced difficulties in raising and maintaining armies, as well as in enforcing discipline in the ranks. In some cases, keeping order on the home front was affected by **class struggle**.

In the North, class inequality had been rising in the years prior to the war. While Northern industrialists wholeheartedly supported war as a means of restoring the Union, the working class was indifferent. The bombardment of Fort Sumter by Confederate forces inspired a wave of nationalism and benefited Northern recruiters, but a string of early war defeats quickly squelched enlistment efforts. The Emancipation Proclamation increased tensions, as white workers feared mass migrations of former slaves to the North. Perceived competition for jobs and lower wages created panic among the working class. The Conscription Act of 1863 pushed the classes further apart as draft riots erupted in New York and other disturbances occurred across the North. The act required that all able-bodied males between the ages of 20 and 45 be subject to military service, but a drafted man who provided an acceptable substitute or paid the government $300 was excused. The $300 exemption resulted in the cry "rich man's war, poor man's fight," alluding to the fact that many in the **upper class** bought their way out of the war. Democratic leaders added to the tension by calling the Conscription Act unconstitutional. Significant numbers of working-class Irish and German immigrants were conscripted into the Union Army with no ability to avoid service. Harsh treatment of **lower class** enlisted men by upper-class officers added to the tension. The New York draft riots pitted large numbers of Irish immigrant workers against abolitionists and blacks. Widespread looting, property destruction, and violence characterized the riots. A black orphanage was burned, leaving children homeless. Police, militia, and Naval and Army forces as well as West Point cadets were called in to restore order. The New York riots cost between $1 and $2 million and approximately 1,000 lives.

Class struggle in the South during the war was equally destructive. Like the North, the white working class in the South was not completely supportive of a war many saw as a vindication of the aristocratic, slave-owning class. Poor, Southern, white workers had long felt the effects of **slavery** and had little chance for economic advancement. Confederate officials feared a Southern abolitionist party might emerge. Like the Conscription Act in the North, the Confederate draft of 1862 had similar repercussions. In the South, not only could a man avoid the draft by paying an exemption fee, but slave owners with twenty or more slaves were automatically free from obligation. "Rich man's war and poor man's fight" was heard in the South as well.

The rift between the aristocracy and the working class intensified during the war as the North's blockade and invading troops disrupted food production and distribution. The women and children of the South faced starvation, as most available food was reserved for Confederate troops. The continual reliance on cash generated from cotton sales kept farmland from being converted to food crops. The overproduction of cotton led to food shortages that had drastic effects on poor working-class women, left at home by men in the military. Speculators increased the tension by inflating prices on the few food items available. Faced with starvation, many women embraced violence and theft to survive. Richmond, Mobile, and every major city in Georgia experienced food riots as desperate women descended on army depots and took food reserved for soldiers. With mothers, wives, and children at home facing such conditions, many Confederate soldiers deserted for family preservation. With the fall of Vicksburg and the defeat at Gettysburg in July 1863, desertion rates rose for the duration of the war. The draft and food shortage, combined with deep class-related animosities, sowed the seeds of destruction for the Confederacy as a better fed and equipped, numerically superior opponent wore down the will of the South.

Although class conflict was not the single cause of the war, class struggle and long-standing disputes between the working class and the elites created problems for both the North and the South. Class conflict influenced the final outcome of the war, and it shaped **Reconstruction** in the years that followed.

Suggested Reading

Lorien Foote, "Rich Man's War, Poor Man's Fight: Class, Ideology, and Discipline in the Union Army," *Civil War History* 51.3 (2005) 269–287; Barnet Schecter, *The Devil's Own Work: The Civil War Draft Riots and the Fight to Reconstruct America*, 2005; David Williams, Teresa Crisp Williams, and R. David Carlson, *Plain Folk in a Rich Man's War: Class and Dissent in Confederate Georgia*, 2002.

CLASS CONSCIOUSNESS

FRANK A. SALAMONE

In **Marxist** terms, a social class consists of a group of people who share the same position in the social hierarchy regarding the **means of production**. Class consciousness refers to the awareness members of that group or class have of their membership in that group. Moreover, included in consciousness is the ability of the class to act in furthering its self-interests. The extent to which individuals are aware of their own class and their allegiance to that class is also important in the definition.

Unfortunately, Marx never completed his work on class consciousness, leaving its precise definition to be contested. Many Marxists contrast class consciousness with **false consciousness** even though Marx never specifically used the latter term. Marxists do agree that true consciousness is a rational acceptance of one's class, a desire to work with the fellow-members of one's class, and an awareness of its history and purpose.

Interestingly, while the concept of social class goes back to ancient societies that had complex economic distinctions, the term itself entered the English language only in the 1770s. Basically, social classes at the top of the hierarchical scale are elites. Classes with greater power subordinate those with less power. Identification with members of one's own class coupled with an understanding of its relationship with other classes is the core of the concept of class consciousness.

There are, then, two major elements of class consciousness. The first is recognition of membership in a group, which has a position in society. The second is a commitment to changing that position through political activity.

Many observers argue that American workers have seldom developed class consciousness, whereas European workers have often exhibited it. Historians have put forward a number of reasons for this phenomenon. Foremost among them is the divide-and-conquer effect of the racial and ethnic divisions within the workforce and **labor movement**. Moreover, until recently at least, there has been the promise of movement into the **middle class** because of higher wages and open **social mobility**. Some scholars also point to the importance of the idea of political **democracy** in the United States traceable to the **American Revolution**. Many scholars, however, are dubious of explanations that posit **American exceptionalism** as an explanation for weak class consciousness.

Although labor unions in the United States provided some political power to the working class, labor membership has seldom been as high as 25 percent of eligible members. Since the 1970s, that percentage has dropped steadily. Thus, even membership in unions as a means for providing and fostering class consciousness has not proved strong in the United States. There is a strong aversion to the very concept of class in America. Beyond the reasons given above, there is resistance to anything remotely connected with Marxism or **socialism** in the United States. There is also a strong cultural value placed on the belief in upward social mobility and the possibility of a **Horatio Alger**–like rags-to-riches shift in material comfort. The rarity of actual mobility does little to dampen the dream.

Suggested Reading

Peter Blau and Otis D. Duncan, *The American Occupational Structure*, 1967; Anthony Giddens, "Class Structuration and Class Consciousness," in Giddens and David Held, eds., *Classes, Power, and Conflict*, 1982; Erik O. Wright, *The Comparative Project on Class Structure and Class Consciousness: An Overview*, 1989.

CLASS DEFINITIONS

See Conflict Theory; Continuous/Discontinuous Views of Class; Corporate Class; Functional Elite Theory; Gender Stratification; Inequality Theory; Lower Class; Managerial Class; Marxism/Marxist; Middle Class; Objective Method; Poverty; Power Elite; Prestige; Race, Racism, and Racial Stratification; Reputational Method; Status Inconsistency; Subjective Method; Underclass; Upper Class; Working Class.

CLASS FORMATION

JOHN F. LYONS

Class formation is the term used by **Marxists** to describe the process whereby individuals in the social relations of production start to attain and articulate a common outlook. Karl Marx believed that class was objectively determined by one's relationship to the **means of production** but that class formation also entailed subjective consciousness of class interests and the translation of these interests into collective action. Marx, who lived in Europe in the nineteenth century, believed that two new classes, the **bourgeoisie** and the **proletariat**, had formed in Western Europe and that similar classes would soon form in the rest of the world, especially other advanced capitalist nations such as the United States.

For Marx, the European bourgeoisie went through a period of class formation under feudalism and monarchism. The bourgeoisie were small property owners such as traders and master craftsmen who opposed the economic and political restrictions of feudalism and monarchism. They grew in number and influence and became conscious of themselves as a class. Starting with the English Revolution of the 1640s and continuing with the French Revolution of 1789, the bourgeoisie overthrew the monarchy, abolished feudalism, and created a capitalist society. Subsequently the bourgeoisie, according to Marx, became a powerful class of owners of **wealth** who controlled the economic and political system.

Marx believed that as **capitalism** matured a new class, the proletariat, or working class, would also go through a period of class formation. The proletariat owned no wealth and made a living by working in the factories and mills owned by the bourgeoisie. The proletariat would endure low wages and increasingly poor working conditions while the bourgeoisie increased their wealth. According to Marx, workers would become conscious of their common plight and the need to organize to overthrow capitalism and to establish a communist society. Eventually, the workers would expropriate the capital and take control of the means of production themselves.

Followers of Marx differed on how workers would gain revolutionary communist **class consciousness**. Some—such as the **Communist Party** of the U.S.A., which championed the ideas of the Russian revolutionary V. I. Lenin—believed that workers were incapable of gaining revolutionary consciousness unaided. A party of full-time revolutionaries must educate the workers, organize revolution, and control the state in the post-revolutionary years. Others—such as the **Industrial Workers of the World** (IWW), formed in 1905—held that the proletariat would gain class consciousness through trade union struggles at work and would seize control of the workplace and run society without the aid of outside intellectuals.

Marx's theory of class formation has proved particularly difficult to transplant to the United States. European-style feudalism and monarchism were never replicated in the United States. The widespread ownership of private property and company shares, and the growth of **white-collar** occupations, has made it difficult to clearly distinguish between the bourgeoisie and the proletariat. Indeed, opponents of Marx have questioned the degree of working-class consciousness in the United States and believe that divisions based on ethnicity, gender, and race have hindered class solidarity. Others argue that American workers are conditioned by **individualism** and **consumerism** and thus view themselves not as exploited workers but as **middle-class** citizens. Whatever the reason, U.S. workers have not chosen to follow the revolutionary path prescribed to them by Marx.

Suggested Reading

Rick Halpern and Jonathan Morris, eds., *American Exceptionalism: US Working-Class Formation in an International Context*, 1997; Ira Katznelson and Aristide R. Zolberg, eds., *Working-Class Formation: Nineteenth Century Patterns in Western Europe and the United States*, 1986; Karl Marx, *The Poverty of Philosophy*, 1847.

CLASS STRUGGLE

JOHN F. LYONS

Class struggle, as defined by **Marxists**, is conflict generated by economic inequality and exploitation. Karl Marx believed that there had been an original primitive society in which equality and cooperation had prevailed, but that conflict between classes emerged with the development of private property. Classes, as defined by one's relationship to the **means of production**, were divided into exploiters and exploited, or between those who controlled the **wealth** and those who created the wealth. According to Marx, this class conflict eventually leads to major historical changes and different ways of producing wealth. In the ancient world, the major classes were master and slave, and in the feudalistic Middle Ages the lord and the serf. Feudalism eventually gave way to modern industrial **capitalism** and the emergence of two new major classes: the **bourgeoisie** and the **proletariat**.

As in previous societies, the conflict between the bourgeoisie and proletariat lay in economic exploitation. The bourgeoisie consisted of the capitalists, who owned the means of production such as mines and factories, while the proletariat comprised those who were propertyless and were forced to earn a living by working for the bourgeoisie. Yet the worker would not receive the full fruits of his or her labor. Instead, the bourgeoisie would compensate the workers for only a portion of their work and keep for themselves as profit what Marx called the "surplus value." Moreover, the employer seeks to increase his profit by lowering wages, by increasing the pace or hours of work, or by introducing new machinery. In contrast, the worker wants higher wages, to spend less time and expend less effort at work, and to enjoy better working conditions. These irreconcilable differences between the demands of the bourgeoisie and those of the proletariat produce class struggle. Workers indulge in sabotage and slowdowns to restrain the pace of work, and they form labor unions and take strike action to achieve higher pay and better working conditions. In contrast, employers fine and fire uncooperative workers and use any means to defeat **strikes** and break unions.

According to Marx, class conflict between the bourgeoisie and the proletariat would intensify because of polarization between classes, a growing deprivation and wretchedness of the proletariat, and declining rates of profit. Unable to compete with large-scale capitalist production, farmers and craft workers would be pushed into the ranks of the proletariat and the ownership of capital would be concentrated among ever fewer. The capitalist economy also produced cycles of boom and slump as capitalists tended to produce more goods than they could sell. This would lead to periods of economic depression, lowering of wages, plant closings, and **unemployment**. Marx, however, argued that these periods of depressions would become increasingly frequent and severe as capitalists spent more income on expensive machinery and their rate of profit declined.

Marx believed that eventually the workers would become aware of their exploitation and the need for collective ownership of property. Workers would join together across industries, confront the army and the police, overthrow capitalism, and take over the means of production. For a time, what Marx termed a "dictatorship of the proletariat," where the workers would rule society, would ensue. With the establishment of the dictatorship of the proletariat, class struggle would continue against remnants of the bourgeoisie until all classes were finally abolished and a classless communist society established. Private property would no longer exist and society would function on the principle "From each according to his ability, to each according to his need."

Conflict between workers and employers, whether in the form of boycotts, strikes, or riots, has been a constant feature of U.S. history. Violence between employers and workers characterized nineteenth-century labor relations, and workers formed labor unions to further their interests. In the nineteenth century, workers formed local labor unions and national unions such as the **Knights of**

Labor and the **American Federation of Labor** to seek higher wages and better working conditions. In the twentieth century, the **Congress of Industrial Organizations** organized across lines of skill and race.

Even though class conflict has existed in the United States, fewer American workers joined the organized **labor movement** than did their European counterparts, nor did they forge large **socialist** or **communist** parties. Many factors have ameliorated class conflict in the United States. Many workers have sought and gained reforms through the political process. **Middle-class** occupations have grown, and public education has given many workers access to these jobs. Class friction has lessened because of the growing affluence and **consumerism** of American workers. Many see race or gender identity as more important than class in igniting conflict in U.S. history.

Whatever the validity of Marxist revolutionary philosophy, many sociologists suggest that class conflict remains a feature of American society. A 2006 survey, for instance, revealed that only 18 percent of Americans making $100,000–$150,000 per year felt there was "a lot" of tension between the rich and poor, yet 41 percent of those making under $30,000 said there was "a lot." Disparities in wealth, unequal access to health and education, and poor working conditions continue to plague American society, and workers seek redress of their grievances through the political process and in unions and strikes.

Suggested Reading

Herbert G. Gutman, *Power and Culture: Essays on the American Working Class*, 1987; Karl Marx, *The Communist Manifesto*, 1848; Robert H. Zieger, *American Workers, American Unions. 1920–1985*, 1994.

CLASS SUBCULTURES

JACQUI SHINE

A subculture is any group with modes of appearance, style, behavior, and beliefs that contrast with mainstream and dominant forms of expression; those whose appearances and behaviors are common across a particular social class are called class subcultures. Usually based around issues or identifiers such as **ethnicity**, sexual expression, political affiliation, or class, the presence of subcultures usually reflects tension within and without the dominant culture. Such identifiers can be either self-selected or imposed onto the members of the subculture by the dominant culture; hence subcultural deviance can be read as either a response to the pressures of cultural conformity, or a response to ostracism and rejection by the dominant culture. Subcultures enact, express, and respond to social rejection through a set of behaviors, aesthetics, and beliefs that make up a separate style.

Class subcultures often reference those subcultures arising from social class identifications, particularly the experiences of **working-class** and **lower-class** young people. Additionally, class subcultures are often heavily shaped by **race** and ethnicity. A recent example of a class subculture is the **punk movement** of the late

1970s, which arose first among working-class white youth in postindustrial, suburban Great Britain. National **unemployment** and inflation collided with a critical mass of young people, many of them undereducated, and produced national disaffection and restlessness that was neither acknowledged nor remedied by the dominant culture—politically, musically, or socially. Punk bands such as The Clash debuted, formed by young musicians with little formal training or native talent. Loud, spontaneous, and fervent, The Clash offered lyrics that addressed the circumstances of working-class teenagers, who formed their fan base. Adorned in deconstructed, ripped clothing, the band developed a style, aesthetic, and message around which their fans could organize. Mainstream society was suitably shocked by this visceral expression of white working-class anger.

The vitality of a subcultural group's style and message is usually fairly short-lived, and the punk movement was no exception, though it did spread to the United States, where it spawned the grunge movement. As a subcultural movement's visibility grows, other groups, usually with mainstream social affiliations, adopt the movement's styles and behaviors, often as a way of managing its threat and mediating its influence. Shortly after its birth, the punk movement attracted the attention of **middle-class** young people, who detached the attitudes, anger, and **alienation** from punk culture and reworked punk's do-it-yourself aesthetic as a ready-made-for-sale-in-stores fashion statement. Once adopted by the mainstream culture it seeks to reject, the subculture's threat is managed and its resistance assimilated. Punk may have allowed working-class people to challenge a mainstream culture that limited their options for success, but only until the dominant culture began to imitate and reenact the styles that had expressed resistance.

The punk rock movement is but one example of a class subculture. Virtually any group operating outside the mainstream that evolves a distinctive set of values and practices could be considered a class subculture. Among the working class, those deeply involved in the **labor movement** could, in some situations, be considered a subculture. Urban **gangs** often exhibit antisocial, subcultural behaviors. But virtually any sort of behavior, positive or negative, operating outside accepted norms could become the basis for a class subculture. As the example of punk shows, however, it is generally easier for the mainstream to co-opt subcultures than for the latter to overthrow the mainstream.

Suggested Reading

Ken Gelder, ed. *The Subcultures Reader*, 1997; Dick Hebdige, *Subculture: The Meaning of Style*, 1979; David Muggleton, *Inside Subculture: The Postmodern Meaning of Style (Dress, Body, Culture)*, 2002.

CLASSISM

CHUCK BARONE

Classism can be defined as the systematic mistreatment of one socioeconomic group by another. It operates on personal, social, cultural, and institutional levels.

Classism, both as an ideology justifying economic and social inequality and as a system of oppression, has largely been ignored in spite of the historical and contemporary existence of class-based societies. Classism is a form of oppression analogous to other forms such as **racism** or sexism, and it is often intertwined with these. Depending upon the level, oppression manifests itself differently as aware and unaware prejudice (attitudes, stereotypes, and behavior); discrimination (**power**); and **institutional discrimination** (control and social reproduction). Classism is rooted in economic distinctions that include one's position within the system of production and distribution, **income**, the material conditions of life, levels of education, **life chances**, and sociocultural differences. Class oppression ultimately rests upon a structure of rules and social customs embodied in institutions, linguistic conventions, unwritten customs, and legal practices. It often embodies aspects of snobbery.

Classism includes prejudice and stereotypes projected toward **working class** and/or the **lower classes**. The actual content of classism is elitist; in other words, class oppression and class privileges are defended on the basis of one person or group claiming to be more important, smarter, better, more deserving, or more qualified than another. These attitudes frame class behavior and thus govern interclass social relations. The oppressed person/group—usually the lower class and poor—is viewed as less worthy intellectually, socially, and economically. Such views can be unintentionally patronizing or they can be vicious. Classism is usually linked to **power** and hierarchy, though bottom-up prejudices often exist. Members of the working class, for example, often presume that members of the upper and middle class are snobs, or that they are exploitative.

Classist patterns and attitudes are the source of much prejudice and have been used to denigrate and discriminate against working and lower-class people, and to rationalize current and past oppression of these groups the world over. Failure to address the economic needs of working families for adequate incomes, housing, and health care; attacks on **welfare** and the poor; widespread anti-union sentiments; and negative media stereotypes of working-class people are examples of classism in action.

The primary institutional basis of contemporary classism is economic, especially within systems in which one social class has power and **authority** over others. In **capitalism** the dominant class includes those who own and manage corporations. This unequal dynamic often results in the exploitation and mistreatment of workers. Classism manifests itself when some are treated as expendable or with less than complete human dignity. It includes being compelled to work long and hard under difficult and often dangerous conditions for compensation that is far less than the value of one's contribution. Classism also often includes being denied due process at work and the democratic right to control one's own production/distribution process.

Suggested Reading

Margaret Anderson and Patricia Collins, eds. *Race, Class, and Gender: An Anthology*, 5th ed., 2004; Chuck Barone, "Extending Our Analysis of Class Oppression: Bringing Classism More Fully into the Race & Gender Picture," *Race, Gender, and Class*, 6.3 (1999), pp. 5–32; Class Action: Building Bridges across the Classes (http://www.classism.org/index.php); Janet Zandy, ed., *Liberating Memory*, 1994.

CLOWARD, RICHARD ANDREW (December 25, 1926–August 23, 2001)

ROBERT E. WEIR

A social activist and sociologist, Cloward's work on **poverty** remains influential decades after its initial conception.

He was born in Rochester, New York, the son of Donald Cloward, a radical Baptist minister, and Esther Fleming, an artist. Cloward spent his entire academic career at Columbia, where he obtained his bachelor's degree, his master's, and his doctorate. He joined the School for Social Work faculty in 1954, shortly after completing his PhD.

Cloward's first notable work was *Delinquency and Opportunity*, a 1960 work coauthored with Lloyd Ohlin. Cloward and Ohlin put forth a contentious "opportunity theory," which argued that juvenile delinquency was a rational response for poor, inner-city youths whose access to legitimate economic opportunity was limited. Although many decried this work as condoning lawlessness, Cloward put his theory into action by creating the Mobilization for Youth program in New York City. He rejected the prevailing paternalism of social work and brought gang members into active leadership roles. This program inspired several **Great Society** initiatives in the mid-1960s. On a personal note, Cloward met **Frances Fox Piven** through the Mobilization program. The two married and were collaborators for the rest of Cloward's life.

During the mid and late 1960s, Cloward and Piven stirred controversy by organizing the poor for militant action. In particular, they actively recruited poor people to swell the **welfare** rolls and hence spur social reform. Their actions included picketing, occupying welfare offices, and other acts of civil disobedience. These ideas and activities ripened into the path-breaking 1971 book *Regulating the Poor*. Coming on the heels of cataclysmic urban riots, Cloward and Piven embraced **class struggle** as a legitimate response for poor Americans. Welfare, they argued, has two primary functions. In stable times it suppresses wages by stigmatizing recipients so that the near-poor will work harder, stay off welfare rolls, and make few financial demands. During times of social unrest, however, welfare's function is to restore order. This is done via a carrot-and-stick strategy in which the government provides basic needs, but only if the poor behave themselves. Both functions, they argued, are insidious blame-the-victim strategies designed to keep the poor in their place. For some recipients, welfare becomes a **self-fulfilling prophecy** in which they internalize their **status** and lose hope. Because the poor lack political clout, their only access to **power** is to be disruptive, especially during times of social upheaval when politicians wish to restore order. (Note: Social movement history reveals that groups that use a limited amount of violence routinely obtain more concessions than those that eschew it or those that engage in wholesale violence. This was true, Cloward and Piven noted, even of **New Deal** programs, which resulted from social upheaval rather than government benevolence.) Evidence suggests there was merit to their arguments; during the quiescent 1950s welfare spending increased just 17 percent, but in the 1960s it increased by around 225 percent.

Cloward and Piven cofounded the National Welfare Rights Organization to advocate for welfare rights, arguing that ongoing militancy was necessary to retain welfare benefits. As they warned, decreased protest paved the way for the **Reagan** and **Bush** administrations of the 1980s to slash benefits. Cloward and Piven were outspoken critics of presidents Reagan and George H.W. Bush. Conservative claims that rises in crime, single-parent families, gang violence, and addiction were due to moral breakdown, they argued, were based on ignorance and cruelty. They pointed especially to draconian cuts to Medicaid and Aid to Families with Dependent Children to argue that welfare cuts were attacks on the **working poor** that served to widen the wealth gap.

In *Why Americans Don't Vote* (1988, 2000), Cloward and Piven opined that the American economic and political systems had effectively closed the door on the **lower classes**. Although many of the institutional aspects of their work—including their assertion that multiparty systems are superior to U.S. two-party dominance— were ignored, their point that registration difficulties served to disenfranchise the poor factored in to the passage of the 1993 National Voter Registration Act— sometimes nicknamed the "Motor Voter Act"—which allows one to register to vote at welfare offices and when renewing drivers' licenses.

Cloward remained to his death a steadfast apologist for political activism. *Regulating the Poor* is still assigned reading in many university sociology and social work classes.

Suggested Reading

Francis Fox Piven and Richard Cloward, *Regulating the Poor: The Functions of Public Welfare*, 1971; Piven and Cloward, *Poor People's Movements: Why They Succeed, Why They Fail*, 1977; Piven and Cloward, *Why Americans Don't Vote*, 1988 (updated 2000).

COLD WAR

FRANK A. SALAMONE

The Cold War was a time of heightened East-West tensions in the years between 1946 and 1991. It resulted from the clashing economic and geopolitical interests between **communism** and **capitalism** as embodied by the Union of the Soviet Socialist Republics (USSR or Soviet Union) and the United States. It is generally dubbed a "cold" war to denote the ideological nature of the conflict, as opposed to armed "hot" war clashes. Both sides, however, also engaged in military action.

The seeds of the Cold War were sown in the midst of World War II. The allies consisting of the Western democracies plus the USSR discussed postwar potential settlements at major conferences in Tehran (1943), Yalta (1945), and Potsdam (1945). Problems between the democracies and the Soviet Union began to develop even before the war ended.

Soviet control of Eastern European states led British leader Winston Churchill to warn in 1946 that an "iron curtain" was descending through the middle of Europe. The USSR's Josef Stalin responded that, because World War II was the logical outcome of Western "capitalist imperialism," future wars were possible. In the meantime, military blocs emerged on both sides. An arms race resulted, and each side sought to exert its influence in the Third World. At times, armed conflict erupted but never between the Soviet Union and the United States. After Stalin's death there were alternating periods of calm and tension that finally ended in 1991, when the Soviet Union collapsed after many Eastern European nations had already cast off communism. Many parts of the former USSR became independent nations.

The Cold War and the ensuing competition had consequences for classes in the United States. After a brief postwar recession, a period of prolonged U.S. prosperity drove out vestiges of the **Great Depression**. The **military-industrial complex** that provided arms during World War II continued during the Cold War, and many American firms also profited from the rebuilding of Western Europe and Japan. Plentiful jobs resulted in great **social mobility** in postwar America. **Incomes** increased greatly; the median family income, for example, nearly doubled between 1945 and 1960. Likewise, the percentage of Americans in the **middle class** increased dramatically, from one-third during the Depression to two-thirds after the war by one reckoning, though other analysts place the figure at closer to 40 percent.

Many things contributed to this growth. Low **unemployment**, new opportunities, and federal spending, based on the exigencies of the Cold War, spurred on prosperity. The G.I. Bill of Rights, officially the Servicemen's Readjustment Act, the building of new factories, low-interest government loans for housing, and other initiatives hastened the expansion of **suburbia**. Indeed, 85 percent of all new homes built in the 1950s were suburban homes.

Between 1946 and 1966, the country underwent a "baby boom." At its peak, 1957, a new baby was born every seven seconds in the United States, and nearly 76 million Americans were born before the boom ended in 1966. These new Americans sparked economic growth. Suburbanites needed new cars to commute, since there was little public transportation in the suburbs. Sales of new cars fueled the economy, as did easy credit to buy houses, appliances, and other important consumer goods. Women entered the job market in large numbers, further pushing the economy upward. President Eisenhower promoted the creation of the interstate highway system, which made car travel and truck deliveries easier. Between 1940 and 1950, the number of cars in the United States jumped from 40 to 60 million.

The government, as part of its defense measures during the Cold War, promoted college education. The new middle class followed the **upper class** in sending its children to college. The 1958 National Defense Education Act provided low-cost loans to college students and money for teacher training and material for instruction. The government aided research, especially in scientific and engineering pursuits. Fully one-third of all university scientific and engineering personnel in universities worked on government projects.

The fear of the "red menace" of communism worked to help workers attain greater benefits. The **Red Scare** put limits on the arbitrary power of business over their workers as the United States sought to win the hearts and minds of people under communist rule through example. This worked to ensure unprecedented gains for American workers in wages and benefits. The ruling class sought to win the Cold War by convincing workers at home and abroad that American capitalism created a higher standard of living than was possible under communism. Statistics were quoted to prove that American workers had to work less to buy cars, houses, and household appliances. Western leaders and businessmen conveniently ignored the cost of things such as medical care, rent, housing, education, transportation, and other subsidized services that were cheaper in the socialist world.

Many of the advances American workers made must be understood in light of the Cold War and the global competition between capitalism and communism. This competition also helped African Americans during the Civil Rights struggle. After all, it was difficult to seek to capture the hearts and minds of Africans, Asians, and Latin Americans while allowing Jim Crow laws, lynching, and attacks on civil rights demonstrators to run rampant. Some American leaders, in fact, put their arguments for equality in precisely such image-conscious terms. Often, social justice mattered less than promoting American-style capitalism.

During the Cold War Americans began to perceive themselves as a middle-class nation. Unprecedented gains were made in working conditions, benefits, and public services. For many, **consumerism** supplanted **class consciousness**. The **labor movement** saw a marked decline in militancy, in part because workers felt more content and in part because its own leaders bought into middle-class ideals. The 1955 merger between the **American Federation of Labor** and the **Congress of Industrial Organizations** buried the hatchet between the two former rivals, but plans to use their mutual might to reverse antilabor bills such as the Taft-Hartley Act foundered. The head of the AFL–CIO, **George Meany**, was an ardent supporter of postwar economic planning and of American policy objectives. He too was infused with notions of the United States as a middle-class society and took a dim view of radicalism among the rank and file. Meany's views played badly among younger workers when the Vietnam War became unpopular.

The upper classes prospered financially during the Cold War, and especially benefited from the decline in working-class consciousness and militancy. The illogic of organized labor's quiescence with Cold War policies came to bear in the 1980s, as the Cold War was winding down and the anti-union administration of **Ronald Reagan** came to power. Since the 1980s labor union membership has fallen precipitously, and it has become harder for unions to convince American workers converted to middle-class ideology that they possess interests antithetical to those of the business community.

Suggested Reading

Gordon Adams, *The Iron Triangle: The Politics of Defense Contracting*, 1981; James L. Clayton, ed., *The Economic Impact of the Cold War: Sources and Readings*, 1970; Nils Gilman, Mark H. Haefele, and Michael E. Latham, eds., *Staging Growth: Modernization, Development, and the Global Cold War*, 2003; Lewis H. Siegelbaum, *The Politics of Industrial Mobilization: A Study of the War Industries Committee*, 1983; Robert Teitelman, *Profits of Science: The American Marriage of Business and Technology*, 1994.

COLES, ROBERT (12 October 1929–)

FRANK A. SALAMONE

Martin Robert Coles is a psychiatrist whose work has had far-reaching consequences. In addition to psychiatry, Coles has been a social philosopher who has critically examined not only what psychiatry is doing but also why practitioners are doing it. Coles was born in Boston, Massachusetts. His father, Philip, an engineer, was English and his mother, Sandra Young Coles, hailed from Sioux City, Iowa. Coles attributes his concern for social justice to their example, stating that one of his early memories was that of his mother reading **Dorothy Day**'s *Catholic Worker* with delight.

Coles attended Boston Latin prior to Harvard College, where he majored in English, studying with Perry Miller. His senior thesis was on a work of William Carlos Williams. The thesis so impressed Williams that he analyzed it for Coles, who had sent it to him. Eventually the two became close friends and Williams became a strong influence.

It was Williams, a physician as well as a poet, who helped Coles enter the Columbia University College of Physicians and Surgeons. Coles first studied pediatrics but switched to child psychiatry. He served in the Air Force as chief of neuropsychiatry in Biloxi, Mississippi. In 1965 he worked as a teaching fellow for Erik H. Erikson at Harvard. The following year he became a lecturer in general education. Coles was in steady contact with Anna Freud, with whom he conducted a regular correspondence. In the midst of all this activity, he managed to become a prolific writer, receiving the Pulitzer Prize in 1973 for volumes two and three of *Children of Crisis.*

Coles has based himself at Harvard, where he has taught and conducted research. He became a professor of psychiatry and medical humanities at Harvard Medical School in 1977, continuing to combine his scientific and humanistic interests. In 1981 he received a MacArthur Fellowship, being in the first group of honorees. He has received numerous other honors in his career, including being visiting professor at Dartmouth and being instrumental in establishing the Center for Documentary Studies at Duke University.

Coles is the founding editor of *Double-Take* magazine, combining photography and writing in an effort, he says, to help people change the way they view the world. It fits in with the general tenor of his work, examining the lives of Americans, especially the disadvantaged. Coles finds a dignity in the lives of the oppressed who display a remarkable resiliency.

Coles has chronicled the lives of children from many backgrounds. His books narrate the lives of children from many regions of the United States as well as those from other countries of the world. These studies display his deep commitment to ethics as well as child psychiatry. Indeed, he has taught social ethics in a number of academic settings, including medical schools, business schools, law schools, and schools of education.

Coles has been a prolific writer. His opus includes 1300 articles and sixty books, including *Children of Crisis* (in five volumes); *The Moral Life of Children*; *The Political Life of Children*; *Dorothy Day: A Radical Devotion*; *The Call of Stories: Teaching and the*

Moral Imagination; and *Doing Documentary Work*. Many of his works deal with young children living in extreme **poverty**. Indeed, his five-volume *Children of Crisis* series is considered by many to rank among the classic works of the effects of poverty on children and their families. His books survey the ways children from a variety of ethnic and **socioeconomic statuses** negotiate moral and social dilemmas. Among the children Coles studied were African Americans, **Latinos**, **Native Americans**, Inuits, and the offspring of **sharecroppers** and **migrant workers**. He has even looked at the ways in which **upper-class** children confront their own privilege.

Coles demonstrates the manner in which poverty affects both the physical and the intellectual well-being of children. The social implications of poverty carry on throughout their lives though, like **Jonathan Kozol**, Coles expressed admiration for the perseverance demonstrated by children in difficult straits. Coles is a fervent opponent of **segregation**, though he maintains that merely busing school children within the city limits is not enough. The rich white **suburbs** need to be included in any comprehensive goal of integration. Not doing so, Coles maintains, ignores the class dimensions of economic status.

"The ultimate reality is the reality of class," Coles proclaims. Working-class whites and blacks, he said, "are both competing for a very limited piece of pie, the limits of which are being set by the larger limits of class, which allow them damn little, if anything." Coles has argued for a class-based affirmative action policy, one that would not pit black against white but would face the reality of class in America.

Suggested Reading

Robert Coles, *Children in Crisis*, five volumes, 1967–1977; Coles, *The Moral Life of Children*, 1986; Coles, *The Call of Stories: Teaching and the Moral Imagination*, 1989; Coles, *The Call of Service: A Witness to Idealism*, 1993; Bruce A. Ronda, *Intellect and Spirit: The Life and Work of Robert Coles*, 1989.

COMMONS, JOHN R. (October 13, 1862–May 11, 1944)

ROBERT PAUL "GABE" GABRIELSKY

John Rogers Commons was an economist, a political scientist, and the father of the modern discipline of American labor history. His perspective was explicitly non-**Marxist**, and he endeavored to explain and justify the **American exceptionalism** embedded in the U.S. **labor movement**, in particular the lack of a mass social democratic or labor-based party in the United States. The pragmatism of American labor unions, another aspect of their exceptionalism, is often labeled "business unionism" and is, in comparison to its European counterparts, extremely conservative and essentially nonideological in its approach to political and economic objectives. This business unionism typically has an exclusive orientation toward a narrow "bread and butter" concern for better hours, wages, and working conditions for the members of each individual union to the exclusion of workers outside the unions, any broader political course of action, or any theory or conception of the working class as a whole.

Commons was born in Hollandsburg, Ohio, attended Oberlin College, and did graduate work at Johns Hopkins University under Richard T. Ely. He never received a doctorate, but he went on to teach at Wesleyan University, Oberlin, Indiana University, and Syracuse University. He also worked for several nonacademic groups before going to the University of Wisconsin in 1904, where he was to spend the balance of his academic career until his retirement in 1932.

The historian Fredrick Jackson Turner had been Commons's classmate at Johns Hopkins, and Turner's notion of the disappearance of the frontier as a primary influence on American economic development greatly influenced Commons's first published book, *The Distribution of Wealth* (1894). Commons's next book, *Proportional Representation* (1896), reflected his belief in a democratic, voluntary society in a system balanced by conflicting pressures.

Commons established his scholarly reputation while at Wisconsin with the publication of *A Documentary History of American Industry* (10 vols., 1910–11). His work culminated in two important books: *Trade Unions and Labor Unions* (1905) and his best-known work, *History of Labor in the United States* (4 vols., 1918–35), written in collaboration with his students.

Commons's institutional approach to labor history and his theory of the labor movement were generally accepted, and they became the basis for the "Wisconsin school" of labor analysis and political economy. Indeed, the perspective that he developed went largely unchallenged until the 1960s, when a new generation of younger labor historians, influenced by the British **New Left** and particularly by the work of E. P. Thompson, began to emerge.

Commons was very much a part of the Progressive tradition and drafted much of the social legislation that made Wisconsin an example for other states and a model for later federal legislation under the **New Deal** in areas of **civil service**, public utilities, workers' compensation, and **unemployment** insurance. His later works include *Legal Foundations of Capitalism* (1924) and *Institutional Economics* (1934). Among those most directly and greatly influenced by him were Selig Perlman, Harry Millis, David Saposs, Ira Cross, Philip Taft, and Wayne Morse.

Suggested Reading

Jack Barbash, "John R. Commons: Pioneer of Labor Economics," *Monthly Labor Review* 112 (May 1989), pp. 44–49; John R. Commons, *Myself* (1934); Commons et al., *History of Labor in the United States*, 4 volumes, 1918–1935.

COMMUNIST PARTY

ROBERT E. WEIR

A **Marxist**-based political party devoted to **class struggle**, the Communist Party in the United States (CPUSA) is a legally registered political organization.

The CPUSA was founded in 1919 by American delegates who attended the Communist Third International. It formed just two years after the Bolshevik Revolution in Russia, and many of its early U.S. leaders were former **Socialist Party** members inspired by the potential for revolutionary upheaval in America, an outcome Karl Marx himself had predicted in his writings. Marx noted that the advanced industrial development of the United States had created an impoverished **working class** that would soon suffer **alienation** because it was divorced from control over the **means of production**. He also saw the growing **labor movement** as evidence that potential revolutionary networks were forming. In the latter spirit, many members of the CPUSA hoped to convert labor unions into communist cells.

The Bolshevik Revolution represented hope to many dispirited American leftists. By 1919 the **Industrial Workers of the World** had been rendered ineffective by repeated government raids, indictments, and repression. Ballot-box **socialism** had also proved disappointing as a national movement, and, on the local level, **municipal socialism** had proved more pragmatic than socially transformative. Moreover, in the conservative backlash following World War I, socialists faltered badly at the polls. Early on the CPUSA argued for a "boring within" relationship with trade unions, whereby communists would seek to gain control over affiliates of the **American Federation of Labor** (AFL) through a front group known as the Trade Union Educational League TUEL). The TUEL also served to insulate communists from the **Red Scare** backlash following World War I. TUEL members worked to convince unions to convert from craft unionism to industrial unionism in the belief that organizing workers according to what they produced rather than by specific skills would build **class consciousness**. Communists were emboldened by a series of general strikes in 1919, but ultimately the AFL proved too conservative. In 1929 the CPUSA set up the independent Trade Union Unity League (TUUL).

The creation of the TUUL also marked a change in relations with the Soviet Union. Early on, the CPUSA maintained a great degree of autonomy, with delegates to the various Communist Internationals arguing that local conditions dictated local strategies. By the mid-1920s, however, Moscow began to direct CPUSA policies, which had the unintended effect of dragging American communists into ideological debates, such as the decision to denounce **Trotskyists**. For the next several decades American leadership ranks were occasionally disrupted by ideological infighting.

The CPUSA experienced its greatest growth period during the **Great Depression** of the 1930s and the oncoming struggle against fascism. Most scholars peg its peak membership at around 75,000 in 1940–41. Its overall influence was far greater, though. Communists proved able organizers, especially in depressed urban areas, where they operated **soup kitchens**, organized rent strikes to protect the **working poor**, ran language classes for immigrants, and galvanized protests against decaying economic conditions. They also rose to prominent leadership positions in numerous unions, including those of autoworkers, furriers, longshoremen, maritime workers, meatpackers, and steelworkers. Many of these unions affiliated with the **Congress of Industrial Organizations** (CIO), which split from the AFL in 1935 and embraced the industrial unionism model favored by the CPUSA. Although only a handful of unions contained substantial numbers of communists, CPUSA leaders did much to help build unions in the 1930s.

Communism's major political appeal lay in its alternative, collectivist economic vision. The severity of the Great Depression led some Americans, especially intellectuals, to question the long-term sustainability of **capitalism**. Communists were further aided by Moscow's shifting tactics in the mid-1930s. As the fascist threat grew, the CPUSA was given permission to cooperate with capitalists to overcome the greater threat. Between 1935 and 1939, a coalition of the left known as the Popular Front united many communists, socialists, labor activists, and radicals.

The CPUSA suffered a blow to its prestige in 1939, when the Soviet Union signed a non-aggression pact with Nazi Germany in a cynical move to annex parts of Poland. Germany's invasion of the Soviet Union in June 1941 led the CPUSA to reestablish its support for **Franklin Roosevelt**, whom it officially endorsed for the presidency in 1944. Communists also proved loyal defense workers, signing no-strike pledges during the war and cooperating with efforts to streamline factory production. Some communists openly asserted that "communism is twentieth-century Americanism," and they were cheered by the U.S./USSR alliance that defeated fascism. For a brief moment the CPUSA was dissolved as a political party and reorganized as a political association.

The postwar period saw alliances unravel quickly and dramatically. With Soviet armies occupying much of southern and eastern Europe, wartime cooperation gave way to adversarial relations known as the **Cold War**, which exacerbated the ideological differences, contrasting territorial designs, and divergent economic visions of the United States and the Soviet Union. American communists were placed in the untenable position of being called upon to subvert their own government and of surviving a postwar Red Scare aimed at destroying them. The 1947 Taft-Hartley Act outlawed many of the militant tactics favored by communist labor activists and required all labor leaders to sign affidavits that they were not members of the CPUSA or any other communist group. The support many communists gave to Henry Wallace's quixotic 1948 campaign for the presidency further isolated them from the American political mainstream.

The Red Scare reached fever pitch between 1949 and 1956. In 1950 the CIO, once a bastion of communist strength, expelled eleven unions and nearly a million members because of supposed ties to the CPUSA. The House Un-American Activities Committee and several Senate Select Committees held near-constant hearings on alleged communist subversion, and numerous prominent CPUSA leaders were jailed. The American public was fed a steady diet of fear and propaganda, which was intensified by the arms race, dramatic spy trials, the Chinese Revolution of 1949, the outbreak of the Korean War, and the ravings of such demagogues as Senator Joseph McCarthy. More than 15,000 federal employees lost their jobs because of security concerns, as did untold others in the private sector. The entertainment industry was under constant scrutiny, and many within it found themselves blacklisted. Nationwide, one in five Americans had to sign loyalty oaths as a condition of employment, while employers found red-baiting an expedient way to derail unionization drives. The CPUSA was forced to go underground merely to survive.

Anticommunist hysteria held sway into the 1960s, often abetted by actions of the Soviet Union, such as its 1956 invasion of Hungary, the building of the Berlin Wall in 1961, its attempt to erect missile sites in Cuba in 1962, its 1968 suppression of a freedom movement in Czechoslovakia, and its support for North Vietnam during the Vietnam conflict. For Americans growing up during the Cold War, communism was synonymous with treason, suppression of freedom, and the threat of nuclear warfare, not the **class struggle**. Revelations of the excesses of former Soviet leader Josef Stalin and allegations—some of which were later substantiated—that Moscow was funding domestic spying within the United States served further to discredit the CPUSA. Unlike the 1930s, the CPUSA was unable to capitalize on 1960s militancy, even though it again surfaced as an open political party and took steps to gain independence from Moscow. For the most part, the CPUSA was eclipsed by the **New Left**.

CPUSA supporters claimed a membership of around 25,000 in the early 1970s, but that figure is surely inflated. Its support weakened as the Soviet Union itself declined, first during Mikhail Gorbachev's reforms in the 1980s, then with the collapse of the Soviet Union in 1991. It was also weakened by its continuing penchant for internecine battles. Today the CPUSA still runs candidates for office, and copies of the *Daily Worker* are still hawked by activists (many of whom are idealistic college students). Most observers claim it has about 2,500 official members and that its current impact on American politics and economic policy is minimal.

Suggested Reading

Mary Jo Buhle, Paul Buhle, and Dan Georgakas, "Communist Party, U.S.A.," in *Encyclopedia of the American Left*, 1992; Harvey Klehr, *The Heyday of American Communism*, 1984; Patricia Sexton, *The War on Labor and the Left*, 1991.

COMMUNITY COLLEGES

WILLIAM DeGENARO

Community colleges are institutions of post-secondary higher education that usually provide two years of instruction for students. Virtually all community colleges are open admissions, which means those with high school diplomas or the equivalent qualify for admission. Community colleges offer lower tuition costs and tend to attract more working-class college students than four-year schools. Although some community colleges are beginning to build residence halls, most remain exclusively commuter schools and provide access to higher education both to traditional and to older, nontraditional students who live in the surrounding communities. Because they have the reputation for attracting students with weak high school records, community colleges are sometimes dubbed "second-chance" schools, or "thirteenth grade."

Community colleges were originally called "junior colleges," because they were envisioned as institutions that would eventually allow four-year (or "senior") colleges to stop teaching the first two years of coursework. Early college planners imagined that the new two-year campuses could help universities weed out less-prepared students who weren't "college material." The first such institution, Joliet Junior College, opened in 1901 in Illinois. By the 1960s, a decade of boom for two-year colleges, the new brand of college had morphed into a multipurpose learning center whose mission and scope, which now included vocational and certification programs as well as academic transfer programs, transcended service to universities. "Community college," a name that reflected this broader mission, became the preferred designation for two-year colleges.

Currently over 6 million students—39 percent of all college students in the United States—matriculate at community college campuses. All fifty states have community colleges, but California has a particularly extensive system. Programs at community colleges include associate degree programs in the arts and sciences, pursued in large part by students wishing to transfer to four-year schools. Community colleges also offer vocational programs and certification in technical or career-oriented areas ranging from medical assistance to nursing to broadcasting to computer repair to heating/cooling repair to welding. Community colleges frequently create partnerships with local businesses to provide job training and other forms of instructional support. The colleges also regularly partner with local high schools for dual enrollment programs wherein high school students receive college credit for courses taken during their eleventh- or twelfth-grade years.

Critics such as sociologist Burton Clark claim community colleges serve a "cooling out" function, managing and decreasing the aspirations of working-class and racial minority students. Further, the critics maintain, public community colleges provide the state a further opportunity to discipline working-class malcontents who might otherwise disrupt the workings of the corporate state. By giving first-generation college students both a trade (via a two-year vocational degree) and a sense of **democracy**, taste, and decorum (via liberal arts requirements), community colleges construct citizens who can contribute to economic and civic life. Indeed, empirical data suggest that students become less prone to high aspirations during their tenure at community colleges and more amenable to a "practical," more realistic set of objectives. Finally, the critics point out that community college students miss out on the opportunities for socializing and the aesthetic qualities that four-year institutions offer.

In contrast to the critics, community college boosters praise community colleges for opening the doors of higher education to a broader cross section of the U.S. population. Many students who could not otherwise afford to attend college take advantage of low costs at community colleges and the fact that close proximity to home allows students to continue working jobs to support families or augment family incomes. Some research also suggests that working-class students—like students who grow up in ethnic enclaves—are more likely to have ties with their home communities that would be broken by "going away" to school. Finally, community colleges boast accessible faculty and student support networks such as tutoring centers that help students learn the culture of higher education; this kind of support is particularly important to first-generation college students, most of whom come from the working class.

Suggested Reading

George Baker, *A Handbook on the Community College in America: Its History, Mission, and Management*, 1994; Arthur M. Cohen and Florence B. Brawer, *The American Community College*, 1996; Kevin J. Dougherty, *The Contradictory College: The Conflicting Origins, Impacts, and Futures of the Community College*, 1994.

COMPANY TOWN

ROBERT E. WEIR

Company town is the term applied to a municipality where a single industry or employer supplies the bulk of employment, owns significant amounts of real estate, and (often) exercises undue political power over local decision making. Historically the term referred to places that were often literally owned by an employer, including housing and utilities. More recently it has come to designate any town and city whose economy relies disproportionately on a single employer.

Company towns owe their origins to the early days of American **capitalism** and were tied to ideas such as individual entrepreneurship and paternalism. Many observers see Samuel Slater's textile operation in Pawtucket, Rhode Island, as the prototype for company towns. Slater owned the mill, required workers to live in the company boarding house, controlled water rights on the Blackstone River, and even paid some workers in scrip redeemable only at the company store. Slater expanded his operation northward along the Blackstone River, often creating new company towns whenever a new mill was constructed.

Textiles and coal mining made up the bulk of pre–**Civil War** company towns. **Lowell**, Massachusetts, was one of the more famous company towns; by the mid-1830s its several dozen mills employed more than 20,000 workers, most of whom were employees of the Boston Associates business conglomerate. The Boston Associates represented a departure from the local, paternal model of Slater. As corporations grew larger, absentee ownership became more common, with towns and factories being administered by an imported managerial class. The Boston Associates, for example, also developed mills in such places as Chicopee, Holyoke, and Lawrence, Massachusetts; Dover, Manchester, and Nashua, New Hampshire; and Biddeford and Saco, Maine. In each place the mill became the dominant (or sole) employer and the towns either overt or de facto company towns.

Other industries followed suit. Lynn, Massachusetts, applied company town principles to the shoe industry, Troy, New York, to iron manufacturing, and Lynchburg, Virginia, to tobacco processing. Both before and after the Civil War, company town principles proved easiest to apply in remote areas. Coal-mining hamlets in Pennsylvania, Colorado, Indiana, Iowa, Kentucky, Ohio, and West Virginia were often company towns, as were silver- and gold-mining operations in California and the Great Basin, timber outposts in the Pacific Northwest and Upper Great Lakes, and copper mines in Arizona. Perhaps the two most famous examples of company towns in the late nineteenth century were the privately owned sleeping car manufactory of Pullman, Illinois, and the greater Pittsburgh, Pennsylvania, region, many of whose towns were solely dependent on steel mills.

The Pittsburgh suburb of Homestead and Pullman suffered cataclysmic strikes in 1892 and 1894, respectively, but the company town ideal outlasted such upheaval. In fact, in the early twentieth century it even expanded. Tobacco- and textiles-dominated company towns crisscrossed much of the South, many New England towns remained under the sway of textile manufacturers, and mining operators continued to operate according to nineteenth-century models. Moreover, the rise of new industries created new de facto company towns—the wave of the future.

Many industrial capitalists preferred to exercise indirect economic power rather than direct social control over towns and property. Detroit, for example, was not a traditional company town per se, but the economy was so dependent upon auto manufacturing that, for all intents and purposes, Ford and General Motors controlled it. The same could be said of the steel industry in Gary, Indiana, and Birmingham, Alabama; the rubber-making industry of Akron, Ohio; machine tool production in Springfield, Massachusetts; and meatpacking in Kansas City, Missouri, and Des Moines, Iowa. The twentieth century even retained old-style paternalist company towns, such as the chocolate domain of Milton S. Hershey, who until the 1950s owned most of the housing stock, charitable organizations, and cultural institutions of Hershey, Pennsylvania.

In the later twentieth century, though, the trend was for towns and cities to diversify their economies. This does not mean, however, that the company town concept disappeared. Ironically, trends such as **deindustrialization** and **globalism** actually revitalized it. Those municipalities that did not diversify became even more dependent upon single employers and often granted tax abatements, funded infrastructure improvements, and offered various economic enticements aimed at preventing corporations from closing or relocating. Even more ominously, communities often ended up competing against each other in bids to lure industries seeking cost containment. (This phenomenon was not new; many New England towns had seen textile mills flee to the low-wage, non-union South before World War II.)

In terms of social class, company towns past and present have had profound implications for those on the lower end of the **socioeconomic status** scale. By exercising economic leverage, powerful business elites tend to exercise undue social and political **power**. Labor unions, for example, find it quite difficult to organize in de facto company towns; corporate critics experience obstacles in publicizing their grievances, and oppositional cultures of all sorts struggle against prevailing norms that are often stamped with the values of corporate leadership. Even town spending tends to tilt toward the interests of the upper **middle class**. This is true even in towns dominated by universities and colleges, which tend to be more liberal politically. That said, many academic enclaves operate as intellectual company towns where local budgets and referenda often disproportionately cater to the middle class.

There are many examples of company town influence in contemporary society. Boeing Corporation and Microsoft exercise tremendous influence in the greater Seattle area, as does the U.S. Marine Corps near Parris Island, South Carolina. Much of central Florida is either owned or controlled by the Walt Disney Company, and many communities in the Northwest continue to bow to timber interests.

Suggested Reading

Stanley Buder, *Pullman: An Experiment in Industrial Order and Community Planning*, 1967; Linda Carlson, *Company Towns of the Pacific Northwest*, 2004; Margaret Crawford, *Building the Workingman's Paradise: The Design of American Company Towns*, 1995.

COMPARABLE WORTH

PAT REEVE

Comparable worth is the concept that workers are entitled to equal pay for work of comparable value. In 2006 members of the nonpartisan National Council of Women's Organizations (NCWO) endorsed policies aimed at increasing women's economic security. Among these was comparable worth, a notion closely related to **equity pay**. Central to both is the idea that gender and racial bias have contributed to the systematic undervaluing and **segregation** of work performed by women and people of color.

NCWO and other women's organizations contend that the Equal Pay Act of 1963 does not protect workers in gender and racially segregated occupations. For this reason, comparable worth supporters call for legislative and contractual remedies that institute wage parity across occupations and labor markets.

Current demands for pay equity build on a century of campaigning for equal pay for equal work. Over time **wages** have been a lightning rod for what historian Alice Kessler-Harris calls "a contest over visions of fairness and justice." Classical economic liberals explain wage setting as a neutral function of supply and demand. Their critics, notably those in the **labor movement**, argue that wage determination reflects prevailing gender and racial biases. At stake in these debates is a worker's right to self-sufficiency.

In 1963 civil rights activists and feminists successfully campaigned for the Equal Pay Act, which amended the Fair Labor Standards Act (1938), and Title VII of the 1964 Civil Rights Act. Thereafter it was illegal to pay lower wages to female rather than male employees for "equal work" or jobs. The judiciary extended protection to greater numbers of female workers in *Schultz v. Wheaton Glass Co.* (1970), U.S. Court of Appeals for the Third Circuit, and *Corning Glass Works v. Brennan* (1974), U.S. Supreme Court.

Still, women earn substantially less than male workers. In 2002 women earned 77 cents for every dollar earned by a man. In April 2004 the Institute for Women's Policy Research (IWPR) reported the earnings of white men and women of different races, concluding that the highest-paid women earned 25 percent less than white men in comparable positions.

Beginning with the 1945 federal Women's Bureau, comparable worth supporters have advocated for data collection to document the causes and effects of job segregation. Recommended are comparative appraisals of job content, qualifications, and working conditions across occupations.

In 1974 Governor Daniel Evans (R) of Washington ordered the nation's first pay equity wage study in response to pressure by the Washington Federation of State Employees (WFSE), American Federation of State, County, and Municipal Employees, Council 28. The ensuing study of 121 job classifications revealed that women in state service earned 20 percent less than male public employees in comparable jobs.

Lawmakers failed to act on pay inequalities documented by the state-commissioned study, causing the WFSE to file suit in U.S. District Court in 1982. In 1983 U.S. District Judge Jack E. Tanner found for WFSE. Plaintiff Helen Castrilli recollected her reaction: "I thought, Oh my God. This is big. This is going to impact hundreds of thousands of people." The state appealed the decision and won. Nonetheless, the union maintained public pressure for a remedy. In 1985 Washington settled with the union and approved $101 million in pay increases for female employees.

Litigation for comparable worth, previously unsuccessful, now promises to narrow the wage gap between men and women. In June 2004 a U.S. district judge in northern California allowed the class action suit *Dukes, et al. v. Wal-Mart Stores, Inc.* to go forth. Plaintiffs, 1.6 million past and present female employees, allege that **Wal-Mart** systematically pays women less than men in comparable positions. *Dukes* is the largest sex discrimination case ever brought against a private employer, and Wal-Mart is the world's largest private employer. The retail giant has appealed the decision.

The climate for Congressional action on pay equity has also improved since 2000. That year the Senate Committee on Health, Education, Labor, and Pensions heard testimony on gender-based wage discrimination. In succeeding sessions, sponsors of the Fair Pay Act have introduced a bill to mandate "equal pay for equivalent jobs." In 2005 Tom Harkin (D, IA) introduced that year's bill, asserting, "In nearly 10 million American households, the mother is the only breadwinner. These families struggle to pay the rent or make mortgage payments, buy the groceries, cover the medical bills and save for a child's education." Echoing earlier generations of advocates for pay equity, Harkin concluded, "We simply must do something about the longtime pattern of wage discrimination. We can start closing the pay gap right now by simply paying women what they're worth."

Suggested Reading

Linda M. Blum, *Between Labor and Feminism: The Significance of the Comparable Worth Movement*, 1991; Sarah M. Evans and Barbara J. Nelson, *Wage Justice: Comparable Worth and the Paradox of Technocratic Reform*, 1989; Margaret Hallock, "Pay Equity: Did It Work?" in *Squaring Up: Policy Strategies to Raise Women's Incomes in the United States*, ed. Mary C. King, 2001; Alice Kessler-Harris, *A Woman's Wage: Historical Meanings and Social Consequences*, 1990.

COMPETITIVENESS

ROBERT E. WEIR

Competition is a central tenet of **capitalism**. Proponents from Adam Smith on have argued that competition is the best way to mediate supply and demand. In theory, competition produces efficiency and economic growth. Consumers can expect to benefit from this, with competitors providing goods and services either at lower prices or with higher quality in order to keep up with their rivals. More recently competitiveness has become a shorthand way to express the economic pressures of **globalization** as they impact American business interests.

There can be little doubt that the United States no longer dominates world economic markets to the degree that it did immediately following World War II. It now faces global competition, not just from Europe and Japan, but also from low-wage competitors in developing nations in Southeast Asia, the Indian subcontinent, and Latin America. Often lost in the discussion of making American business more competitive is the domestic impact of such policies. Most American politicians, economists, and business lobbyists favor **free trade** policies that treat much of the planet as a single market for the movement of goods, services, and labor. Free trade capitalist enterprises can become more competitive through innovation or improved efficiency, but one of the primary ways is to reduce labor costs. Such reductions have profound implications for the American class system.

One way that American business cuts labor costs is by relocating operations to low-wage areas, whether they are non-unionized sections of the United States or abroad. Still another way is to wrest concessions from the workforce. This is frequently done when companies face bankruptcy; Chrysler Corporation got $673 million in employee wage cuts, pension reductions, and fringe benefit givebacks in 1979. Similarly United Airlines demanded more than $5 billion in concessions from its employees under a 2002 reorganization plan.

Since the 1980s, however, even profitable businesses have insisted upon wage, pension, and benefits concessions from employees, often in the name of global competitiveness. In numerous cases employers simply closed U.S. plants and located outside U.S. borders in order to cut labor costs. Critics have charged, with considerable merit, that many of these moves use the rubric of being more competitive to disguise the true motive of greater profit taking for stockholders and other investors. The impact of this on the working class is profound. Studies of the impact of the North American Free Trade Act (NAFTA), enacted in 1994, show that more than 200,000 American jobs were lost in the first five years of its passage, 70 percent of which were formerly high-paying manufacturing jobs. NAFTA has also had a negative effect on environmental standards and on U.S. trade deficits.

Competitiveness has, to date, served to widen the **income and wealth** gap in America. When adjusted for inflation, the average hourly wage has declined steadily since 1975. By 1995 the average hourly wage had declined to just $4 of real buying power, down from more than $13 just twenty years earlier. The gap is even more acute for workers under the age of twenty-four. Ironically, the productivity of American workers has soared since 1975. Nonetheless, wages fell in real terms from 1970 to 1990, and they rose less than 0.05 percent in the next decade. The statistics become even more alarming when one factors in lost benefits. In 2005 Delphi Corporation put forth a plan that would slash wages and benefits by two-thirds for its employees. Labor unions also charge that employers further undercut wages by hiring illegal immigrants; one 2004 study reveals that as many as 20 percent of all construction jobs now go to illegal aliens being paid in cash off the books.

Competitiveness is an attractive buzz phrase, but whether the **American dream** can be realized by workers receiving drastically reduced compensation is, at best, problematic. Early signs are not encouraging; nearly all studies reveal a widening gap between rich and poor.

Suggested Reading

Thomas Friedman, *The World Is Flat: A Brief History of the Twenty-First Century*, 2005; Kent Hughes, *Building the Next American Century: The Past and Future of American Economic Competitiveness*, 2005; Barry Lynn, *End of the Line: The Rise and Coming Fall of the Global Corporation*, 2005.

CONFLICT THEORY

ROBERT E. WEIR

Conflict theory is a major school of social science analysis that posits the inevitability of fundamental clashes of economic interest in most societies, especially those in which **capitalism** is the dominant exchange mode. Conflict theory derives largely from a **Marxist** critique of **power**, though not all modern conflict theorists are Marxists. Lewis Coser is one example of a non-Marxian conflict theorist. During the 1960s and 1970s, Coser argued that conflict—both among and within groups—is often an important factor in shaping in-group identity. Likewise it can serve to reinforce groups and institutions by revitalizing them and preventing social calcification. Another non-Marxist conflict theorist is **Ralf Dahrendorf**.

Most conflict theorists, however, see much of society as marked by competing interests rooted in social, political, racial, gender, and economic inequality. Marx and others argued that **class struggle** was inevitable, though they held out hope that positive social change would come from it. Marx famously argued that class conflict would ultimately yield a one-class society in which future clashes would vanish along with private property, private wealth, and inequality. **C. Wright Mills** later argued that the dominance of the **power elite** muted the voices of the masses in decision making. Although he too believed that class conflict was probable, Mills also imagined a pessimistic premise in which class issues would be subsumed in geopolitical conflicts whereby militarization led to World War III.

The predictions of such theorists as Marx and Mills notwithstanding, conflict theory's greatest contribution to date has come from its analysis of power and clashing interests. Some academic fields—labor history, black studies, and feminist studies, for instance—are dominated by conflict theorists. In a vaguely Darwinian way, most conflict theorists see society as a struggle to control finite and scarce resources. In such a scenario, powerful interests can become more so only by claiming resources from the less powerful. Hence, competition, conflict, and change are inexorably linked. Clashes can occur along any of society's social divisions, as well as between ideological systems and nation-states, but conflict theory is most often employed by scholars to critique social class.

Conflict theorists insist that social stratification is inherently dysfunctional and destabilizing. It limits opportunities for those with less social power, degrades the **life chances** of the non-wealthy, and supports the social status quo, even when it is based on nonrational, nonscientific, and socially inefficient criteria such as family origin, **ethnicity**, **race**, **gender**, and class. Ultimately it fosters discontent, resentment, and social upheaval. Dahrendorf went so far as to suggest that conflict within stratified societies was inherent in their design. Marx noted that capitalism was particularly vulnerable to conflict because it rested on a set of social problems that were not in the best interests of capitalists to resolve. Low wages, for instance, can be addressed only by reducing profits to investors. Likewise, a permanent and replenishable reserve of unemployed workers was necessary for capitalist enterprises to expand; otherwise businesses would have to compete with each other to secure workforces.

Conflict theorists have also been at the fore of studies on the causation of **poverty**. In sharp contrast to conservative critiques that shift much of the explanation onto individuals, conflict theorists point to the built-in structural impediments that prevent poor people from enacting the **self-reliance** nostrums favored by conservatives. In contemporary society, for example, conflict theorists point to systematic campaigns to cut labor costs, cripple the **labor movement**, slash social services for the poor, prevent the equalization of educational spending, and work on other factors whose net effect is to deny opportunity to those most in need.

Suggested Reading

Joseph Healey, *Race, Ethnicity, Gender, and Class: The Sociology of Group Conflict and Change*, 2005; Harold Kerbo, *Social Stratification and Inequality: Class Conflict in Historical and Comparative Perspective*, 2005; Rhonda Levine, ed., *Social Class and Stratification: Classic Statements and Theoretical Debates*, 1998.

CONGRESS OF INDUSTRIAL ORGANIZATIONS (CIO)

SARAH CROSSLEY

Originally the Committee for Industrial Organization, the CIO was founded within the **American Federation of Labor** (AFL) in 1935 by **John L. Lewis** of the United Mine Workers and several other union leaders. After 1937, when it was expelled, the CIO was an independent labor federation and a rival to the AFL. It remained so until 1955, when the two groups reunited.

Its purpose was to organize the unskilled workers on an industrial basis instead of having them placed into various craft unions. Founders of the CIO felt that, with the onset of industrialization and mass production, most workers were part of integrated production processes, so that all workers within a given sector should be organized regardless of their skill level. Historians note that grassroots uprisings among unorganized industrial laborers had already shown their mettle and potential strength by pressuring politicians to enact significant legislative gains such as the **Wagner Act**.

Contrary to the goals of the fledgling CIO, the AFL was content to organize skilled tradesmen within their particular trade. They believed that skilled workers could maintain more control over a given industry through craft unions because their particular skills gave them leverage over production. AFL leaders argued that bargaining power would be diminished if craft unions organized across an industry rather than by specific skills. Many also argued that unskilled pools of labor dominated by poor **immigrants** were difficult, if not impossible, to organize given language and culture barriers. One AFL leader contemptuously referred to such workers as "the garbage of the **labor movement**."

Lewis and other industrial union advocates saw more opportunities than obstacles. The CIO in 1935 began mobilizing exactly those workers deemed unorganizable. Initially, it consisted of eight unions with about a million members. Within two years, it nearly quadrupled its membership, with thirty-two unions, more than 6000 locals, and about 3.7 million members. The CIO's initial successes occurred in 1937. A sit-down strike by the United Auto Workers (UAW) against General Motors (GM) exhibited the power of grassroots activism on the shop floor. In addition to workers taking over GM plants, a UAW women's auxiliary was formed, the **Socialist Party** formed the Women's Emergency Brigade, and even **Eleanor Roosevelt** made a monetary donation in support of the strike. The UAW's victory catapulted the CIO into the public consciousness, and its focus on workplace **democracy** and working-class solidarity was pivotal to its initial success. By the late 1930s the CIO had succeeded in unionizing numerous industries that hitherto had weak unions or none at all: automobiles, electronics, rubber, steel, and textiles, for example. It also enjoyed a reputation as being the most socially progressive mainstream federation since the **Knights of Labor** in the late nineteenth century.

The grassroots militancy of CIO unions existed in part because of the nature of their organizing. The AFL sought to turn highly skilled tradesmen into a part of the **middle class**. By virtue of their skills, the task was difficult but not impossible. By contrast, CIO industrial unions embraced working-class identity. The CIO wanted similar economic stability for unskilled workers but recognized that unity against big business was the only way to secure that goal. Hence, CIO unions tended to be more confrontational than AFL unions. CIO unions also had an open-door policy in regard to **race, gender**, nationality, and religious affiliation. Constitutions were adopted among affiliate unions forbidding any form of discrimination, exclusion, or segregation, and members were often required to take a pledge promising never to do so.

The culture of solidarity that spread through CIO unions was part and parcel of the leftist perspective that made up much of the CIO, including **communists**. Some scholars credit radical leaders with advancing **class consciousness** and class solidarity over racial, gendered, or political barriers. Their presence did, however, make the CIO vulnerable to Red-baiting. In May 1938 the U.S. House of Representatives established the Committee to Investigate Un-American Activities. John Frey, representing the AFL Executive Council, appeared before Congress and offered the names of hundreds of CIO leaders affiliated with the Communist Party.

Although the CIO's first head, John L. Lewis, had previously attacked communism, he welcomed Communist Party members into the CIO, as he understood how the Communist Party's emphasis on working-class solidarity often resonated among rank-and-file industrial workers. He also admired the skills of Communist Party organizers, which he hoped to use for his own purposes. Lewis resigned as CIO head in 1940, and his successor, Philip Murray, initially maintained friendly relations with communists. Over the next eight years, however, infighting and political divisions caused an irreparable rift between CIO leaders and the Communist Party. The 1947 Taft-Hartley Act forbade communists from holding union leadership positions, and it was another factor in the CIO's decision to expel numerous unions and nearly a million workers from the federation in 1948.

By the 1940s, cracks also appeared in the CIO's progressive mission. Not all CIO unionists agreed on how to create worker solidarity or, more importantly, which workers belonged in the union. For instance, some United Auto Workers locals called spontaneous "wildcat" strikes to protest the promotion of African American workers from service jobs to production jobs. The CIO took limited actions against racism, but failed to deal sufficiently with high levels of racism within the rank and file. Sexual discrimination also often took a backseat to other issues. Prior to World War II, even unions whose membership was predominately female—such as the International Ladies' Garment Workers' Union—had no female leaders. Even after the war, when women entered the industrial workforce in droves, the situation was slow to change.

By the late 1940s the CIO was on the defensive. New antilabor bills robbed the CIO of cherished weapons such as the sit-down strike and led to an overall drop in the militant spirit that had led to its rapid rise. This, plus leadership's squabbles and a purge of communist unions, greatly reduced the CIO's strength. When the CIO and the AFL finally agreed to merge in 1955, CIO president **Walter Reuther** made a number of demands for racial and gender equity that reflected the spirit of the early CIO, and he extracted promises to promote industrial unionism. Unfortunately, his weak bargaining position in relation to the stronger AFL meant that the new organization failed to implement many of these concessions.

Despite the CIO's official demise as a federation separate from the AFL, its early spirit remains an inspiration to current labor activists. Grassroots organizing campaigns in service industries often evoke the CIO, including movements such as the Service Employees International Union's Justice for Janitors campaign, or Domestic Workers United (not affiliated with the AFL–CIO). Additionally, in the summer of 2005 several unions bolted from the AFL–CIO to form the Change to Win Coalition, the latter likening itself to the renegade CIO and making analogies between 1930s industrial workers and twenty-first-century service industry workers.

Suggested Reading

Harvey Levenstein, *Communism, Anticommunism, and the CIO*, 1981; Nelson Lichtenstein, *Labor's War at Home: The CIO in World War II*, 2003; Robert Zieger, *The CIO, 1935–1955*, 1995.

CONSPICUOUS CONSUMPTION

VICKY HILL

Coined by the economist and social critic **Thorstein Veblen** in his 1899 classic, *The Theory of the Leisure Class*, the term *conspicuous consumption* refers to the acquisition and display of expensive luxury items for the purpose of demonstrating one's social status and wealth.

Veblen argued that American society was ruled by a "leisure class," a wealthy elite that maintained its position and **status** through demonstrations of conspicuous leisure and conspicuous consumption, since its members enjoyed the privilege of not having to work for a living. His observations of the **Gilded Age** elite were among the first to articulate the now-commonsensical connection between consumption and groups' attempts to solidify and demonstrate their place in the social hierarchy. At the time Veblen wrote, however, this idea was a departure from mainstream economic thought, which insisted that human economic activity was governed by a rational individual desire to accumulate wealth for utilitarian purposes. Veblen was the first analyst to suggest that impressing other people was an important economic motivation for many individuals. He was also the first to articulate the importance of the cultural meanings attributed to goods, clearly linking consumption and class for the cultural theorists who followed.

Taking an anthropological perspective on economics, Veblen pointed out that in early societies, high status was awarded to excellent hunters or warriors. These talented individuals could also command more physical resources than other members of the society—the hunters could catch more food, for example. But the relatively greater wealth of the individual was a result of his status, not the cause of it. However, over time, wealth itself came to be viewed as a reason to hold its owner in high esteem. Once that shift occurred, those who had wealth wanted to be sure that others knew about it. They learned to display visible symbols of their wealth, not only to illustrate their own standing, but to aggressively compare that standing with others'. This competitive aspect of conspicuous consumption was key for Veblen; he insisted that the main motive for consuming conspicuously was to outdo others and to widen the status distance between oneself and one's rivals. Conspicuous consumption also had to be wasteful; if it merely served a utilitarian function, it couldn't display and solidify its user's status.

As culture developed, elite individuals could no longer consume enough by themselves to display their wealth properly. They resorted to giving lavish feasts and gifts and maintaining servants, wives, and children to consume vicariously for them. Veblen was the first to describe how the ruling class used women to display their husbands' status via idleness, expensive leisure activities, and the ostentatious display of expensive clothing, decoration, and housing.

Modern theorists argue that conspicuous consumption is no longer the sole province of the leisured elite; in fact, some scholars claim that a form of conspicuous consumption—or displaying one's financial resources, taste, and identity through commodities—is a primary social function in modern mass consumer culture.

Suggested Reading

Stephen Edgell, *Veblen in Perspective: His Life and Thought*, 2001; Roger Mason, *The Economics of Conspicuous Consumption: Theory and Thought Since 1700*, 1998; Thorstein Veblen, *The Theory of the Leisure Class*, 1899.

CONSUMER PRICE INDEX

See Poverty Calculations

CONSUMERISM

ROBERT E. WEIR

Consumerism is the practice of accumulating/using goods and services that are generally purchased rather than produced by individuals. It can be used generally to refer simply to the purchasing patterns of Americans, but is more commonly referenced as a debatable economic pattern that defenders claim celebrates the prosperity and choices created by American **capitalism**, and which critics argue induces an unhealthy materialism that is harmful to individual livelihoods, community welfare, and social stability.

Although consumerism is not necessarily synonymous with capitalism, within the United States the two have developed in tandem. Prior to the **Industrial Revolution** most American families produced most of what they consumed, bartered for goods and services they did not produce, or engaged in highly selective and infrequent monetary transactions to secure necessities. The articulation of regional and national markets occasioned by the development of the **factory system** in the early nineteenth century shifted economic transactions to an emphasis on money that hastened the separation of production and consumption, led to the rise of the **wage** system, and changed the way Americans defined necessity and desire. Some, including **labor movement** activists and **Marxists**, viewed these changes with alarm. Labor reformers feared that, if the wage system became permanent, it would undermine **self-reliance** and foster dependency in ways that **agrarianism** and proprietorship did not, while Karl Marx and others argued that a consumer society bred **alienation** by cheapening the value of labor. Marx predicted that the marketplace rather than work would set the value of goods and services. Marx and many neo-Marxists such as **Louis Althusser**, Theodor Adorno, and Herbert Marcuse also argued that consumerism leads to commodity "fetishization" in which objects assume an artificial value that creates its own (often irrational) desire.

Gilded Age society saw the creation of new objects and fabulous fortunes, but also widening gaps between rich and poor. As wealth became increasingly measured in material terms rather than older measures such as land and social deference, critics such as **Thorstein Veblen** argued that **conspicuous consumption** was supplanting things of true value. Veblen's *The Theory of the Leisure Class* (1899) remains a relevant work for those studying contemporary consumerism. Although consumerism has waxed and waned according to economic cycles, by the early twentieth century mass production of goods, efficiency, market- and money-based economic exchange, and created desires came to define American economic activity. **Advertisers** and merchants linked their wares to comfort, leisure, and novelty. The constant flow of new goods, new models, and changing trends dovetailed nicely with the ideology of **individualism**; consumers were encouraged to seek self-expression through their purchases.

Historian Gary Cross notes that products such as the assembly-line–manufactured Model-T Ford and new venues such as **department stores**, amusement parks, and movie theaters strengthened consumerism to the degree that it could withstand challenges such as the **Great Depression**. The post–World War II economic boom democratized consumption by making objects such as television, electronics, and household appliances affordable to the **masses**. Americans were steadily told that the United States had become a **middle-class** society, with consumption standing as a marker of said **status**. In fact, social critic Dwight Macdonald argued that consumerism converted Americans into passive and uneducated shoppers who accepted the enticements of advertisers, retailers, and marketers without reflection. American consumer patterns were also exported. As Victoria De Grazia shows, by the 1950s much of Europe and parts of Asia had come to embrace American-style market consumerism.

The triumph of consumer ideals meant that even the anti-consumerist ideologies found among the **New Left**, the counterculture, and ecology groups sometimes had the ironic effect of reinforcing materialism. Capitalists often view **class subcultures** as good business, as they encourage new styles that can be packaged and marketed, just as environmental awareness spawns the production of T-shirts, bumper stickers, and other salable movement paraphernalia. By the 1980s groups such as **Yuppies**, though a much-exaggerated social phenomenon, openly celebrated shopping and spending.

Consumerism has not gone unchallenged, and economic factors perhaps threaten to erode it. As observers such as Cross, **Ralph Nader**, and **Juliet Schor** have argued, recent patterns of American consumerism differ from those of the past in that the reference group for consumers has changed. Americans no longer compete with their economic peers or even aspire to achieve a hypothetical middle-class standard; rather they are encouraged to compare themselves to the affluent and spend their way to **prestige**. Although these critics may err in assuming this is a new development—working-class women of the nineteenth century often copied the fashions of the middle class, for example—they do correctly point out that modern consumerism often rests upon accumulating debt. More than half of Americans feel they are too deeply in debt, and economists generally agree that family debt is too high and savings rates too low to sustain current consumer patterns.

There is also evidence that many Americans are uncomfortable with consumerism as currently constituted. A 2004 poll of Americans older than twenty-four conducted by the Center for a New American Dream confirms this: 88 percent of Americans feel that society has become too materialistic and 95 percent feel that youths have been bombarded with advertising that has made them "too focused" on consumerism. The poll also surprisingly revealed that 91 percent think American **lifestyle**s are wasteful, that 83 percent think we consume too many resources, and that 57 percent feel that greedy consumerism harms U.S. foreign relations. Such opinions do not necessarily translate into behavioral changes, but several trends suggest that there may be changes on the horizon. Sixty-four percent of those polled believe that it is harder to obtain the **American dream** now than ten years ago, and 48 percent have made lifestyle changes through which they have opted to work less, earn less, and buy fewer things in order to create more leisure and family time.

Academics such as Craig Thompson and James Twitchell counter that such data are alarmist and that consumerism is a positive thing that authenticates American prosperity and provides outlets for expressiveness. They even suggest that consumerism critics are latter-day **Puritans** trying to impose their values onto the American mainstream. Whether American consumer capitalism can continue to be pervasive and malleable is an open question that engenders intense debate.

Suggested Reading

Gary Cross, *An All-Consuming Century: Why Commercialism Won in Modern America*, 2000; Victoria De Grazia, *Irresistible Empire: America's Advance through*

Twentieth-Century Europe, 2005; Sarah Roberts, "Survey Confirms That Americans Overworked, Overspent and Rethinking the American Dream" (http://www.newdream.org/newsletter/survey.php); Juliet Schor, *Do Americans Shop Too Much?* 2000.

Continuous/Discontinuous Views of Class

Robert E. Weir

Class may be viewed as being continuous or discontinuous. In brief, those who hold that social class ranks are continuous argue that class can be ranked from low to high on a spectrum. As such, there are various ranks and sub-ranks, all of which exist within a coherent social system. By contrast, supporters of discontinuous rankings see sharp divisions between classes, the differences being so magnified as to enhance the possibility of **class struggle**.

Functionalist sociologists are often among those who favor continuous class ranking, and this continuity undergirds theories such as the **Davis-Moore thesis**. Class is viewed as analogous to a scale whose boundaries are fuzzy and indistinct because the individual classes naturally blend into one another. What, for example, distinguishes the upper **lower class** from the lower **middle class**? Ultimately such delineations rest on **subjective methods** that are imprecise, but nonetheless real. Subjectivity is also socially useful in that it promotes consensus and social stability.

Those functionalists who argue for continuous class rankings do not deny that social classes exist; rather they see a very broad social distribution of **income**, **status**, and wealth that precludes creating hard, fast, and **objective methods** of measuring class. Because criteria for establishing class are so murky, the development of **class consciousness** in a **Marxist** sense is improbable. Some advocates of the continuous perspective go so far as to suggest that many Americans cannot conceive of, let alone perceive, the reality of social class.

Those holding discontinuous views of class rankings see the continuous position as a convenient myth that attempts to hide the very real, objective realities of social class in America. They see opposition and breaks, not consensus and flow. In their view the social system has very sharp divisions of income, status, **prestige**, and wealth, all of which can be measured. Moreover, these divisions are so dramatic as to cast doubt on the variegated class continuum postulated by those holding a continuous view of class. Karl Marx felt that society consisted primarily of the **bourgeoisie** and the **proletariat**, and that the division and inequalities that existed between them rendered class conflict inevitable.

Many modern scholars see Marx's dichotomous view of class as too sharply drawn, but **conflict theorists** nonetheless argue that very real and very obvious class differences exist. Far from building consensus, class stratification is dysfunctional, unjust, and unstable. Rather than focus on subjective (some would say delusional) constructions of class, scholars of the discontinuous school measure **life chances** and other objective factors.

Suggested Reading

John Creswell, *Research Design: Qualitative, Quantitative, and Mixed Methods Approaches*, 2002; David Rose and David Pevalin, *Researcher's Guide to the National Statistics Socio-Economic Classification*, 2003; Alex Thio, *Sociology: A Brief Introduction*, 2000.

CONTRADICTORY CLASS LOCATION

VICKY HILL

Sociologist Erik Olin Wright developed the concept of *contradictory class location* to describe, within a generally **Marxist** framework, the class position of some contemporary members of the **middle class**.

Karl Marx's foundational analysis of class was based on his perception that two main classes existed, the **bourgeoisie** and the **proletariat**, and that the two were engaged in an epic struggle because the bourgeoisie necessarily exploited the proletariat to maintain their own class position. However, Marx wrote in the late nineteenth century, before the dramatic expansion of the middle class. Further, he had assumed that as capitalism progressed, the middling classes that had existed would eventually diminish as a few members ascended into the bourgeoisie and the rest were forced into the proletariat. Subsequent scholars found it difficult to incorporate the increasingly widespread and influential middle class into Marx's broader framework.

In response to this theoretical problem, a handful of theorists, most notably Wright, recognized in the late 1970s and early 1980s that many people in the wage-earning middle classes experience characteristics of both traditional class positions. For example, many middle-class workers have supervisory jobs and thus exploit the workers who report to them, but they are also exploited by their own supervisors. Similarly, many executives who do not directly supervise employees do have control over a company's money or its physical means of production, which would indicate a bourgeois position, but they are still subject to the control of their own supervisors, the possibility of being fired, and exclusion from ownership of capital assets. Wright described this situation as a "contradictory class location" because the two traditional classes have inherently contradictory class interests and to embody them both is necessarily to have contradictory class interests within oneself. Though Wright has since moved away from the idea that these intermediate class locations must, in every case, have contradictory interests, the concept of contradictory class position remains a useful one for class theorists in describing some middle-class situations.

Suggested Reading

Erik Olin Wright, *Class Boundaries and Contradictory Class Location*, 1978; Wright, *Classes*, 1985; Wright, *Class Counts: Comparative Studies in Class Analysis*, 1997.

CORPORATE CLASS

ROBERT E. WEIR

The term *corporate class* refers to individuals in government and business whose high rank and far-reaching influence gives them extraordinary social, economic, and political **power**. Some scholars postulate that this group has largely supplanted the **upper class** in influence in contemporary America; others argue it *is* the modern upper class; and some doubt its very existence. If there is a corporate class, many traditional class definitions and stratification theories are outmoded.

Debates over the influence of financiers and manufacturers have circulated since the implications of the **Industrial Revolution** became apparent during the **Gilded Age**. To some degree, however, the rising industrial elite often found itself at odds with the top stratum of the upper class, which viewed this group as gauche parvenus and sought to block their social and political ambitions. Under advanced **capitalism**, however, the economic ground shifted from under the property-endowed upper classes by making money-based **income and wealth** more important than property ownership. The **Great Depression** may have forestalled the rise of the corporate class, but by the 1950s many social commentators began to argue that this group was in ascendancy and the upper class in decline. **C. Wright Mills** presaged contemporary thinking in his **power elite** studies, and in 1961 President Dwight Eisenhower famously warned of an emergent **military-industrial complex** whose sway over economic and political decision making was ominous.

The corporate class is now said to consist of a select group of **CEOs**, presidents, vice-presidents, and board members from powerful corporations. It may also include politicians with close ties to those corporations. Many members of the administration of George W. **Bush**, for example, have had extensive ties with Halliburton, a Texas-based oil and chemical company that also routinely wins large government contracts. Members of the corporate class tend to move capital, advance government policy, and command bureaucracies rather than hold extensive amounts of property as the traditional upper class does. This has implications for **Marxist** views of class, which usually link class to ownership of the **means of production**: the corporate class controls rather than owns the means of production.

The corporate class is closely linked to what is often called "economies of scale": that is, its members come from very large (often international) corporations; hold vast amounts of stock, securities, and other investments; and are often linked through **social networks** and various interlocking boards, charity organizations, fraternal organizations, and decision-making bodies. Their overall clout gives them great leverage over political fundraising; hence the corporate class exercises political influence disproportionate to its size.

It is clear that there is tremendous overlap among top firms. A handful of banks such as BankAmerica, Citibank, and Chase Manhattan, for example, are also major stockholders of global corporations and seat their representatives on the boards of those enterprises. What is less clear is what this economic reality means in social terms. **Conflict theorists** and **critical elite theorists** often view the corporate class as a cabal whose power imperils **democracy**, perpetuates the exploitation of the working **masses**, and manipulates society to serve its own interests. By contrast,

functional elite theorists see corporate elites as a necessary force to negotiate the complex global economy. They see the corporate class as efficient, technically proficient guardians of the public interest.

Still others altogether discredit the existence of a corporate class. Pluralist social theorists argue that modern society is too complex, that interests (including ideology) are widely divergent, and that countervailing groups and structures (such as laws and regulations) blunt the potential of a corporate class. Still others argue that common economic interests are not enough upon which to base social class. This group finds no evidence of **class consciousness**, which is seen as crucial to class formation. These critiques are minority views in the academic community, the bulk of which assumes the existence of a corporate class, though it hotly debates the importance, need for, and influence of it.

Suggested Reading
Bennett Harrison and Barry Bluestone, *The Great U-Turn: Corporate Restructuring and the Polarizing of America*, 1988; Harold Kerbo, *Social Stratification and Inequality: Class Conflict in Historical and Comparative Perspective*, 2004; Michael Useem, *The Inner Circle: Large Corporations and the Rise of Business Political Activity in the U.S. and U.K.*, 1984.

CORPORATE WELFARE

FRANK A. SALAMONE

Corporate welfare is a term applied to government programs and policies that benefit business and industries. There are two major types of government programs that benefit this sector: subsidies and tax breaks. Those in favor of these programs argue that they aid American business in gaining a competitive edge. However, many others argue that these aids are nothing more than handouts to corporations with great political influence. Moreover, they argue, these handouts stifle rather than increase competition.

Newly enacted corporate benefits cost taxpayers an additional $570 billion over a five-year span. Much of this money comes from **middle-class** and **working-class** wage earners, who can least afford subsidizing wealthy corporations. The growing government deficit is also fueled by these subsidies. Often subsidies go to wealthy, established corporations such as oil companies. The Strategic Petroleum Reserve, for example, supposedly guards against depleting supplies during a war. This is no longer the case, yet the subsidies continue, and they serve to raise the cost of oil by creating an artificial demand for the product.

There are many similar examples of corporate welfare unnecessarily funding programs that no longer need them. Thus, although the family farmer has been largely supplanted by **agribusiness**, the farm subsidy program continues, aiding the farm corporations that drove family farms from the landscape. The biggest example of government favoritism to private interests, however, is that to corporations exploiting natural resources.

What many term the "Granddaddy of All Giveaways" is that given to the mining industry. The 1872 Mining Act allows the mining industry to take and excavate hard-rock minerals on land belonging to the public. It does so at bargain-basement prices and without paying any royalties. Moreover, it purchases the land for between $2.50 and $5.00 per acre. Thus, Congress has given away billions of dollars in public lands and resources. The taxpayers, additionally, pay for the cleanup of the lands and the rivers, which industry leaves polluted.

Subsidies and tax breaks to corporations have many deleterious effects. Certainly, they decrease government revenues. They shift the tax burden to those who can least afford it while allowing the wealthiest corporations to avoid taxes. Additionally, programs to aid those most in need of help are often cut for lack of funds.

Stephen Moore and Dean Stansel have compiled a list of ten targets they would like to eliminate from the corporate welfare list. These targets include the 1872 Mining Act, the Forest Service's building of timber roads, the Clean Coal program, the National Ignition Facility, the GT-MHR Gas Reactor, the National Parks concession contracts, the I-69 highway extension plan, and the USDA Marketing Promotion program. Consumer advocate **Ralph Nader** is among the most vocal opponents to corporate welfare; Senator **Bernard Sanders** is another.

Corporate welfare hurts government, the consumer, and **capitalism** itself. It ties business and government too closely together, but tends to favor interests that in many ways are antithetical to the interests of the consumer. It also hinders free competition, favoring wealthy businesses, especially those involved in resource exploitation, over others. The majority of taxpayers are hurt for the benefit of a few. Members of the **lower class** and the **working poor** are especially impacted, as money spent on corporate welfare is unavailable for programs aiding the socially and financially disadvantaged.

Suggested Reading
Corporate Welfare Information Center (http://www.corporations.org/welfare/); Stephen Moore and Dean Stansel, "Ending Corporate Welfare As We Know It" (http://www.cato.org/pubs/pas/pa225.html); Ralph Nader, *Cutting Corporate Welfare*, 2000.

COUNTRY CLUBS

ADAM R. HORNBUCKLE

Country clubs are venues to recreate, play golf and tennis, swim, and socialize, especially for high-income Americans of the **upper** and **middle classes**. Originating in the late nineteenth century, the country club is essentially an imitation of the country estates of English aristocracy or moneyed gentry. In England the upper classes often lived in the country and belonged to urban social clubs, but in America the privileged classes tended to live in the cities and seek an approximation of the

English country manor in rural areas. One mark of social distinction was to approximate European aristocratic privileges by keeping servants and maintaining private preserves in which to indulge outdoor activities such as hunting, fishing, horseback riding, and other activities.

Established in 1882, the first country club in the United States was in Brookline, Massachusetts. The official history of the Brookline Country Club unabashedly states that the club was established to cultivate, promote, and preserve the exclusiveness of **Boston's Brahmin** elites. The Brookline group zealously guarded social borders and constructed a realm in which **social reproduction** of privilege was the order of the day. The Country Club became a venue in which **social networks**, including socially endogamous marriages, were arranged. With the Brookline Country Club as an example, the American country club stood in stark contrast to the English country estate as a buffer placed between the upper and middling classes. In comparing the English athletic club to the American country club, Englishman George Birmingham observed that the members of the English clubs became acquainted through their common pursuits, whereas those in American country clubs drew upon preexisting sociability to encourage mutual participation in sports. Citing New York's Tuxedo country club as an ideal, Birmingham noted that "it not only fosters, it regulates and governs the social life of the place."

During the nineteenth and twentieth centuries, country clubs spread throughout the nation as a result of the growing interest in golf. Joseph M. Fox, a successful Pennsylvania businessman, and John Reid, a Scottish immigrant and executive of a Yonkers, New York, iron works, introduced golf into the United States in 1887. Reid organized the first golf club in the nation, the St. Andrews Club, named after the famed Scottish golf course. The first professionally designed golf course came in 1891, at the Shinnecock Hills Golf Club in Southampton, New York, where many wealthy New Yorkers had summer homes. By the end of the century, golf had become the favorite pastime of the upper crust in New York, Boston, Philadelphia, and Chicago, and they built their own golf courses based on the Shinnecock Hills model. During the early twentieth century, golf had spread into the South, where the nation's elite built lavish golfing resorts for their winter pleasure. Throughout the twentieth century, golf became the favored sport of business and professional men, who stood a rung or two down from the wealthy elite on the nation's social ladder. Golf provided this social niche not only a symbol of conspicuous status, but also an escape from the confines of the urban office to the open countryside. For many businessmen, however, the golf course became an outdoor boardroom, where final touches could be made on business deals or the foundations laid for future deals.

The majority of contemporary country clubs center on golf, with once-central pursuits such as hunting, fishing, horsemanship, and swimming relegated to secondary roles. Nearly all country clubs charge membership fees, the cost of which mirrors the clientele to which they cater. Clubs designed for the **working class** are few, but some middle-class clubs charge day rates and greens fees for those using their facilities, thus democraticizing country clubs to some degree. For the most part, however, country clubs remain what they have always been: zones of social exclusivity.

Suggested Reading

George Birmingham, "The American at Home and in His Club," in *America in Perspective*, ed. Henry Steele Commager, 1947; Frederic Curtiss and John Heard, *The Country Club, 1882–1932*, 1932; Benjamin Rader, *American Sports: From the Age of Folk Games to the Age of Televised Sports*, 2004; Steven Riess, *City Games: The Evolution of American Urban Society and the Rise of Sports*, 1991.

COUNTRY MUSIC

MICHAEL T. BERTRAND

Commencing in the mid-1920s, country music has reflected the tensions related to the adaptation of tradition to modernity. Its underlying themes of individual alienation and vulnerability have possessed universal appeal, and have helped country music attain a large global audience. Indeed, by the turn of the twenty-first century, country music enjoyed unprecedented popularity and represented a multibillion dollar corporate enterprise recognized around the world.

Yet commercial country music has not always enjoyed widespread acclaim. For most of its history, a problematic pedigree circumscribed its allure. It did appeal to a Southern rural white **working class** lacking in political power, status, and material affluence. Like other aspects of Southern culture, country music allowed natives to create a space for themselves, a virtual autonomy that indulged self-expression, psychological release, creative sustenance, and personal satisfaction. Because country artists generally emerged from the audiences they entertained, their articulated hopes, fears, dreams, doubts, desires, and anxieties necessarily corresponded to those enjoyed and endured by the larger community. On the surface, country music conveyed an authenticity not usually associated with commercial culture.

The origins of country music can be indirectly traced to one of the founding fathers of American modernity and commercial culture: Henry Ford. Ford, who despised the modern sounds and rhythms of 1920s **jazz**, sought to counter the syncopated rage by popularizing old-time music. Ford dealerships across the country sponsored fiddling contests. Extremely popular with audiences composed of recent migrants from the South, these fiddling competitions soon found their way to radio. Hoping to translate rather random and informal affairs into a permanently profitable enterprise, radio executives created an efficient formula that endured for much of the twentieth century: rustic costumes and personas; sentimental and nostalgic song repertoires; homespun group names such as the "Gully Jumpers," "Skillet Lickers," "Fruit Jar Drinkers," and "Possum Hunters"; and, most important, the sense that country performances were unstructured and spontaneous.

The appeal of the "hillbilly formula" diminished during the **Great Depression**. Its affected images of **poverty**, personified by performers wearing overalls and other rural regalia, often reminded audiences of conditions they were anxious to forget. Soon wool hats, galluses, and dobro guitars gave way to Stetsons, chaps, and singing cowboys. The West, with its wide-open spaces and romanticized past, provided a complementary motif that country music promoters, performers, and audiences were very willing to adopt. No doubt driven by commercial considerations, the "Country and Western" character of country music nevertheless suited artists and listeners searching for signs of their own material and social progress. While the "formula" may often have been concocted, the symbols it referenced certainly seemed familiar to large numbers of people.

Saturday night radio barn dance programs—such as the *WLS National Barn Dance*, *The Grand Ole Opry*, and *WSB Barn Dance*—contributed greatly to the informality and down-home familiarity associated with country music. They also launched the stars who dominated the field prior to World War II, including Bradley Kincaid, Uncle Dave Macon, DeFord Bailey, the Delmore Brothers, Roy Acuff, and Red Foley. The post–World War II era witnessed the birth of other significant wireless barn dance programs, including the *Louisiana Hayride*, the *Big D Jamboree*, and the *Ozark Jubilee*.

No single phenomenon helped popularize country music more than World War II, as migratory patterns allowed the displaced of Dixie to disseminate their music to a wider audience. Transferred Southern-born soldiers brought their musical tastes with them, and country music package tours performed for military units on a regular basis. The jukebox, a mechanical record-playing machine found in many establishments catering to the working class, also popularized the music beyond its original borders. War-related industries in the South likewise exposed new listeners to the sounds of country music. Anecdote holds that Japanese attacks on American troops in the Pacific were accompanied by shouts of "To Hell with Roy Acuff!"—a testament to the unexpected ubiquity of country music.

Country music continued to gain popularity after World War II, although songs rather than artists generally crossed into the popular music mainstream. Indeed, pop stars regularly mined the repertoires of "hillbilly" vocalists for hit records. The song-writing talents of Hank Williams, for instance, brought him national fame, yet as a performer, his provincial singing style and mannerisms did not resonate far beyond regional working-class audiences. The same could be said for most of the artists who attained prominence during this period, including Ernest Tubb, Lefty Frizzell, Hank Snow, and Webb Pierce.

The next generation of performers, led by Merle Haggard, Buck Owens, Conway Twitty, George Jones, Charley Pride, and Willie Nelson, arguably enjoyed country music's golden age. The success of episodic rural-based television shows such as *The Beverly Hillbillies* contributed to this upsurge, as it suggested that country music fans watched television. A large number of country music–themed shows were regularly aired in syndication, and major networks briefly featured programming that included *Hee Haw* and the *Glen Campbell Goodtime Hour*. From 1969 to 1971, ABC-TV produced the *Johnny Cash Show*, an innovative program that effectively linked country music's past and present to contemporary popular music.

In the years between 1960 and 1980, the country music industry fashioned a product that creatively reflected the various upheavals disrupting American and Southern life. As a result, country music penetrated further into the national consciousness than ever before. The music's popularity fluctuated for the remainder of the twentieth century, however, with much of its appeal seemingly tied to its association with often lightweight motion pictures, opportunistic politicians, and the cyclical whims of the market. Acts such as Ricky Skaggs, Randy Travis, Alabama,

George Strait, and Dwight Yoakam consciously worked to reconcile innovation with convention and newer listeners with older traditions.

Although bound in imagery that exaggerates the exclusivity of its rural white male working-class attributes, country music has an inclusive folk history. Never, for instance, has it operated as a separate male preserve; countless women, from the Carter Family, Coon Creek Girls, Patsy Montana, Minnie Pearl, and Kitty Wells to Patsy Cline, Loretta Lynn, Tammy Wynette, Dolly Parton, and Reba McIntire have found their voice in country music. Although country songs often appear to endorse a world of **gender stratification** in which women are systematically subjugated, they also reveal glimpses into the lives of women who have endured and overcome such oppression. Country music has expressed self-assertion and strength as well as dependence and vulnerability.

Country music has been dynamic and adaptive. Jimmie Rodgers, the "Father of Country Music," for instance, was an eclectic entertainer who transcended categories and served to remind listeners of country music's deep connections to African American **blues**. Country music fostered such racial boundary–bending performers as Rodgers, Jimmie Davis, and the young Gene Autry, who established precedents that eventually gave rise to rockabilly. Elvis Presley and other Southern **rock 'n' roll** artists were infatuated with rhythm and blues (R&B) and emerged from a country-blues tradition embraced by earlier performers such as Bob Wills, Bill Monroe, and Hank Williams.

Soul music also reflected the influence of country music. Many recording studios in the South brought together black and white musicians schooled in both R&B and country, a common musical heritage that defied a segregated past. At the height of his career in the early 1960s, Ray Charles, the lead architect of soul, ventured to Nashville to produce a country music album, *Modern Sounds in Country and Western Music*. Although the album did not single-handedly break down racial barriers erected by marketing and record executives in the 1920s, its tremendous popularity demonstrated that country music's appeal was not and never had been as racially restricted as conventional wisdom suggested.

Much of country music's storyline has been linked to a subplot involving the South's long-delayed entry into (and alienation from) the national mainstream. Southerners have long attempted to reconcile modernity with tradition, **middle-class** ethics with working-class realities. And contrary to Henry Ford's dictates, country music has also responded to the interests of a more affluent yet socially apprehensive audience. Even bluegrass, often considered a safe haven for "old time music," is an innovative subgenre derived from sources both old and new. Although built around acoustic instrumentation, its hard-driving, jazz-influenced improvisations diverged from pre-commercial techniques. With its reliance on blues, jazz, black and white gospel, vocal harmonies, and rural repertoires, bluegrass represents a "modern" form of expression. It is, as one writer put it using language more appropriate to the automobile age, "folk music in overdrive."

Country music has evolved to address issues and experiences common to ordinary people. At times nostalgic, comical, quixotic, and escapist, it is a music generally couched in personal rather than political terms. Country songs express the innermost desires and frustrations of alienated individuals coping with the uncertainties of everyday life. Played at an assortment of venues and through multiple media, country music (or any one of its other contemporary appellations and sub-genres, such as "old familiar tunes," "country folk," "Country and Western," "Western swing," "bluegrass," "honky tonk," "rockabilly," or "country pop") provided more than a soundtrack to the lives of its disaffected adherents.

Suggested Reading
Mary Bufwack and Robert K. Oermann, *Finding Her Voice: Women in Country Music, 1800–2000*, 2003; Curtis Ellison, *Country Music Culture: From Hard Times to Heaven*, 2001; Bill Malone, *Country Music U.S.A.*, 2002; Malone, *Don't Get above Your Raisin': Country Music and the Southern Working Class*, 2002; Richard A. Peterson, *Creating Country Music: Fabricating Authenticity*, 1999; Charles Wolfe, *A Good-Natured Riot: The Birth of the Grand Ole Opry*, 1999.

CREATIONISM

ROBERT E. WEIR

Creationism, a religious view associated primarily with Western Christianity, holds that God created the universe. It is at odds with scientific teachings on evolutionary development. There is no one Creationist movement per se; Biblical literalists, taking their lead from the book of Genesis, hold that creation took place in six days, and some ultraconservatives use Old Testament genealogies to assert—as did the sixteenth-century Irish Bishop James Usher—that the world was created in 4004 BC. More recent manifestations of the creationist debate have surfaced among supporters of Intelligent Design. Proponents of Intelligent Design insist that the universe is so complex as to demand the existence of a higher power that made order from chaos. Some hold that Intelligent Design is compatible with science, with the latter being an explanation of how life emerged, and the former a rationale for why it occurred. This view is held by some scientists who are also religious. However, the bulk of Intelligent Design supporters reject scientific explanations altogether and call evolution merely a theory for which there is little credible evidence.

The creationism debate has implications for **class consciousness**, class identification, and a host of other social issues. It is not a new debate in American society. Charles Darwin's publication of *On the Origin of the Species by Means of Natural Selection* (1859) caused a hailstorm of controversy within American churches. By the end of the nineteenth century, many liberal Protestant denominations had reconciled themselves with Darwin's assertion that present-day life evolved from lower forms, but fundamentalists and conservative Christians largely rejected evolution. Educated Americans, concentrated disproportionately in the **upper** and **middle classes**, were also more comfortable with evolution, a principle that soon became well established in the curricula of American universities. In the famed Scopes Trial of 1925, a Tennessee public school teacher was tried for teaching evolution to high school biology students in violation of state law. This case was seen as a cause celebre that pitted superstitious, rural, **lower-class** Americans against modern, scientific, urban sophisticates. Although John Scopes was found guilty, creationists were discredited and their efforts lost steam.

The teaching of evolution slowly became the norm in public schools, but the centrality of religion in American public life guaranteed that it would not go unchallenged. Religious supporters were angered by a host of court decisions during the 1960s and beyond that placed restrictions on public religious expression, struck down school prayer as unconstitutional, and affirmed secular school curricula. When conservatives began to reassert political power in the 1980s, especially during the administration of **Ronald Reagan**, creationists were among those seeking to revisit domestic policy. Since then the Republican Party has courted creationists and other religious conservatives, using morals as a wedge issue to attract groups such as the **working class**, **Catholics**, white Southerners, and others who had for decades preferred Democrats.

The composition of the revitalized creationist movement differs significantly from its predecessors. It cuts across social class boundaries, but some of its greatest strength is among the white suburban middle class; in a 2005 poll, 52 percent of this group supported the teaching of Intelligent Design in public schools. Many modern-day creationists are also profoundly antiscience in their perspective. In a recent National Science Foundation survey, 80 percent of creationists rejected the notion that Earth is 4 billion years old, and 40 percent of them feel that scientists are "dangerous"; indeed, 25 percent of them blame science for what they see as America's spiritual decline.

Creationism has spawned several very high-profile public battles. The state of Kansas mandated teaching creationism along with evolution in 1999. The Kansas Board of Education reversed this mandate in 2001, after suffering great ridicule, but reinstated the policy in 2005. In 2004 the Dover, Pennsylvania, school board also mandated that the biblical view of creation be taught alongside Darwin's evolutionary studies. This too caused great controversy, and in 2005 most of the school board was replaced by candidates vowing to remove creationism from the curriculum.

Because creationism is not class specific, it further muddies the study of class in America. Some critics argue that social class no longer corresponds to values, breeding, education, **prestige**, or any other traditional class definitions. To such individuals, class is strictly defined by purchasing power. One need not agree with that assessment to see how wedge issues such as creationism, abortion rights, and others associated with the **culture wars** challenge constructions of class that give the greatest weight to economic determiners. Indeed, some analysts assert that cultural issues are cynically manipulated by elites to divert attention from the existence of economic inequality. More prosaically, issues such as creationism suggest that social theorists need to pay more attention to **subjective** factors when discussing **class formation**.

Suggested Reading

Douglas Eichar, *Occupation and Class Consciousness in America*, 1989; Michael Shermer, *Why People Believe Weird Things*, 1997; Clyde Wilcox and Ted Jelen, *Public Attitudes towards Church and State*, 1995.

CREATIVE DESTRUCTION

DIETER BÖGENHOLD

Creative destruction is an ambivalent term originated by Joseph A. Schumpeter (1883–1950), an Austrian economist who held professorships in Austria and Germany before joining the faculty at Harvard University in the early 1930s, where he spent the rest of his career. It refers to the economic processes by which old systems, technology, innovation, and thinking are destroyed by the new. Examples of creative destruction in the music industry include the evolution from wax cylinders to vinyl records to compact discs and MP3 files. Schumpeter saw creative destruction as a logical byproduct of **capitalism**, but not necessarily as a good thing.

From a contemporary perspective Schumpeter was truly interdisciplinary, and his many works span fields such as sociology, finance economics, and politics. Over a time span of nearly fifty years, Schumpeter published numerous articles and books. *Capitalism, Socialism, and Democracy* (1942) contained the expression "creative destruction." The book's chapter entitled "Creative Destruction" deals with the modus operandi of competition. Schumpeter argues against some predominant economic thought of his time, which characterized economies as being static. In opposition to that, Schumpeter conceptualized economy as being in a constant flux of economic and social change. Schumpeter frequently discussed the parallels and divergences of his thought and **Marxism**: "The essential point to grasp is that in dealing with capitalism we are dealing with an evolutionary process. It may seem strange that anyone can fail to see so obvious a fact which moreover was long ago emphasized by Karl Marx."

Schumpeter is regarded as one of the pioneers of "evolutionary economics." He viewed capitalism as a "form or method of economic change." Creative destruction is a contradictory expression that seeks to highlight the fact that competition and inherent processes leading toward monopolistic and oligopolistic competition are only one part of the overall economic game. Too often neglected are simultaneous processes of the creation of new firms, new ideas, and even new business leaders elsewhere in an economy. Deaths and births—of business enterprises and of individuals—are two sides of the same coin, and Schumpeter dubbed creative destruction an essential fact about capitalism.

Creative destruction has to be seen in a wider context of innovation and entrepreneurship for which Schumpeter is well-known. Entrepreneurs are treated as agents to introduce new inputs into the economy. He defined an entrepreneur as a person who comes up with "new combinations" (new goods, new methods of production, new markets, new sources of supply, new organizations of any industry, or combinations of these items), which are commonly called *innovation*. Entrepreneurs are driven by a set of diverse motivations, and their activity is fundamental for economic development. Innovation is the infusion of "fresh blood" through new ideas and people who keep the "capitalist machine" vital. However, creativity is always combined with destruction elsewhere. When new products appear, consumer demands change, and existing production and related markets are rendered obsolete. In some cases entire communities are negatively impacted when the production of new products locates elsewhere. Labor historians and economists have long studied the fallout from **deindustrialization**. There are, for example, cities and towns throughout the Northeast and Midwest that have yet to recover from the economic decline associated with the closure of textile and steel mills.

Capitalism always exists as a development with a fragile balance of "coming" and "going" of firms, entrepreneurs, goods, ideas, mentalities, and ideologies. Although Schumpeter is often regarded as the academic hero of entrepreneurship and innovation, he was highly skeptical about the endogenous ability of capitalism to achieve a balance between creativity and destruction. In one chapter he posed the question "Can capitalism survive?" and did not hesitate to answer "No, in my opinion not." He actually felt that **socialism** would eventually supplant capitalism. So far, Schumpeter can be said to have underestimated the potential innovation sources of capitalism. Nevertheless, Schumpeter's ideas remain in vogue, and an international Joseph A. Schumpeter Society was founded in the 1980s. Schumpeter has found a firm place as one of the most important economists of the twentieth century.

Suggested Reading

S.E. Harris, ed. *Schumpeter: Social Scientist*, 1951; J. Stanley Metcalfe, *Evolutionary Economics and Creative Destruction*, 1998; Joseph Schumpeter, *Capitalism, Socialism, and Democracy*, 1942.

CRIME

CHUCK BARONE

Studies show a strong connection between **socioeconomic status (SES)** and crime. Those from the lowest SES groups are over-represented among the more than 2 million prisoners in the United States, a country with one of the highest incarceration rates in the world.

Criminal behavior is sometimes believed to be the result of flawed individuals, which in this case means that such individuals are disproportionately from lower SES groups. Others believe that a social environment of **poverty** and **unemployment** creates economic pressures that can result in criminal behavior. Evidence in support of this contention includes statistical studies that show a strong correlation between the rate of unemployment and the rate of crime. Furthermore, social psychologists have found a high correlation between socioeconomic inequality and violence.

Whatever the individual cause, the existence of these "dangerous classes" has been historically associated with the development of industrial **capitalism**, which created specialized social (penal) institutions to contain, punish, and rehabilitate criminals.

Some view the criminal justice system (CJS) itself as reflecting and serving the dominant class interests of the larger society. The very purpose of the CJS is in this view questioned, as a system that not only contains and makes the public safe from the "dangerous classes," but also as a system of social control—a way of regulating the poor and **working classes**. In a highly stratified class-based society, such as the United States, where class divides are great and growing wider, dominant class interests are often reflected in the nature of the CJS.

The extent that the CJS reflects such interests depends upon the ability of **upper-class** groups to influence the decisions of legislators who decide which behaviors/acts are to be criminalized; the decisions of police and prosecutors who arrest and charge; and the decisions of judges and juries who convict and sentence. For example, the economic cost to society of **white-collar** crime far exceeds the cost of street crimes, yet far fewer resources are devoted to enforcing and prosecuting white-collar crimes, and punishment is usually much less severe. Another example is the criminalization of drug use in the United States and the way such laws have been selectively enforced and prosecuted so as to disproportionately affect those from lower SES groups, especially but not only racial minorities.

The rapid growth in the prison population in the United States has resulted in a corresponding growth of the prison system to house, guard, supervise, feed, and clothe prisoners. This has become a rapidly growing and profitable billion dollar industry that some call the "prison industrial complex," an intricate web of corporate and local interest groups that benefit financially from its expansion. The rapid growth of government expenditures on the CJS has been offset by less growth in other areas of government, including education, **welfare**, and other programs that are targeted for lower-income families. The growing use of cheap prison labor by some of our largest corporations raises interesting questions about exploitation, a captive labor force, and the impact of this particular kind of internal "outsourcing" on domestic labor markets.

Suggested Reading

Gregg Barak et al., eds., *Class, Race, Gender, and Crime: Social Realities of Justice in America*, 2001; Barbara Chasin, *Inequality and Violence in the United States*, 1997; Norval Morris and David J. Rothman, *The Oxford History of the Prison: The Practice of Punishment in Western Society*, 1995; Christian Parenti, *Lockdown America: Police and Prisons in the Age of Crisis*, 2000; Jeffrey Reiman, *The Rich Get Richer and the Poor Get Prison: Ideology, Class, and Criminal Justice*, 1998.

CRITICAL ELITE THEORY

MAURO STAMPACCHIA

Critical elite theory is based on the assumption that in every society only a minority retains power, whether it be political, economical, or cultural, while the vast majority is deprived of it. This assumption can be purely descriptive; however, most elite theory focuses mainly on the retention and exercise of *political* power.

Ancient, medieval, and modern history show us many examples of aristocratic or oligarchic power, where the two words indicate respectively "the rule of the best," or "the rule of the few." But elite theory was formalized at the end of the nineteenth century, when the idea of **democracy** coincided with notions of the sovereignty of the people. Many elites were critical of government by the people, for the people, and of the people, including many of America's **Founding Fathers**. Elites often described mass democratic processes as mere appearance and ritual, while the very substance of political processes operated at the highest levels and filtered down to the masses. Critical elite theorists thus look at the ways political elites acquire legitimacy and consent. The political elite does not perfectly coincide with the **ruling class**, or the **bourgeoisie**, as it was defined by **Marxists**. It is, rather, a professional, specialized group, and its behavior could be described, according to some, as appropriate and beneficial.

Gaetano Mosca, a professor of political thought, pointed out the unique role of what he named the "political class." Likewise, Vilfredo Pareto, an economist and a sociologist, wrote about the "circulation of the elites," the political conflict that leads one elite to overcome other elites. Robert Michels, a student of **Max Weber**, used critical elite theory to analyze political parties and organizations, with a focus on the European **socialist** parties. He argued that elites were originally skeptical of democratic processes and social reform. The emerging elite used social conflict language and adopted socialist ideas only to chase the established elite from power, and were thus not part of the **working class**. But the elite theory proved to be open also to a democratic and progressive interpretation.

In the United States, critical elite theory had a renewed fortune during the **Great Depression** of the 1930s. Harold Lasswell wrote about the presence of not just a single elite, but also of middle strata of intermediate elites. He stressed that democracies needed elites who could manipulate propaganda in such a way as to ensure that the **masses** accept what is in their best interest. In this regard, the social structure does not depend on the absence or presence of a political elite, but on the quality of the relations between elites and masses, and elites are judged by how they exercise political power. Lasswell's thinking was, in some ways, a marriage between **functional elite** and **power elite** theory.

Not surprisingly, apologists for critical elite theory inspired critics (hardly surprising, considering that Michels was a fascist). In his influential 1941 work, *The Managerial Revolution*, the **Trotskyist** James Burnham argued that **capitalism** and democracy were imperiled, but doubted a socialist future. Instead, he foresaw political dominance by a new class of managers, technocrats, bureaucrats, and the military, whose power relied not on owning the **means of production**, but rather on controlling them through social knowledge and managing functions. His views anticipated theories of the **military-industrial complex** and those of **C. Wright Mills**. Mills provocatively raised doubts about the role of the "common man" in America, and argued that a selective and exclusive power elite controlled positions that offered strategic control over political **power**, wealth, celebrity, and high **status**. The stable positions held by the "power elite" in politics, the economy, and the military are instrumental to the unchallenged control elites exercise on the society as a whole.

Wright's ideas were themselves subject to dispute. Robert Dahl criticized the idea of a monolithic ruling elite and argued that the **pluralism** of American society meant that different elites shared power and/or competed in every major aspect of society. From the political left, Paul Marlor Sweezy argued that Mills overstressed the influence of military and political elites over corporate capitalism. He and other theorists of a **corporate class** returned critiques of critical elite theory to the economic base of classical Marxism. Most modern theorists suggest that any construction of elites needs to be nuanced.

Joseph Schumpeter noted that elites competing for power through the popular vote were the very essence of a "democratic elitism," and the concept of a divided elite runs through thinkers such as Raymond Aron, as does the idea that elites are continuously influenced by political and social needs from below. **Ralf Dahrendorf** proposed a model of society in which social inequalities are determined not by the economic structure, but by **authority** relations that shift and are constantly renegotiated.

Suggested Reading

James Burnham, *The Managerial Revolution*, 1941; Robert Dahl, *Democracy and Its Critics*, 1989; Steve Fraser and Gary Gerstle, eds., *Ruling America: A History of Wealth and Power in a Democracy*, 2005; Harold Lasswell, *Politics: Who Gets What, When, How*, 1936; Paul Sweezy and Paul Baran, *Monopoly Capitalism*, 1966.

CULTURAL CAPITAL

SHANNON J. TELENKO

Cultural capital is **Pierre Bourdieu**'s (1930–2002) sociological concept for the abstract cultural gains that someone can make because of social background, upbringing, education, and other experiences. Similar to financial capital, such as money and material things, one can also accumulate cultural capital. In addition, like financial capital, the more cultural capital one has, the more cultural capital that person can obtain. The effect is exponential. In addition, in order to obtain it at all, one must know how to go about doing so and know that cultural capital even exists. Most people do not know the term cultural capital, but all are familiar with what it represents.

Examples of cultural capital include anything of cultural significance that is of value to some segment of society. Categories of cultural capital include **literature**, **film**, music, **art**, language, **fashion**, food and drink, and general cultural knowledge. Middle- and **upper-class** segments of society have some common tastes and goals when it comes to accumulating cultural capital. Thus the **middle class** is commonly accused of trying to emulate the upper class. **Lower-** and **working-class** segments of society might have a different ideal when it comes to accumulating cultural capital and may use their values as a form of resistance against the more elite members of society. A good illustration of such resistance is the relationship between teenagers and parents. Younger Americans will come up with ways to keep out the older generations, through music, dance, language, and clothing. This is both a protest of adults' control over them and a way to form identity with peers.

Cultural capital can be both symbolic of what a segment of society finds important for understanding life, and a means for **social mobility**. Although everyone accumulates cultural capital regardless of age, **income**, or **socioeconomic status**, certain types of cultural capital will allow entrance into certain segments of society. If one is trying to gain admission into something that is traditionally and institutionally set up to accept those from middle- and upper-class backgrounds, it will be much easier if one is born into a family that is in the upper classes of society and knows how to go about accumulating the proper type of cultural capital for the situation.

What is most vital in understanding cultural capital, in the way Bourdieu originally intended, is that certain kinds of cultural capital are more valuable for attaining higher class status. The higher status one tries to attain, the more difficult and expensive it becomes to accumulate cultural capital. In this way cultural capital also works as a barrier to entry into certain social circles. It can be a tool for sustaining racist, classist, and sexist practices.

Cultural capital gives the message to others that one belongs or could belong to a certain segment of society. Since cultural capital is accumulated by already having cultural capital or the knowledge of its existence, Bourdieu argues that it serves to secure power for select members of society.

Suggested Reading

Pierre Bourdieu, *Distinction: A Social Critique of the Judgment of Taste*, 1984; Pierre Bourdieu and Jean-Claude Passeron, *Reproduction in Education, Society and Culture*, 2nd ed., 1990 [1977]; David Swartz, *Culture & Power: The Sociology of Pierre Bourdieu*, 1997.

CULTURAL TOURISM

LISA L. HEUVEL

Cultural tourism identifies the motivation for people who travel to destinations with cultural institutions, historic sites, and cultural events. Along with heritage tourism or cultural heritage tourism, it describes the activities, travel-related industries, and worldwide economies impacted by tourists interested in learning more about their own culture or other cultures. Although camping, boating, and other recreational activities may be part of vacationers' overall plans, cultural tourism involves experiencing unique regional or cultural lifestyles for pleasure and education.

Culture entails the overall beliefs, customs, arts, and institutions of a given society at a particular time, and cultural tourism destinations are as varied as the restored eighteenth-century capital of Williamsburg, Virginia, France's Louvre Museum, and Gila Cliff Dwellings National Monument in southwestern New Mexico.

Whether it involves museum going, sight seeing, dining, or other pursuits, the essence of cultural tourism is experiencing another culture in meaningful and personally enjoyable ways. A significant market niche has been created by the growing adult baby boomer generation of the United States: both the travel and tourism industries concentrate research and marketing on people with the affluence and leisure to plan vacations around such experiences. According to Travel Industry of America statistics for 1997, 25 percent of U.S. adults (53.6 million) took at least one trip that included a historic place or museum, and 17 percent of U.S. adults (33 million) took at least one trip that included a cultural event or festival. In 1990 tourism constituted an estimated 5.5 percent of the world gross national product, according to the World Travel & Tourism Council. However, it should be pointed out that cultural tourism is not necessarily limited to places and events customarily considered **high culture**. A case can be made that any vacationer's travel, whether to Disney World or the Taj Mahal, can be considered cultural tourism because it presents a different perspective than the tourist's familiar, everyday world.

Among the issues cultural tourism raises is the potent attraction of unique or real-life environments, lifestyles, and cultures. The consequences of marketing these features successfully may be increased social, economic, and political gain for related tourist industries and the destination sites. However, they may also include negative impact from environmental damage and other tourist-related overuse.

A further cause for concern is the impact on populations who on one hand welcome tourism for economic gain, but on the other hand fear exploitation of the unique characteristics that set them apart. In some cases, indigenous communities worldwide may be impacted through this interface with tourism, speeding acculturation that otherwise might have been delayed to some degree.

Another aspect of cultural tourism is driven by supply and demand. Entrepreneurs often package experiences for marketing value, moving them away from a "way of life" authenticity for broader appeal to potential consumers. When this happens, underlying cultural realities, historical narratives, and social concepts may be sublimated because of other determining factors: length of stay, competing area attractions, and budget may all affect the cultural tourism equation.

Suggested Reading
Priscilla Boniface, *Managing Quality Cultural Tourism*, 1995; "Cultural Tourism," National Endowment for the Humanities pamphlet; Clare Gunn and Turget Var, *Tourism Planning: Basics, Concepts, Causes*, 4th ed., 2002; Bridget Beattie McCarthy, *Cultural Tourism: How the Arts Can Help Market Tourism Products, How Tourism Can Help Provide Markets for the Arts*, 1992.

CULTURE OF POVERTY

ROBERT E. WEIR

The *culture of poverty* is a controversial concept popular among some interactionist sociologists and conservative political theorists. They postulate that poverty can become self-perpetuating and that many programs designed to assist the poor actually do more harm than good. To proponents of a culture of poverty theory, poverty is part of the socialization process, with those raised in poverty more likely to see their lifestyles as normative, even when they engage in antisocial behavior. The term is often credited to Oscar Lewis (1914–71), an anthropologist whose work with Mexican and Puerto Rican families in the 1960s led him to see poverty as pathology.

From a culture of poverty vantage point, the everyday interactions of the poor make them prone to fatalism, feelings of inferiority, and antisocial behaviors and values. Among the latter are a desire for instant gratification (including sexual), a rejection of long-term planning, pessimism, and a generalized disregard for social conventions and laws. The longer any individual lingers in poverty, the more likely it is that he or she will pass on these values to other family members, with children being especially vulnerable to having their value systems distorted. A child growing up amid single-parent families, drug dealing, and violence may come to see these things as normal. That child might even overtly reject mainstream values such as work and embrace hustling or crime as the means to material gratification.

Few sociologists would deny the baleful effects of poverty, but culture of poverty theory becomes especially controversial when blended with social policy, as controversial conservative policy analyst Charles Murray has done. Some argue, for instance, that **welfare** programs are partly responsible for creating a culture of poverty and should be curtailed, reduced, or eliminated. Some conservatives even advocate strains of **individualism** and **self-help** that hark back to the **Gilded Age**, when social problems were largely viewed as individual failings.

Culture of poverty theory has many critics. Some see it as little more than blaming the victim, perhaps little more than disguised racism and nativism. Other critics excoriate proponents for refusing to address the structural causes of poverty, and a small number of scholars even view antisocial values as a top-down imposition on the **lower class**. The most substantive attacks have come from scholars who say that the concept is just too simplistic. The desire for material gratification, for example, seems to indicate that the value systems of the poor do not depart very much from the American mainstream. Herbert Gans and **William Julius Wilson** are among the critics who view culture of poverty as a stereotype that assumes all poor are alike when, in fact, communities of poor people are as heterogeneous as any other social group. Wilson and others have even argued that much of what passes for antisocial behavior is, in fact, a coping mechanism employed by individuals who currently have little access to mainstream lifestyles. Thus poor people might engage in what Richard Della Fave and others dub a "value-stretch approach." Stretched values, however, are not necessarily permanent or preferred.

Suggested Reading
Herbert Gans, *The War against the Poor*, 1995; Charles Murray, *Losing Ground: American Social Policy, 1950–1980*, 1984; William Julius Wilson, *The Truly Disadvantaged: The Inner City, the Underclass, and Public Policy*, 1987.

CULTURE WARS

RICHARD JENSEN

These "wars" have been part of European and American history for over a thousand years. European culture wars historically pitted **Catholics** against Protestants, from the extraordinarily violent Thirty Years War of the seventeenth century to the nonviolent *Kulturkampf* in Germany in the late nineteenth century, when Bismarck's German Protestant government sought to suppress Catholicism and failed. In the nineteenth and early twentieth centuries the great battles were over cultural and ethnic nationalism, in addition to political contests between clerical and secular forces, especially in France from 1789 to the early twentieth century. Just as violent were the occasional conflicts between Christianity and Islam that led to dramatic battles such as those at Tours (732), Kosovo (1389), Constantinople (1453), and Lepanto (1571). Similar outbursts occurred in Chechnya during the 1990s, and in Britain, France, the Netherlands, Spain, and elsewhere after 2001.

In the Western hemisphere, great violence accompanied culture wars in Mexico from 1810 to the 1930s that saw clerical/conservative alliances battle anticlerical, modernizing forces. In Canada mostly nonviolent cultural tension between English and French ethnic groups has simmered from 1760 onward. Finally, in the 1990s Canadians opted for a multicultural compromise that downgraded British heritage and Canadian nationalism in general. There remain, nonetheless, active separatist groups among Francophones and some native peoples.

Since 1789 there has been a persistent global cultural war between the forces of modernization, secularization, and globalization on the one hand, and traditionalists on the other. The latter expressed itself among Roman Catholics in the nineteenth century, and Islamists, Hindu nationalists, and Christian evangelicals in the twentieth and twenty-first centuries. In class terms, the upper **middle class** has typically been the proactive modernizing force, with the peasants and **working classes** (often joined by the aristocracy) acting in reaction.

In American history, culture wars have seldom escalated into violence. In general, the groups at sword's point in other lands coexist in America. The rare exceptions were tensions between Catholic and Protestant Irish in the nineteenth century that erupted in riots in New York (1871), Philadelphia (1844) and elsewhere, though these were quickly quelled. More violence and hatred has surrounded racial tensions between blacks and whites (and between whites and Chinese in the late nineteenth century, and blacks and Koreans in the late twentieth century).

The most important culture wars in America have involved questions of morality. The abolitionist movement was one such expression. Before the 1830s many national leaders, North and South, considered **slavery** a social evil that should be gradually abolished. During the Second Great Awakening, religious evangelicals in the North began preaching that slavery was a personal sin that slave owners must immediately repent. The novel (later a play) by Harriet Beecher Stowe, *Uncle Tom's Cabin* (1851), became a best seller in America and Britain, driving home the horrors of slavery. Across the South those suspected of harboring abolitionist thoughts were driven out. More generally, the South feared various Yankee "isms" (abolitionism, feminism, and reformism) that threatened to destroy the traditional lifestyle of both subsistence yeoman farmers and slave plantations. The North meanwhile was modernizing rapidly and building an educational system that provided the intellectual and interpersonal skills needed for an upwardly mobile middle class to flourish. The South was nearly as rich as the North in 1860, but its wealth depended less on intellectual skills than on the luck of land speculation, gambling, European demand for cotton, and weather. After slavery ended in 1865 and cotton prices plunged, the South fell behind economically and intellectually until it finally broke with cotton and began urbanizing in the 1940s and abandoned **segregation** in the 1960s.

The Second Great Awakening created a series of reform movements that generated culture wars. In addition to abolition was the **Prohibition** movement, which moved liquor from a social nuisance to a personal sin in the minds of many pietistic, low-church, revivalist Protestants and motivated their efforts to destroy the liquor trade and **saloons**. The robust resistance provided by Catholics and liturgical, high-church Protestants such as **Episcopalians** and German Lutherans turned liquor into an ethno-religious issue that polarized the political parties along parallel lines.

Still another spin-off of the Second Great Awakening was Mormonism, whose doctrines of polygamy and theocracy profoundly alienated Americans. Persecuted relentlessly in culture wars in Ohio and Illinois, the **Mormons** journeyed to Utah. There the Mormon subculture grew rapidly because of high birth rates and successful missions to Europe. The anti-Mormon culture wars largely ceased around 1905, when Mormons finally abandoned polygamy and theocracy. A peculiar feature of the Mormon case was the remarkable combination of a high commitment to technological, organizational, and educational modernity among Mormons, who simultaneously clung to traditional religious and ethical views.

The post–World War I South developed a culture based on **fundamentalism** and related antimodernist tendencies. It rallied to its favorite political hero, William Jennings Bryan, already a leader in the prohibitionist cultural wars, when he declared war on ungodly Darwinism in the 1920s. The result was the fiasco of the Scopes Trial in 1925. It took decades to recover, but Southern antimodernism resurged in the 1980s, assisted by a new political mobilization behind the conservatism of **Ronald Reagan**. It was sponsored by the Christian Coalition and other ad hoc alignments led by the ministers of **Southern Baptist** mega-churches. Northern Catholics had long opposed abortion and began mobilizing their own culture war against secularism in the 1970s. In the name of "family values," Southern Baptists, Missouri Lutherans, Mormons, and fundamentalists joined in the new culture war, attacking abortion, feminism, homosexuality, obscenity, and government support for the arts and humanities. African Americans joined the ad hoc coalition to oppose gay rights. After 2000, stem cell research also became a culture war target. To reach their antiabortion and anti–stem cell position, the culture warriors had to reinterpret 2000 years of Christian teaching on the centrality of the birth experience and argue that life begins upon fertilization. Southern Baptists, who expanded nationwide after 1945, reignited their crusade against Darwinism as taught in the public schools and lobbied for the teaching of various forms of **creationism** as an alternative.

By the 1980s educational levels, more so than social class, aligned culture war partisans and spilled over into presidential elections. Republicans increasingly attacked public schools, higher education, and the arts, as they became a party of college dropouts and lost their historic support among the better educated. The injection of **immigration** issues into politics after 2005 opened a new front in the culture wars by reinvigorating nativist themes that had been dormant since the 1920s. Immigration, however, has proved problematic for Republicans, as Republican nativists often denounce the Republican business interests that attracted illegal **Latino** immigrants in the first place with irresistible job opportunities.

Suggested Reading

Morris P. Fiorina with Samuel J. Abrams and Jeremy C. Pope, *Culture War? The Myth of a Polarized America*, 2004; James D. Hunter, *Culture Wars: The Struggle to Define America*, 1992; Richard Jensen, "The Culture Wars, 1965–1995: A Historian's Map," *Journal of Social History* 29 (October 1995), pp. 17–37; Adam K. Webb, *Beyond the Global Culture War*, 2006; Jonathan Zimmerman, *Whose America? Culture Wars in the Public Schools*, 2002.

D

DAHRENDORF, RALF (May 1, 1929–)

ROBERT E. WEIR

Ralf Gustav Dahrendorf is a European sociologist whose work on **conflict theory** continues to influence the way social class is debated among scholars.

Dahrendorf was born in Hamburg, Germany, earned his PhD from the University of Hamburg in 1952, and did advanced studies at the London School of Economics (LSE) in 1954. He has taught at various German universities and served in the government of the former West Germany, and he was an official with the European Economic Community from 1970 to 1974, the director of the LSE from 1974 to 1984, and warden of Anthony's College, Oxford, from 1987 to 1997. In 1988 Dahrendorf became a British citizen and in 1993 was knighted by the Crown. He has been honored by numerous other governments and is a member of many prestigious societies, including the American Philosophical Society.

Many observers credit Dahrendorf with reshaping the way sociologists deal with social class. His view is a bold synthesis of **Marxist** views of class and those of functionalists, especially **Max Weber**. Dahrendorf observes that social change is inevitable, ubiquitous, and contentious. Moreover, since most social change is rooted in some form of coercion, class conflict is also a common feature of society. Like Marx, he sees class conflict as a clash between two competing groups, which he calls the "superordinate" and "subordinate" classes. Class conflict results because the former wishes to maintain the status quo at the expense of the latter, which resents its inferior status and wishes to alter existing social relations.

Dahrendorf departs from both Marx and Weber in how he defines class. Whereas Marx located it in the relationship to the **means of production** and Weber in market relations, Dahrendorf sees class as deriving from **authority** relations. In advanced societies it is simplistic to define class in purely economic terms, he argues, as individuals and groups often seek nonmonetary and nonmaterial rewards, such as freedom, **status**, or leisure. Possession of authority, defined as the likelihood that one's desires will be carried out, is the key to accessing resources in complex societies. He agrees with Weber that shared **life chances** are a better indicator of social class, though he feels that status groups also influence these, not just market relations.

Overall, authority and **power** are more complex than Marx's dichotomous **bourgeoisie/proletariat** construct would suggest. What sociologists call the "managerial revolution" complicates matters because authority and private property are no longer necessarily linked. Marx's view was based in a family-centered **capitalism** that is now outmoded. Owners frequently cede power and authority to managers, boards of directors, and others who work hand-in-hand with government.

The expansion of and changing nature of the **middle class** and its ambiguous position within the social system also complicates matters. In essence, Dahrendorf sees social class as embedded within the social system. He uses the cumbersome term "imperatively coordinated associations" (derived from Weber) to describe social organizations with built-in authority relations. These establish the norms that define which social roles are most valued and structure how both individual and group interests are granted or denied. Unlike the functionalists, he does not believe that the norms are necessarily rational or benign. Conflict is inevitable because those in superordinate positions seek to maintain their position at the expense of those below them. Conflict also occurs because individuals (and, to a lesser extent, groups) are part of numerous associations, each of which may entail a different relationship to authority. The intensity of conflict, he argues, is dependent upon factors such as the amount of mobility an individual has, whether the conflict results from social **pluralism** or an autocratic act, careful calculations of cost and probability of success, and the degree to which the conflict seems a permanent fixture of the imperatively coordinated association.

Dahrendorf's theories have been extended to industrial and political conflict to show how interest groups form, how conflict is mediated, and how change occurs or is resisted. He is consistent, however, in seeing society as coercive by nature, though he sees conflict as potentially creative as well as destructive. He has been instrumental in forcing scholars to see the degree to which power-based class conflict is structural, not the result of economic crisis or the dawning of **class consciousness**. Because it is normative, other traditional theoretical constructs—such as attributing **false consciousness** to members of the **working class** who seemingly buy into **capitalism**, or the Marxist assertion that revolution would end class conflict—are open to critique.

Dahrendorf's work is also open to criticism. **Critical elite theorists** continue to ascribe essential and rational social roles to those who hold power, not the self-serving motives Dahrendorf postulates. Some functionalists charge that his view of inevitable and constant conflict is absurd, as it would preclude the existence of any meaningful social life; others assert that social change results more from social consensus than from conflict. Dahrendorf has also been criticized for his uneasy mix of complexity and reductionism. If individuals in society belong to as many overlapping associations as Dahrendorf claims, why continue to assert that one either has or does not have authority? Where does one draw the line between the superordinate and the subordinate classes? Given the possibility that some might be members of both classes, depending upon which associational role is in question, how does one determine which class identifies an individual given the murkiness of Dahrendorf's view of class consciousness? Indeed, why assume a correlation between occupation, authority, and class? Some scholars feel that Dahrendorf should have repudiated Marx's dualistic construction of social class altogether.

The criticisms of Dahrendorf's work should rightly be viewed as confirmation of their enduring importance. Most serious work on social class in America wrestles with the implications of his theories.

Suggested Reading

Ralf Dahrendorf, *Class and Class Conflict in Industrial Society*, 1959; Dahrendorf, *The Modern Social Conflict*, 1989; Dahrendorf, *Life Chances: Approaches to Social and Political Theory*, 1991.

DAVIS, KINGSLEY

See Davis-Moore Thesis.

DAVIS-MOORE THESIS

ROBERT E. WEIR

Among the better known postulates in **functional elite theory** is the Davis-Moore thesis. It is named for Kingsley Davis (1908–97) and Wilbert Moore (1914–87), two sociologists who worked on questions of stratification. In the 1940s Davis and Moore attempted to explain the primary function of stratification and concluded that it was to guarantee that society's most important roles and positions were occupied by those most qualified to fill them. This is particularly the case in the economic, political, religious, and technological sectors of society.

Like all functionalists, Davis and Moore concentrated on those consensus-producing roles and norms they felt were necessary for society to survive and thrive. In a 1953 analysis of their work Melvyn Tumin delineated seven key components of the Davis-Moore thesis. First, some social roles are more important than others and require specific abilities to fill. Second, these roles are so specialized that only a few are capable of mastering them. Third, those roles require special training, and fourth, said training is difficult to obtain and hence must be rewarded. Fifth, those rewards can come in the form of special privileges that are harder for others to obtain. Sixth, those in the elite receive **prestige**, **power**, and other perquisites that tend to institutionalize inequality. Finally and most controversially, this level of inequality is desirable, positive, and functional. In essence, talent is scarce and ought to be rewarded.

The Davis-Moore thesis has been and remains contested. Some critics accused the two of constructing an illogical tautology that could not be tested; others charged **classism** and ideological biases. **Conflict theorists** question functionalist assumptions at their core, and several note that Davis and Moore treated society as if it always operated as an ideal **meritocracy**, when in truth elite status often derives from factors other than merit, such as **social networks**, **Ivy League** education, inheritance, and in some cases exploitation of the **lower classes**. Their model also assumes competency and benevolence on the part of elites, a thesis often at odds with reality. **Harold Kerbo** further challenged the Davis-Moore thesis on the grounds that, even if they were correct, their postulates do not justify the degree of inequality that pervades American society.

The Davis-Moore thesis is no longer in vogue, but it nonetheless retains value. It remains a good explanation concerning the process by which some forms of elite **status** is attained, and, protestations of ideals notwithstanding, their argument that stratification in an advanced **capitalist** society is inevitable has yet to be refuted. Moreover, although it is seldom evoked by name, variants of the Davis-Moore thesis underpin many of the arguments made by economic and political conservatives.

Suggested Reading

Leonard Beeghley, *The Structure of Social Stratification in the United States*, 2000; Kingsley Davis and Wilbert Moore, "Some Principles of Stratification," *American Sociological Review* 7 (1945), pp. 242–249; Harold Kerbo, "Marxist and Functionalist Theories in the Study of Social Stratification," *Social Forces* 55 (1976), pp. 191–192.

DAY, DOROTHY (November 8, 1897–November 29, 1980)

MATTHEW PEHL

An important **Catholic** activist, Day has influenced the thinking of many socially conscious church members through her work among the **working class** and the poor. She came of age in a left-wing, militantly secular milieu, but by the time of her death she was recognized as the most influential Roman Catholic laywoman of the twentieth century and a pioneer of Catholic radicalism.

Born to a **middle-class** family, Day embraced **socialism** during her student days at the University of Illinois and moved to New York where she lived in the years surrounding World War I. While in New York, she worked as a radical journalist for such magazines as the *Call* and *Masses*, and she also became familiar with staples of the bohemian art scene such as Floyd Dell and Eugene O'Neill. Day's personal life during these years was tempestuous, characterized by rocky romances and what she later termed a "long loneliness."

After the birth of her daughter, Tamar, in 1927, Day decided to baptize her child in the Catholic Church. Following the baptism, Day endured her own crisis of faith; ultimately, she abandoned Tamar's atheist father and converted to Catholicism herself in 1927. The turning point in Day's life came in the early 1930s when she met an eccentric French peasant and philosopher, Peter Maurin. Maurin urged Day to channel her Catholic spirituality and left-wing politics into a newspaper, *The Catholic Worker*. Sold for a penny outside radical meetings and along the picket lines at major **strikes**, the paper gradually became a movement infused with Day's religious sensibilities.

Practically, the Catholic Worker movement spread with the success of the newspaper (which reached a circulation of 100,000 in the 1930s) and with the rise of "houses of hospitality." These houses offered a refuge for the poor and **unemployed**, and they provided Catholic Workers an intellectually stimulating environment in which they could enact— and, to some extent, reinvent—their faith. Catholic Workers distrusted the modern state, and instead proclaimed a kind of neo-medieval belief in organic society and human brotherhood. Day's own voluntary poverty reflected her belief in the spiritually exalted status of the poor, and served as an inspiration for a new generation of Catholic activists. Likewise, Day's insistence on what she termed "personalism"—the personal responsibility of all people to each other—offered her many admirers a way to practice the corporal works of mercy so central to Catholic Worker theology. Finally, Day remained an unwavering pacifist, even as America entered and fought World War II. Day's commitment to nonviolence cost the Catholic Worker movement a great many members and

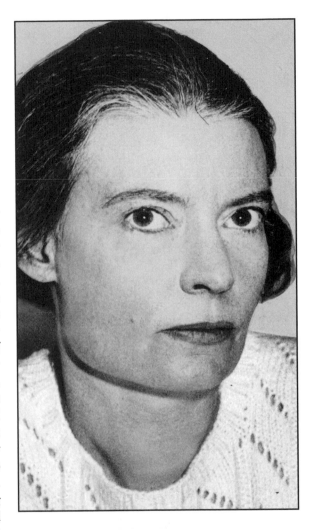

Dorothy Day, ca. 1934. Courtesy of the Library of Congress.

dramatically reduced the number of houses of hospitality during the 1940s.

In time, however, Day's pacifism laid the groundwork for the major peace movements of the 1950s and 1960s. Other aspects of Catholic Worker thought continued to reverberate throughout the religious left; the movement's most famous influence, perhaps, was on the young Catholic Worker **Michael Harrington**, who went on the write *The Other America* in 1962 and helped prompt President Lyndon Johnson's **War on Poverty**. Slowed by age in the 1970s, Dorothy Day died in 1980.

Suggested Reading

Robert Coles, *Dorothy Day: A Radical Devotion*, 1987; Dorothy Day, *The Long Loneliness*, 1993; James H. Forest, *Love Is the Measure: A Biography of Dorothy Day*, 1997.

Day Trading

Robert E. Weir

Day trading is the legal, but controversial, practice of purchasing and selling stocks and securities for quick profit. To its defenders, day trading has democratized the stock market and afforded small-scale investors opportunities once reserved for the **upper class** and corporations. To its detractors, day trading is more akin to **gambling** than wise investing, and it is more likely to incur debt than attainment of the **American dream**.

Day trading in the United States is a by-product of loosened regulations of the New York Stock Exchange (NYSE), competition, and technological change. The price of securities fluctuates according to daily trading on the NYSE and other exchanges. Investors make purchases and sales through brokerages licensed to transact exchanges. Very few investors pay face value up front for stocks or securities they purchase; rather they put down a percentage of the price, which is called the "margin." Investors also pay fees to the brokerage firms. Making money on stocks is done two ways: one can hold them for a long period and collect dividends paid to investors (generally on a quarterly basis), or one can sell the stock for a higher price than one purchased it.

Day traders nearly always pursue the second option. Some critics compare modern day trading to market conditions of the 1920s. Stock prices rose spectacularly in the 1920s, and some investors made fortunes. (A rising market is known as a "bull market"; a declining one is called a "bear market.") The supercharged market of the 1920s lured numerous small investors, especially members of the middle and lower ranks of the **middle class**. Margins were very low in the 1920s, a condition that led to speculation based mostly on confidence. Purchases were made for which little money actually changed hands; hence, when the market crashed in 1929, billions of dollars of debt accrued for which no assets existed to secure them.

In 1934 the Securities and Exchange Commission (SEC) was established to regulate stock exchanges. Much higher margins were required for purchasing stocks and securities (generally from 25 to 50 percent). Brokerage commissions were also regulated.

Great Depression–era reforms stabilized market transactions for several decades, but technological change made certain SEC and NYSE practices outmoded. By the 1970s it was possible to conduct exchanges electronically, an advantage over the slower procedure of making personal contact with a broker. In 1971 NASDAQ (National Association of Securities Dealers Automated Quotations) formed to compete with the NYSE and to facilitate electronic purchases. Brokers subsequently began listing securities electronically and could even conduct business when exchanges were closed. NASDAQ also inspired day traders. By the mid-1970s numerous brokerages could list their products on NASDAQ's Electronic Communication Networks (ECNs), which operate much the way that real estate multilisting services operate. Anyone with computer access can search various ECNs to see what is available for purchase. In the 1970s personal computing was still in its infancy, but by the 1980s it became widespread. The introduction of high-speed Internet connections in the 1990s made day trading even easier. In 1994 NASDAQ exchanges surpassed those on the NYSE. In 1998 NSADAQ merged with the American Stock Exchange to form an even more powerful challenge to the NYSE.

Also influential for day traders was a 1975 SEC ruling that banned fixed brokerage fees. Most had been based on a percentage of the sale price, usually 1 percent. Brokerage fees dropped dramatically, with most charging low flat rates per transaction—often as low as $10—regardless of the value of stocks being traded. This benefited ECNs, who take in profits through "spreads," rather than by processing transactions. (NASDAQ's inventory is offered at prices that are slightly higher than their actual value, the difference being the "spread").

In 1997 an SEC ruling forced NASDAQ to offer the same spreads to small investors that had previously been available only to large-scale investors. This was fortuitous for both NASDAQ and the NYSE, as it coincided with a bull market in technology stocks. NASDAQ was heavily invested in technology stocks; hence its value more than quadrupled from 1997 to 2000, the same period that saw feverish day-trading activity. Some technology stocks were sold several times in the same day, and a handful of day traders made big profits.

Stories of day-trading fortunes made their way into popular culture and led to an explosion of day trading, especially among members of the middle class. The technology stock boom coincided with retrenchment in many **white-collar** businesses, encouraging some displaced professionals to take up day trading. In some cases, day traders borrowed money and speculated wildly. Most inexperienced day traders based purchase decisions on news trends and sought quick profit, not long-term investment plans. The 1920s analogy proved prophetic when, in March of 2000, technology stocks tumbled (the **dot-com bubble**) and NASDAQ's value returned to its pre-1997 levels. This led to huge losses on the part of many day traders, some of whom had taken out second mortgages or had invested student loans.

In 2001 the SEC set new rules to govern day trading. It distinguished between "occasional" traders and "pattern" traders, the latter being those who trade four or more days out of five. Occasional traders are required to have at least $5,000 in equity, pattern traders at least $25,000. Automatic triggers suspend trading activity if daily purchases exceed the buying power of those securities. Margins must be paid within five trading days. The SEC also publishes guidelines warning investors of the risks involved in day trading. Estimates suggest that just 20 percent of day traders realize profits.

Suggested Reading
Shannon Henry, *Dinner Club: How the Masters of the Internet Universe Rode the Rise and Fall of the Greatest Boom in History*, 2002; Maggie Mahar, *Bull!: A History of the Boom, 1982–1999: What Drove the Breakneck Market—and What Every Investor Needs to Know about Financial Cycles*, 2003; Securities and Exchange Commission, "Day Trading: Your Dollars at Risk" (http://www.sec.gov/investor/pubs/daytips.htm).

DEBS, EUGENE (November 5, 1855–October 20, 1926)

BILL BARRY

Eugene Debs was a labor leader, **socialist** agitator, and five-time candidate for president of the United States.

Born in Terre Haute, Indiana, Eugene Victor Debs (named by his father for French novelists Victor Hugo and Eugene Sue) followed the course of American industry and the **labor movement** from low-capital enterprises marked by personal relations between owners and skilled workers, to bitter confrontations between thousands of organized workers and national **robber barons**—the latter supported by military force, the legal system, and other arms of the federal government.

Debs began working in the railroad yards of Terre Haute when he was fifteen. In 1871 he became a fireman on the Terre Haute and Indianapolis Railroad. After five years of sporadic employment, Debs took a position as organizer and recording secretary for a lodge of the Brotherhood of Locomotive Firemen (BLF). Craft unionists of the time believed that a combination of high skills and responsible, sober attitudes would lead employers to recognize labor unions as partners in the emerging industrial landscape. Debs dreamed of eliminating conflict between workers and employers, and he believed that social harmony required that workers and bosses meet as equals. Debs was so convinced that railroads were the fulcrum of progress that he distanced himself from the 1877 railroad **strike**, even though his BLF lodge was technically on strike and federal troops secured the Terre Haute depot.

Debs served as secretary-treasurer of the BLF and editor of the *BLF Magazine* until 1892, by which time he had grown critical of craft unionism and its conciliatory attitude toward railroad owners, who were growing more powerful and more hostile to their workers. He was also becoming more interested in politics. In 1879 Deb was elected Terre Haute's city clerk as a Democrat; he also served one term (1884 to 1886) in the Indiana General Assembly.

By early 1893 Debs had grown suspicious of the possibility of a peaceful capital/labor accord. In June he cofounded one of the country's first industrial unions, the American Railway Union (ARU). The ARU found itself in immediate conflict with the craft "aristocracy": engineers and conductors. Still, the ARU grew rapidly, especially on the western rail lines of the Union Pacific, the Southern Pacific, and the Santa Fe. Shortly after winning a dramatic strike in April 1894, against James J. Hill's Great Northern Railroad, the ARU was drawn into one of labor history's most famous episodes: the Pullman Strike of 1894.

Rising against the oppressive paternalism of the Pullman Corporation (maker of railroad cars and operator of an infamous **company town**), workers from the Pullman Palace Car shops walked out in May 1894 and came to the ARU's first convention in Chicago for support. Over Debs's objections, the ARU agreed to support the strike, but the determined Pullman management, bolstered by court injunctions and the intervention of federal troops authorized by President Grover Cleveland, broke the strike and devastated the ARU. At one point in the strike, an ARU delegation asked **American Federation of Labor** (AFL) president

Samuel Gompers for support, but Gompers refused. Debs never forgave Gompers's betrayal.

Part of the U.S. mail was transported in Pullman cars. As part of its intervention, the federal government had used the mails as pretext to obtain injunctions against ARU leaders. Debs continued his strike activities but was arrested and in June 1895 was sent to prison in Woodstock, Illinois, for six months. While in jail, Debs claimed to have experienced a near-apocalyptic conversion to socialism. He read widely, claiming that "in the gleam of every bayonet and the flash of every rifle, the **class struggle** was revealed." In January 1897, after campaigning in 1896 for William Jennings Bryan, Debs announced his belief that socialism was labor's ultimate salvation.

Debs ran for president five times—in 1900, 1904, 1908, 1912, and 1920—as a **Socialist Party** (SP) candidate. The 1908 campaign featured "The Red Special," a train that toured the country in true whistle-stop fashion, and in 1912 Debs amassed almost 1 million votes, nearly

Eugene Debs, ca. 1912. Courtesy of the Library of Congress.

6 percent of the total, in the four-way race for the presidency ultimately won by Democrat Woodrow Wilson.

In addition to socialist politics, Debs continued to support industrial unionism. In June 1905 Debs appeared at the founding convention of the **Industrial Workers of the World** (IWW), a new organization rooted in principles of revolutionary industrial unionism. As the IWW struggled against bitter opposition from the bosses, the majority of its members—many of them transient workers—rejected the political action that Debs so forcefully advocated. This prompted Debs to quit the IWW. He spent the rest of his life speaking across the country in support of socialism.

As World War I began, Debs and other prominent radicals voiced opposition to what they saw as a capitalist war. In a June 16, 1918, speech in Canton, Ohio, Debs urged workers to hold fast to the principles of international socialism. Debs insisted that wars were made by the "master class" and fought by the "subject class"; hence the master class "had all to gain and nothing to lose, while the subject class has had nothing to gain and all to lose—especially their lives."

Debs placed his opposition to the war within the protection of the U.S. Constitution, but his speech became the basis for a ten-count indictment for violation of the Espionage Law of 1917. In his defense, he claimed to be part of a tradition that began with "Washington, Paine, [and] **Adams**," but he was nonetheless convicted and sentenced to ten years in federal prison. In court, Debs delivered one the most dramatic courtroom speeches in American history, proclaiming that "while there is a lower class, I am in it; while there is a criminal element, I am of it; while there is a soul in prison, I am not free."

While serving his sentence in a federal prison in Atlanta, Debs was once again a candidate of the Socialist Party for president. In the 1920 election Debs drew nearly 1 million votes (3 percent of the total). Yet even as Debs ran his unique campaign, his Socialist supporters fragmented in the wake of the Russian Revolution. Many SP members quit and joined with **communist** groups that they hoped would hasten revolution in the United States.

On December 23, 1921, President Warren Harding commuted the sentences of Debs and twenty-three other political prisoners. He returned to Terre Haute in frail health to confront the various factions of the left and to resume friendships with Midwestern colleagues such as **Sinclair Lewis** and Carl Sandburg. In 1923 he became the national chairman of the Socialist Party, but conceded that a working-class party had no chance in the 1924 elections. Instead Debs supported Robert M. LaFollette's fledgling Progressive Party, a decision denounced by the new Communist Party.

Debs never fully recovered his health after his release from the penitentiary. He spent time in a sanitarium near Chicago and witnessed the virtual collapse of the Socialist Party after 1925 amid the reactionary politics of the 1920s. Debs died on October 20, 1926, the same day he received a cheerful letter from anarchist Nicola Sacco, himself standing in the shadow of the gallows.

Suggested Readings

J. Robert Constantine, ed., *Gentle Rebel: Letters of Eugene V. Debs*, 1995; Ray Ginger, *The Bending Cross: A Biography of Eugene Victor Debs*, 1949; Nick Salvatore, *Eugene V. Debs, Citizen and Socialist*, 1982.

Debutantes

Neda Maghbouleh

Debutantes, or "debs," are young women formally introduced to society at the age of eighteen. The selection and presentation of debutantes was first observed in the **Gilded Age** of the late 1800s and practiced by the most wealthy, aristocratic segments of U.S. society. In their earliest form, debutantes were presented as both girls on the cusp of womanhood and as eligible bachelorettes. In fact, some scholars contend that "debbing" surfaced at the same time that historically entrenched **upper-class** families were losing economic traction to the rising **bourgeoisie**. The debutante as commodity fulfilled a basic economic function by infusing her cash-strapped noble family with "new money." And in welcoming a deb to the family, the wealthy but hopelessly bourgeois family could hope for some social cache to rub off and legitimate their claims to social elitism.

During the **Great Depression**, debutantes highlighted the anxieties and injustices of class in a supposedly classless America. The debutante cotillions and "coming out" parties were extravagant spectacles of privilege, bringing into sharp relief the ever-widening gap between the haves and have-nots. And it was during this same period that public thirst for debutantes reached fever pitch, fueling many American girls' fantasies of wealth and **social mobility**. Newspapers printed breathless accounts of the New York social season, and party sponsors enjoyed seeing their names alongside genuine newsmakers, politicians, and entertainers of the time. A new trope of the "poor little rich girl" arose as journalists detailed various dysfunctions of wealthy families—with adulterous, suicidal, or neglectful parents, a debutante was sufficiently humanized for public consumption. The rise and fall of Brenda Frazier, a deb who became a nightclub darling and—in a first for the era—commercial spokesperson, perhaps provides a prototype for celebrity culture today. The suffering masses no longer saw the deb as a tea-pouring, virginal "bud," but rather as everything glamorous, aspirational, and unattainable about the 1930s.

Although our cultural expectations of debutante-like behavior may have shifted, modern-day debutantes still dress as they always have—in long gloves, pearl necklaces, and formal gowns, usually in white or a muted pastel. They are often linked with upstanding young men as "escorts," performing elaborate dances at cotillion. And yet the cotillion, like the deb, has changed over time. Now framed as a charity event in which cash contributions are donated to an arts or civics organization, the modern cotillion somewhat obscures the fact that wealth and class still determine whose daughters are transformed into debs.

"Coming out" has retained a formality of dance and dress, but debutantes now come out as college students, prospective interns or employees, and of course, potential daughters-in-law within the privileged classes. It is noteworthy that debutantes and cotillions enjoy particular importance within varied ethnic and racial communities across the United States and that "coming out" is both an expression and an event more closely associated with today's gay community. But perhaps the most significant change to the debutante tradition is in the cotillion's democratization and reinvention as "prom" in our nation's public and private high schools, making the average American girl a deb for a day.

Suggested Reading
Michaele Thurgood Haynes, *Dressing Up Debutantes: Pageantry and Glitz in Texas*, 1998; Karal Ann Marling, *Debutante: Rites and Regalia of American Debdom*, 2004; Emily Post, *Etiquette: In Society, In Business, In Politics, and At Home*, 1922.

DEFERENCE

ROBERT E. WEIR

Deference refers to the respect one is expected to give to an elder, social superior, or person of a higher rank, position, or class. Although concepts of courtesy and civility are embedded within an act of giving deference, it also usually involves an implied **power** relationship; that is, the person receiving deference is seen as a superior whose bidding should be done by the social inferior.

Insofar as it can be determined, the first use of the verb *defer* specifically relating to class dates to the late fifteenth century; by the seventeenth century it was an integral feature of the British social system. Long before the term actually came into use, the practice of deference was long established in Western society. By the Middle Ages society was rigidly hierarchical, with those of noble and aristocratic birth commanding deference from serfs, independent yeoman, merchants, and others of non-aristocratic lineage. It was not only expected; it was customarily and legally proscribed. Even the ranks of nobility were highly stratified, and one was always expected to defer to those higher on the social scale. In England a separate class of prosperous landowners known as the gentry emerged; although many in the gentry were **nouveau riche** and lacked noble title, their great **wealth** placed them in a position to command deference from all other than the aristocratic classes.

British models of deference were imported to the American colonies as settlements developed. Some historians even claim that an excess of nobles demanding deference but lacking practical skills retarded the early development of colonies in the Chesapeake region. Attempts were made to replicate British government and class systems in America, but distance and differing conditions were not always ideal for this reproduction. Class tension emerged early in the British colonial experience and can be seen in such events as the **Anne Hutchinson** trial in Massachusetts and **Bacon's Rebellion** in Virginia. Deference was, however, an integral part of the relationship between masters and their **indentured servants** and **slaves**. It was also a customary, if contested, practice throughout Colonial society, with an elite group of wealthy landowners exercising political and social power in most places. Some church officials were also among society's top ranks.

Recent studies suggest that deference was breaking down on the eve of the **American Revolution**, and examples abound of commoners refusing to behave in a deferential manner. It would be naïve, however, to say that the American Revolution swept away systems of deference along with British political authority. Although aristocratic titles were abolished, such founders as John Adams and Thomas Jefferson believed fervently that "worthy" men should rule and that the masses should defer and follow.

The **masses** often proved intractable. By the early 1800s commoners complained bitterly of property requirements for voting, imprisonment for debt, and other "special privileges" that accrued to the rich. After the War of 1812, most states abolished many of the more blatant class-based laws, but enough remained for the Workingmen's parties of the late 1820s and early 1830s to make "equal rights" a centerpiece of their activities.

By mid-century, however, deference was alive and well; it had simply assumed other forms. The antebellum Southern social code was laden with faux chivalric ideals that were rooted in deference; likewise, **slaves** who failed to defer faced beatings and other sanctions. (Many slaves evolved complex subterfuges to disguise acts of defiance as acts of deference.) In the North, a new industrial capitalist class was emerging that demanded that wage earners submit to long hours, low pay, and substandard working, housing, and sanitary conditions. Many industrialists even demanded that their workforces accept the moral codes of their employers.

In the post–Civil War period, the rising **middle class** accelerated its embrace of the set of social norms often deemed **Victorianism**. Many aped English practices, including codes of deference. Civility, refinement, manners, and social interactions came to be defined by elite and middle-class norms, with those lower on the social scale expected to recognize the superior breeding of their alleged betters.

In the twentieth century deference took more subtle forms. The advent of mass, popular culture had a leveling effect insofar as one saw more convergence between the middle classes and **working classes**. One response of the **upper classes** and the **social climbers** seeking to join their ranks was to isolate themselves in educational, cultural, and social circles that positioned them to exercise power and hence command deference through the positions they held. **Ivy League** and other elite colleges, for example, remained exclusive bastions for the wealthy until the 1960s, and many remain less diverse than society at large. Elites also formed **social networks** designed to perpetuate class power and maintain control over such cultural institutions as the **opera** and **museums** that are designed, in part, to cultivate a sense of refinement that (they hope) sets them apart.

Deference has also taken on a less-savory connotation: the expectation that underlings owe unflinching deference to corporate executives. Although much has been made recently of imperious **CEO**s, overbearing executives such as **Donald Trump**, and bullying bosses, the phenomenon is not new. In the 1950s, for example, William Whyte warned of the dangers of the "organization man" who did not question his superiors and blindly carried out assigned tasks. Indeed, one could easily assert that both past and deference are conditions endemic to **capitalism**, which is, at its heart, a power dynamic; thus the line between due respect and abuse of position is easily transgressed.

Suggested Reading

John Kasson, *Rudeness and Civility: Manners in Nineteenth-Century Urban America*, 1990; Gregory Nobles, "A Class Act: Redefining 'Deference' in Early American History" (http://www.uga.edu/colonialseminar/Nobles2.pdf#search='deference%20and%20class); William H. Whyte, *The Organization Man*, 1956.

DEINDUSTRIALIZATION

ROBERT E. WEIR

The decline of the factory system in terms of its overall importance within the American economy is often called *deindustrialization*. As such it is a relative term; there are still more factories in contemporary America than there were during the nineteenth-century **Industrial Revolution**, but they are of declining rather than expanding importance within the overall economy.

By the end of World War I, the United States was the world's leading industrial power, and in the 1920s about 30 percent of all American jobs were in manufacturing. The United States retained its manufacturing might despite the **Great Depression** and emerged from World War II as even more dominant. This was especially the case of "smokestack" industries such as steel and iron production, automobiles, rubber, glass, electronics, consumer appliances, apparel, and textiles. Many of these factories were the backbone of **blue-collar** employment and provided livelihoods for members of the **working class**. In 1950 about one-third of all American jobs were in the manufacturing sector, a figure that remained little changed until the 1970s. By 1984, however, just 18.5 percent of American workers were employed in blue-collar factory jobs and by the early twenty-first century just over 10 percent.

In April 2006 roughly 13.2 million Americans worked in manufacturing, a figure that represented a loss of over 2 million jobs since 1970. Some of the decline was due to the pressures of **globalism**. By the 1960s the war-ravaged economies of Western Europe and Japan had recovered and begun to contest U.S. dominance in global markets. Although conservatives often cite overly high **wages** forced upon employers by the **labor movement** as a reason why American firms did not respond well to global competition, other observers cite U.S. **Cold War** policy as a central factor. According to the latter critique, the **military-industrial complex** siphoned research and development money and talent from the consumer sector and plowed it into weapons production. Many firms found military contracts more lucrative and neglected other manufacturing lines. This conspired to leave the nation with aging factories to compete against the state-of-the-art technology of economic rivals. Inefficient factories were hard hit by surges in energy costs that first took effect in the 1970s. The hyper-inflation that ensued meant that capital improvements were often neglected, the costs of American products soared, and cheaper imports undercut U.S. goods. Even the automobile industry—often considered the bellwether of American manufacturing health—lost market shares to companies such as Volkswagen, Toyota, and Nissan (originally imported as Datsun).

Deindustrialization also occurred because of changes in tax and trade laws. Tax cuts enacted by presidents Jimmy Carter and **Ronald Reagan** were partly aimed at lowering the corporate tax burden to encourage reinvestment. The cuts—especially those under Reagan—were lauded by fiscal conservatives, but they served far better as **corporate welfare** than as a **trickle-down** stimulus. This was especially true of large firms. U.S. Steel, for example, saved over $450 million in taxes, but rather than reinvest in steel production it gave large bonuses to shareholders and deemphasized manufacturing. From 1991 to 2001 it even operated as USX Corporation to signal that much of its revenue came from non–steel-related ventures: shopping malls, real estate transactions, engineering consultation, financial services, and so on. The 100 largest American firms pocketed huge profits in the 1980s, yet created less than 0.5 percent of all new jobs for the decade.

The effects of deindustrialization have been devastating for many communities, especially in the Northeast and Midwest, areas unflatteringly dubbed the "Rust Belt." Particularly hard hit were cities whose economic base was heavily tied to manufacturing, such as Akron, Buffalo, Detroit, Erie, Flint, Pittsburgh, and Youngstown. Youngstown, immortalized in song by **Bruce Springsteen**, has become an emblem of ongoing problems associated with deindustrialization. In addition to higher rates of **unemployment**, areas impacted by deindustrialization report above-average rates for social problems such as alcoholism, crime, divorce, domestic violence, drug addiction, and chronic illnesses. Studies also reveal that very few workers displaced by deindustrialization obtain new jobs that pay as well as those they have lost.

Deindustrialization has also been fueled by deregulation and changes in trade policy. Deregulation took away many of the safeguards from dangerous work conditions, how worker pensions were invested, how jobs were assigned, and how grievances were settled. Some firms seized the initiative to raid pension funds and smash labor unions, but the biggest impact has been the freeing of capital for use in other investments. The net result is that many firms decided to sell off assets, downsize operations, and eliminate jobs. Changes in trade laws made it easier for "American" firms to close plants in the United States and open them in low-wage nations. In some cases entire lines of work are outsourced. Even before the signing of the 1993 North American Free Trade Agreement (NAFTA), many firms had set up shops in Mexico, but an additional 880,000 U.S. jobs were lost in the next nine years. In the early twenty-first century more than 700,000 jobs were outsourced to India. Such vaunted American firms as Levi Strauss and Maytag now produce all their products abroad, and firms such as American Motors, Bethlehem Steel, TRW, and Youngstown Sheet and Tube have gone out of business. By 1987 only Zenith still offered American-made television sets, and by 1993 it merely assembled sets in two U.S. plants; the nation that perfected television now imports all of its receivers. Deindustrialization touches even American children; no mass-produced American-made bicycles have been manufactured since 1999, and 80 percent of all toys are manufactured in China and Southeast Asia.

Some commentators claim that deindustrialization is exaggerated and that the history of **capitalism** is that some enterprises falter while others rise. They point out that American cultural exports remain strong, that the United States is a pioneer in medical technology, that capital goods remain 49 percent of all U.S. exports, and that information services are in demand. This rosy assessment is not shared by all economists, many of whom wonder how the United States can sustain a high standard of living within an economy in which just 20.7 percent of the gross national product comes from durable goods and a whopping 78.3 percent is tied to the service sector. Of even greater concern is that America now imports much more than it exports and hence suffers from massive balance-of-trade deficits. In 2005 alone, the United States imported over $1.7 trillion worth of goods while exporting just $927.5 billion worth of goods and services.

Current trends suggest that deindustrialization has not peaked. In 2005 General Motors—once the world's largest corporation—announced plans to close nine U.S. and Canadian plants and eliminate 30,000 jobs in the process. Ford Motor announced similar plans. The overall decline of manufacturing as a percentage of the total economy is evident. In 1965 it made up 53 percent of the total; by 1988 that had sunk to 39 percent and by 2004 it was just 9 percent. Although the analysts who see these trends as cyclical readjustments may prove to be right, the social and economic impact on the working and **middle classes** could be quite traumatic.

Suggested Reading

Donald Bartlett and James Steele, *America: What Went Wrong?* 1993; Randy Colwell, *Most Un-American Event Ever: Deindustrialization and the Maytag Sellout*, 2005;

Jefferson Cowie and Joseph Heathcott, eds., *Beyond the Ruins: The Meanings of Deindustrialization*, 2003; Steven High, *Industrial Sunset: The Making of North America's Rust Belt, 1969–1984*, 2002.

DELMONICO'S

ROBERT E. WEIR

One of several New York City restaurants famed in the **Gilded Age** as social and dining destinations for the well-heeled, Delmonico's is often evoked as a metaphor for both the opulence of the late nineteenth century and its tendency toward excess. Dining at Delmonico's was surely a marker of social class, as only members of the **upper** and upper **middle class** could afford it. In the 1880s millionaire banker August Belmont was reputed to have a monthly wine tab of around $20,000. Delmonico's is sometimes credited with being the first formal public restaurant in the United States, the first to offer an à la carte menu rather than fixed meals, and the first to introduce European-style fine dining. Such culinary delights as Lobster Newberg, Baked Alaska, avocados, terrapin soup, and chicken à la king were said to have debuted at Delmonico's, as well as its namesake steak and a potato dish.

Delmonico's began rather humbly when Swiss émigrés Giovanni and Pietro Del-Monico opened a pastry shop and café on South William Street in 1827. Two years later they opened a restaurant that quickly became known for innovative cooking at a time in which American fare could charitably be called basic. In 1831 nephew Lorenzo Delmonico arrived from Switzerland, got involved with the restaurant, and began to cater to a more upscale clientele. He parlayed the **Europhilia** of New York's social elites into a profitable enterprise by modeling various New York establishments on Parisian restaurants. By 1838 the Delmonico's menu was 100 pages long and featured 370 separate items.

The Delmonicos moved their enterprises numerous times, often following population shifts uptown, but a centerpiece was its 2 South William Street restaurant, nicknamed "The Citadel" because of its grandeur. Another branch opened on Chambers Street near City Hall in 1856, catering to bankers, stockbrokers, and high society. By then, Delmonico's was associated almost entirely with wealthy patrons. An 1876 restaurant opened at 26th and Fifth Avenue surpassed even The Citadel in opulence, featuring chandeliers, mirrors, fountains, frescos, and a ballroom. In the 1870s, the Delmonicos operated four separate upscale restaurants.

Delmonico's contracted upon Lorenzo's death in 1882, and by 1888 operated only two establishments. In 1891, however, a new eight-story restaurant opened on William Street, and five years later another debuted at 44th and Fifth that was renowned for its Palm Garden and which was reputedly the first restaurant to feature an orchestra playing as patrons dined. By the end of the nineteenth century, however, Delmonico's began to lose its grip on New York society, which had gravitated to its many imitators. It closed its 26th Street restaurant in 1899, was embroiled in propriety law suits from 1904 to 1907, and began to hemorrhage money. The flagship William Street establishment closed in 1917, and the firm filed for bankruptcy in 1919. It was sold to Edward L.C. Robins, who had the misfortune to take over the business just as Prohibition put a damper on the high-end liquor trade once enjoyed by posh patrons. It was raided for liquor violations in 1921 and closed in 1923. Since then several other hotels and restaurants have used the Delmonico's name, but they bear little relationship to the original, despite efforts to associate themselves with its eminence.

During its heyday, Delmonico's clientele formed a compendium of Gilded Age wealth and fame from both America and abroad. Its diners included James Blaine, Diamond Jim Brady, Charles Dana, Charles Dickens, Jenny Lind, **Theodore Roosevelt**, Lillian Russell, Sir Walter

Delmonico's Restaurant, New York, ca. 1890–1910. © Photo Collection Alexander Alland, Sr./Corbis.

Scott, Mark Twain, Stanford White, Queen Victoria, and numerous governors, presidents, lawyers, merchants, and politicians. It was also the site of lavish banquets that some critics viewed as sybaritic displays of wretched excess. Infamous dinner parties featured acts of **conspicuous consumption** such as $100 bills rolled into cigarettes, the presentation of a $15,000 dog collar, and pearls embedded in dinner oysters.

Suggested Reading
Lewis Erenberg, *Steppin' Out: New York City and the Transformation of American Culture, 1890–1930*, 1981; Matthew Josephson, *The Robber Barons: The Great American Capitalists 1861–1901*, 1934; Joe O'Connell, "History of Delmonico's Restaurant and Business Operations in New York" (www.steakperfection.com/delmonico/History.html).

DEMOCRACY

ARTHUR HOLST

By definition, democracy is a form of government in which policies and laws are for the most part defined by the preference of the majority, usually through the process of election or referenda. More recently, the rise of nations and changing governments have been closely linked with the specific ideals of American democracy. According to a freelance research group, approximately 117 of the 192 countries in the world are democratic in nature. The rise of more constitutional forms of government has been closely associated with a reduction in global tension, rapid socioeconomic development, and social stability. Democratic governments are generally viewed as more peaceful while dealing with neighbors and better at educating their citizens, igniting human initiative, fostering productive ambition, and unleashing energy for constructive purposes, wealth origination, and economic growth.

In the contemporary age, democratic descriptions are used to denote situations and lifestyles—not just an ethics system or personality type. In essence, the basic principles behind democratic notions are to incorporate the differences and personal identities of an entire group and give each a fair share of input toward government actions, whether on a local or national level. In a pure democracy all opinions would be valued equally, and minority groups, as such, would not exist. It is clear, however, that most democracies deem some viewpoints as more valuable, especially those emanating from individuals with wealth.

For democratic systems to be effective, more is required of a country than voting equality for its citizens. The success of democracies is based largely on the premise of political **legitimation**, that is, a generalized acceptance of a political system. American democracy is conceptually thought of as a liberal democracy, a form of representative democracy in which the political power of the government body is regulated by a constitution that protects the liberties and freedoms of individuals and minorities. However, in the United States less than 2 percent of the population controls over 95 percent of the country's wealth and monetary **power**. American **capitalism** is controlled primarily by those who have the means to do so, meaning that it is easier for the more advantaged to make their opinions known and heard. So one may wonder how the United States is able to run a legitimate and functional democratic system.

For a democracy to function correctly, a population must first be divided into hypothetical "winners" and "losers," as not every citizen is going to be happy with the election of a particular official who received the majority of a vote. Even though these "losers" might be unhappy with an election, they know that the premises of democracy ensure that any rules or laws enforced will not be completely abhorrent; a democracy must take into account its minorities or it will lack legitimacy. Yet when such a small percentage controls the nation's wealth, the "minority" can potentially make up most of the American public. With the obvious presence of a wealthy **upper class**, there conversely must be a lower, **poverty**-ridden class. Thus, the presence of a **middle class** is often thought to be a determinate factor of democracy.

One of the most important ideologies of democracy is the notion that all citizens are able to participate in political decision making. It is often explicitly stated or at least implied that the government's power in a democratic state belongs to the people. However, more than 20 million people are living within U.S. borders as **immigrants**; unless they obtain citizenship, these people are not given the opportunity to participate in government. It is not a coincidence that many of these immigrants are part of the lower classes.

The middle class and **working class** make up the largest segment of the American population. Hypothetically, a large portion of the laws should be passed in the favor of these groups, but this is not always the case. Even though the middle strata represent the majority, the upper classes retain much of the power needed to control the country's laws. The upper classes, because of their class power, have the ability to influence outcomes and decisions to benefit their interests relative to those of other classes. This can be seen in the ways in which those with wealth assert political capital to secure the passage of **corporate welfare** benefits. Another example of class stratification is in the education system. Those in lower classes are usually forced to attend schools with fewer resources, which in turn leads to long-term negative results and retards upward **social mobility** for those at the bottom.

Democracy is often criticized for the possibility of a "tyranny of the majority," an idea first suggested by **John Stuart Mill**. This term implies that a government reflecting majority opinion will oppress minorities. This can be accomplished by dictating which social classes get certain benefits. Ironically, though, modern democracy is often more prone to tyranny by the (numerical) minority: the upper classes.

Overall, the existence of a democracy in the United States creates and keeps many of our social classes separate, without much individual hope of climbing or establishing oneself in a different class. Democracy in practice often limits human ambition and inhibits the redistribution of the wealth. In essence, democracy keeps the rich rich and the poor poor.

Suggested Reading
Thom Hartman, *What Would Jefferson Do? A Return to Democracy*, 2005; Pat McGuire, *The Nonpartisan League and Social Democracy in the U.S.: Social Networks, Class Power, State Occupancy, and Embedded Class Biases*, 2002; Alan Wolfe, *Does American Democracy Still Work?* 2006.

DEPARTMENT STORES

JANEAN MOLLET-VAN BECKUM

Large retail establishments that sell a wide variety of products, department stores grew out of the **lower-** and **middle-class**–owned peddler carts and specialized shops. The first true department store was founded in Paris in 1838 by L.A. Boileau; it was named Le Bon Marché (the good market). The first American department store is usually considered to be Alexander Stewart's New York City establishment, which opened in 1846, but department stores developed in earnest after the **Civil War**, many created by talented entrepreneurs such as Rowland Macy, Marshall Field, and Richard Sears and Alvah C. Roebuck.

These early stores employed mainly **working-class** women but catered to the upper middle and **upper-class** consumer. The store owners' policy of hiring cheap labor while serving high-class clientele created conflict. Workers often dressed above their perceived station in life to attract desirable customers to the store. In turn, they began to see themselves as equal to those they served, a notion of which the upper class disapproved.

Department stores were one of the driving forces toward a more egalitarian society, especially for women. Jobs created by the stores gave the women who held them a respectable alternative to other work outside the home. Although department store jobs often entailed long hours and low pay, many women preferred them to factory work, which generally involved even longer hours, lower wages, and more dangerous conditions. They also allowed the female consumer to meet her shopping needs on her own in one location. Although catering to the upper classes, cheaper prices of the mass-produced goods sold meant that the lower classes could afford some of the cheaper items.

Department stores were also essential in the distribution of mass-produced goods of the **Industrial Revolution** as well as the dissemination of new technologies and innovations. They were often the first to offer new goods to the public. Being able to buy in quantity helped to keep prices low, and this in turn democratized consumption and influenced both urban and rural values and lifestyles.

Along with the department store came mail order catalogs, the remedy for the rural customer. For many rural consumers the U.S. Mail was the only way to purchase uncommon items not stocked by the local general store. As nearly 70 percent of the country's population lived in rural areas until the 1920s, there was a huge market for the mail order service. The most widely known mail order catalog was Montgomery Ward's, created by former shopkeeper Aaron Montgomery Ward in 1872. With mass production in full swing, and transportation and mail service across the United States improving, Ward built a company that by 1882 did more than $1 million in sales. The availability of nearly everything large-city dwellers could buy created more equality between the urban and rural communities. Today, the Internet has taken over many of the services mail order catalogues of the past served, allowing consumers to purchase from retailers worldwide.

Catalog sales notwithstanding, department stores would not have been possible without the dramatic expansion of urbanization and industrialization during the **Gilded Age**. Mass migrations of workers from rural areas to cities created a need for more and less-expensive goods. Department stores also spawned innovation and employment in areas other than retail. Because of the sheer size of the stores, architectural advancements were needed to make them run smoothly. New and different building materials and designs, as well as improved heating, cooling, and lighting technology, were driven by the needs of department stores.

Department stores inspired discount stores, which offered a wide array of goods at even cheaper prices. Discounters such as F.W. Woolworth, J. J. Newberry, and W.T. Grant began their enterprises in the early twentieth century and by the 1950s provided stiff competition for department stores. By the 1970s discounters such as K-Mart routinely outperformed department stores, which were badly hurt by stagflation and high overhead. Moreover, the flagships of many department store chains were located in **inner cities** rocked by urban riots and social problems. Although department stores opened branches in suburban shopping malls, many venerable names had perished or merged by the early twenty-first century: Hudson's, Steiger's, Wannamaker's, Jordan Marsh, Filene's, Field's. Even Sears and Roebuck recently merged with K-Mart. Some analysts consider old-style department stores a sunset enterprise that will soon be eclipsed by specialty stores and discounters such as Target and **Wal-Mart**. Wal-Mart in particular has been demonized as destructive of small stores and department stores alike. It provides goods at lower costs, in part, because of high-volume wholesale purchases, but also because it pays low wages and provides very few benefits to its employees. If the

Wal-Mart model prevails, links may be severed in the historical associations between department stores, community pride, **status** mobility for clerks, and opportunities for women.

Suggested Reading
Susan P. Benson, *Counter Cultures: Saleswomen, Managers, and Customers in American Department Stores, 1890–1940*, 1988; Robert Hendrikson, *The Grand Emporiums: The Illustrated History of America's Great Department Stores*, 1979; Bill Lancaster, *The Department Store: A Social History*, 1995.

DESIGNER GOODS
See Luxury Goods

DISCONTINUOUS VIEWS OF CLASS
See Continuous/Discontinuous Views of Class

DISENFRANCHISEMENT
CARMELITA N. PICKETT

Disenfranchisement is the deliberate act of depriving a group of people or a person of civil or electoral privileges.

When America was founded in 1789, **voting rights** were granted only to white male property owners, thus disenfranchising African Americans, white women, poor white men, and ethnic minorities. During **slavery** African Americans were considered three-fifths of a person for tax purposes. The issue of slavery ripped the country apart, finally coming to a head when Abraham Lincoln issued the Emancipation Proclamation on January 1, 1863. After the **Civil War** ended in 1865, Congress passed the Thirteenth Amendment abolishing slavery; in 1868 the Fourteenth was passed, granting African American citizenship rights. This amendment was followed by the Fifteenth Amendment, granting voting rights to African American males but still excluding all women.

During the Reconstruction era (1865–77) blacks began to gain political power, but after the election of Rutherford B. Hayes, progress halted. Southern whites, who resented African Americans running for office, used intimidation and violence to maintain white supremacy. Supreme Court decisions such as *The United States v. Cruikshank* (1875) and *Plessy v. Ferguson* (1896) undermined the Fifteenth Amendment and upheld "separate but equal" principles that were thinly veiled disenfranchisement mechanisms. By the early twentieth century most Southern states had adopted legal policies, such as grandfather clauses, literacy tests, and poll taxes, that denied African Americans the right to vote.

Women gained voting rights in 1920 with the enactment of the Nineteenth Amendment to the Constitution. Although this was a celebrated accomplishment, its full impact was felt mostly by white women; African American women and men still faced obstacles if they attempted to vote.

There were occasional small victories for African American political empowerment. In 1928 a black Republican, Oscar De Priest, was elected to Congress from Chicago. But it took another seventeen years before another African American, Adam Clayton Powell, was elected to Congress, representing **Harlem**, New York. After African Americans returned from World War II, many realized they had been fighting for freedom abroad but were denied freedom in their own country. Many became committed to gaining true citizenship in the United States. The 1954 Supreme Court decision *Brown vs. the Board of Education of Topeka* struck down many of the assumptions of "separate but equal" clauses. This led many African Americans to realize that their quest for full citizenship in America was progressing and that **segregation** would soon be outlawed. Congress followed the Supreme Court decision with the Civil Rights Act of 1964. This act outlawed segregation in all public areas in America, meaning that African Americans could drink from the same water fountains as whites, ride the bus without giving up their seats to whites, and dine in restaurants without going to the back door. These changes were definitely significant, but without political representation in the South, African Americans could still be deprived of their civil rights. The Voting Rights Act of 1965 abolished discriminatory practices that were practiced by Southern states. This act gave not only African Americans the right to vote but also other ethnic groups such as **Latinos** and **Asian Americans**.

During the 2000 presidential election many Americans watched George W. **Bush** claim the presidency while losing the popular vote. Al Gore, the Democratic candidate, finally conceded after thirty-seven days, while many Americans watched in disbelief. Political analysts speculated about voter irregularities in Florida. Many Americans asserted there was something wrong with the electoral process. The U.S. Commission on Civil Rights investigated the voting irregularities that occurred on Election Day in Florida and reported that polling locations were relocated without proper notification, defective machines were used, African Americans were prohibited from voting because of inadequate resources at polling sites, non-felons were removed from voter registration lists based on unreliable information, and persons with disabilities had limited access to certain polling sites. All of this suggested that disenfranchisement was still a feature of American society. Congress finally agreed to the Election Reform Bill. It required states to develop nondiscriminatory and uniform voter registration lists, and created provisional paper ballots to replace Florida's punch-card voting machines until the latter are replaced. Americans were finally faced with the reality of disenfranchisement: when votes are not honored, **democracy** is dishonored.

Suggested Reading

Lucias J. Barker, *African Americans and the American Political System*, 4th ed., 1999; Derrick Bell, *Race, Racism, and American Law*, 2000; John Fund, *Stealing Elections: How Voter Fraud Threatens Our Democracy*, 2004.

DOMHOFF, G. WILLIAM, JR. (August 6, 1936–)

ROBERT E. WEIR

George William Domhoff Jr. is a prominent psychologist and sociologist whose work in **conflict theory** is often invoked by scholars. He authenticates many of the suppositions of **C. Wright Mills**, illumines the inner workings of the **upper class**, and challenges the supposed openness of American **social mobility**.

Domhoff was born in Youngstown, Ohio, the son of George W. and Helen S. (Cornet) Domhoff. He obtained a BA in psychology from Duke in 1958, an MA in psychology from Kent State in 1959, and a PhD in psychology from the University of Miami in 1962. He taught at Los Angeles State College from 1962 to 1965, at which time he joined the faculty at the University of California–Santa Cruz, where he has taught psychology and sociology since. His work in the latter field is what most pertains to the study of social class.

Domhoff has studied the myriad ways in which upper-class **power** penetrates American society. Much like Mills's famed **power elite** studies, but in a more analytical and less ideological fashion, Domhoff posits the existence of an elite whose far-reaching agenda shapes everything from textbook content to the way the media present free enterprise. The elite also dominate political life, foreign policy decisions, university policies, and the construction of ideology. His work is a direct challenge to **pluralists**, who argue that the complexity of American society tends to diffuse power among numerous groups.

Domhoff takes his cue from **E. Digby Baltzell** in defining the American upper class. To be a member of the upper class, one is usually listed in the ***Social Register***, attends the proper prep schools and colleges, belongs to exclusive private clubs, and is either born or marries into wealth. Education is of utmost importance; like Baltzell, he argues that the proper schools act as "surrogate families" whose job it is to acculturate rich children into an upper-class subculture. This means that children attend prestigious prep schools, such as Andover, Groton, Hotchkiss, or Saint Mark's, and go on to elite colleges, the top four preferences being Harvard, Yale, Princeton, and Stanford, followed by remaining **Ivy League** schools and select private schools.

Domhoff also treats club activities, **debutante** balls, lavish parties, jet-set vacations, **yachting**, and upper-class retreats more seriously than many. Far from being exercises in frivolity or **conspicuous consumption**, he argues, this lifestyle solidifies group identity and facilitates the creation of networks that give the upper class its power. For example, members of the upper class often belong to social clubs in various cities, a practice that makes policy coordination or business deals easier to execute. This point is crucial; Domhoff dismisses the popular notion of the upper class as a leisure class. The upper class *does* work; business and finance are the favored professions, followed by law, then medicine and other pursuits such as architecture and museum administration. There is a tendency toward patriarchy among the upper class, with men engaging in professions and women in volunteer and **philanthropic** ventures.

Domhoff views this group as a true power elite. His 1983 study of top industrial, financial, communications, and utility firms revealed that more than half of their directors came from the upper class. Among the trustees of leading universities and colleges, 45 percent are found on the *Social Register*. Even more surprising is their presence on boards at state colleges and universities. Domhoff and others have also noted the prevalence of upper-class members in presidential cabinets, in the diplomatic corps, in **think tanks**, and in various government positions. Domhoff's work also suggests that political affiliation is of little consequence; Democrats and Republicans alike are equally beholden to powerful and wealthy patrons.

The consequences of upper-class penetration of American institutions are far-reaching. First, it poses an obstacle to upward mobility. Rather than a **meritocracy**, Domhoff sees "sponsored mobility" systems that favor members of the upper class. His work closely parallels others that show occupations are inherited far more often than the conventional myth of self-made individuals holds. Class is often the determiner of who gets recruited for certain careers or tasks. This is decidedly the case in politics, where the candidates selected to run are seldom those emerging from the grass roots.

Second, the upper class possesses extraordinary resources that ensure its values and beliefs are put forth favorably. For example, the media put forth a relentlessly pro-business spin on the news, seldom bothering to point out the way in which the American economy is controlled by interlocking networks or the ways in which business decisions negatively impact workers. In a like manner, few Americans are told that foreign policy initiatives are often driven by think tanks and policy boards dominated by corporate leaders. The upper class even exerts control over how Americans are socialized through the pressure it exerts on school curricula, teacher training, and textbook content.

Of particular concern is the ability of the upper class (through public officials) to plant disinformation. In the 1960s and 1970s, for example, campaigns were launched against several protest groups based on misleading or false information. It was found, for instance, that many anti-Vietnam War groups were riddled with FBI informers and that some acts of violence blamed on such groups were actually the work of government agents provocateurs. Likewise, through upper-class control over the media the American public can be led astray on an array of government initiatives, ranging from economic plans to military decisions.

Although few would deny that the upper class exerts disproportionate influence in American society, Domhoff's suggestion that a **business aristocracy** rules America with scant regard for **democracy** or the **masses** is highly controversial.

Suggested Reading

G. William Domhoff, *Who Rules America?*, 1967 (updated as *Who Really Rules?*, 1978, and *Who Rules America Now?*, 1983); Domhoff, *The Power Elite and the State: How Policy Is Made in America*, 1990; Domhoff, *Changing the Powers That Be: How the Left Can Stop Losing and Win*, 2003.

DORR REBELLION

ARTHUR HOLST

The Dorr Rebellion took place in Rhode Island in 1841–42; it was named for its leader, Thomas Wilson Dorr, and was a struggle for change in Rhode Island's electoral system. Rhode Island had historically experienced problems within its system of voting. Originally established as a colony by King Charles II of England in 1663, Rhode Island retained property requirements for voting long after such provisos were abolished elsewhere. Originally only white landowners had the right to vote. Later changes excluded even some of them and stipulated that one had to have property valued at $134 or more (over $2,300 in 2005 dollars) to vote. After the **American Revolution**, Rhode Island saw a pop-

TYRANTS PROSTRATE   LIBERTY TRIUMPHANT.

A polemic applauding Democratic support of the Dorrite cause in Rhode Island. "Tyrants Prostrate" is a pro-Dorr statement, praising the support of the movement by Democratic candidates Polk and Dallas while portraying Whigs Henry Clay, Theodore Frelinghuy, and Daniel Webster as enemies of the freedom of religion. Courtesy of the Library of Congress.

ulation increase, as it was one of the earliest states to experience the **Industrial Revolution**. By 1840 nearly 60 percent of white males were ineligible to vote because the state was still operating under its charter of 1663. By then Rhode Island was the only state without a universal suffrage system for white males.

The initial 1841 rebellion lacked support, but in October 1842 Dorr and his supporters held an extralegal People's Convention, which declared all white males eligible to vote after a period of one year's residency. Dorr wrote a lengthy convention report, which he sent to the official legislature. This set off a tit-for-tat chain of events that exacerbated tension. The Rhode Island legislature formed a Freemen's Constitution that went against Dorr and the People's Convention. The latter promptly voted on and defeated the Freemen's Constitution.

The Chepachet Free Will Baptist Church played a big role in the Dorr Rebellion. The founder of the Chepachet Free Will Baptist Church Society, Job Armstrong, was against Dorr's rebellion. Nonetheless, three leading Dorrites came from the Society—Samuel Young Atwell, Amasa Eddy, Jr., and General Jedediah Sprague—and it provided more supporters among its members than any other organization in the state. About 300 of the Chepachet supporters were armed. In early 1842 both Dorr and the "Charterites," who supported Governor Samuel Ward King, held competing elections.

Predictably, rival polls only increased tension. On May 18 Dorr and his followers tried to seize a state **armory** but were forced to retreat to Chepachet, where they tried to reconvene the People's Convention. Governor King issued an arrest warrant for Dorr on June 8, along with a reward that increased over time from $1,000 to $5,000. Dorr fled the state but returned later in 1842. Faced with the potential for expanded armed conflict, the Rhode Island General Assembly (legislature) met at **Newport** and created a new constitution that greatly liberalized the requirements for voting. It opened voting to any white man who could pay a $1 poll tax.

Dorr was not destined for hero status. He was found guilty of treason against the state of Rhode Island and was sentenced to life imprisonment and hard labor. His harsh sentence was widely condemned, and one year later Dorr was released for health issues. Dorr suffered mental disability for the rest of his life, though his civil rights were restored in 1851 and the court's judgment against him overturned three years later. He died in 1854.

Suggested Reading

Joyce M. Botelho, *Right & Might: The Dorr Rebellion & the Struggle for Equal Rights*, 1992; Paul Buhle, Scott Molloy, and Gail Sansbury, eds., *A History of Rhode Island Working People*, 1983; Marvin Gettleman, *The Dorr Rebellion: A Study in American Radicalism, 1833–1849*, 1973.

DOT-COM BUBBLE

JESSICA LIVINGSTON

The term *dot-com bubble* refers to the period of speculative frenzy surrounding Internet and technology companies in the late 1990s. A stock market bubble is a self-perpetuating boom in the price of stocks in a particular industry. Speculators notice a stock rising rapidly in value and buy it in hopes of further increases rather than because the company itself is undervalued. Companies can become overvalued, as were many dot-coms in the 1990s. When the bubble burst in 2000, stock prices plummeted and many companies went out of business.

During the boom, venture capitalists and entrepreneurs were often more focused on using companies to create stocks and increase shareholder value than on building a company. Because the number of stocks in Internet companies was limited, the prices of stock skyrocketed. Stocks rose even for nonprofitable companies. For example, Webvan, a company that sold groceries online and delivered them, was valued at $8 billion in its initial public offering (IPO) in November 1999. The company, which had been in existence for less than a year, was operating on a deficit and was expected to lose more than a half a billion dollars in its first three years of operation. Even the stock values of successful companies such as America Online, Yahoo!, and Amazon.com exceeded the companies' value. During 1998 America Online's stock rose by 593 percent, Yahoo!'s by 584 percent, and Amazon.com's by 970 percent.

The media contributed to the bubble. Rather than engaging in investigative reporting, the media offered tip-sheet journalism. They celebrated successful businessmen such as Steve Case of America Online and Jeff Bezos of Amazon.com. The press was not interested in exposing the unsound business practices of Webvan and other failing companies. A number of new magazines, such as *Wired* and *Fast Company*, devoted themselves to information technology and Internet businesses. Journalists and media companies had a vested interest in *not* reporting that the economy was in the midst of a bubble because they themselves were benefiting from this bubble. Overall, they helped to popularize investing in the stock market.

The Federal Reserve, which was created after the **stock market** crash of 1929 to prevent speculative excess, failed to stop this speculative frenzy. While a rising trade deficit, a dropping savings rate, and increasing indebtedness indicated that the economy was in an increasingly precarious position, the Federal Reserve did nothing. Chairman of the Federal Reserve Alan Greenspan, a committed free-market conservative, resisted pressure from colleagues to raise interest rates.

A belief in the "New Economy"—that the Internet was transforming the American economy—buoyed the dot-com bubble. This idea appealed to many, and Wall Street analysts and Internet investors frequently touted the virtues of the "New Economy" and the economic benefits of technology. This New Economy argument, however, exaggerated the role that information technology plays in the economy. From a historical perspective, the New Economy arguments about a "new era without depressions" were similar to those made in the 1920s about the "new economics." In retrospect, most bubbles are mass deceptions.

Suggested Reading
John Cassidy, *Dot.Con: How America Lost Its Mind and Money in the Internet Era*, 2002; Philip J. Kaplan, *F'd Companies: Spectacular Dot-com Flameouts*, 2002; Roger Lowenstein, *Origins of the Crash: The Great Bubble and Its Undoing*, 2004.

DREISER, THEODORE (August 17, 1871–December 28, 1945)

JACQUI SHINE

Dreiser was an American novelist, journalist, and social critic whose fiction explored American class differences through the lens of urban life. Best known as a novelist, though prolific in multiple genres, Dreiser published eight novels among his twenty-seven books. He also had a long career of prominent social and ideological activism. He enjoyed associations with such prominent radicals as **Emma Goldman**, and a visit to the Soviet Union in the late 1920s cemented his interest in the **Communist Party** as an alternative to the American economic system. A writer and activist until late in his life, Dreiser died of heart failure in California, where he had made his home for several years prior.

Born into a large family headed by a German immigrant whose declining fortunes in the wool industry coincided with Dreiser's childhood years, Dreiser left home in Indiana at 16 to work as a reporter in Chicago, a move that would become central to some of his most famous fiction. He attended, but did not graduate from, Indiana University.

His first novel, *Sister Carrie*, was published in 1900. *Sister Carrie* was an early example of American literary naturalism, which sought to portray life—particularly urban life—with careful attention to detail and attention to the causative factors, such as heredity and circumstance, that influence behavior. The novel's titular heroine, seduced by city life, leaves her family's home in rural Wisconsin to go to

Theodore Dreiser, 1943. Courtesy of Eon Images.

Chicago, where she begins her urban life in a crowded apartment that she pays for with her sweatshop **wages**. By the end of the story, however, Carrie's fortunes have risen considerably, though not through the usual "pluck and luck" of earlier fictional heroes. Carrie, by contrast to **Horatio Alger**'s hard-working young boys whose courage and fortitude brings them success, instead becomes a happily kept woman and adulteress; when her second husband's fortune fails, she leaves him and becomes a successful actress. Her disgraced husband eventually ends his life in a transient hotel.

In presenting the story of Carrie's life without judgment and with the clinical detachment that is a hallmark of naturalism, the novel emphasizes that class distinctions have less to do with character, ambition, and moral turpitude than with sheer luck—less with what one deserves than what one stumbles into. Dispensing with the moralistic and proto-religious tone of earlier American fiction that equated economic poverty with ideological or moral **poverty**, Dreiser's *Sister Carrie* marked a significant shift in literary portrayals of class.

Following the novel's publication, Dreiser, suffering from writer's block, worked several years as a reporter and magazine editor, bringing his interest in social reform to his work with the women's magazine *The Delineator*. His second novel, *Jennie Gerhardt*, was published in 1911; much in the vein of *Sister Carrie*, the eponymous heroine has an affair with a senator and gives birth to his illegitimate child.

Dreiser then began exploring social class from the perspective of American business and economic institutions with 1912's *The Financier*. The first in his "Trilogy of Desire," also known as the "Cowperwood Trilogy" after the series' fictional analogue for Chicago transportation magnate Charles Yerkes, *The Financier* follows Frank Cowperwood's ambitious ascent to **power** and wealth. His acquisitive greed shapes his career in the railroad industry and includes aggressive and illegal investment practices. Yet even after Cowperwood is arrested and jailed, he is not reformed; the character and the characterization are amoral. There is no redemptive experience for Cowperwood or for the reader, because the novel's conceit is dispassionate observation, not moral judgment.

Dreiser's work was suppressed and censored by publishers and editors over the course of his career; *Sister Carrie* was met with deep resistance from the literary community and even from Frank Doubleday, his publisher, who considered it sordid and immoral. Support from public literary figures such as H.L. Mencken and the publication of 1925's *An American Tragedy*, based on a 1906 murder, as well as a growing international reputation, began bringing Dreiser greater acclaim.

Now known more for his pioneering naturalism than for his sometimes overburdened writing style, Dreiser is recognized as a major literary force whose work helped to change attitudes about **social mobility** and character.

Suggested Reading

Theodore Dreiser, *Sister Carrie*, 1900; Dreiser WebSource, University of Pennsylvania (http://www.library.upenn.edu/collections/rbm/dreiser/); Yoshinobu Hakutani, ed., *Theodore Dreiser and American Culture: New Readings*, 2000.

DRUG POLICY

ROBERT E. WEIR

The use of physical and mind-altering substances in the United States is widespread. How society responds, however, is inconsistent and controversial. In the public mind, the term *drug* usually implies an illegal substance. Medically speaking, though, a drug is any introduced agent that changes the way the human body or psyche responds on its own accord.

Public policy on drugs is and has been incongruous. Now-banned substances such as marijuana, cocaine, and LSD were once legal; in essence, the use of certain drugs is viewed as a social problem only when the legal system has so defined it. Many drugs are considered the purview of the legal system rather than the medical profession; hence possession and use of some categories of drugs are sometimes prosecuted out of proportion to the actual social danger they represent, and serious conditions such as addiction often incur legal sanctions rather than medical treatment.

Drug policy within the United States is rife with instability, injustice, and intolerance. The very definition of an "illicit" drug is an example. From a medical and sociological standpoint the most-abused drugs in the United States are alcohol and tobacco, both of which are regulated only for minors. Mortality studies for the 1980s show that more than 5 million Americans died of tobacco-related problems during the decade, 1 million more from alcohol abuse, and just 350,000 from all other addictions combined. Alcohol is, by far, the most serious drug in terms of its link to social problems. Throughout the 1990s, approximately half of all fatal auto accidents and homicides were alcohol related. Alcohol abuse also correlates highly with rape, domestic violence, and a host of illnesses including heart disease and cirrhosis. Alcoholics are seven times more likely to divorce and twice as likely to miss work as nonabusers. One estimate from 1990 claimed that alcohol-related problems cost Americans $86 billion per year, whereas those associated with illegal drugs cost only $58 billion. By 1999 National Institutes of Health statistics pegged alcohol abuse–related problems at $184.6 billion annually, greater than the $151.4 dollar loss associated with drug abuse in a Letwin Group study. (The latter figure is deceptive as a raw number because it also includes abuse of prescription drugs, a figure that has soared in the wake of rising HIV rates.)

Nonetheless, by the 1990s 36 percent of all federal arrests were for possession, sale, or distribution of illegal drugs, a figure that had doubled since 1980. Those percentages have continued to rise. As the much-ballyhooed "war on drugs" intensifies, class and race inequities have become more obvious. Members of the **lower class**, African Americans, and **Latinos** are disproportionately prosecuted for drug offenses, even though studies reveal that members of the **middle** and **upper classes** use certain types of drugs with greater frequency. This is especially the case for powder cocaine, an expensive drug whose use is more common among affluent users. In pure form, powder cocaine is more addictive and dangerous than "crack" cocaine, which is smoked. Crack is more common among less-affluent users, and those arrested for crack offenses routinely receive much harsher sentences than are meted out for powder cocaine arrestees. **Conflict theorists** link this disparity to **racism** and **classism**.

In fact, contemporary drug abuse is often presented as synonymous with **ghettos**, **poverty**, and minority groups, much as drug abuse was associated with hippie subculture in the 1960s. Upper- and middle-class drug use is often ignored altogether, or is considered a medical problem when abuse occurs. In the nineteenth century, for example, many middle-class women used an opium-based substance known as laudanum; likewise, some scholars believe that the largest group of drug abusers in American history was **suburban** women of the 1950s whose abuse of legally prescribed tranquilizers dwarfed that of ghetto heroin addicts. Conservatives often associate drug use with permissive liberal values, but the link between political ideology and drug use is weak. In fact, cocaine use was highest in the 1980s, when conservative Republican **Ronald Reagan** was in office, and many who snorted cocaine were wealthy. When conservatives abuse drugs, however, as in the much-publicized revelation in 2003 that right-wing radio host Rush Limbaugh was addicted to painkillers, the focus tends to shift from enforcement to treatment.

After tobacco and alcohol, the next most used drug in the United States is marijuana (pot). Pot use cuts across social class and ethnic barriers and is so widespread that many consider it a recreational drug like alcohol, though alcohol consumption is far greater than pot smoking and the use of marijuana has declined steadily since 1980. Medical and social problems associated with smoking pot are few; nonetheless, an average of about 500,000 people are arrested annually for possession of marijuana. Some police and urban politicians argue that the cost of prosecuting such trivial offenses robs resources from more serious crime-fighting initiatives. Calls for legalization of marijuana have run into ideological barriers, but in some locales simple possession is now akin to public-order offenses that result in minor citations.

This is decidedly *not* the case for sale and distribution, however, and this is another area in which social class and ethnicity become visible. Dealers are often members of socially or economically disadvantaged groups; as the middle link between users and suppliers, they are more visible and far more likely to get arrested. Suppliers are frequently quite affluent, and some have ties to organized crime; most are many levels removed from individual drug transactions and are therefore seldom caught. Suspicions run high that a sizable percentage of money deposited in Florida banks comes from high-stakes drug supplying, but it takes careful and time-consuming investigation to crack drug rings. Instead, officials touting progress in the war on drugs often elevate the arrest of low-level dealers as evidence of "getting tough on crime."

Amphetamine and barbiturate abuse largely cut across social class lines, though there is a slight tendency for middle-class addicts to be dependent on painkillers such as OxyContin rather than illegally manufactured compounds. Members of the lower class are also more likely to support drug habits through crime; amphetamine use is particularly associated with incidents of violent crime in poor neighborhoods. According to the Drug Enforcement Agency nearly 20 million Americans have at some point used painkillers illegally.

In addition to crack there are several drugs that are more commonly abused by members of the lower and **working class**. Among these is the hallucinogen PCP (phencyclidine), often known as Angel Dust. It is now the fourth most consumed drug in America. Heroin addiction is also higher among those of lower socioeconomic and educational levels. The high cost of heroin nearly guarantees that its users will commit other crimes; heroin use correlates highly with prostitution, burglary, theft, robbery, and drug dealing. Data suggest that as high as 75 percent of serious crime in urban areas is associated with drug addiction. Heroin use is also correlated with hepatitis and AIDS, as injection needles are often shared.

Why an individual uses or abuses drugs varies, but there are several class markers. Researchers assert that availability is the single greatest predictor of drug use. This is why drug use is high among doctors, for example, and it also explains why ghettos contain large numbers of addicts. Peer groups also exert great influence, which is why teens, young adults, and **gang** members are more likely to use drugs. Poverty is also a factor; those with reduced **life chances** sometimes use drugs to ameliorate despair. There are also data that link drug use with prolonged periods of **unemployment**. The poor are also more prone to be in **one-parent families**, another associated factor for addiction.

Addiction is a serious social problem, but critics of current drug policy argue that little progress can be made until the social focus shifts from law enforcement to social justice and medical treatment. They also point to the hypocrisy of how society views drug users. Athletes use a variety of drugs to enhance their performance, some of them illegal—as in the case of major league baseball stars Jose Canseco and Mark McGwire and football's Lyle Alzado, who used steroids, and those such as basketball's Len Bias, who died from drug use. The scandals notwithstanding, **advertising** saturates the airwaves and newspapers with appeals to use legal drugs, perhaps creating a pill-popping culture. Although it is true that those from the lower classes have higher addiction rates than those of the upper and middle classes, those with resources are *more* likely to experiment with drugs.

Suggested Reading

Paul Galigher, *Illegal Drugs: A Complete Guide to their History, Chemistry, Use and Abuse*, 2003; James Inciardi, *Drug Control and the Courts*, 1996; Inciardi and Karen McElrath, eds., *The American Drug Scene: An Anthology*, 1998; Office of National Drug Control Policy, *Pulse Check: National Trends in Drug Abuse*, 1997.

DRURY, VICTOR (February 24, 1825–January 21, 1918)

ROBERT E. WEIR

Victor S. Drury was a French-born radical active in the **Knights of Labor** in the 1880s. Although Drury is little known today, a series of articles he wrote for *The Socialist* in 1876 and gathered into book form as *The Polity of the Labor Movement* (1885) was exceedingly influential among **working-class** radicals in the late nineteenth century. Indeed, *The Polity of Labor* ranked with the writings of Karl Marx and **Henry George** among American **anarchists**, **socialists**, and other radicals.

During his long life Drury himself dabbled in numerous oppositional political forms, always from the perspective that work ennobled individuals and that non-producers were social parasites. As a young man he participated in an attempted overthrow of the French government of Louis Philippe in 1848. He was present at the first International Working Men's Association (IWMA) meeting in London in 1864, where he witnessed the debate between anarchist followers of Mikhail Bakunin and those adhering to the path laid out by Marx and Engels in *The Communist Manifesto*.

At first Drury sided with Marx and emigrated to New York City in 1867 to establish French-speaking chapters of the IWMA. He was in New York when the IWMA met there in 1872, just one year after the collapse of the Paris Commune, which had given hope to **communists** worldwide. By this time, however, Drury was beginning to question orthodox Marxism, especially Marx's assertion that the **labor movement** and trade unions would be the vanguard of a revolutionary movement. Drury was particularly influenced by the **utopianism** of Charles Fourier and Albert Brisbane, as well as Ferdinand Lassalle's insistence that Marx undervalued the role of the state.

When Drury wrote *The Polity* in 1876, he brought all his influences together. Like Fourier and Brisbane, he rejected the possibility of finding justice within **capitalism** and insisted that worker-owned cooperatives were integral to overthrowing the profit system. Like the Lassalleans, he grew distrustful of trade unions, which he privately viewed as parochial self-interest groups, although he generally spoke positively of them in public. He also envisioned that the state itself would be the vehicle for reforming society and urged workers to seize control through the ballot box. He was prepared, as many orthodox Marxists were not, to be patient as the working class consolidated its power.

Like most nineteenth-century reformers, Drury was also an advocate of land for settlers. His attacks on landlords, speculators, and absentee owners were quite popular among readers. He was respectful of the Grange and Greenback movements, but he chided each for placing too much hope that the monetary or banking systems could be reformed. In his view, only government ownership of things in the public interest—transportation, communications, property, exchange systems—would benefit laborers, and it was necessary that these things not be subject to economic forces of supply and demand.

Drury's views on labor won him many friends. As long as labor was viewed as a commodity, he argued, it would fall prey to what David Ricardo called the "iron law of wages"; that is, employers would drive wages down to subsistence level and workers would be denied upward **social mobility**. Drury argued there were only two social classes: producers and non-producers. The latter group commanded

80 percent of all society's resources, and Drury argued that society's "golden age" would emerge only when that percentage shifted to producers.

Drury also attacked nationalism and warfare, wrote about land redistribution in ways that anticipated (and perhaps influenced) **Edward Bellamy**, and put forth tax schemes consonant with Henry George and the **single tax**. Overall, though, it was his passionate defense of the labor theory of value—that it is the amount of labor imbued in any product or endeavor that sets its worth—that made *The Polity* so popular among workers. Many embraced Drury's thesis that they were being exploited by greedy and dishonest **robber barons**.

Drury moved sharply to the left, even as workers devoured his writings. By the early 1880s he had become an anarchist and no longer advocated the patience about which he wrote in *The Polity*. In 1883 he sponsored Johann Most's lecture tour of North America, and he coauthored the Pittsburgh Manifesto, a fiery document that espoused violence. During this time Drury was also active with the Knights of Labor (KOL) in New York City and became the center of an internecine struggle within the organization. Many New York Knights were Lassalleans who felt that KOL leader **Terence Powderly** was too cautious and that he kowtowed to trade unionists. Drury led an internal sect called the Home Club and used his own *Polity of the Labor Movement* as a proselytizing tool to gain support for an attempted takeover of the KOL.

The Home Club occupied much of the KOL's energies between 1882 and 1890, and it probably controlled the organization from late 1885 through 1887. Eventually both the Home Club and Drury were brought down, ironically with help of orthodox Marxists led by Daniel DeLeon. Drury began to modify his views in the 1890s and spent his remaining years as a mystic Christian socialist. Many of his late writings reflect a return to Fourier and Brisbane. By the time of his death in 1918, he was largely forgotten.

Nonetheless, Drury's obscurity—heightened in no small part by his mania for secrecy—should not blind scholars to his importance in articulating social class for nineteenth-century workers. His simple bifurcation of producers and non-producers was a typical viewpoint and serves as a reminder that capitalism was contested, that many workers rejected the idea that they held common interests with employers, and that late nineteenth-century laborers held more **class consciousness** than do most contemporary workers. They may also have been more politically educated and astute.

Suggested Reading

Victor Drury, *The Polity of the Labor Movement: A Synopsis*, 1885; Leszek Kolakovski, *Main Currents of Marxism*, 1978; Robert E. Weir, "'Here's to the Men Who Lose!': The Hidden Career of Victor Drury," *Labor History* 36.4 (Fall 1995), pp. 530–556.

Du Bois, W. E. B. (February 23, 1868–August 27, 1963)

Veronica C. Hendrick

Du Bois was an important African American civil rights advocate, prominent radical, and crusader for social justice.

W. E. B. Du Bois. Courtesy of Eon Images.

Du Bois was born five years after President Abraham Lincoln signed the Emancipation Proclamation (1863) and two years after the passage of the Thirteenth Amendment (1865), which constitutionally abolished **slavery** in the United States. He was raised in Great Barrington, Massachusetts, a free state since 1780, and graduated from its public high school. While just a teenager, he began to write a newspaper column for *The New York Globe*, which catered to a black readership. In 1884 he received a scholarship to attend Fisk University in Nashville, Tennessee. After graduating, he transferred to Harvard, where he received both a bachelor's and master's degree. Still hungry for knowledge, Du Bois pursued two years of doctoral study at the University of Berlin before returning to the United States as a teacher and completing his PhD at Harvard.

Despite enjoying the privilege to pursue his education and attend one of the nation's top schools, Du Bois focused his attention of the overall situation of black Americans. He was very concerned with the lack of social progress made by freed slaves and their descendants. To receive his PhD from Harvard, Du Bois wrote a dissertation titled "The Suppression of the African Slave Trade to the United States of America, 1638–1870." This project, along with his other writings, demonstrates the seriousness of his attention to the struggling **lower class** of black Americans.

Du Bois was a leading civil rights figure during the late 1890s and into the first half of the twentieth century. He focused upon improving the social, economic, and political conditions of black Americans. Du Bois is most famous for creating the Niagara Movement (1905), which demanded full civil rights for blacks. He was also involved in the creation of the National Association for the Advancement of Colored People (**NAACP**). Various civil rights leaders developed the NAACP, but Du Bois became one of its most famous members. He was responsible for editing the NAACP's magazine, *Crisis*, from 1910 to 1934.

The works presented in *Crisis* and Du Bois's other lectures and writings discussed civil rights and equality for black Americans. He believed political and legal action could force the United States to recognize these civil rights. Unlike his colleague Booker T. Washington, Du Bois felt it was a mistake to accept the small concessions offered to American blacks, especially in relationship to voting rights and education. Also unlike Washington, Du Bois stressed the need for intellectual and cultural advancement of blacks. He believed that a percentage of the black race should strive to excel in **education** and industry, thereby paving the way for future generations. In his 1903 article titled "The Talented Tenth," Du Bois argued that African American liberation would be led by its "exceptional men." Ultimately, Du Bois fell away from the NAACP. He did not like the organization's push to have black culture blend completely into white culture. Du Bois wanted to highlight the strength and beauty of African American society.

Politically, Du Bois was concerned with issues of **segregation** and education, although he also had a deep appreciation for the cultural and artistic experiences of African Americans. Du Bois's interest in the welfare of people of color extended beyond America's borders. He asserted that the treatment of blacks worldwide was an issue of class. Du Bois organized a series of Pan-African conferences to unify blacks throughout the world in order to combat global racism. These conferences inspired him to dig into African history and write several books. Later in life, Du Bois became unhappy with the progress that black Americans had made in terms of equality and social status. He also moved politically to the left, becoming a member of the **Communist Party** when he was 93. He became increasingly involved with Pan-Africanism and, in 1961, moved to Ghana. Disgusted with the lack of progress in America, Du Bois gave up his U.S. citizenship to become a citizen of Ghana, where he died in 1963.

Suggested Reading

Seamus Cavan, *W.E.B. Du Bois and Racial Relations*, 1993; David L. Lewis, *W.E.B. Du Bois—Biography of a Race, 1868–1919*, 1993; James Neyland, *W.E.B. Du Bois*, 1992.

DYE, THOMAS (December 16, 1935–)

ROBERT E. WEIR

Thomas Roy Dye is a political scientist whose work on the entrenched **power** of the **upper class** parallels that of sociological **conflict theorists** such as Randall Collins and **G. William Domhoff**.

Dye was born in Pittsburgh and was educated at Pennsylvania State University, where he obtained his BA in 1957, his MA in 1959, and his PhD in 1961. He taught at numerous colleges and universities before joining the government department of Florida State University (FSU) in 1968. He has been a visiting professor at Bar Ilan University, the University of Arizona, and the Brookings Institute. He also directed the FSU Policy Sciences Center from 1978 to 1991 and remains affiliated with it. Professor Dye has won numerous awards and research grants.

Much of Dye's research has looked at the relationships between power, wealth, and decision making. He is among those scholars who posit the existence of a **corporate class** that operates as a de facto **power elite**. Americans like to view their society as open and tell stories of upward **social mobility** and institutional leadership based on **meritocracy**, but Dye is dubious of these cherished myths. He has argued that who gets what, when, and how is often more a function of social standing than merit, and his meticulous analyses of political and social institutions back his assertions. He notes that access to and use of bureaucratic structures is one way that power is obtained and retained among elites. In studies of the corporate class from the 1970s on, Dye has shown that, within top corporations, roughly 90 percent of the top officials come from either the upper class or the upper **middle class**. The **Horatio Alger** saga of rising from **blue-collar** labor to the upper class is, in truth, quite rare.

Like Domhoff, with whom he has collaborated, Dye argues that the corporate class has influence that stretches far beyond company boardrooms. Because of interlocking directorships and **social networks**, the corporate class also dominates college and university trustee boards, **think tanks**, foreign policy committees, lobby groups, and decisions on research and grant funding. It also has greater access to politicians. Dye's *Who's Running America?* series has focused on the corporate class's influence on presidencies from Jimmy Carter to George W. **Bush** and shown the consistency with which the economic interests of American elites are given priority.

Dye argues that decision making in America is mostly a top-down process that often disregards the wishes and best interests of average Americans. A study of the roughly 7,000 elites associated with the George W. Bush administration shows that decisions are hammered out by law firms, interest groups, think tanks, and foundations, not in accordance with public opinion or social need. In fact, earlier Dye studies reveal the degree to which the media are used to sell and reinforce elite points of view. By 1995, for instance, just fifteen newspaper chains controlled more than 50 percent of the papers sold in the United States. Likewise, television networks are owned by corporate interests that make certain that pro-business stories are reported and which (can) operate as censors. NBC, for example, is owned by RCA, while ABC is owned by Disney; Viacom owns CBS, and the Fox network is part of the media empire formed by the controversial Rupert Murdoch, whom some have regarded as a right-wing ideologue.

Dye's work suggests that American **democracy** often takes a back seat to class and economic interests.

Suggested Reading

Thomas Dye, *Who's Running America?* 1976 (revised 1979, 1983, 1986, 1990, 1994, 2001); Dye, *Top Down Policymaking*, 2001; Dye, *Power and Society*, 2004.

E

ECONOMIC OPPORTUNITY ACT OF 1964 (EOA)

ARTHUR HOLST

The Economic Opportunity Act of 1964 (EOA) was an important antipoverty measure passed during the administration of President Lyndon B. Johnson.

After the assassination of John F. **Kennedy** in 1963, Vice President Johnson took the reins of the presidency with an internal agenda to improve the general welfare of the United States. With the nation knee-deep in the **Cold War** and after seeing the hardships of broken populations in poor countries, President Johnson spoke of a **Great Society** in his first inaugural address in 1964. Johnson declared an overall **War on Poverty** to improve the lives of the most vulnerable Americans.

The centerpiece of Johnson's antipoverty measures was the implementation of the EOA in the legislative arena. The EOA was passed in August 1964 after having been drafted in the previous February. Johnson stated that the EOA's primary focus was to "mobilize the human and financial resources of the Nation to combat poverty in the United States," so as to "not make the poor more secure in their **poverty** but to reach down and help them lift themselves out of the ruts of poverty and more." The EOA was originally coordinated by the Office of Economic Opportunity, but presently many of its original sections have been rescinded and the remaining functions transferred to other federal agencies.

President Johnson believed that, through the "Great Society" and the EOA, all American citizens would be able to achieve their full economic and societal potential, as would the United States as a nation. This could only happen if each person contributed to the development of society, whether through the workforce or in some other manner. To that end, educational and vocational training were central to the EOA's mission.

Johnson recognized that in most cases it is best to start education or useful work experience at a young age; therefore, he set up the **Job Corps**. The Job Corps was (and is) available to those between the ages of sixteen and twenty-one, and it provided for both rural and urban residential centers for education, vocational training, and basic work experience. Education was also provided for adults, and the Economic Employment Act of 1964 also provided loans to **small businesses** attempting to establish roots. Other programs set up by the EOA included **Head Start**, VISTA (Volunteers in Service to America, a domestic version of Peace Corps), and the Neighborhood Youth Corps, which created projects and jobs for high-risk inner city children. There were also programs devoted to family planning, adult education, community health, expanded legal services, summer youth programs, senior centers, work study programs, and meal preparation for seniors and the poor.

The EOA also set up community action agencies (CAAs) to deliver direct help, which currently reaches about 96 percent of the nation's poor. Since 1964 the EOA has established more than 1,600 CAAs at the local level to assist in the implementation of the standards set on the federal level. Since then community action agencies have helped more than 13 million people nationwide. Each CAA is conducted and supervised by residents of the local area only. They deliver assistance in forms ranging from immediate emergency food and housing needs to long-term educational, nutritional, and health programs.

The EOA has been the target of conservatives and advocates of **self-reliance**, who see its programs as fostering dependency. Some of its critics have correctly identified waste within some programs. Nonetheless, the EOA has played a vital part in improving the quality of life for disadvantaged Americans.

Suggested Reading

Community Action Partnership, http://www.communityactionpartnership.com/default.asp; Richard H. Davidson and Sar A. Lefvian, *Antipoverty Housekeeping: The Administration of the Economic Opportunity Act*, 1968; Richard Worth, *Poverty*, 1997; David Zarefsky, *President Johnson's War on Poverty*, 1986.

EDGE CITY

ROBERT E. WEIR

Edge city is a commonplace term among urban planners and urban sociologists that refers to commercial, retail, and technology centers and other enterprise clusters that emerge on the fringes of municipalities. Quite often these appear at the intersections of interstate highways or along the "beltline" feeder roads to them. Some see edge cities as an extension of **white flight** to the suburbs and as entities that further erode the vitality of nearby cities. The fact that many of them lie in unincorporated lands outside the control of any elected government adds to the controversy.

The term was coined in 1991 by *Washington Post* journalist Joel Garreau, whose prototype is Tysons Corner, Virginia, a collection of shopping malls, hotels, and business offices that arose at the junction of Interstates 495 and 66 outside of Washington, D.C., and close to Dulles International Airport. Tysons Corner sports several hundred retail stores, more than 3,000 hotel rooms, and over 100,000 jobs. Garreau set five criteria for edge city status: more than 5 million square feet of office space, over 600,000 square feet of retail space (often in the form of malls), more jobs than homes, an attempt to provide for basic human commercial and recreational needs in a single environment, and the emergence of said activity in an area that had recently been undeveloped.

Garreau identified 123 edge cities in 1991 and another 83 that were in the process of becoming so. The bulk were located along the crowded urban corridors of the East and western California, but the phenomenon appears across the United States; new edge cities have emerged since Garreau's original study.

A definitional complication has arisen in that some edge cities have begun to spawn construction of new homes. If this trend continues, Garreau's criterion that edge cities tend to be commuter areas whose populations decline after work hours will lose its validity. This has led some critics to question the legitimacy of the concept and to view edge cities as simply another manifestation of urban sprawl: in essence, an extension of the **suburbs**. The greater Los Angeles area, for example, now encompasses an area that surpasses the state of Rhode Island in size.

Still another point of view disputes Garreau's criticism that edge cities tend to erode further already declining urban centers. Some view edge cities as economic engines that create new opportunities and serve as magnets to draw new residents seeking economic opportunity, visitors, and regional investors who would otherwise avoid nearby cities. A recent study of Chicago-area edge cities such as Rolling Meadows, Deerfield, Oak Brook, Des Plaines, and Rosemont suggests that edge cities provide a higher quality of life and greater stability than either urban Chicago or its closest suburbs.

The future of edge cities is uncertain, but their immediate impact on urban areas and social class is clearer. Edge cities may indeed serve as economic generators in some areas, but for the most part they drain more jobs from cities than they replace. Retail and commercial activities that once formed the backbone of **inner city** economic life have tended to shift further away from the urban core. Urban shoppers often have fewer options and often pay more for consumer goods, groceries, and entertainment than more prosperous suburbanites or upwardly mobile families that have easy access to edge cities. Moreover, edge cities entail longer commutes for those in nearby cities who often hold the bulk of service sector jobs. In essence, edge cities serve to exacerbate **stratification** rather than act as levelers.

The vast majority of those who hold high-paying jobs in edge cities go there to shop or be entertained, and live near or in them, are white, upwardly mobile, and members of the upper levels of the **middle class**. As economic activity gets further from the urban core, inner cities have become repositories for people of color, immigrants, and the poor. The population of Washington, D.C., for example, is 60 percent African-American and its economic profile is significantly lower from the population residing near Tysons Corner. Data from a 2002 Chicago study showed that the median income for the city was around $36,000, while those in edge cities enjoyed incomes of $57,500. Atlanta, another city ringed with edge cities, is over 61 percent black; Detroit's population is almost 82 percent African-American, and Birmingham, Alabama's, is over 73 percent. The same pattern of minority inner cities surrounded by white edge cities prevails where large **Latino** populations cluster, such as East Los Angeles, El Paso, and Miami, whose inner city Latinos make up 97, 77, and 66 percent of the populations, respectively.

The lack of political accountability in edge cities is also troubling. Because many are not part of any municipal body or regional authority, residents of these areas get to vote on matters that affect nearby cities without having to deal with the consequences of their decisions. In the Chicago study, 31 percent of edge city residents called for cuts to welfare programs, as opposed to just 17 percent of Chicago residents. Similarly, just 44 percent of edge city dwellers supported subsidized housing for low-income workers, an idea favored by 60 percent of Chicagoans; 72 percent of the city's residents identified unfairness in school funding schemes, but just 48 percent of edge city residents agreed.

Some observers predict that it is inevitable that edge cities will be absorbed by metropolitan or regional governments and authority boards. If edge cities do indeed evolve into new suburbs—already dubbed technoburbs, suburban cores, and perimeter cities by those who project this process—it does not necessarily bode well for regional cooperation, if examples from existing suburbs can be taken as a measure. If that pattern is replicated, edge cities will simply replicate existing racial and economic stratification trends.

Suggested Reading

Richard D. Bingham, ed., *Beyond Edge Cities*, 1997; Woody Carter, Robert Frolick, and Tim Frye, "Edge Cities or Edge Suburbs," (www.roosevelt.edu/ima/pdfs/edge-cities.pdf); Joel Garreau, *Edge City: Life on the New Frontier*, 1991.

EDUCATION

ROBERT E. WEIR

Education has traditionally been (and remains) a key factor in upward **social mobility**. Nonetheless, the quantity and quality of education that individuals receive often depend on class, ethnicity, **race**, and **gender**. This is true on all levels of the educational system, but it is acutely the case for primary and secondary education. The United States, unlike many democracies, does not have a national curriculum, nor does it fund schools equitably. Local school districts must raise part of their operating expenses from taxes; this practice tilts the balance heavily in favor of wealthier communities. **Upper-** and **middle-class** families also have **private education** options that are generally unavailable to poor families.

Quality education historically corresponds with **wealth**. In Colonial society, many individuals had rudimentary reading skills and men might have had some background in mathematics and accounting, but a college education was a **status** marker for a small number of upper-class individuals. Early universities such as Harvard (1636), Yale (1701), and William and Mary (1693) trained mostly ministers and dilettante scholars. By the end of the eighteenth century, most of the **Ivy League** colleges had been established, and nearly all of their students came from wealthy families. Benjamin Franklin is generally credited with advancing the idea of practical education aimed at training professionals, but this was not widespread practice until the nineteenth century.

The concept of free public education was bolstered by the **American Revolution**, initially as a way of advancing ideals of republicanism and patriotism. In 1789 Massachusetts became the first state to require towns to provide tax-funded public elementary education. Because of the advocacy of women such as Judith Sargent Murray and Abigail **Adams**, girls were also educated in Massachusetts. Upper-class women, however, were generally sent to private academies, and it remained the custom elsewhere for females to receive little (if any) formal education. In 1800 there were no public schools outside of New England. Southern states also enacted laws that forbade teaching **slaves** to read or write, and even in the North very few African Americans obtained formal education.

By 1860, however, all states had enacted some form of public education. Federal land sales stipulated that money be set aside for that purpose, and urbanization led to renewed emphasis on the need for practical education. Horace Mann championed free universal education and formal teacher training, as did reformer George Henry Evans, who saw education as necessary for members of the **working class** to advance. Education was also bolstered by government legislation such as the 1862 Morrill Land Grant Act, which set aside land for agricultural colleges. Many state colleges and universities began as land grant colleges. During **Reconstruction** African Americans of all ages flocked to schools. Some **Native Americans** also received education, although much of it came in the form of forced assimilation programs aimed at "civilizing" Indians.

Educational opportunities expanded for white men and women during the **Gilded Age** but contracted for African Americans. Educational opportunity went hand-in-hand with industrialization, and scholars generally agree that a latent function was to delay the entry of males into the job market. By the late nineteenth century, more students were entering high schools, and the number of colleges nearly doubled between 1870 and 1900. Single women made up the bulk of all teachers outside of colleges, and the profession was poorly paid. **Segregation** laws also meant that black students were educated separately from whites, a principle enshrined in the 1896 *Plessy v. Ferguson* Supreme Court decision. In practical terms it meant that, in many places, African Americans received inferior education—and many got none whatsoever beyond elementary school. By 1911 just sixty-four high schools in the entire South accepted black students, and no state universities did so. It was not until the 1960s that public colleges in the South were forced to lower racial barriers.

Reforms during the **Progressive Era**, spearheaded by individuals such as John Dewey, finally shifted American education toward a pragmatic curriculum for all. By 1920 there were nearly 600,000 students enrolled in colleges, almost half of them women. Female teachers, however, remained poorly paid, and most states fired women educators who married, a trend that accelerated during the **Great Depression**.

The post–World War II period shaped many of the parameters of contemporary education. The federal government did much to promote education, in part because it linked an educated citizenry with **Cold War** objectives of touting American values and of developing scientific knowledge that might be of military value. The structure of the **military-industrial complex** began to emerge in the 1950s. The GI Bill sent thousands of veterans to college after World War II, stimulating an overall growth of the university system, especially among public institutions. Overall, college enrollments soared from 2.3 million in 1940 to 7.4 million in 1970.

Public education expanded greatly during the 1950s, with the population surge resulting from the baby boom leading the way. The 1954 Supreme Court decision *Brown v. the Board of Education of Topeka* paved the way for black students to expand their educational horizons, though a bitter civil rights struggle was needed to make *Brown* operational. *Brown* also presaged ways in which American education became inextricably entangled with politics and social tension. The upheaval of the 1960s, fueled in part by a rising tide of baby boomers attending college, raised questions about many assumptions of education and society. Demands for black studies, women's studies, and critical social theory convulsed college campuses, and an influx of non-European immigrants touched off debates over **bilingualism** in public schools.

Tensions associated with the increasing diversity of American society have often leached into American schools, where they have mixed with social class to create a toxic brew. Liberals and conservatives routinely spar over **culture war** agendas such as sex education, **creationism**, funding girls' sports on par with those of boys, negotiating with teachers' unions, and a host of other values-based issues. Even more serious are disputes over who gets what sort of education.

Although strides have been made in some areas of gender equity, and nearly all colleges and universities now admit women, female students continue to complain that they are treated differently from males on all levels. In 1972 Title IX linked federal funding to equal spending for females, but the 1984 Supreme Court decision *Grove City v. Bell* limited the scope of this equality to specific programs, not entire institutions. Early in the twenty-first century the percentage of women attending college surpassed that of males, but sexism has yet to be vanquished.

Inequality is more obvious when applied to race and **socioeconomic status**. In 1944 **Gunnar Myrdal** noted problems associated with segregated school systems. Yet studies done fourteen years after the *Brown* decision showed that 77 percent of black students still attended segregated schools. That figure had dropped to 64 percent by 1984, but **Reagan**-era attacks on affirmative action caused the numbers to climb again, and by the twenty-first century, American schools were more segregated than they had been at the time of *Brown*.

This increased segregation has been due largely to white flight from urban areas, including in the North and Midwest, which had abandoned legal segregation well in advance of *Brown*. Rising crime rates in **inner cities**, resistance to court-ordered busing mandates, and racism coupled with school problems such as assault, vandalism, and falling achievement scores have led many whites to move from the city or to enroll their children in private schools. Currently schools are segregated by de facto population shifts rather than statute, but suburban parents also exert their political will to resist efforts to alter the racial profiles of their schools.

Given that most schools rely on local funding, many black students, as well as poor whites and **Latinos** who cannot move to other districts, receive inferior educations. In his numerous studies of urban schools, **Jonathan Kozol** reveals a "savage inequality" in how children are educated. Detroit, for example, has a student body that is 90 percent black, but per-pupil expenditure is just 60 percent of what nearby affluent white suburbs such as Grosse Pointe or Bloomfield Hills spend. Kozol also reports on **Harlem** schools where students lack basic resources such as textbooks, paper, and sanitary facilities.

Minority students also complain that low expectations become **self-fulfilling prophecies**, a charge backed by evidence showing that African Americans, Latinos, and the poor are more likely to be placed in special education programs, business tracks, or **vocational** programs. **Conflict theorists** charge that one of the functions schools perform is to weed out students so that prime opportunities are reserved for children of the middle and upper classes. By 2003 nearly 90 percent of all Caucasians over the age of twenty-five had a high school diploma, but just 80 percent of all African Americans and only 57 percent of Latinos. Moreover, inner city schools often do a poor job of preparing minority students for college. According to a 2004 Education Trust report, 57 percent of all Caucasian students who enter college graduate, but just 44 percent of all Hispanic and but 39 percent of all African American students obtain their bachelor degrees.

Minorities and the poor have also fought rearguard actions against attacks on compensatory education programs such as **Head Start**. In 1969 Arthur Jensen advanced a **eugenics**-like assault on compensatory education by arguing that African Americans were intellectually inferior, as evidenced by IQ tests. Subsequent studies have verified that the tests have built-in white biases and that compensatory education works to raise IQ scores, but this has not prevented conservatives such as Charles Murray from resurrecting inferiority claims in less overtly racist terms.

Wealth plays an enormous role in how children are educated. About 29 percent of Americans aged twenty-five to thirty-four had a college degree in 2000. According to the Department of Education, students from upper-income brackets are twice as likely to enroll in college as those from low-income families, and far more likely to graduate. Nearly two-thirds of qualified black students claim that they lack the financial resources to attend. Deep cuts in federal grant and loan programs have further eroded access for poorer students. In recent years critics have warned of an emerging two-tier higher educational system. Although Ivy League and other prestigious schools are more diverse today than in the 1950s, the trend is for **elite** schools to revert to pre–World War II patterns, with smaller state schools and **community colleges** becoming bastions of lower-income students. At Yale, for example, just 15 percent of the 2006 student body came from families earning less than $60,000 per year. There is a decided correlation between attending prep schools, being a **legacy**, or having college-educated parents and acceptance to top-rated schools.

Public education is currently under attack from political conservatives. The 1993 *A Nation at Risk* study from the National Commission on Excellence in Education painted a bleak picture of falling SAT scores, high drop-out rates, "dumbed-down" curricula, and ill-prepared teachers within American classrooms. The tone was alarmist, and some of the "evidence" was simply wrong: SAT scores, for example, dropped initially because many more students were taking them, but they have been remarkably stable since 1975. Nonetheless, there have been calls to "return to the basics," and many states have enacted teacher and student tests before granting certification or diplomas. Conservatives have also touted merit pay based on student achievement as a condition for teacher raises—a move critics charge would penalize teachers in poor districts. Some have also called for **school vouchers** to allow parents to send children to any school of their choice, but these remain problematic, as vouchers would divert tax dollars into private education. Other controversial ideas include scrapping **school tracking**, increasing the length of the school day, mandating homework, and making students wear uniforms. What remains off the table in most places is equalizing school spending, standardizing curricula, or making college education affordable for all. Indeed, states such as California and Vermont, which have enacted laws to try to reduce spending gaps, have faced stiff challenges to overturn such legislation. Education can be a great equalizer, but it is not and never has been a portrait of equality.

Suggested Reading

Jonathan Kozol, *Amazing Grace: The Lives of Children and the Conscience of a Nation*, 1996; Rosalyn Mickelson and Stephen Smith, "Education and the Struggle against Race, Class, and Gender Inequality," in *Mapping the Social Landscape*, ed. Margaret L. Andersen and Patricia Hill Collins, 2006, pp. 289–304; Gary Orfield and Susan Eaton, *Dismantling Desegregation: The Quiet Reversal of* Brown v. Board of Education, 1997.

EHRENREICH, BARBARA (August 26, 1941–)

STACEY INGRUM RANDALL

Barbara Ehrenreich is the author of fourteen books that focus on women's issues related to health, welfare, and economics, including the *New York Times* bestseller *Nickel and Dimed*. Ehrenreich is a prolific author and activist who believes that women have been controlled by the status quo in the United States. Recent works examine the lives of American women who are working **blue-collar** jobs, trying to survive and take care of their families. She is a frequent contributor to the *New York Times*, *Harpers*, and the *Progressive* as well as a contributing writer to *Time* magazine. *Bait and Switch: The (Futile) Pursuit of the American Dream*, was published in 2005, expounds on the problems of low-wage workers.

Ehrenreich was born Barbara Alexander in Butte, Montana, in 1941. Her father made his living as a copper miner and attended night classes in order to attend Carnegie Mellon. Though Ehrenreich's father was lucky enough to escape the mines of Montana, neither he nor his daughter ever abandoned concern for the **working class.** The image of the struggles of wage-earning families was deeply ingrained in Ehrenreich's mind and spurred her later work on the poor. Ehrenreich attended Reed College, where she studied chemistry and physics. She went on to graduate school at **Rockefeller** University, where she earned a doctorate in cell biology in 1968 at the age of twenty-seven. A self-described nerd and reader of Dostoevsky and Conrad, Ehrenreich became involved in the antiwar activism of New York, and it was there that she met her first husband, John Ehrenreich.

This focus on activism led Ehrenreich to the first of several books that focused on women's issues and **gender stratification**. She wrote two booklets on women's health along with Deirdre English: *Witches, Midwives, and Nurses: A History of Women Healers* and *Complaints and Disorders: The Sexual Politics of Sickness*. These two works were extremely influential to the women's health movement of the 1970s and continue to be read today. Ehrenreich and English questioned the social control that existed over women, particularly the **power** exerted by male physicians and the medical community. They argued that the swift transition from an **agrarian** to an industrial society had left American women at loose ends as to their place in society. In older, preindustrial societies women were subordinate, but their work was necessary and indispensable for the family's survival. Women were also skilled healers and midwives who were respected for their knowledge as they held a valuable place in society. Modern **capitalism** had shattered the world into two spheres—public

Author Barbara Ehrenreich promotes her book *Bait and Switch* at Book Expo 2005 NYC. © Nancy Kaszerman/ZUMA/Corbis.

and private—which stand in opposition to one another. In this new world, men worked in the public realm and women stayed at home, which meant that traditionally feminine roles such as that of midwives became increasingly taken over by men. Women's health care was moved from the home into the hospital and became increasingly standardized and sterilized, excluding most women from being anything other than a patient. Ehrenreich's works with English were among the founding documents of the women's health movement and are seen as pathbreaking.

Ehrenreich's *Fear of Falling* is often cited by scholars of the American **middle class**. This work is controversial in that she does not see the middle class as the bedrock of American society. Instead she views the middle class as fragile, endangered, and frightened. Its tenuous hold on **status** and prosperity has led to an internalized "fear of falling" that has made it insular, self-absorbed, and intolerant. She traces its slow abandonment of liberal social values and its retreat into mean-spiritedness and self-aggrandizement. She calls on the middle class, which she argues is imperiled, to join forces with the equally endangered working class.

Ehrenreich has been the recipient of numerous grants and awards, including a Ford Foundation Award for Humanistic Perspectives on Contemporary Society (1982), a Guggenheim Fellowship (1987–88), and a grant for Research and Writing from the John D. and Catherine T. MacArthur Foundation (1995). She shared the National Magazine Award for Excellence in Reporting (1980) and has received honorary degrees from numerous universities, including Reed College, the State University of New York at Old Westbury, the College of Wooster in Ohio, John Jay College, and La Trobe University in Melbourne, Australia. Her work has been and remains controversial. Her critics view her as a polemicist and decry political views they interpret as sentimental **socialism.** Ehrenreich's many fans hail her as a champion of the downtrodden and a woman who is not afraid to take on entrenched power.

Suggested Reading
Barbara Ehrenreich, *Fear of Falling: The Inner Life of the Middle Class*, 1990; Ehrenreich, *Nickel and Dimed: On Not Getting By in America*, 2001; Ehrenreich, *Bait and Switch: The (Futile) Pursuit of the American Dream*, 2005; Ehrenreich, *For Her Own Good: Two Centuries of the Experts' Advice to Women*, 2005.

ELITISM

See Classism.

ENTITLEMENTS

GERALD FRIEDMAN

Entitlements are benefits, money, goods, or services that individuals receive automatically if they meet fixed criteria. These are bestowed without any discretion on the part of the granting agency. Some entitlement benefits are universal; among these are the rights to practice religion, to receive due process of law, or to move freely in society. Other entitlements depend on one's previous work record, such as **Social Security** retirement income, unemployment insurance, Medicare benefits, or the tax deduction received for employer-provided health insurance. Finally, there are means-tested entitlements, which are dependent on one's income, such as food stamps, Medicaid, or Transitional Assistance to Needy Families (TANF). Individuals receive these only if their income is below a certain threshold level. Different categories of entitlements have different distributional consequences because they generally go to different people.

Because it depends on the population that meets prescribed rules, entitlement spending does not rely upon the annual appropriation process in which Congress or state legislatures vote particular sums for particular programs. Entitlements, therefore, can grow without being subject to annual review. Perhaps for this reason, entitlement spending has grown faster than discretionary spending. Including both direct expenditures and "tax expenditures," where individuals who meet certain criteria are able to lower their income taxes, federal entitlement spending was over $1.6 trillion in 2005. As half of total federal direct expenditures of $2.6 trillion and tax expenditures of over $700 billion, entitlements are 14 percent of the entire United States economy. Most entitlement spending is in the areas of health care and elderly assistance; because spending in these areas is expected to grow rapidly with the aging of the population, one can anticipate that entitlements will also grow as a share of the federal budget.

Most entitlement benefits in the United States are linked to past work experience. The $125 billion tax benefit for employer-provided health insurance, for example, is exclusively for workers with relatively good jobs; the 45 million workers without employer-provided health insurance get nothing from this entitlement, and low-wage workers gain less than do better-paid workers and managers who pay taxes at a higher rate. Other entitlements also favor the relatively well-to-do. Originally available for only a third of the workforce, Social Security retirement is still not available for workers in agriculture and some service occupations. Retirement benefits are tied to past earnings, so workers who earn more in their working years receive larger pensions. **Unemployment** insurance also favors the relatively well off: benefits are available only for workers with a stable work history, and benefits are tied to past earnings.

In all, about 80 percent of entitlement benefits are associated with past work. This American accent on work-reinforcing entitlement benefits makes a contrast with countries where there are more universal benefits provided to all citizens. By associating entitlement benefits with work experience, the American approach rewards those who have done well in the labor market. This may reflect an attempt to encourage more productive market work; and Americans do work more than workers in other advanced **capitalist** countries, devoting 170 more hours per year to market work than do the British, 300 more hours than the French, 400 hours more than the Germans, and 500 hours more than the Norwegians.

By linking entitlements with work and by giving entitlements to those who are already doing well in the labor market, the United States limits the redistributive effect of entitlements. This approach also limits the impact of entitlement spending on **poverty** rates; American government programs have dramatically less effect on poverty rates than do programs in other countries. This approach is a conscious political decision. In many other countries, universal entitlement programs have been sponsored by radical and **socialist** political movements as part of a broader program to reduce inequality and to limit the scope of the labor market. Without a strong socialist political movement, there has been little support for universal programs and fewer challenges to market hegemony in the United States. Those who advocate government entitlement programs, therefore, have had to make their arguments consistent with the dominant market ideology by showing how their programs mimic market outcomes and even reinforce the market. Politically, they have had to attract supporters among political groups not inclined to favor socialist programs for universal entitlements. The Social Security Act of 1935, for example, was carefully structured to mimic insurance programs provided by capitalist firms, and to attract the support of well-paid workers without challenging existing capitalist retirement or other insurance programs. Sponsors of the act wanted to steer benefits to the poor, but in a hostile political and ideological climate they knew that they had to bring such entitlements in through the back door without distracting from the main attraction of a retirement program for those who were already relatively well-off.

American patterns of linking entitlements to work have bred a curious ideology. The vast majority of those receiving entitlements do not view them as such. They see entitlements as "rights" that emanate from and accrue because of hard work, as if they were **self-reliance** savings accounts. By contrast, needs-tested entitlements such as many of the **welfare** programs serving the **lower class** are seen as "give-aways" and are often resented by members of the **upper** and **middle classes**, and even some members of the **working class**.

Suggested Reading

Michael K. Brown, *Race, Money, and the American Welfare State*, 1999; Gosta Esping-Andersen, *The Three Worlds of Welfare Capitalism*, 1990.

ENVIRONMENTALISM

See Zoning.

EPISCOPALIANS

HOWELL WILLIAMS

Episcopalians are members of a Protestant denomination called the Episcopal Church, which was established as an American branch of the Church of England, or Anglican Church, in 1789. Traditionally, Episcopalians have occupied a prominent place in the nation's aristocracy, as they represented one of the wealthiest and best-educated denominations. However, historians are careful to point out that such generalizations exclude the diversity of Episcopalians and those who were not representative of America's ruling class. Although no religious group is class exclusive, one might notice a homogeneous social class at local levels and in church governance. Today the Episcopal Church of America has over 2 million members and comprises 1 percent of the U.S. population, but the denomination has been responsible for eleven U.S. presidents. Why have Episcopalians been historically so influential?

In Colonial America, Anglicanism was the dominant religion of the English colonies. Anglicans held the first service in America in Jamestown, Virginia, in 1607, and Anglicanism became the established state church in the southern colonies and several New York counties. Prominent southern families and wealthy planters were leaders in the church, as the aristocracy identified with the powerful and wealthy English government. According to historian Henry May, Anglicans in America considered themselves to be modern, rational, moderate, and enlightened, or in other words, English. They built elaborate church structures as evidence of their **power** and **prestige**. However, not all Colonial Anglicans appreciated the established church's connection with the upper echelon of society.

For example, in the eighteenth century Anglicans divided their loyalties. Some clergy remained loyal to the English crown while other colonists associated Anglicanism with British oppression and dominance by the elite. In fact, two-thirds of the people who signed the *Declaration of Independence* were Anglican, as was the first president, George Washington. Soon after independence, Anglicans in America established their own branch of the church, thereafter known as the Episcopal denomination.

In the beginning of the nineteenth century, the Episcopalians did not join in efforts with the **Baptists**, Methodists, and Presbyterians to evangelize the frontier, and many clergy returned to England. However, there were concentrations of Episcopalians called "low church," such as those in Virginia, who expressed more of an evangelical tradition, emphasizing preaching and salvific personal conversion. Other Episcopalian churches, in New York and Tennessee, developed a more sacramental, or "high church," tradition. These worship styles were not determined by geography, or necessarily by social class, but rather a preference for worship style and reactions to revivalism and emotionalism.

American religious history scholars have long been familiar with the popular stereotype: "The Baptists came on foot, the Methodists on horseback, and the Episcopalians in parlor cars." This trope contains some truth, in that Baptists and Methodists experienced rapid growth on the southern and western frontiers through Methodist itinerant preachers and Baptist farmer-preachers. The sheer magnitude of Baptist and Methodist growth, as well as the emergence of Presbyterians as a competitor for elite church members and patrons, challenged the powerful position of the Episcopal Church as a church of the **upper classes**.

Nonetheless, in the Victorian era the Episcopalians, Congregationalists, and Presbyterians formed the "establishment," or what were considered the most prestigious and influential denominations. For example, Episcopalians founded the University of the South in Sewanee, Tennessee, shortly before the **Civil War** as a university for the **elite**. The powerful men of the Confederacy, Robert E. Lee and Jefferson Davis, were also Episcopalian. On the **slavery** issue, northern and southern Episcopalians agreed to disagree, never officially dividing over the issue as other Protestant denominations did. Episcopalians never took an official stance, but the church in the South was generally supportive of slavery and **segregation**. Episcopal bishops Leonidas Polk of Louisiana and Stephen Elliot of Georgia were two of the largest slaveholders in the country.

The Episcopalian Church reached its apex during the **Gilded Age**, and many urban churches contained well-heeled industrialists who supported **Social Darwinism**. Yet the Episcopalians' liberal theology also fostered numerous individuals at the fore of the **Social Gospel** movement. Episcopalians rarely experienced schism, but in the late twentieth century, debates over women's ordination, a revised *Book of Common Prayer*, and sexuality caused more conservative, traditionalist groups to leave the Episcopal Church.

Today one can find Episcopal churches all over the United States, but the membership is not as nationally vast and encompassing as in the late nineteenth century. Its traditional geographic presence has been in urban areas, the Northeast, the Midwest, and the Tidewater South near concentrations of wealth and influence. Thus, in a contemporary age, one can continue to recognize some denominations not only by their religious ideas but also by their social **status**.

Suggested Reading

David Hein and Gardiner H. Shattuck Jr., *The Episcopalians*, 2004; John K. Nelson, *A Blessed Company: Parishes, Parsons, and Parishioners in Anglican Virginia, 1690–1776*, 2001; Peter W. Williams, *America's Religions: From Their Origins to the Twenty-First Century*, 2002.

EQUITY PAY

ROBERT E. WEIR

The term *equity pay* refers to plans that would close the wage gap that currently exists for many workers. Women, ethnic groups, and people of color tend to collect lower wages on average than white, male workers. In 2002, for example, white female workers made 72 cents to every dollar earned by male workers, African-American women 64 cents, and Latinas just 52 cents.

The wage gap has been a long-standing feature of the **wage** labor system and has served to drive down wage structures for all workers. In the mid-nineteenth century, for example, Irish and Chinese railroad crews worked for lower wages than native-born Caucasians, but the latter found their own struggle for higher pay frustrated by the presence of low-paid workers. As new immigrants poured into the United States between 1870 and 1920, the problem intensified. Employers frequently sought to replace disgruntled native workers with immigrants, women, and African Americans. Some within the **labor movement**, notably the **Knights of Labor** (KOL) and the **Industrial Workers of the World** (IWW), sought to include most workers within their fold, but the reaction of the **American Federation of Labor** was more defensive; many of its constituent unions made it difficult for marginalized workers to join. The decline of the KOL and IWW meant that many workers were excluded from the labor movement until the rise of the more inclusive **Congress of Industrial Organizations** (CIO) in the mid-1930s, although even the CIO was often slow to consider women. Several pieces of **New Deal** legislation even went so far as to justify a male/female wage gap, and a 1942 plan by the War Labor Board to equalize pay was not put in place by the time World War II ended. African Americans and ethnic minorities gained some protection under the 1941 Fair Employment Practices Act, but the scope of the law was too narrow and enforcement too spotty to make significant impact.

The 1963 Equal Pay Act finally mandated that men and women must receive equal pay for the same work, and the 1964 Civil Rights Act banned employment discrimination of women and people of color. Also in 1964, the Equal Employment Opportunity Commission was established to hasten hiring of minorities and protect them on the job. This was the beginning of modern affirmative action programs. Both law and intent have proved easy to circumvent, however, through devices such as creating classifications within jobs, writing job qualifications in ways designed to exclude certain groups, not revealing company wage structures, and devising deceptive job categories. Moreover, Supreme Court decisions in the 1970s and 1980s ended most mandated **quota systems** and weakened many affirmative action plans. Pay equity and "comparable worth" campaigns have become grassroots political causes for women and minorities, but thus far a proposed Paycheck Fairness Act designed to close wage gaps across the nation has not been passed.

The wage gap remains quite significant, and critics charge its major purpose is to create a secondary labor force whose debased economic status suppresses wages across the board. Labor union officials point to the large numbers of workers willing to cross strike picket lines as a measure of how employers conspire to keep wages low. They also point out that the richest 1 percent of Americans control over one-third of the nation's total wealth, and the bottom 80 percent command just 16 percent of the wealth. The wage gap is acute for racial and ethnic minorities. Overall, the median income for white families in 2002 was $55,885 but just $34,293 for African Americans and $34,968 for Latinos. These data render problematic the conservative view that equal opportunity exists in modern America and gives weight to the charge that pay inequity reinforces the existing class structure and institutionalizes inequality.

Suggested Reading

Jeanne Gregory, Ariane Hegewisch, and Rosemary Sales, eds., *Women, Work and Inequality: The Challenge of Equal Pay in a Deregulated Labour Market*, 1999; Michael McCann, *Rights at Work: Pay Equity Reform and the Politics of Legal Mobilization*, 1994.

ETHNIC ENCLAVES

ROBERT E. WEIR

Ethnic enclaves are areas dominated by individuals of a particular cultural heritage. They are frequently the neighborhood of choice for first-generation **immigrants**, though many evolve into established centers for people of a specific background. African Americans have also tended to cluster, by forced **segregation** or by choice.

Ethnic enclaves are a logical outgrowth of the desire of newly arrived immigrants who have not yet acculturated to American society to be among those with whom they share language, culture, and lifestyles. Although cities like Philadelphia sported a section called Germantown and New York City had districts dominated by Dutch descendants, ethnic enclaves were not very visible until the spread of urbanization in the mid-nineteenth century. In many respects, the **Irish** were the first to draw attention to ethnic enclaves. Unlike earlier immigrants, the Irish were viewed in negative terms by many of those who fancied themselves to be natives. Some Irish were forced to live in defined sections, located on the outskirts of town, while others located among other Irish out of cultural solidarity. The Irish tended to settle in towns and cities touched by the **Industrial Revolution**, as these provided employment opportunities. Many towns and cities had enclaves unflatteringly given nicknames such as Shanty Town and Hungry Hill, the latter a reference to the "Famine Irish" who had fled the potato blight. Conditions were debased in many of these enclaves as many of the Irish lived in **poverty**. They were, however, vibrant culturally and supported such institutions as the **Catholic** church, fraternal organizations, and music clubs. In essence, Irish enclaves were **ghettos**, with all the negative and positive attributes such a designation entails.

Prior to the **Civil War**, the only other group to cluster to the degree of the Irish was the Chinese. "Chinatowns" were likewise areas in which Chinese immigrants could find familiar cultural practices, understand each other, and feel more secure. The latter became of the utmost importance after the Civil War, as anti-Chinese sentiment prevailed in American society and culminated in the passage of various laws to stop Chinese immigration. Chinatowns became self-contained centers that met the needs of residents, as well as providing services such as commercial laundries, which were not widely provided outside Chinatown.

The waves of massive immigration between 1870 and 1920 led other groups to set up ethnic enclaves. Soon American cities were dotted with Little Italys, Greektowns, Hunkyvilles (Slavs), and Jewtowns. As the names suggest, outsiders viewed these centers and their residents with suspicion, if not contempt. This was exacerbated by customs that struck long-time residents as odd, by the high population density of many of the enclaves, and by the high rates of poverty among recent immigrants. Like most centers of high poverty, ethnic enclaves had higher rates of crime, disease, and other social problems—though the reality of these seldom matched the sensational rumors that spread.

Ethnic enclaves have played an important role in assimilating immigrants. Many groups saw a three-generation model in which original immigrants clung to their culture to such a degree as was possible, while their children sought to Americanize. The second generation, however, was often caught between two worlds, and it was therefore the third generation that succeeded in assimilation. Assimilation, however, often entailed spatial mobility. Ethnic enclaves often fluctuate in their makeup, with groups such as the Irish moving up the social ladder and out of the enclave, while others supplant them both socially and spatially. A section that was originally Irish might become Polish, and later give way to Puerto Ricans or Cubans. Today that neighborhood might be inhabited by Eritreans or Haitians.

When **Jacob Riis** photographed New York City ethnic neighborhoods in the late nineteenth century, he noted the myriad social problems associated with them. Although some of his language bristles contemporary sensibilities, many of his observations remain relevant. Today's ethnic neighborhoods remain centers where groups seek to integrate into the American mainstream, yet maintain cherished cultural traditions. For a time the model enclave was **Harlem**, which spawned black-owned businesses, black organizations, and one of the most creative cultural flowerings in American history. Harlem, like areas such as Roxbury in Boston and the Sweet Auburn section of Atlanta, was a place where African Americans felt secure and which fostered racial pride. It began to fade in the 1940s and by the 1960s had become a ghetto, but its traditions were such that it is currently undergoing a revival.

Whether they are **Latino** barrios, Little Saigons (Vietnamese), Little Havanas (Cubans), or Russians living in the Brighton Beach section of Brooklyn, contemporary ethnic enclaves conform to many of the same patterns of those of the past. In each case, newer immigrants seek to survive and older ones seek to find their niche. All struggle to overcome nativism, nourish their culture, and seek physical and financial security.

Suggested Reading

Jacob Riis, *How the Other Half Lives*, 1997 [1890]; David Varady, *Desegregating the City: Ghettos, Enclaves, and Inequality*, 2005; Min Zhou, *Chinatown: The Socioeconomic Potential of an Urban Enclave*, 1994.

ETHNIC STRATIFICATION

NEDA MAGHBOULEH

Ethnic stratification is a form of social ranking that describes enduring relationships of inequality between different ethnic or racial groups. Ethnic stratification specifically pinpoints the existence of a hierarchical social system that positions ethnic groups relative to one another based on the political exigency, economic **wealth**, and class status members may or may not enjoy. In addition, ethnic stratification indicates patterns of **institutional discrimination** and injustice that determines a particular ethnic group's quality of life, or "**life chances**," as described by **Max Weber**.

In order to consider ethnic stratification in the United States fully, it is first necessary to interrogate the terms *ethnicity* and **race**, as the terms are often (incorrectly) used as synonyms for one another. One of the better definitions of ethnicity comes from the British sociologists Ellis Cashmore and Barry Troyna, who define it as "a subjective feeling of oneness or unity that a racial group may feel in certain contexts." In an American context, Cashmore and Troyna's definition falls short, eliding as it does the complex interactions between race and ethnicity, between (fallacious) sociobiology and culture. *Race*, which implies genetic ancestry, has been a powerful organizing principle in the United States, permeating every aspect of history, from Jim Crow to civil rights legislation. *Ethnicity* has served as a more politically neutral catch-all term, taken to mean a population's supposed genetic traits as well as its cultural qualities. Perhaps it is for that exact reason that the term *ethnic stratification* has held far more traction in American social thought than *racial stratification* has.

Therefore, given these definitions, ethnic stratification occurs as a result of unequal interactions between two or more populations deemed culturally or physically different from one another. And for this particular form of stratification to take place, ethnic groups once isolated from one another must come into contact. From antiquity to the present day, urbanization, colonization, territorial expansion, and human migration have contributed to the ethnically heterogeneous societies we see today. Stanley Lieberman, in his seminal 1970 article *Stratification and Ethnic Groups*, parses out historically "superordinate migrations" (conquest or annexation) from comparatively "subordinate migrations" (compelled by political refuge, **slavery**, or labor), signaling the potential for future societal inequality. Followed to its logical end, it is apparent that the nature by which diverse ethnic groups initially meet is a critical factor in explaining ethnic stratification. The distinction between voluntary and involuntary migration is consequently an important one.

Around the same time that Lieberman was exploring the historical origins of ethnic migration, sociologists such as Donald Noel proposed a theory of ethnic stratification, delineating the specific social conditions necessary to advance a patterned system of social inequality such as this. Noel and others argued that four factors, particular to an interethnic social environment, ultimately led to ethnic stratification: universal needs and wants (all groups seeking similar resources and life goals), competition (typified by scarce means or mutually exclusive goals such as political domination), ethnocentrism (the belief that one's own group or culture is superior to all other groups or cultures), and unequal power (the ability of one group to dominate or otherwise compel other groups to acquiesce). That these four factors are quite common to multiethnic environments suggests that ethnic stratification is not surprising and perhaps even to be expected.

Once a multiethnic society has come into being and ethnic stratification has taken hold, several ideologies and systems have over the course of modern history worked to further rationalize or perpetuate this stratification. Most notorious are the "biological" explanations for ethnic stratification, widely disseminated as recently as 1994 with the publication of Charles Murray and Richard Herrnstein's *The Bell Curve*. The authors, a political scientist and psychologist respectively, claim that American social stratification is the inexorable, natural outcome of genetic IQ differences between whites and nonwhites (the former essentially deemed a permanent, biologically determined **underclass**). Though many mainstream scholars have roundly discounted such an intellectually outdated, pseudoscientific explanation for inequality, similar ideas continue to fuel heated national debate on issues such as affirmative action.

Other explanations offered for ethnic stratification are perhaps as problematic or speculative as the biological explanation, only more subtly so. Anthropologist Oscar Lewis offered a "cultural" explanation in his famous 1966 ethnography *La Vida: A Puerto Rican Family in the Culture of Poverty, San Juan and New York*. While Lewis accepted ethnic stratification and inequality as systemic in the United States, he nevertheless claimed that this stratification was born out of the formation of autonomous ethnic subcultures, perpetuating particular values that ultimately advanced **poverty**. Specifically, Lewis was concerned that black and Hispanic children are socialized into behaviors and attitudes (distrust of authority and early sexual activity, among others) that propagate their powerlessness in escaping the underclass. Although the **culture of poverty** thesis has been contentious since its beginning, the notion still carries much weight, especially in public policy conversations about welfare reform.

Sociologist Stephen Steinberg capably elucidates a third explanation for ethnic stratification in *The Ethnic Myth*. He argues that the behavior patterns characterized by scholars like Lewis as "cultural" are actually symptomatic of existing and historically determined class inequalities between various ethnic groups, with particular attention paid to their (often limited) ability to participate in the U.S. economy. Steinberg takes on, for example, the myth of an intellectual, adaptable, and economically successful **Jewish-American** community. He contends that the timing and locality of Jewish **immigration**, coupled with the specific occupational skills Jews had acquired in Europe, in due course translated into favorable life circumstances for this particular group in a multiethnic United States. It is not, he asserts, biology or culture that accounts for ethnic stratification, but rather social class.

Other scholars, including Melvin Oliver and Thomas Shapiro, argue that historically established networks of wealth accumulation and dispersion—not social class per se—perpetuate ethnic stratification. In their 1995 book *Black Wealth/White Wealth*, Oliver and Shapiro analyzed wealth (measured in total assets and debt) rather than **income** (a standard measure of inequality) to explain ethnic stratification in the United States. With particular attention paid to the legacy of prejudice and discrimination against black Americans, the authors investigate barriers and restrictions against wealth accumulation—for example, the access denied to black Americans in finding, financing, and ultimately owning a home. **Home ownership** is important symbolically (as the ultimate "American dream") but even more so economically (as a home is typically the most significant asset an American will have). Thus, Oliver and Shapiro argue that the narrowing income gap between blacks and whites will not curtail ethnic stratification. Rather, the authors argue that cumulative and self-perpetuating networks of wealth accumulation, denied to blacks and other ethnic minorities, are what uphold ethnic stratification.

Another subject of intense theorizing by social scientists is whether there are potential alternatives to ethnic stratification in the multiethnic United States. These alternatives are often posited as fundamental or eventual social outcomes, though the four explanations for ethnic stratification discussed above do not necessarily anticipate such optimistic or seemingly innocuous results. The most familiar alternative outcome to ethnic stratification is **assimilation**, best explained by Robert Park and other Chicago School theorists of the early twentieth century. Often referred to as "melting pot theory," Park's vision of multiethnic integration is based on his observations of the ethnic mosaic in Chicago, conceptualizing urban ethnic life as a series of concentric circles of acculturation—the core being an "ethnic **ghetto**" and assimilation represented by a group's eventual suburban migration farther and farther from the ethnic core. Although Park allowed for both large and small degrees of ethnic resistance, he believed that assimilation was both unavoidable and preferable for American society.

Some scholars have since recognized that the melting pot theory does not account for the perseverance of inequality and thereby assert a cultural **pluralist** model. Originating with Horace Kallen's *Cultural Pluralism and the American Idea* (1956) and popularized by Nathan Glazer and Daniel Moynihan's *Beyond the Melting Pot* (1963), the cultural pluralist theory offers ethnic groups a coping mechanism for ethnic stratification—that is, the nurturing of distinctive cultural, organization, and behavioral characteristics to manage discrimination. Cultural pluralist theory has been distilled into popular culture through the ubiquitous use of the term "multiculturalism," the "salad bowl" metaphor for a multiethnic America, and Reverend Jesse Jackson's vision for a Rainbow/PUSH Coalition inclusive of workers, women, and people of color. There are nearly as many criticisms of cultural pluralist theory as there are of assimilation theory, the most frequent being that pluralism still does not account for the broader social forces—such as the previously mentioned disparities in housing quality and secure neighborhoods—that sustain stratification.

An effective, long-lasting solution to ethnic stratification in the United States has not yet translated into public policy. Modern academia cannot even come to any shared conclusions about its origins—never mind its future—as demonstrated by the wealth of disparate research on the issue. Scholars will unfortunately agree, however, that sizable disparities in wealth are the rule, and not the exception, across centuries of interethnic contact.

Suggested Reading
Ellis Cashmore and Barry Troyna, *Introduction to Race Relations*, 1983; Michael Omi and Howard Winant, *Racial Formation in the United States*, 2nd ed., 1994; Stephen Steinberg, *The Ethnic Myth*, 3rd ed., 2001; Mary Waters, *Ethnic Options: Choosing Ethnic Identities in America*, 1990.

EUGENICS

David V. Healy

Eugenics is a pseudoscientific theory born from misinterpretations of Darwin's theory of evolution. Eugenics, which arose in the mid-1860s, was developed, and named, by Sir Francis Galton as an explanation of the essence and performance of the human race. Though considered a reputable scientific discipline for many decades, its beliefs proved dangerous for many. From its inception, eugenics was infused by the prevalent **racist** and **classist** ideologies of the time. Eugenicists were quick to identify and decry "traits" of nonwhites and members of the **lower classes**, and to use those conclusions to influence government policies. At first, eugenics-guided policies led to registration and tracking of "undesirables," typically through analysis of family trees.

However, even more invasively, eugenicists were also involved in forced **birth control**, selective breeding, and **immigration** control. Typically, policies such as forced birth control were imposed on the poor and minorities as part of punishments for criminal violations, though this was not always the case. Miscegenation laws, including immigration laws, were based on the fears of legislatures and the populace of the times, but were justified by the propositions of eugenicists. Overall, eugenicists were responsible for creating a greater racial consciousness, and using that consciousness to justify the racial enmity common in the late nineteenth century and beyond.

The racial ideologies of eugenics were also partly responsible for the policies of colonialism and imperialism. Leaders of European and American powers used their influence, justified by eugenics, to "prove" that colonized peoples were better off under their control. This "white man's burden" continued well into the twentieth century until colonial systems collapsed because of resistance by colonized peoples.

It was also during the earlier twentieth century that eugenics would be tied to the Third Reich of Germany. Nazis, who held an ideal of Aryan racial purity, utilized eugenics as one of their primary propagandistic enterprises in convincing the German public of their beliefs. Nazi eugenicists theorized an ideal German and then used that concept to weed out "undesirables," including Jews, Gypsies, homosexuals, and others. These theories would eventually be implemented in the Final

Solution, whereby the Nazis rounded up thousands and forced them into extermination camps to be killed en masse. After World War II the extremes of eugenics would discredit the field. Though many of its endorsed practices would continue, they would no longer be under the aegis of eugenics as a scientific field.

The United States, the second-most frequent user of eugenic policies, no longer officially supported the field after World War II. However, numerous eugenics-based laws would persist well into the 1980s and 1990s, including forced sterilization and immigration control. Today, concerns over eugenics are tied into the controversies over genetic engineering. Critics have pointed out the similarities in eugenic and genetic engineering terminology and goals, and some consider genetic engineering to be simply a more modern and technologically sophisticated danger.

Though eugenics is no longer a popularly supported field, it does have its proponents, including several academic journals and advocacy groups. Some writers have drawn upon (or alluded to) eugenic theories to argue that women and certain ethnic groups are (or seem to be) intellectually inferior to **WASP** (white Anglo-Saxon Protestant) males. Charles Murray and Richard Herrnstein's 1994 study, *The Bell Curve*, created controversy in this regard. Murray has insisted that the work has been misconstrued, but there is little doubt that some conservatives embraced it as part of an overall attack on affirmative action and other programs delivering services to minority groups.

Suggested Reading

Edwin Black, *War against the Weak: Eugenics and America's Campaign to Create a Master Race*, 2003; Francis Galton, *Inquiries into Human Faculty and Its Development*, 1883; Richard Lynn, *Eugenics: A Reassessment (Human Evolution, Behavior, and Intelligence)*, 2001.

EUROPHILIA

ROBERT E. WEIR

Europhilia refers to the practice of adopting European manners and culture as a way of separating oneself from the **masses**. It was quite popular among Americans of the **upper** and upper **middle class**es throughout the nineteenth century and remains an unheralded trend in contemporary society.

Many Colonial settlers came from Europe; thus before the **American Revolution** it was customary to associate with one's ancestral lands. For upwardly mobile families, the ability to furnish homes with English goods or to dress in clothes imported from Europe was a mark of **status**. Even as the English colonies matured, **luxury goods** were normally associated with European rather than domestic production.

On the eve of the American Revolution, many Colonists launched boycotts of such English goods as tea and cloth, but even then elites enjoyed French goods when they could get them. During and immediately after the war for independence, Great Britain turned the tables and banned exports to her rebellious American colonies or else demanded cash rather than credit. This had the net effect of encouraging American factories, but **elites** retained the idea that domestic goods were less fashionable and of lower quality. Many wealthy families were frustrated by their inability to obtain European imports, and many, particularly in New England, were furious when President Thomas Jefferson signed the Embargo Act of 1807, which forbade British and French imports and exports in hopes of preventing America from being dragged into the war between the two nations. Some merchants were ruined by the embargo. The War of 1812 further disrupted trade with Britain, but the war's aftermath led to a surge of patriotism that removed some of the stigma against American-made products.

Elite prejudices against American goods began to wane at about the same time that they came to embrace European culture. In the early nineteenth century, there was less distinction between **high culture** and mass culture. **Working-class** theaters performed Shakespeare, **opera**, and popular music, even as they took liberties with the presentation and content. As the cultural system known as Victorianism began to develop during the **Gilded Age**, however, many upper- and middle-class Americans came to canonize theater, opera, symphonic music, literature, and art. Part of this process was to ape the manners of Europeans, while denouncing working-class culture as common, crude, and vulgar.

Victorian members of the upper and middle classes often adopted the style and moral concerns that developed in England during the long reign of Queen Victoria (1837–1901). Upon the death of her husband, Prince Albert, in 1861, Victoria's cultural and moral tone became more severe and dour, expressions that made their way across the Atlantic. Like their English cousins, American Victorians heightened concern for being proper and evolved elaborate social rituals to reinforce their sense of order, morality, and taste. By the late nineteenth century, American Victorians mimicked the social and cultural values of European aristocrats, which contrasted markedly with what one saw among immigrants and laborers. Cotillions, formal balls, orchestral music, literary societies, promenading, fancy dress, and dinner parties were common among America's upwardly mobile families, and the works of certain composers, playwrights, and artists were canonized as high culture. German opera and symphonies, unadulterated Shakespeare, the novels of Charles Dickens, and the works of European academic artists became part of a "cultivated" person's cultural world.

Even language came under scrutiny. "Standard" English has always competed with various regional expressions and colloquialisms, but many Victorians became more obsessed with grammar. Jeremiah Wharton's 1654 spelling guide was rediscovered and the dictionaries of Samuel Johnson (1753) and Noah Webster (1784) were often consulted, the latter noteworthy for its expulsion of Irish and Scottish expressions that Webster feared had polluted the English language. Some Victorians even spoke with affected English accents.

Nineteenth-century elites vacillated between seeing European-style culture as a moral tool with which they could instruct and refine the lower classes and viewing it as a retreat that marked their class distinctiveness. The latter course was adopted when popular culture became mass culture as the twentieth century dawned. Many in the lower middle class embraced popular culture. Movies, recorded music, radio, and sports were usually more American in content and form. Elites quickly relegated these to "low" culture status and retreated more deeply into art, **symphonies**, and opera dominated by Europeans.

Although American artists, composers, and conductors made their marks in the twentieth and twenty-first centuries, European works still dominate high culture. In music, for example, works by Mozart, Bach, Beethoven, and other European masters are still performed more often than the works of American composers such as Leonard Bernstein, Aaron Copeland, or Charles Ives, and there have been very few successful American operas. An exception has been theater, where American playwrights came to dominate, though works by Moliére, Goethe, Marlow, and Shakespeare remain popular. Moreover, the high price of theater tickets in most American cities has once again bifurcated theater by class. In community and popular theater one is more likely to see bold liberties taken with past masters, whereas elites often see such innovation as crass. This is particularly true when, for example, Shakespeare is made into movies. Although such films as Mel Gibson's truncated *Hamlet* (1990), Kenneth Branagh's *Much Ado about Nothing* (1993), and Michael Radford's *Merchant of Venice* (2004) got reasonably good reviews in the mainstream press, they did not fare well in elite publications. Filmed revisions of Shakespeare, such as *My Own Private Idaho* (1994) and *10 Things I Hate about You* (1999), were especially scorned, though they did well at the box office.

Europhilia often shows up as affected snobbery, especially in language. Former Secretary of State Dean Acheson (served 1949–53) was excoriated by right-wing critics for his affected British accent, yet conservative commentator William F. Buckley, Jr. has also adopted an affected accent. Even the pop singer Madonna has adopted a faux British accent, and British actors and actresses are a staple in American popular culture. Recent polls suggest that many Americans feel that people with British accents sound more intelligent and, despite an outbreak of anti-French xenophobia when France refused to support the war against Iraq in 2003, many Americans continue to associate France with cultural and gustatory sophistication. Corporations have also long understood the cachet of associating products with Europe, and many American firms have adopted vaguely European-sounding product names.

If the trend toward popularizing Europhilia continues, it bears watching whether culturally and socially isolated elites will continue to view Europeans as arbiters of style and taste.

Suggested Reading

Jackson Lears, *No Place of Grace: Antimodernism and the Transformation of American Culture 1880–1920*, 1981; Lawrence Levine, *High Brow, Low Brow: The Emergence of Cultural Hierarchy in America*, 1988; Robert McCrum, Robert MacNeil, and William Cran, *The Story of English*, 2002.

EVANGELICALISM

See Creationism; Culture Wars; Religious Fundamentalism; Sexuality; Southern Baptists.

F

FACTORY SYSTEM

ROBERT E. WEIR

Factory system is the name generally given to the emergence of industrial manufacturing in the United States during the early nineteenth century. It led to profound changes in the way social class was constructed.

Although factory production and **wage labor** strike most contemporary Americans as normal, neither was widespread at the time of the **American Revolution**. Many of the **Founding Fathers**, including Benjamin Franklin and Thomas Jefferson, were suspicious of factories, and everywhere **agrarian** ideals reigned supreme. Jefferson even went so far as to recommend that Americans import the few manufactured goods that could not be made by independent yeomen or master artisans, lest the United States fall prey to social problems and inequality associated with British factories. Although Colonial society and the early American republic included wage earners, particularly domestic servants and journeymen artisans, collecting wages was seen as a temporary status until a woman obtained a husband or a journeyman established his own shop.

Samuel Slater's Pawtucket, Rhode Island, textile mill opened in 1793 and is generally viewed as the first American factory. Agrarianism remained the dominant ideology, however, and into the 1830s, most American factories hired small numbers of predominately seasonal laborers. In certain industries, though—notably textiles, shoes, and iron production—factories began to hire hundreds, even thousands, of workers who toiled under a single roof, often for corporations centered far from the factory. Still, by the outbreak of the Civil War, most American factories had just a few employees, production lines were not organized into assembly lines, and skilled workers usually controlled their tools and work patterns. After 1870, American manufacturing entered its economic takeoff phase, and by the turn of the twentieth century, the United States was an industrial giant and wage labor had become institutionalized.

Although the development of manufacturing unfolded at a slow and uneven pace, its social implications emerged earlier. By the 1820s there were already Americans who spent their entire work lives as wage earners, a condition Benjamin Franklin once feared would foster dependency. Throughout the nineteenth century, American workers dreamed of owning a farm, but by the late 1820s a distinct **working class** had emerged in the United States. **Class consciousness** seldom developed as later **Marxist** theorists said it would (or should), but the bulk of working-class Americans did come to view themselves as a separate social class. The nascent **labor movement** likewise began to articulate itself, with unions emerging from older journeymen's associations and mutual aid societies and beginning their long struggle to improve the lives of workers.

The modern **middle classes** also emerged coterminous with the factory system. Earlier American society contained a fair number of **middling sorts**—shopkeepers, small business owners, and professionals—but their numbers were few and most identified with other Colonial and early republican social groups. The expansion of the American economy and the rise of factories created new opportunities in commerce, business, manufacturing, and the professions. Like the working class, most in the middle class also worked for wages rather than possessing large amounts of land or inherited wealth. Most, however, identified culturally and socially with elites and **nouveau riche** manufacturers, investors, and speculators. Also like the working class, however, those in the middle classes also came to see themselves as a class apart.

Although their mutual rise was as much coincidental as planned, one could easily make the case that the emergence of the factory system and the beginnings of the contemporary social **stratification** are inextricably linked.

Suggested Reading

Martin Burke, *The Conundrum of Class: Public Discourse on the Social Order in America*, 1995; Stephen Innes, ed., *Work and Labor in Early America*, 1988; Bruce Laurie, *Artisans into Workers: Labor in Nineteenth-Century America*, 1989.

FAITH-BASED CHARITIES

ROBERT E. WEIR

The term *faith-based charity* refers to the principle of funneling resources designed to help the poor, needy, and unfortunate through religious organizations. Although churches, synagogues, mosques, and other religious bodies and their ancillaries have historically played a major role in dispensing aid, the practice has received renewed attention in the wake of President George W. Bush's call for faith-based initiatives to receive an increased share of federal taxpayer dollars to carry out their work.

Bush made his initial "Charitable Choices" call in 2001 and stated his desire to create a White House Office of Faith-Based and Community Initiatives. The

House of Representatives passed HB 1407, allowing some taxpayer funds to go to religious groups, provided that the money go solely to administrative costs, that the charity not deny any client on the basis of personal beliefs, and that no money be used for proselytizing. By 2004 some $3.7 billion of federal money was being dispersed by religious groups.

As noted, religious groups have long been involved in philanthropic work over and beyond missionary efforts. Religious groups have operated poor houses, emergency shelter programs, work-relief efforts, **soup kitchens**, **settlement houses**, food banks, and after-school programs. At various junctures in history, the philanthropic impulse has found strong adherence among religious followers, one notable example being the **Social Gospel** movement of the late nineteenth and early twentieth centuries. Historically, black churches and mosques have been socially active. That said, there also have been periods in which religious groups have tended more toward moral and political conservatism. In the mid-nineteenth century, for example, many Christians allied themselves with **Social Darwinism** and tended to view **poverty** as punishment for sin and unworthiness rather than a condition to alleviate. In recent years, there has also been a tendency for many Christian and Jewish groups to embrace the **self-help** ideology of the modern conservative movement.

Even more troubling has been the tendency for religious charity to wax and wane according to how flush the sponsoring group might be. During the **Great Depression**, for instance, private charities of all sorts proved wholly inadequate for dealing with the staggering human need occasioned by the collapse of the economy. The **New Deal** programs of the 1930s were fashioned in part because of the failure of private charity. New Deal programs formed the very foundation of how subsequent charity and assistance schemes became the domain of the federal government, and in the 1960s, **Great Society** programs dramatically enhanced the role of the federal government in addressing social issues.

This uneven record of private groups is among the reasons many social workers, liberals, and philanthropists fear the renewed emphasis on faith-based charity. As they see it, social problems are too large to be addressed willy-nilly by a disconnected array of private groups, many of which have other agendas that further complicate matters. In this critique, only governments can marshal the needed resources to attack systemic problems.

Local, state, and federal bodies have, however, seen a decrease in available funding, and the trend has been for social budgets to be reduced. This, in part, has fueled calls for private charities to fill the void. However, another part has been ideological. Many conservatives fundamentally disapprove of what they dub "social engineering," object to using tax revenues to fund social welfare policy, and argue that government handouts destroy individual initiative. Some even call government programs forms of "creeping **socialism**" and attempt to paint them as un-American. Only a few extremists would deny the need for some forms of assistance, however; thus, many conservatives have come to embrace the idea of allowing the private sector to address those needs, especially faith-based charities.

This has proved very polarizing because many faith groups discriminate in ways inconsistent with federal law. Many religious charities discriminate in their hiring practices, link aid to proselytizing programs, or fail to delineate clear boundaries between social work and other agendas. Some object to tax credits for **Catholic** charities, for example, on the grounds that the church also funnels money into campaigns to undermine abortion and birth control rights. Similarly, some groups associated with the Rev. Jerry Falwell openly discriminate against Muslims. Many liberals, in fact, see faith-based charities as part of a "compassionate conservatism" smokescreen whose ideology-driven purpose is to dismantle all publicly funded programs from welfare to public education.

Still others, including the American Civil Liberties Union, feel that any public support for religious groups violates separation of church and state principles; the first amendment to the U.S. Constitution states, "Congress shall make no law respecting an establishment of religion, or prohibiting the free exercise thereof." They also point out that religious groups are not values-free in their approach; some, for instance, treat alcohol and drug abuse as personal sin rather than as diseases, as they are officially classified. Thus, whether Congress intends to promote religion or not, diverting public money to religious charities is a de facto promotion of religion. Indeed, this question is so thorny that some religious conservatives themselves are troubled by it; the Rev. **Pat Robertson** criticized the Bush initiative as opening a "Pandora's box" for people of faith that might force them to act in ways contrary to their beliefs in order to meet federal guidelines, such as working with the Nation of Islam or other groups that Christian conservatives find objectionable. Many religious leaders, however, see opportunity in the Bush program. Many have counterattacked secular critics by accusing them of religious bigotry. Some have also tarred past relief efforts as failures or products of the political left.

The entire debate has become so polarized that the diversity of groups affected by "Charitable Choice" gets overlooked. It does indeed funnel money to conservative Christian groups such as Focus on Family and Campus Crusade for Christ, but also to Jewish organizations, more liberal groups such as Habitat for Humanity, and such American icons as the YMCA and YWCA. Lost also is the fact that in the short term, it is extremely unlikely that Congress will fund social programs at New Deal or Great Society levels. Those who argue that faith-based charities fill needs probably have a point.

There is, however, little reason to think that faith-based charities can supplant public charities. Their track records are strongest in meeting immediate needs and taking on small projects, but they have proved anemic at implementing long-term programs that truly reverse the gap between haves and have-nots. Goodwill and good deeds have yet to translate into changing the social class structure.

Suggested Reading

Mark Chaves, *Congregations in America*, 2004; Chaves, *Financing American Religion*, 1999; Lizabeth Cohen, *Making a New Deal: Industrial Workers in Chicago, 1919–1939*, 1990; Stanley Kurtz, "The Faith-Based Left: Getting Behind the Debate," *National Review Online*, February 5, 2001 (http://www.nationalreview.com/comment/comment020501b.shtml).

FALSE CONSCIOUSNESS

MICHAEL A. VASTOLA

"False consciousness" is the phrase applied to the classical **Marxist** definition of ideology that refers to the manner in which **capitalism** tricks individuals into misunderstanding the way in which it works. Karl Marx himself never used the phrase, but in 1893 Frederick Engels explicitly referred to ideology as a process of false consciousness that aims to mystify real capitalist motives.

This definition fits a conception of the historical causes of ideology upon which Marx and Engels had long relied. These causes were based on material circumstances—such as the production and distribution of resources—rather than the psychological assumptions of the Enlightenment tradition that preceded Marx and Engels. Consequently, their materialist theory of ideology was inseparable from the revolutionary politics they saw as precipitating the end of philosophical inquiry—or at least the need for such inquiry—in the form of a **communist** society.

For Marx, the illusory consciousness that typified pre-capitalist society lacked sufficient coherence to be considered ideological. False consciousness arises out of the thought processes embedded in a social order in which division of labor and class-stratification systems lead intellectuals to advance ideals harmful to the **proletariat** in the service of maintaining existing social relations, including the domination characteristic of capitalism. In *The German Ideology* (1845), Marx and Engels understood ideology as strictly illusory or mystifying, and its opposite would be a clear understanding of class domination and the historical necessity of **socialism**. In *Capital* (1867), on the other hand, material reality becomes fundamentally inconsistent with clear thought because it is mystified by capitalist modes of production and the blurring of distinctions between the products (or services), the desire to obtain them, and the **power** relations involved in producing them, a process Marx called *commodity fetishism*. For example, if an individual desires expensive clothing without thought of impoverished workers making it, that clothing is being treated as a fetish by that individual. In Marxian terms there is a need for a special "scientific" discourse that will make evident the real meaning of this structuring.

Both definitions of ideology, with their assumptions about a false worldview, no longer fit the more contemporary conceptions of the term. First, they insist upon a level of certainty—a way of truly "knowing"—that is not theoretically tenable by today's standards. But they also presume an almost complete lack of agency on the part of those allegedly afflicted with false consciousnesses, and they fail to take into account a calculated dimension of belief that would allow individuals to behave as though certain social relations were necessary and permanent, without actually believing that they are. In essence, it may be possible for individuals to engage in economic activities without necessarily approving of them. Moreover, in the wake of the rise and fall of socialist bureaucracies in places such as the former Soviet Union, it is problematic to hold that the **masses** are blind to the truth and a small group of the intellectual elite is endowed with pure vision.

Since the 1950s Marxist and post-Marxist theory has actively engaged with the idea of ideology as something other than false consciousness. This new focus was a logical result of the failure of the proletariat to recognize their historical mission.

Most modern Marxists understand that the construction of ideology is complex and that appeals to false consciousness have not been useful in convincing workers that capitalism has exploited them. Aspects of false-consciousness theory linger in some circles, however, especially in **hegemony theory** and among those citing Frankfurt School theorists, who evoke notions of commodity fetishism, which, as discussed above, serves to hide the economic, political, and ideological relations between humans and systems of production.

Suggested Reading

Terry Eagleton, *Ideology: An Introduction*, 1991; Jorge Larrain, *The Concept of Ideology*, 1979; Slavoj Zizek, ed., *Mapping Ideology*, 1994.

FAMILY TRUST

TINA MAVRIKOS-ADAMOU

A family trust is a form of estate management that has been around for centuries. Family trusts have served many purposes, but they mainly secure the transference of a family business or family estate from one generation to the next. Sometimes, family trusts are called "living trusts," which refers to the legal document that defines title to and ownership of real property and assets. By creating a living trust, one legally establishes a transfer ownership of assets to a "trust," but does so without relinquishing control over those assets. The "grantor" or "settlor" has control over all assets while alive and therefore can make changes at any time. Upon death, those designated as "beneficiaries" inherit the remaining assets. The legal reasoning behind setting up a family trust is that one can avoid costly and time-consuming probate, which is the legal process of taking one's name off a title of an asset and replacing it with a new owner.

There are all kinds of trusts, that is, legal agreements created for specific purposes. There are charitable trusts, welfare funds, unit trusts, and will trusts, for example, but what is specific about family trusts is that they are started within a family, and the beneficiaries are restricted mostly to just family members who are explicitly selected to inherit these assets.

Family trust defined in this way is a form of asset management and estate planning, and it is considered the principle way for the wealthy and those of the **upper class** to ensure that their family property and wealth are transferred to the next generation intact. It is therefore a way for the upper class to keep the wealth in the family and maintain the family name and legacy. The economic life cycle (and lifestyle) is passed down from one generation to the next, and therefore, family trusts have been perceived as forms of **social reproduction**. **Elite** theorists contend that an upper class based in inherited wealth wields a great deal of economic power and likewise has great influence over political outcomes and public policy. They also maintain that America is run by a small group of very powerful elites who monopolize control over the economic, political, and military arenas and who do not allow **pluralism** to function as it should.

Many well-known companies and businesses in the United States are family-controlled. Powerful families often own large numbers of shares in supposedly publicly traded companies, and hence, they have major sway over strategic decisions made in these firms. It is estimated that families in the United States control between 35 and 45 percent of the stock in America's 500 largest companies, including **Wal-Mart**, in which the Walton family owns approximately 38 percent of the shares; and Ford Motor, in which the Ford family controls 40 percent of the voting shares. These facts further the elite theory's premise that there is an unequal and unfair economic environment present in the United States today.

Today, however, the practice of setting up a family trust is being utilized by more families as a way to specify precisely how, when, and in what way they want their assets dispersed once they are deceased. Evidence of this increase can be found in the rise in the number of fiduciary income tax returns that are reported by the Internal Revenue Service (IRS). The United States Income Tax Return for Estates and Trusts (Form 1041) is used to report income and deductions. Increasingly, families of modest assets are turning to family trusts and are not relying solely on wills. Thus, as the use of family trusts gains popularity, elder-care lawyers and other legal experts are being called upon to provide advice for people who want to utilize this more explicit method of organizing their assets. Family trusts are gaining public interest also because people are using them alongside living wills as a way to plan for medical expenses related to possible disabilities in old age or to make medical choices now in the event that they become unable to speak for themselves.

Suggested Reading

American Bar Association Staff, ABA, *The American Bar Association Guide to Wills and Estates*, 2004; James E. Hughes, *Family Wealth: Keeping It in the Family*, 2004; George E. Marcus, *Lives in Trust: The Fortunes of Dynastic Families in Late Twentieth-Century America*, 1992.

FARRELL, JAMES (February 27, 1904–August 22, 1979)

ROBERT E. WEIR

James Thomas Farrell was an **Irish American** novelist whose best-known works appeared in the 1930s and 1940s. His works are lightly regarded by many literary scholars, but some historians cite his work as examples of **proletarian literature** during the **Great Depression**, especially his Studs Lonigan trilogy.

Farrell was born in Chicago and lived in a South Side **slum**. His Irish American parents were of **working-class** stock, but like many "lace curtain Irish," held **middle-class** pretensions. By the early twentieth century, Irish Americans were several generations removed from **immigrants** fleeing famine, and many assumed an exaggerated sense of propriety and respectability. Farrell attended the University of Chicago, but middle-class values never set well with him. Much of Farrell's writing deals with the clash between Irish American ideals and the rough and raw ways of the street, the domineering influence of the **Catholic** church, religious bigotry, and **poverty**.

Farrell's most famed works are *Young Lonigan* (1932), *The Young Manhood of Studs Lonigan* (1934), and *Judgment Day* (1935). These books center on William "Studs" Lonigan from his Chicago adolescence to his death. The trilogy deals with Lonigan's journey from idealistic teen to realistic young adult to his frustrated and debased adulthood. They take place against a backdrop of mean streets, economic depression, violence, and sexual assault. At the time, many hailed the trilogy for its frankness of language, its social realism, and the boldness with which it attacked hypocrisy and social airs. Critics, however, complained his work was stilted and read like fictionalized sociological treatises. Farrell was not a great stylist, though his defenders upheld his work as an example of naturalism. His use of stream-of-consciousness writing often led to jolting lapses in structure, a problem that became especially pronounced in later writings.

Farrell not only wrote about the chaos of the 1930s; he participated in it. The anger he felt toward poverty and **capitalism** led him into radical politics. He joined the Socialist Workers Party (SWP), a **Trotskyist** group devoted to a revolutionary vision of **Marxism**. His SWP affiliation led him into contact with the **labor movement**, especially the 1934 Teamsters' **strike**, the Teamsters then having a strong Trotskyist presence. **Communist** groups were fractious in the 1930s, and the SWP was highly critical of Joseph Stalin's regime in the Soviet Union. Farrell became immersed in factionalism as World War II approached. He supported helping the Soviet Union, a position at odds with SWP leadership. After the war, he grew disenchanted with both Stalinists and Trotskyists, became an outspoken anticommunist, and supported **Cold War** programs such as the Marshall Plan to rebuild Europe. He nonetheless went on to join various **socialist** parties and supported socialism for the rest of his life. Many of Farrell's writings directly or obliquely reference radical factionalism in the post–World War II period.

Farrell wrote more than fifty novels as well as numerous nonfiction works, but the only other work that received much notice was his five-book, 2,500-page Danny O'Neill series written between 1936 and 1953. It plows many of the same furrows as the Studs Lonigan trilogy, although O'Neill escapes the streets and lives a more respectable and less tragic life than Lonigan. Once again, a major theme is the tension between the generations of Irish American families, and most commentators see Danny O'Neill as Farrell's autobiographical persona. These books lack the dramatic tension of the Lonigan trilogy, and parts are artlessly written.

By the 1960s Farrell's literary reputation was faltering, though his output remained prodigious. He angered many young radicals with his denunciation of the **New Left**—Farrell rather inexplicably supported U.S. involvement in the Vietnam War—and his personal life was tumultuous; he divorced his first wife, remarried and divorced, and then remarried his first wife, Dorothy. By the 1970s Farrell was using vast quantities of amphetamines to prop up his sixteen-hour writing marathons, though few were reading his work. He died in 1979.

Contemporary critics are largely divided between those who place Farrell in a literary tradition with figures such as Sherwood Anderson, **Theodore Dreiser**, and **Sinclair Lewis** and those who see him as a writer of turgid prose whose reputation was exaggerated by his brief ability to capture the social zeitgeist of the

1930s. Feminists often find Farrell's earthy and aggressive male world hard to stomach; however, the African American novelist **Richard Wright** is among those writers inspired by Farrell's stark realism.

Suggested Reading

James Farrell, *Reflections at Fifty*, 1954; Pete Hamill, ed., *James T. Farrell: Studs Lonigan, a Trilogy*, 2004; Robert Landers, *An Honest Writer: The Life and Times of James T. Farrell*, 2004.

FASHION

JANEAN MOLLET-VAN BECKUM

Fashion consists of the latest and most admired styles, usually in clothing, but can also be extended to cosmetics, hairstyles, and behaviors. These trends are often set by people who are admired and in the public eye, such as movie and music stars, political figures, and the wealthy. Many factors contribute to what is considered fashionable in a society, and ideals can vary within a culture across social, religious, and cultural boundaries. Fashion is the way in which individuals express themselves outwardly to the world. It is one of the most visible forms of consumption we have, expressing moods, social class, gender, and occupation.

Sumptuary laws are proof that what one wears is attributed to social class. Sumptuary laws are regulations prescribing what different social classes can and cannot wear. Examples of these laws appeared throughout history, from the Greeks to the first European immigrants to North America to the **caste** system in India. English immigrants to the American colonies often transplanted sumptuary laws, though many fell out practice after **Bacon's Rebellion** in Virginia. Some scholars argue that the decline of sumptuary laws was a strategy by **elites** to prevent **lower-class** whites from allying themselves with **slaves** or **indentured servants**.

Before the **Industrial Revolution**, clothing was one of the most valuable possessions a person owned. For this reason, the poor probably never saw new clothes, and the wealthy willed them to deserving relatives upon their death. Even murder for, and theft of, a person's clothes was known, the perpetrator then pawning the clothing for cash value. Preindustrial society clothing indicated very precisely social status, gender, and often occupation and regional variation.

Although not common in locations where **social mobility** was possible, those who were able to move up in social rank usually adopted the clothing styles of those of higher social ranks. However, **nouveau riche** individuals were not completely accepted by their new peers because their refinement and tastes were still of their class of origin. The nouveau riche was only one of the groups scorned for their upward mobility. As with all mass-produced goods, the Industrial Revolution changed how fashion was perceived.

By the late nineteenth century, clothing was less expensive and more accessible to all classes. It is widely believed that this was the beginning of democratization of the fashion and clothing industry because all social classes were able to adopt similar styles at the same time. Many **upper-class** people were upset by the idea that the **lower class** could now dress in the same fashion as they. One example comes from **department store** workers. Mainly **working-class** women were employed in these new stores, but stores catered primarily to the **middle-class** and upper-class consumers, so clerks often dressed in high-class fashion, advertising the products they sold. Seen as "uppity," these female workers were looked down upon by the upper-class customers.

There are two main social theories as to why what is considered fashionable changes. In the first theory, **Georg Simmel** (1858–1918) believed that fashion change was caused by a process of imitation. Lower social classes attempted to emulate the upper classes as best they could on a lower income, though the upper classes always tried to be distinct in their dress and behavior. By the time the lower classes achieved a passable level of imitation, fashion among the upper classes had changed so that elites could distinguish themselves from the **masses**.

Pierre Bourdieu (1930–2002) took a similar, but more complex, approach to why fashion changes. Bourdieu believed lower classes were prevented from complete assimilation of the upper classes' fashions because of economic, educational, and socialization differences. In this regard, imitation had limits. He also believed different social classes used fashion on the basis of their individual cultural needs. For example, a farmer would not wear a high-priced suit to work the field. He would want practical, functional, and durable clothing, not only aesthetically pleasing clothes.

Clothing remains symbolically important in modern society, though it is now often an expression of individuality or membership in a subculture rather than a show of direct social status. These subcultures, however, often project or represent perceived views of social class. For example, an office worker who wears an expensive suit to work is perceived to be of the middle or upper class, whereas the same person in punk or hip-hop street fashion is perceived of a lower class. Changes in a person's daily fashion can also allow them to move between subcultures. For example, the office worker may wear a suit during the week and belong to the **white-collar** subculture. But on weekends, when relaxing with friends, he may opt to wear clothing related to the hip-hop or punk subculture, thus changing his association and perceived class with a change of his clothing.

Despite the ways in which fashion has become more malleable and varied, haute couture remains the preserve of the wealthy. Original clothing, shoes, and accessories from top designers such as Christian Dior, Versace, or Gucci cost many thousands of dollars, and even mass-produced lines are beyond the reach of the average consumer. Since the 1980s, fashion consciousness, the cult of supermodels, and **advertising** have enticed shoppers of modest means to don items bearing fashion-designer labels, but these are seldom the same items worn by wealthy individuals. The same impulses have given rise to markets for knock-offs, simulacra, and counterfeit apparel. This suggests that the fashion preferences of the upper classes have perhaps attained a hegemonic status akin to that of the nineteenth century.

Suggested Reading

Malcolm Barnard, *Fashion as Communication*, 2002; Christopher Breward, *The Culture of Fashion*, 1995; Diana Crane, *Fashion and Its Social Agendas: Class, Gender and*

Identity in Clothing, 2000; David Muggleton, *Inside Subculture: The Postmodern Meaning of Style*, 2000.

FEDERALIST PARTY

See Founding Fathers.

FEDERALIST SOCIETY

See Think Tanks.

FEMINIZATION OF POVERTY

GERALD FRIEDMAN

Women constitute a growing share of poor people in the United States. In 2003 adult women were 40 percent more likely to be impoverished than were men. Among adults, women make up nearly 60 percent of the poor, with 14 million adult women living in **poverty**, compared with only 9 million men. Relatively high rates of poverty among women reflect the combination of women's low market earnings with a decline in the flow of funds from fathers to mothers and declining state support for **one-parent families**.

Poverty is rarer among adults able to work full-time or in husband-and-wife households where the husband is present. Poverty is heavily concentrated in households where a single adult is responsible for children without significant outside support. Single-parent households are more likely to be impoverished because the expenses of raising children all fall to a single wage earner and because single parents cannot devote as much time or energy to paid employment because of their responsibilities as caregivers. Poverty is especially common among women because labor-market discrimination lowers their wages; the poverty rate for unmarried women without children is 15 percent higher than for unmarried men without children. But poverty is also more common among women because they are three times more likely to be responsible for children than are men and because single mothers are more likely to be impoverished than single fathers. The presence of children raises the poverty rate among single men; among households with only an adult male resident, the poverty rate is over 13 percent, twice the poverty rate for men in two-parent households. Among single mothers, the combination of low wages for women and responsibilities for children doubles the poverty rate again to 28 percent. The chart on page 258 illustrates these categories.

The costs of raising children explain poverty among parents only if we expect custodial parents to bear the costs of child raising themselves. This is not how we approach poverty among the elderly. Among Americans over age sixty-five, government programs, notably **Social Security**, reduce the poverty rate by over

Adult Poverty, 2003

	Male		Female	
	Number (000s)	Poverty Rate (%)	Number (000s)	Poverty Rate (%)
Adults	117,295	8.0	123,154	11.1
Single Parents	4,711	13.5	14,129	28.0
Married Couples	57,685	5.4	57,685	5.4
Other Singles	54,899	10.2	51,340	12.8
Non-singles	112,584	7.7	109,025	8.9

80 percent. Among younger Americans and their parents, however, government programs do little to reduce poverty. In the 1990s government programs lowered the poverty rate among the non-elderly by less than 20 percent; the effect is even less since the Aid to Families with Dependent Children's program was repealed in 1995. Now, barely 25 percent of single mothers receive *any* welfare assistance. Some single parents receive child support from the absentee parent. But over 60 percent of single mothers and almost 80 percent of single fathers in poverty are not promised any support, and the proportion receiving any support at all is even lower. Almost 90 percent of single fathers living in poverty in 2003 received no financial support from the absentee mother, and almost 80 percent of single mothers in poverty received no support. When single parents do receive child support from the absentee parent, the amount is often very low. The average (mean) child support received annually is less than $4,300 for all parents, and it is even lower for single parents living in poverty, where it is barely $3,000 for all children, or less than $2,000 per child. By contrast, the United States Census Office estimates that each additional child adds nearly $3,300 to the minimum annual budget needed to remain out of poverty.

Poverty need not be inevitably associated with women having children. The time women spend in caregiving roles, including performing housework and shopping for the family, inevitably reduces their earnings by reducing the time they can give to paid labor. **Institutional discrimination** also lowers women's wages so that full-time employed white women earn only 76 cents for every dollar that men earn. (Black women average 66 cents and Latinas just 55 cents.) As a result, in 2002 the median income for a full-time male worker was $40,668 per annum, compared with just $30,724 for women; women with college degrees earned only as much as male high school dropouts. Effective programs against discrimination and support for parents are both necessary to end the feminization of poverty.

Suggested Reading

Nancy Folbre, *Who Pays for the Kids? Gender and the Structures of Constraint*, 1994; Victor Fuchs, *Women's Quest for Economic Equality*, 1988; Christopher Jencks, *Rethinking Social Policy: Race, Poverty, and the Underclass*, 1992.

FIFTH AVENUE

ROBERT E. WEIR

Fifth Avenue is a major boulevard in New York City. It begins at Washington Square Park in Greenwich Village, and its Manhattan course continues north into **Harlem**, where its name changes at 135th Street. Fifth Avenue runs roughly through the middle of Manhattan and officially separates the East Side from the West Side of the city. It is most famous, however, for its associations with the **upper class**. Although today many of its neighborhoods are quite diverse, the very evocation of Fifth Avenue continues to conjure images of **wealth**, high society, and elegance.

Much of the opulence associated with Fifth Avenue is a product of the **Gilded Age**. It was then that such tycoons as **J. P. Morgan** and Henry Clay Frick built homes on or near Fifth Avenue. The first **department store** appeared in 1869, and soon fashionable establishments proliferated. Famed architects such as Richard Morris Hunt and Stanford White built lavish homes for members of New York City's **elite**. The area has also been home to such luminaries as newspaper magnate Joseph Pulitzer and **socialites** Doris Duke and Barbara Hutton. Indeed, so many wealthy members of New York society have lived on or just off Fifth Avenue that a section of Midtown was dubbed the "Gold Coast" and "Millionaires' Row." Several novels by **Edith Wharton** use Fifth Avenue as a backdrop for upper-class life.

Fifth Avenue is also home to such New York landmarks as the Empire State Building, St. Patrick's Cathedral, **Rockefeller** Center, the Metropolitan Museum of Art, the Guggenheim Museum, and the New York Public Library. Also on or near Fifth Avenue are private **men's clubs** such as the Knickerbocker and the Metropolitan. (Some of these clubs now admit women.)

Fifth Avenue is perhaps best known for stores that deal in **luxury goods**. The most famous of these is Saks Fifth Avenue. Saks began life in 1902 as a men's clothing store based in Washington, D.C. It changed its name to Saks Fifth Avenue when, in 1924, it opened a New York City store on Fifth near Fiftieth Street. It also began dealing in high-quality, high-priced goods, and for many decades, Saks label goods were valued by upscale consumers before **designer goods** were fashionable in the rest of society. Today, Saks also deals in luxury labels such as Armani, Chanel, Gucci, Prada, and Ralph Lauren. Other luxury purveyors on Fifth Avenue include Bergdorf-Goodman, Brooks Brothers, Donna Karan, and Lord & Taylor. It is also home to famed jeweler Tiffany and Company, the toy store F.A.O. Schwartz, and Christie's Auction House.

Fifth Avenue's past reputation exceeds its contemporary reality. Fifth Avenue retailers have fallen prey to same competitive pressures that have beset those elsewhere, and chain stores such as Disney and Warner Brothers have opened outlets along the avenue. Even Saks has struggled, and in 2005 it discontinued its own label. Many wealthy residents have relocated to more private locations, and there are parts of Fifth Avenue that can be charitably described as run-down. It has, nonetheless, spawned many imitators. Among the fashionable shopping and upscale housing areas patterned after Fifth Avenue are the Magnificent Mile in Chicago, Newbury Street in Boston, Rodeo Drive in Beverly Hills, Sloane Street in London, and Union Square in San Francisco. In New York itself, Madison Avenue and Park Avenue have long rivaled Fifth Avenue as destinations and domiciles for the wealthy.

Suggested Reading

Jerry Patterson, *Fifth Avenue: The Best Address*, 1998; Kate Simon, *Fifth Avenue: A Very Social History*, 1978.

FILM

BILL BARRY

Movies are among the most popular forms of the popular arts. The **working class** has historically flocked to the cinema, but depictions of working-class life are rarer than workers' presence amid the audience.

Movies depicting workers often reflect larger social movements. In the 1930s, for example, there were some "socially conscious" movies, though these virtually disappeared by the 1980s and are rare today, casualties of the declining **labor movement** and the film industry's emphasis on commercial success. Movies require enormous capital investments, and hence, summer blockbusters, teen-oriented project, and films such as *Star Wars* (1977), with merchandising tie-ins and computer-generated special effects, are more heavily promoted than social dramas.

Movies that portray working-class life can be placed into two basic categories: "labor" movies, which show workers' collective struggles and their organizations, and "worker" movies, which depict workers' lives and situations, often focusing on individual efforts and upward social mobility. Both categories of movies, however, show workers trying to deal with the fundamental class question: how can workers make their lives better?

Labor movies such as *Norma Rae* (1979), *Matewan* (1987), *Silkwood* (1983), *Bread and Roses* (2000), and *10,000 Black Men Named George* (2002) show workers organizing unions in a positive and even inspirational way. In contrast, movies such as *FIST* (1978), *Blue Collar* (1978), *Act of Vengeance* (1986), *Hoffa* (1992), and *North Country* (2004) show unions as corrupt or destructive social movements.

"Worker" movies usually feature ambitious working-class individuals who—far from trying collectively to change class relations—use their skills and ambitions to rise within, or even out of, the working class. Movies such as *Breaking Away* (1979), *Coal Miner's Daughter* (1980), *October Sky* (1999), and *Erin Brockovich* (2000) are typical movies of this type.

The silent movie era, which ran from 1909 to the late 1920s, provided a surprisingly large numbers of labor movies. Describing them as "Capital vs. Labor" films, historian Michael Shull estimates that between 1909 and 1919, roughly 150 films—about two per month—showed workers in confrontation with their employers. Many of these early silent movies—luckily preserved by the Library of Congress—depict typical workplaces: sewing shops, mines, factories, and so on. They also portray the conflicted consciousness of the working class trying to find its way: decent employees are often incited by outside agitators while young working-class women—typified by Mary Pickford in *The Eternal Grind*—fall in love with the children of their employers. Even the famous director D.W. Griffith directed a "labor" movie, *Intolerance* (1916), his follow-up to his glorification of the **Ku Klux Klan** in *Birth of a Nation* (1915).

Historian Steven J. Ross points to the problem of financing and distributing early movies. Although the nascent "flickers" that appeared in the early 1900s required very little capital, the production and distribution of movies was capital-intensive; hence, unions often tried to raise money for working-class stories that could be shown in union halls. These efforts were not terribly successful, and the huge capital investments required for movies has had a marked negative impact on the depiction of workers in movies ever since.

The most famous silent movie depicting working-class life was, ironically, a movie that appeared after the silent era had ended. Released in 1934, Charlie Chaplin's *Modern Times* dramatized a worker driven literally crazy by work on an assembly line. In a vision of **deindustrialization** and the Depression, the worker becomes a service worker and then a migrant worker and even accidentally participates in a **communist** demonstration. Chaplin had showed the difficulties of working-class life for the previous twenty years, and his most famous figure—The Tramp—is a displaced and individualistic worker, a hobo without the support of the **Industrial Workers of the World** (IWW), a group that organized transients. His depiction was generally that of the worker as victim, resourceful but powerless, pitiful and comic at the same time.

In *City Lights*, Chaplin explored for the first time one aspect of social mobility in workers' culture: the sudden, happy, and accidental relationship between a worker and a very wealthy individual who literally makes dreams come true. More modern versions, such as *Working Girl* (1988), *Maid in Manhattan* (2002), and even *Pretty Woman* (1990), reprise the Cinderella (or "Cinderfella") myth of virtuous and ambitious workers who fortuitously find wealth and (presumably) happiness by having relationships above their class.

Although the 1930s could have provided a large number of movies reflecting the rise of industrial unionism, the domination of the movie industry by the Hollywood studios, which were obsessively anti-union, and by the Breen Office (the studios' censorship board, which feared "Reds" as much as sexual innuendo) limited the movies about workers and their struggles. Despite the horrendous economic dislocation associated with the **Great Depression**, Hollywood films were more likely to depict the lifestyles of the **upper class** than those of Americans struggling to survive. This emphasis on glamour, materialism, and wealth remains a staple of Hollywood movies.

Two famous and enduring movies, both directed by John Ford, did take up workers' lives. Although sociologists might argue over the exact class status of tenant farmers in ***The Grapes of Wrath*** (1940), there is no question that the Joad family experienced precipitous downward mobility because of the Depression. Ford's film is more optimistic than the John Steinbeck book on which the film is based, but it nonetheless shows the radicalization of Tom Joad and the difficulties of family survival during the Great Depression. Ford's *How Green Was My Valley* (1941) is a classic depiction of working-class social history and union organizing, though it too focuses on upward **social mobility**, with a coal miner's daughter marrying the son of the mine owner.

A similar social ascension is depicted in *The Valley of Decision* (1945), in which the daughter of a disabled Irish steel-mill hand is hired as a domestic worker at the mill owner's house and then marries the son of the owner.

Two other movies from the 1930s show working-class life in a very different way. *Black Fury* (1935) depicts a bitter miners' **strike**, resolved when an individual miner threatens to blow up the mine, and *Black Legion* (1936) shows the hazards of upward mobility as an ambitious skilled tradesman, played by Humphrey Bogart, joins a hate group after being passed over for promotion in favor of a Polish coworker.

It could also be argued that many of the gangster movies of the 1920s and 1930s depicted class issues, given that their criminal antiheroes are invariably ambitious poor young men, often surrounded by examples of "legitimate" wealth acquired by less than ethical methods. Working-class women are likewise stereotyped in gangster films, often appearing as gun molls and "gold diggers."

The 1940s brought the depiction of workers as energetic and brave patriots in a long string of war movies, usually featuring the class polyglot of ethnic characters in the strict—and unchallenged—class system of the military. *From Here to Eternity* (1953) is perhaps the most skillful of these movies, though it omits the scene from James Jones's book in which the main character is in military prison with a former IWW organizer.

The release in 1954 of two very different movies about workers and their struggles highlights how "labor" movies differed from typical Hollywood fare. Not only was *Salt of the Earth* a movie about workers' struggles, but the workers themselves also helped create the film, and many of them played featured roles. Based on a strike at a zinc mine by a local of the Mine, Mill and Smelter Workers in Bayard, New Mexico, the movie was written, produced, and directed by blacklisted Hollywood talent. It shows a heroic workers' struggle, tangled in gender, ethnic, and family issues. Screenwriter Michael Wilson stayed with striking miners for three months in 1951 to gather material for the script and later returned to let the miners "edit" his draft in a unique collaborative experience. Financed in part by the union and using a crew of blacklisted technicians, director Herbert Biberman featured blacklisted actor Will Geer as an evil sheriff. The depictions of struggling workers in a movie provoked more controversy in real life—officers of the International Alliance of Theatrical and Stage Employees refused to allow unionized projectionists to show the movie.

An opposing view of workers and unions emerged in *On the Waterfront*, written and directed by Elia Kazan and Budd Schulberg, who had cooperated in the expansion of the Hollywood blacklist by "naming names." This movie depicts the longshoreman's union—accurately—as a mobster-controlled organization and provides a starring role for a marginal worker and former boxer who also turns stool pigeon in an attempt to clean up the local. Consistent with other movies about the working class, *On the Waterfront* features an individual inspiring a collective struggle that is as much against the officers of a union as it is against the bosses (the struggle in this case being like the ones depicted in *FIST* or *Blue Collar*). Although not always flattering to either capital or labor, *On the Waterfront*'s gritty realism stands in stark contrast to the rags-to-riches fairy tales that were twentieth-century versions of the **Horatio Alger** myth.

The power of the blacklist and the shift of American culture away from labor movies also impacted gender roles. Sylvia Jarrico, the wife of blacklisted writer Paul Jarrico, noted that after the **Red Scare** of the early 1950s, strong women were considered "sinister" and "manipulative," and hence, one "labor" movie of the period, *The Pajama Game* (1957), featured perky Doris Day as a union officer bedecked in frilly clothes and high heels. In the film, she not only wins a strike but also—in a classic depiction of worker mobility—falls in love with the plant manager. *The Pajama Game* also embodies the ideology of the postwar "classless" society myth. In popular discourse, most Americans were becoming **middle class**. This (false) logic hastened the disappearance of **class struggle** in movies.

Several exceptions stand out; *Norma Rae* (1979) and *Matewan* (1987), *Bread and Roses* (2000), and *10,000 Black Men Named George* (2002) each show union organizing in all its complexities, with the main organizer as the hero or heroine for the movie.

With the growth of the service economy, movies such as *9 to 5* (1980), *Glengarry Glen Ross* (1992), and *Office Space* (1999) were set in modern office workplaces. Among the most overtly ideological portrayals of workers as the century ended was the glorification of scabs during a strike in *The Replacements* (2000), but otherwise the working class and its issues have been virtually eliminated from popular movies in the United States. **Blue-collar** life, if it appears at all, is likely to appear as a mere background detail for film characters. Only a handful of independent directors—such as Barbara Kopple, Michael Moore, and John Sayles—routinely direct their lenses on the working class.

It should be said, however, that direct engagement of class issues has always been rare in mainstream films, with the possible exception of the pre-Hollywood silent era. Mogul Samuel Goldwyn (1882–1974) once allegedly remarked, "Pictures are for entertainment, messages should be delivered by Western Union." His pithy remark is a reminder that movies are a **capitalist** business enterprise. In this regard, it is hardly surprising that they reinforce the status quo far more often than they challenge it.

Suggested Reading
James Lorence, *The Suppression of Salt of the Earth: How Hollywood, Big Labor, and Politicians Blacklisted a Movie in Cold War America* (1999); Steven J. Ross, *Working-Class Hollywood: Silent Film and the Shaping of Class in America* (1998); Michael Slade Shull, *Radicalism in American Silent Films, 1909–1929* (2000); Tom Zaniello, *Working Stiffs, Union Maids, Reds and Riffraff: An Expanded Guide to Films about Labor* (2003).

FIRST FAMILIES OF VIRGINIA

LISA L. HEUVEL

Better known as "FFVs," the First Families of Virginia claim lineal descent from the most prominent colonial families living in seventeenth- and eighteenth-century Virginia. Over the last century, these terms have attracted mixed responses as signifiers of heritage, aristocracy, and ancestor veneration.

The FFVs claim connection to the governing Virginia **elite** who accumulated power beginning in the 1660s. The ruling dynasties of Virginia's colonial era were indirectly founded through the efforts of Sir William Berkeley, who encouraged both the younger sons of English gentry and the Royalist supporters of King Charles II of England to take advantage of Virginia's potential. By law, younger sons could not inherit their family estates, and Royalists found Oliver Cromwell's reign inhospitable after the English Civil War.

In the colony of Virginia, both groups found opportunities for lucrative political office and the accumulation of large land holdings, giving rise to a new Virginia aristocracy that maintained its status until after the **American Revolution**. The original promise of Virginia as a New World unlike the hierarchical society of England slowly faded over time as the colony's new leaders gradually evolved into its **ruling class**. Some of their eighteenth-century descendants, including Thomas Jefferson, Richard Henry Lee, and George Washington, led the fight for American independence from their ancestral country.

This genealogical background is only part of a growing interest in preserving Virginia history and historical sites prior to and after the 1907 anniversary celebrating three hundred years of white settlement in Virginia. In 1889 the Association for the Preservation of Virginia Antiquities was founded to protect Jamestown Island from decay, and it soon expanded efforts to other endangered historic sites. On May 13, 1912, Minnie Gaithright Cook (wife of Henry Lowell Cook) instituted the Order of First Families of Virginia, 1607–1624/5, to recognize descendants of the first settlers of Jamestown sent by the Virginia Company of London. Twelve years later, George Craghead Gregory founded the Jamestowne Society, whose membership is made up of descendants of stockholders in the Virginia Company and descendants of landholders and those who had domiciles on Jamestown Island prior to 1700.

The Order of First Families of Virginia, 1607–1624/5, was incorporated in Virginia on July 22, 1913. In 1915 Lyon G. Tyler, then president of the College of William and Mary, wrote an article for the *William and Mary Quarterly Historical Magazine*, which he edited. Tyler's article described the FFVs not as descendants of the earliest settlers, but as those of the socially and politically prominent families who first served in either the governor's office or colonial council while also maintaining prominence in local affairs.

Tyler listed fifty-seven family names, including Carter, Custis, Lee, and Randolph. Almost a century later, these names are still prominent in Virginia history and place names. However, the historical underpinnings of the FFVs as a formal organization and social classification should also be considered only part of the meaning of FFV in the twenty-first century. Although still considered socially significant by many prior to World War II, by the 1980s the First Families of Virginia were treated as more of an anachronism and less of an aristocracy by most observers. However, the terms FFV and First Families of Virginia continue to be popularly used in Virginia and in general usage as a generic connotation of social class.

Suggested Reading

Ray Allister, "From Allerton to Yardley," *The Virginia Genealogical Society Newsletter*, November–December 1985, p. 1; "Becoming Virginians," *The Story of Virginia: An*

American Experience, Virginia Historical Society (http://www.vahistorical.org/sva2003/virginians.htm); *Roster of Members, Order of the First Families of Virginia 1607–1620*, 1957.

FLAT TAX

GINA L. KEEL

A flat tax is a tax with a single fixed percentage rate for all payers. The flat tax usually refers to an **income tax**, although other bases of taxation can be subject to a single rate as well. It is also called a proportional tax because under it, all taxpayers pay the same proportion of their taxable incomes. A flat tax is distinct from the current **progressive** income tax structure, which uses graduated rates ranging from 10 percent to 35 percent that increase along with income in six brackets.

Advocates of a flat tax on incomes argue that it would improve the simplicity, economic efficiency, and fairness of the system. Simplicity would be enhanced if all or most exemptions and deductions were eliminated; tax returns could be filed on a postcard-sized form. A more simplified system would make compliance easier and reduce the costs of administration, the size of the Internal Revenue Service, and the tax accounting and legal services associated with tax preparation and income sheltering. Proponents also argue that a flat tax would increase incentives to work more and would reduce incentives for legal tax avoidance and illegal tax evasion, thereby efficiently increasing tax yields to the public treasury. A flat income tax appeals to those who see it as more fair because the higher earning classes would pay the same proportion of their income in taxes rather than be penalized for their success by having to pay a higher rate. Also, taxpayers with relatively equal incomes would pay the same tax (horizontal equity) if those who have the means to shelter income, maximize deductions, and avoid taxes could no longer do so. A flat tax could also enhance fairness by ending tax provisions that favor unearned income, such as capital gains and dividends, over wage and salary income.

Opponents of the flat tax argue that progressive or graduated tax rates are fairer because the wealthier have a greater ability to pay taxes, and only higher rates on the wealthier class can approximate equal sacrifice among taxpayers (vertical equity). Beginning in the 1980s, new tax laws reduced rates and collapsed brackets, thereby making the income tax structure much flatter than previous decades. A historic shift to a single-rate flat income tax would immediately benefit those who pay the highest rates and the majority of income taxes and would shift a greater burden onto the middle and lower economic classes.

A flat tax does not require the elimination of exemptions and deductions, although it is usually characterized this way. A standard exemption for all taxpayers, to avoid taxing subsistence needs, would introduce some progressiveness without adding complexity. Many flat tax opponents are skeptical about whether deductions, particularly those benefiting the economically privileged and politically powerful, would be reintroduced into the system, given the nature of interest-group politics in tax policymaking.

Tax systems at the state and national level include flat taxes. For example, states and localities rely heavily on fixed-rate **sales taxes** that are regressive in their impacts, meaning people with lower incomes spend a larger portion of their income on that tax than do people with higher incomes. Federal **Social Security** payroll taxes (FICA) use flat rates on **wages** up to the maximum taxable amount ($94,200 in 2006) and are therefore regressive in their taxing impact. The Social Security benefits system, however, is progressive because it pays higher benefits—relative to taxes paid in—to lower-income workers.

Suggested Reading

"The Flat-Tax Revolution," *Economist*, 375 (April 16, 2005), http://www.economist.com/opinion/displayStory.cfm?story_id=3861190; David R. Francis, "U.S. Already Moving toward a Flat Tax," *Christian Science Monitor*, 97, no. 98 (April 14, 2005), p. 3; Joel Slemrod and Jon Bakija, *Taxing Ourselves: A Citizen's Guide to the Debate over Taxes*, 3rd ed., 2004.

FLOYD, CHARLES ("PRETTY BOY")

See James, Jesse.

FLYNN, ELIZABETH GURLEY (August 7, 1890–September 5, 1964)

RON BRILEY

Elizabeth Gurley Flynn was the "Rebel Girl" active in labor organization and leftist politics from the **Industrial Workers of the World** (IWW) to the **Communist Party** (CPUSA) in the first half of the twentieth century.

Flynn was born in Concord, New Hampshire, to **working-class** parents who were descended from a long line of Irish rebels. In 1900 the family moved to the Bronx, where the Flynn flat became a gathering place for **socialists** and Irish freedom fighters. The Flynn family encouraged their daughter's developing social conscience, and by age fifteen, she was speaking on street corners, advocating causes such as women's suffrage and government support for children in order to reduce working-class women's dependence on men. The next year, she was arrested for speaking without a permit, the first of many arrests, which garnered the young radical considerable media exposure.

In 1906 Flynn joined the IWW, and she was christened the Rebel Girl by Wobbly minstrel Joe Hill. As a "jawsmith," or traveling organizer for the union, Flynn participated in the memorable textile **strikes** at Lawrence, Massachusetts (1912), and Paterson, New Jersey (1913–1914). She was also actively involved with the IWW free speech struggles in Missoula, Montana (1908), and Spokane, Washington (1909–1910).

During the post–World War I **Red Scare**, Flynn labored to provide legal assistance to victims of government harassment. She was one of the founders of the

American Civil Liberties Union, an organization that expelled her in 1940 for her association with the CPUSA. Flynn was active in the defense of Italian anarchists Nicola Sacco and Bartolomeo Vanzetti, who were accused of murder and robbery in Braintree, Massachusetts. Exhausted by her labors and a tragic love affair with the **anarchist** organizer Carlo Tresca, Flynn collapsed in 1928, spending the next decade in Portland, Oregon, recuperating at the home of Marie Equi, with whom she was rumored to have been romantically involved.

Returning to left-wing politics in 1938, Flynn joined the CPUSA, and in 1941 she was appointed to the party's national board. Flynn was never completely comfortable with her leadership role in the party because she considered herself a figurehead who had not risen through the ranks. Nor was she considered a major party theoretician. Flynn, however, was a popular speaker who wrote a regular column for the party newspaper *The Daily Worker*. She also continued to organize among **immigrants**, students, and civil rights activists on behalf of the party.

Flynn and other leaders of the Communist Party were indicted in 1951 under the Smith Act, which made it illegal to belong to a political organization advocating the overthrow of the American government. Flynn spoke eloquently in her own defense, but she was sentenced to a three-year prison term in the Alderson federal penitentiary in West Virginia. While incarcerated, Flynn wrote her autobiography *I Speak My Own Piece* (1955; reprinted as *The Rebel Girl* in 1975).

Elizabeth Gurley Flynn (Mrs. J.A. Jones). Courtesy of the Library of Congress.

Following release from prison in 1957, Flynn published a prison memoir, *The Alderson Story* (1963), and continued her involvement with the CPUSA, becoming the first female national chair of the party in 1961. She traveled extensively on the party's behalf and died in the Soviet Union, where she was visiting and writing. She was given an elaborate state funeral in the Soviet Union, but Flynn had requested that her ashes be scattered in the Chicago cemetery containing the remains of the men hanged for the 1886 Haymarket bombing. Although never a feminist, Flynn carried out important duties in the male-dominated IWW and Communist Party. She remained dedicated to the cause of labor reform throughout her life, always the Rebel Girl.

Suggested Reading

Rosalyn Baxandall, *Words on Fire: The Life and Writing of Elizabeth Gurley Flynn*, 1987; Elizabeth Gurley Flynn, *The Rebel Girl, An Autobiography, My First Life (1906–1926)*, 1955; Flynn, *The Alderson Story: My Life as a Political Prisoner*, 1963.

Food Bank

Robert E. Weir

A food bank is a private or semiprivate charitable agency that delivers direct aid in the form of food to needy individuals. Unlike breadlines and **soup kitchens**, this food is usually unprepared; recipients take it home and consume it individually rather than dining in communal style with others seeking relief from hunger. Food banks—sometimes called "food pantries"—usually stockpile food as a hedge against peak demand, but many operate with minimal resources and volunteer help.

Food banks, soup kitchens, shelters, and other like charities are the products of evolving constructions of **poverty** in America. In Colonial time and during the early years of the republic, seeking relief from poverty was viewed as an individual's responsibility, and hence, institutions such as almshouses and workhouses usually linked assistance with manual labor. During the **Gilded Age**, the idea of **self-reliance** was pushed even further. Members of the **middle** and **upper classes** often viewed poverty as an individual moral failing and decried that well-meaning relief efforts only encouraged irresponsible behavior. American society did not possess well-articulated notions about "social" problems until century's end.

Despite this, some Americans have long felt compelled to assist those in need. This was particularly true of those belonging to religious organizations, with Catholics, Lutherans, Quakers, and the Salvation Army developing charitable wings in advance of the rest of society. New York City Jews formed B'nai Brith in 1843, one of whose tasks was to deliver aid to the poor. The influence of the late nineteenth-century **Social Gospel** movement also helped many see poverty as a social rather than individual concern.

Food banks are organized on the community level and normally deliver assistance on a regional basis. Many belong to nationwide umbrella organizations such as America's Second Harvest, which solicits corporate funding and in-kind donations. It also receives food from the United States Department of Agriculture (USDA). The USDA has long donated surplus food to communities to be delivered through private or quasi-governmental agencies. In 2001 Second Harvest delivered more than two billion pounds of food to needy Americans.

Many food banks also receive some support from state and local governments. Despite broader connections, most food banks rely heavily on donations of canned goods, nonperishable items, and funding from private individuals and community businesses. In 2005 more than 25 million Americans sought sustenance from local food banks. According to a Second Harvest study of those receiving help, more than 9 million were children. Nearly 40 percent of those seeking aid came from among the **working poor**, those families in which at least one member held a full-time job. The elderly constitute another large group served by food banks. The group also reports that many families seeking food already receive food stamps and that 30 percent of them routinely forego medical care in order to pay for food.

The number of people seeking help from food banks has steadily climbed since the 1980s, suggesting that the **wealth** gap between rich and poor is indeed widening and that changes in the American economy have impacted the poor and the **working class** negatively. The **minimum wage**, for instance, has remained frozen at $5.15 since 1997. With traditional **blue-collar** jobs disappearing as a result of **deindustrialization**, a displaced worker forced to take a minimum wage job would earn under $10,800 per annum, which would place a family of four considerably below the **poverty line**.

Structural economics form the basis for one of the very few critiques of food banks. Volunteers and charities are almost universally admired, but some analysts argue that private charities simply ameliorate the symptoms rather than the root causes of poverty. They also point out that private charities cannot possibly marshal the necessary resources to deal with extraordinary events such as the **Great Depression** or Hurricane **Katrina**. Indeed, many food banks and shelters exhaust their resources in the course of a normal winter. From this perspective, the work of nonprofit agencies such as food banks is admirable, but only concerted governmental action can hope to shrink poverty in America.

Suggested Reading
America's Second Harvest (http://www.secondharvest.org); Peter Eisinger, *Toward an End to Hunger in America*, 1998; George McGovern, *Third Freedom: Ending Hunger in Our Time*, 2002.

FOREIGN POLICY ESTABLISHMENT

ROBERT E. WEIR

The term "foreign policy establishment" refers to those charged with envisioning, planning, and implementing American diplomatic, trade, and military objectives vis-à-vis the rest of the world. It refers not only to visible leaders—many of whom are political appointees—but also to career personnel, bureaucrats, and line staff.

The term is fraught with ambiguity and is frequently applied cavalierly to score political points. Foreign policy is complex and sprawling in its formulation and structure. It involves not just the Department of State, but also agencies such as the Central Intelligence Agency, the National Security Council, and the Commerce Department. Policy is often hammered out in various **think tanks**—such as the liberal-leaning Brookings Institute or the conservative Heritage Foundation—that, on paper, have no formal relationship to official channels but that, because of the nature of **social networks**, are highly connected to those in power. Policy is also influenced by private and public trade commissions, corporate **lobbyists**, and groups few Americans know of, including the ostensibly nonpartisan Council on Foreign Relations, which, since 1921, has exerted tremendous influence on policy through task forces, published reports, and access to politicians.

Members of the political right such as **Pat Buchanan** and Rush Limbaugh often denounce the "liberal" foreign policy establishment whenever a cherished global objective is delayed or employment of the military abroad is debated. Likewise, those of the political left such as **Noam Chomsky** invoke a "conservative" foreign policy establishment to decry what they deem needlessly provocative actions toward foreign nationals, neglect toward developing nations, or forceful behavior they interpret as imperialist in nature.

Political rhetoric notwithstanding, American foreign policy objectives enjoyed bipartisan support for most of the twentieth century and beyond. Many political scientists argue that this has been especially the case since World War II. Both Republicans and Democrats, conservatives and liberals, for example, overwhelmingly supported the **Cold War** objective of containing international **communism**, even to the point of offering at least tacit support for **Red Scare** domestic policies. Major military interventions, including the Korean War, the Vietnam War, the invasion of Grenada, both Gulf wars, and unilateral actions designed to curtail terrorism likewise drew support from erstwhile political rivals. Some analysts claim there is no essential difference between the political parties on matters relating to trade, diplomacy, and military intervention.

What is unarguably clear is that diplomacy has historically been and continues to be a career disproportionately staffed by members of the **upper class** and their allies from the upper **middle class**. In the nineteenth century, diplomacy and international trade were viewed as a "gentlemen's" professions and were dominated by graduates from **Ivy League** colleges and the offspring of wealthy families. As the federal government expanded in the twentieth century, however, more jobs fell under the aegis of civil service laws, thereby forcing **elites** to rely on nongovernmental agencies, think tanks, and less official channels to exert influence. The Council on Foreign Relations (CFR), for example, consisted almost entirely of Ivy Leaguers and representatives of **Wall Street**. The efforts of the CFR, like those of the foreign service and intelligence agencies, were largely hidden from public scrutiny. Outside of the academic and political worlds, few Americans considered how foreign policy was made until after World War II.

It was, ironically, conservatives who first called public attention to foreign policy after World War II. Republicans and Southern Democrats invoked national security fears, partly as a strategy to attack the **New Deal** and partly because many were genuinely convinced of an internal communist threat. High-profile spy cases, such as that involving State Department official Alger Hiss, cast light on the foreign policy establishment, as did the demagogic speeches of politicians such as Richard Nixon and Joseph McCarthy. The Soviet Union's development of an atomic bomb and a revolution in China that installed a communist government in 1949 also fueled fears that American foreign policy was flawed and its planners inept. Senator McCarthy was especially adroit in attacking the upper-class background of policymakers.

Despite attacks from the right in the 1950s and attacks by anti-Vietnam protestors on the left in the 1960s, the foreign policy establishment never purged privilege from its ranks. Even President Richard Nixon, who disliked Ivy Leaguers, chose a Harvard man, Henry Kissinger, as his Secretary of State. Kissinger did much to reestablish the anonymity with which agencies such as the State Department and the CIA did their work, while presidents Carter and Reagan worked to rebuild the credibility of the foreign policy establishment following the Vietnam War.

Reagan also deeply politicized the foreign policy establishment. Top posts in government agencies have long been held by political appointees, but many key Reagan posts went to those with such conservative views that liberals cried foul. Since Reagan, more attention has been given to the ideological views of top officials, and sometimes the confirmation process for candidates is bruising. Senator Jesse Helms blocked the 1997 nomination of ex-Massachusetts governor William Weld to become Ambassador to Mexico because Helms deemed Weld too liberal and did not trust him to guard American trade interests. Likewise, liberals (unsuccessfully) battled the 2005 nomination of John Bolton to become U.S. Ambassador to the United Nations because they saw him as too ideologically rigid to negotiate with other nations. Liberals also accused President George W. **Bush** of imposing an ultra-right ideological litmus test for foreign policy (and other) appointees.

Political rancor obscures the fact that the foreign policy establishment represents class interests as much as (if not more than) ideological agendas. What happens beyond the top ranks remains hidden, but the connection between policy-setters like the CFR and the business community is quite clear. Critics as diverse as **G. William Domhoff Jr.** and **Ralph Nader** charge that the foreign policy establishment is an integral part of the **power elite** and is beholden to the **military-industrial complex**. They assert that foreign policy and trade objectives are designed to serve the interests of the business community, not average Americans. This contention is bolstered by the inordinate number of Cabinet, ambassadorial, and government posts held by leaders of the business community. Scholars of the **corporate class** also note these interconnections. More recent work centers on what journalist Ari Berman dubs "the strategic class," a group of foreign policy experts, think tank theorists, and political strategists who thoroughly dominate the behavior of both Republicans and Democrats.

It could be argued that the term "foreign policy establishment" is too imprecise to be meaningful. Whatever position one takes on its usefulness in analytical discourse, the phrase serves to draw attention to the role of social class and **power** in the making and implementation of foreign policy. Even when policymaking is hidden from plain view, the decisions rendered impact millions of Americans.

Suggested Reading

Eric Alterman, *Who Speaks for America? Why Democracy Matters in Foreign Policy*, 1999; Ari Berman, "The Strategic Class," *The Nation*, August 29, 2005; Burton Hirsch, *The Old Boys: The American Elite and the Origins of the CIA*, 1992.

Fortune Magazine

Kevin S. Reilly

Fortune magazine is one of the oldest and most influential general business periodicals. It began its life as a lavish, folio-sized monthly publication in 1930. It was the second magazine developed by Henry R. Luce (1898–1967) and Briton Hadden (1898–1930), the owners and founders of Time Inc. *Fortune* initially addressed "tycoons" and wealthy families but quickly expanded its audience to include important business professionals of all kinds. Ironically, it thrived during the Depression and in the widespread anti-business sentiment of the 1930s and grew to become extremely influential in industry and public policy circles with a circulation of 250,000 by 1945.

Luce created *Fortune* to address the complacency he discerned among American businessmen, whom he faulted for failure to "constitute themselves as a class." Luce encouraged business executives to enter public life—akin to the national aristocracies of Europe—and to be educated leaders with character. *Fortune* was marketed as an intellectual vehicle for visionary leaders in corporate management. The editors were charged with developing business literature that would be a cultural expression worthy of the physical and economic importance of large capitalist enterprise. Talented young writers artfully crafted articles, which were illustrated with color prints and beautiful photographs by Margaret Bourke-White and other well-known modernist photographers. The publishers successfully defined the magazine's role through marketing and design to ensure that it became the bible of the aspiring executive.

The journalistic innovation for which *Fortune* is best known is its "corporation story." These descriptive narratives of companies combined thorough empirical research with colorful analysis of personalities and events within the corporation and with magnificently reproduced photographs of factories and individuals. The formally dressed managers common in *Fortune*'s visual corporate stories were described in terms that framed them as modern male heroes: learned and emotionally reserved, but of rugged constitution and decisive action. This framed the corporate elite in a more flattering light than previous popular images of businessmen. *Fortune* was a consistent voice of corporate modernity. The habits of older rich families were compared unfavorably to the energy of the new corporate professionals. The filthy and brutal labors of mining and meat processing were presented in photographs and words as sanitized narratives of flawless production. Yet men who embraced reform were treated to more flattering coverage than conservatives, and the magazine advocated business-government cooperation consistently from 1930s through the 1950s.

During the 1930s, *Fortune* drew attention for important stories and research innovations. *Fortune* achieved a major franchise with the hiring of Elmo Roper to conduct an opinion poll, the "Fortune Survey," to rival the popular Gallup Poll. After 1932, the magazine also produced significant coverage of foreign affairs and policy. International articles focused on rapid transformations in German, Russian, and Italian industry and society, and its September 1936 issue presciently reported on Japan's military and economic ascendance before other journalists took notice.

Richard Edes Harrison, *Fortune*'s cartographic specialist, produced pioneering maps to accompany this reportage.

The editors were also willing to produce provocative articles critical of American businessmen or politicians. Eric Hodgins's 1934 piece on the international arms industry, "Arms and the Men," was widely quoted and helped spark a Senate investigation into the munitions industry, but such pieces earned condemnation as well as praise. A 1936 series on U.S. Steel contained pointed criticism of the company's executives and their business practices, especially their hostility to the **labor movement**. Although never enamored of most national union leaders, *Fortune* was sympathetic to organized labor within industry and wrote encouragingly of the Roosevelt administration's attempts to curb corporate repression of labor. As a result, some business readers came to consider *Fortune* politically hostile to American capitalism.

Some of *Fortune*'s surprisingly liberal positions on business and politics can be attributed to the makeup of its early staff. Most of the men who did the writing and the women who did the research were young graduates of elite colleges and were deeply engaged in the cultural and political fervor of New York in the 1930s and 1940s. Luce's concern about presenting the best ideas and the best writing led him to hire, among others, Pulitzer Prize–winning poet Archibald MacLeish; James Agee, author of the Depression classic *Let Us Now Praise Famous Men*; and critic and essayist Dwight Mcdonald, who was active in **Trotskyite** politics. During the war, *Fortune* also recruited such well-known men as economist **John Kenneth Galbraith** and writer Alfred Kazin.

The magazine's political vision, however, was far from radical. Its editorial offices operated increasingly like a **think tank** intent on establishing a middle ground between laissez-faire **capitalism** and state **socialism**. Luce and some editors had lost faith in the **New Deal** by the late thirties and cast *Fortune*'s support to liberal Republican businessman Wendell Willkie in the 1940 presidential election. During World War II, the magazine called for the state support of corporate growth and advocated policies that limited competition, kept labor peace, and minimized economic controls. These policies were intended to maximize the production of war material, but they also articulated Luce's vision of large corporations as the key institutions in American society. If government constrained the profiteers and overly aggressive reactionaries, *Fortune* suggested, large corporations and their leaders would produce an era of peace and abundance.

During the **Cold War**, the magazine took a more conservative, explicitly procapitalist turn in editorial direction. In some sense, *Fortune* was more invested in politics during the Dwight Eisenhower administration than it had been previously. *Fortune*'s publisher and Time Inc. vice president C. D. Jackson took leave of the company to write speeches for Eisenhower and ultimately served as a presidential advisor on inter-American affairs and psychological warfare. *Fortune* remained critical of business developments that seemed dangerous to individual liberty, however. In the early 1950s, editor William H. Whyte Jr. produced articles that would become the core of his attack on bureaucratic life, *The **Organization Man***. The magazine also created a genre called "the failure story," which recounted businesses gone awry to give variety to the magazine's litany of success stories. Mostly, large business organizations were celebrated as the primary movers in the American economy. The magazine resisted anti-monopoly prosecution of firms, arguing that the benevolent, rational administration of large companies was not simply one of the great achievements of modernity, but that the material salvation of mankind depended on them. Corporations were the monuments of what *Fortune*, in direct reference to Soviet **Marxism**, called "The Permanent Revolution" of American democratic capitalism.

Fortune's coverage of the troubled American economy and society of the late 1960s and 1970s turned even more libertarian and conservative. The magazine reversed its long-standing acceptance of the idea that business firms had a social accountability beyond their own quest for profit. Government entitlement programs, industry regulations, and federal deficits were all identified as culprits in the national crisis.

Fortune's biggest concern in these later years, however, was its own revenues, as it faced stiff competition from rival business publications. In 1972 its original folio size was reduced because of cost and because young readers found it unwieldy. *Fortune* also changed from monthly to biweekly publication in 1978. Although forced to compete with flashy, though less substantive, business reporting in other periodicals, *Fortune* remains a publication interested in showcasing big ideas about business and political economy. In addition to regular reporting, its staff continues to publish significant essays and books on these subjects.

Suggested Reading

James L. Baughman, *Henry R. Luce and the Rise of the American News Media*, 1987; Daniel Bell et al., *Writing for Fortune: Nineteen Authors Remember Life on the Staff of a Remarkable Magazine*, 1980; Robert T. Elson, *Time Inc.: The Intimate History of a Publishing Enterprise, 1923–1941*, 1968.

FOUNDATIONS

LAURA TUENNERMAN-KAPLAN

Foundations are nongovernmental, nonprofit organizations, incorporated under state or federal law, which have their own funds and programs managed by trustees or directors. In general, they have been established to support—mostly through grant-making activities—educational, social, charitable, religious, or other activities that benefit society. The status of modern foundations is defined in the Internal Revenue Service code section 501(c)(3), which provides for four basic categories of foundations:

1. *Independent foundations* are privately funded organizations that generally give grants to others. These account for a very large percentage of foundations overall.
2. *Company-sponsored foundations* are legally the same as independent foundations but are commonly the charitable arm of for-profit organizations.
3. *Operating foundations* primarily use their funding to do in-house research or service and are often large and well-known.
4. *Community foundations* allow philanthropists to set up tax shelters and bequests that earmark local charities.

Historically, the idea of foundations dates back to early seventeenth-century English legal traditions of charitable trusts. In the United States, however, it was not until the turn of the twentieth century that foundations took on a prominent place in society. At that time, the richest of the rich—families who had amassed fortunes so vast that they could no longer be controlled by any single individual—followed the lead of industrialist and philanthropist **Andrew Carnegie** and began to create a new type of organization, the charitable foundation, which allowed for the careful disbursement of funds through a large, centralized organization.

Shortly thereafter, community foundations arose out of **Progressive Era** concerns about the need for coordinated raising and disbursement of funds. The first such organization was founded in Cleveland, Ohio, in 1914. These foundations, unlike many private foundations, pooled together the wealth of many individual donors in a single community.

Foundations—whether private or community-based—were a departure from earlier forms of **elite** giving in several ways. First of all, the very act of giving signaled the declining appeal of **Social Darwinism**. Second, foundations marked a shift from personal giving, which was often tinged with paternalism, toward organizing giving along more businesslike lines. Although in many cases personal preferences of the benefactors or their family members continued to direct giving, for the most part the actual disbursement of funds was handled not by the benefactors themselves, but rather by paid, professional administrations who were expected to make informed decisions based on the latest scientific and social scientific data available; this process created a perceived aura of professionalism that often increased the perceived credibility of the projects supported by foundations.

Foundations have not flourished without opposition from those who question their legality and altruism. In 1910, for example, an attempt to incorporate the **Rockefeller** Foundation was defeated in Congress. At a time when the Sherman **Antitrust** Act was being used to dismantle Rockefeller's Standard Oil, opponents of the foundation concept suggested that foundations were simply another way for individuals to create trusts in order to perpetuate large fortunes. In 1936 Eduard C. Lindeman, a faculty member at the New York School of Social Work, published *Wealth and Culture*, a study of 100 foundations during the 1920s; his findings suggested that the reasons for the creation of foundations were mostly economic rather than **philanthropic**, and he condemned their trustees for being arrogant members of the elite class. Lindeman questioned whether the wealthy should be responsible for investigating and shaping public policy and funding welfare efforts focused on the **lower classes**.

Because of their nonprofit or tax-exempt status, foundations have also been carefully investigated by Congress. The Tax Reform Act of 1968, for example, placed some restrictions on foundation activities, demanding more regulation and public accountability.

Today, there are thousands of foundations in the United States influencing society on every level. Many are small and focused on supporting a specific educational or cultural institution, for example, whereas others are large and multipurpose. More than 500 of the largest U.S. foundations—including household names such as the Ford Foundation, the Bill and Melinda **Gates** Foundation, and the Russell Sage Foundation—have assets of over 100 million dollars and impact public policy and social services globally.

Suggested Reading

The Foundation Center, David Jacobs, ed., *The Foundation Directory 2005*, 27th ed., 2005; Ellen Condliffe Lagemann, ed., *Philanthropic Foundations: New Scholarship, New Possibilities*, 1999; Paul N. Ylvisaker, "Foundations and Nonprofit Organizations," in *The Nonprofit Sector: A Research Handbook*, ed. Walter Powell, 1987.

FOUNDING FATHERS

ROBERT E. WEIR

The term "Founding Fathers" refers to the leaders who orchestrated the **American Revolution** and went on to write the U.S. Constitution. Within the United States, some members of this group—such as George Washington, Thomas Jefferson, John **Adams**, James Madison, and Benjamin Franklin—are held in quasi-religious awe. The Founding Fathers are often stereotypically cited to evoke ideals of patriotism, **democracy**, and equality.

The Founding Fathers had acute political talent, but most were highly distrustful of democracy and the **masses**. Historians have noted that the very idea of revolution emerged from disputes within the Colonial **upper class**. Newly enriched merchants, distillers, shipbuilders, and lawyers within the North often occupied second-class **status** vis-à-vis older **elites** with ties to Britain. The same was true of newer members of the gentry class and the **slave** importers in the South. These were the individuals who organized protests against various British taxes imposed after 1763. In essence, many of the Founding Fathers were frustrated elites.

They were able to exploit rising **lower-class** anger in the Colonies. **Howard Zinn** notes that there had been untold numbers of riots, and at least eighteen attempts to overthrow Colonial governments, in the hundred years between **Bacon's Rebellion** and the American Revolution. New elites sought to mobilize the lower classes as the American Revolution drew nigh. Revolutionary leaders were overwhelmingly of the upper class, but the Continental Army and various militia groups drew from the ranks of small farmers, landless agrarians, urban manual laborers, and humble craftsmen.

New elites and the lower orders made common cause to overthrow the British, but the Founding Fathers felt little sentimental attachment to their humbler citizens, and the latter grew restive when the American Revolution failed to alter their economic lot. Independence was formalized by the 1783 Treaty of Paris, and the United States first operated under a loose confederation that granted few powers to the central government. Wars with **Native Americans**, problems securing credit, and tumultuous popular uprisings like **Shays's Rebellion** led many of the Founding Fathers to lobby for a more powerful central government, a task realized by the writing of the U.S. Constitution in 1787.

The U.S. Constitution is a remarkable document, but it was also the product of a specific class of men with strong ideas of who should govern society and whose interests best serve the nation. The historian Charles Beard noted that the vast majority of Constitutional signers were lawyers, wealthy property owners, and

George Washington presiding at the signing of the Constitution in Philadelphia on September 17, 1787. Courtesy of the Library of Congress.

businessmen. Moreover, many of them held interest-bearing government bonds that would be jeopardized if the nation's credit could not be secured. A host of other social and economic interests were represented in the Constitutional assembly, including slaveholders seeking to ensure continuation of **slavery**, bankers hoping to curtail inflation, craft and manufacturing interests seeking tariff protection, and landowners with holdings in areas threatened by Native Americans. What was of little interest to them was democracy; nowhere is it mentioned in the Constitution.

Many of the Founding Fathers were well grounded in Enlightenment political theories. According to prevailing notions, democracy was akin to **anarchism** and was often interchanged with the term "mobocracy." Some Founders, including John Adams, Fisher Ames, Alexander Hamilton, Gouverneur Morris, James Otis, and Benjamin Rush, were openly contemptuous of the very idea of common people wielding political power. Hamilton originally proposed that the president—whom he envisioned as a sort of Platonic philosopher-king—and the U.S. Senate be lifetime appointees. Even Thomas Jefferson privately concurred with John Adams that humankind should be ruled by its "**natural aristocracy**."

Jefferson's view was emblematic of those in his social class. The Founders passionately defended **meritocracy** and equal opportunity, but they did not equate these with democracy. They believed that individuals should rise according to their ability, but nearly all believed that ability was circumscribed by breeding and class. These views were somewhat tempered by benign paternalism. Few of the Founders saw any contradiction between their own interests and the health of the

Alexander Hamilton. Reproduction of painting by John Trumbull. Courtesy of the Library of Congress.

nation. If **power** and **wealth** were concentrated in the hands of worthy men, they reasoned, those individuals would act as custodians of the national interest (this line of reasoning endures in forms such as the concept of *noblesse oblige* and the **trickle-down theory** of economics). Their views of meritocracy also served to check the influence of mere wealth. Many of the Founders were just as distrustful of unfettered wealth as they were of the unwashed masses.

Many of the pre-revolution social dynamics surfaced anew as ratification debates for the Constitution took place. Some lesser elites felt excluded from what they saw as a power clique, and it was not difficult to mobilize the disenchanted masses, who, rightly, doubted the document's usefulness to them. The final document was a compromise and included the Bill of Rights, the first ten amendments to the Constitution that secured personal liberties and set other parameters that later became the basis for popular democracy.

Nonetheless, the nation brought forth by the Founding Fathers was a republic, not a pure democracy. There are many aspects of the Constitution that enshrined the Founders' fears of too much public power. Women, Native Americans, and slaves were excluded from full citizenship privileges, and many states imposed property restrictions on white male voters until after the War of 1812. Most significantly, the Constitution created a *representative* government in which elected and appointed officials make decisions. In theory, popular will is expressed through elected officials; in practice, the masses can only express approval or disapproval on Election Day. Moreover, some officials, such as members of the judiciary and (until 1913) U.S. senators, have been appointed rather than elected. The Constitution's famed checks and balances also serve to blunt popular opinion, and the Electoral College can override (and has done so on three occasions) the popular vote in presidential elections.

The Founding Fathers did much to create the enduring American political system. They also wittingly contributed to the equally enduring link between political power and social class.

Suggested Reading

Charles Beard, *An Economic Interpretation of the Constitution of the United States*, 1935; Gary Nash, *Class and Society in Early America*, 1970; Howard Zinn, *A People's History of the United States*, 2003.

FRATERNALISM

ROBERT E. WEIR

Fraternalism refers to the practice of joining voluntary associations whose purposes are fellowship, mutual aid, and (sometimes) public charity. It is a broad term that is applied to semi-secretive societies such as the Freemasons, to civic staples such as the Boy Scouts, and even to hate groups such as the **Ku Klux Klan**. Membership to fraternal (and sororal) orders is generally controlled by existing members, who demand that potential joiners conform to a set of criteria determined by the group. This has tended to segregate American fraternal life by race, ethnicity, gender, religion, and social class.

Modern fraternalism is a remnant of medieval Europe, where upper classes joined various chivalric orders and religious lay societies, and skilled craftsmen, merchants, and manufacturers belonged to guilds. The latter are generally viewed as the forerunners of mutual aid societies and journeymen's associations, which, in turn, were the roots of trade unions. In fact, throughout much of the nineteenth century, the line between unions and fraternal orders was unclear, and groups such as the **Knights of Labor**, the Brotherhood of Carpenters and Joiners, and the American Railway Union retained strong elements of fraternalism.

Most fraternal orders use special rituals designed to build group identity and solidarity. When Europeans settled North America, they brought ritual fraternal practices with them, especially Freemasonry. Freemasons trace their mythical origins to stone workers laboring on King Solomon's temple, but modern practices derive largely from England, where, in 1717, a Grand Lodge was formed to serve as the focal point for all Masons. In 1738 the Catholic Church denounced Freemasonry, and prejudice against it remains strong among Catholic clerics.

From the start, Freemasonry tended to attract more prosperous and **status-conscious** individuals. Many key figures of the **American Revolution**, including George Washington and Benjamin Franklin, were Freemasons. Despite the reputations of such men, Freemasonry and the Order of Cincinnati, a society of Revolutionary War officers and their sons, were viewed as aristocratic and engendered great opposition. Washington served as first president of the Order of Cincinnati from its founding in 1783 until his death in 1799, by which time many of the order's chapters had collapsed in the wake of public outcry against them.

Many Americans feared Freemasonry because of its admission practices and secrecy. Some whites resented the formation of a black Masonic order by Prince Hall in 1775, but a more serious incident occurred in 1826 when a New Yorker, William Morgan, disappeared. Rumor held that Freemasons had murdered him for revealing their ritual. The timing of Morgan's disappearance coincided with a rising of popular republican sentiments associated with **Jacksonian democracy**. Anti-Masonic political parties formed after 1828, some of which exerted political influence on the state and local levels up to the outbreak of the Civil War.

The latter half of the nineteenth century was a takeoff period for fraternal orders in the United States, with the Freemasons claiming over six million members by

1900. Masonry, however, never lost its association with the **upper** and upper **middle classes**, and it was deemed elitist and aristocratic and was considered a secret power cabal to control the **working class**.

Immigrants often formed ethnic fraternal orders to ease their entry into American society, and many societies had distinctive ethnic compositions. The Ancient Order of Hibernians, for example, was popular among the Irish, as were various Turnverein athletic groups with Germans and B'nai Brith among Jews. Most manual laborers preferred fraternal orders dominated by workers, the Independent Order of Odd Fellows proving particularly attractive. By 1900 there were at least 600 separate fraternal organizations in the United States; even the Catholic Church relented, forming the Knights of Columbus in 1882 and Opus Dei in 1928. As noted, even labor organizations infused fraternal practices into assembly life, and as late as the 1930s, organizers for the **Congress of Industrial Organizations** (CIO) reported surges in recruitment when they convinced fraternal order officers to join the CIO.

In the twentieth century, there was less overt ethnic separation and class conflict in American associational life, and most orders relaxed exclusionary rules, though custom continued to segregate groups. Fraternal orders have historically been male preserves, with women often relegated to membership in auxiliaries. Similarly, people of color and ethnic minorities have not been offered a fraternal hand, either because of overt discrimination or because of custom. Those organizations with the highest percentages of working-class participation, such as the Veterans of Foreign Wars, Moose lodges, and the Elks, have generally been more diverse than groups originally founded by elites or the middle class.

American fraternal groups reached their apex around 1910, when as many as one-third of all adult males over the age of nineteen belonged to some sort of nonreligious voluntary association. Membership spiked again in the 1930s, declined in the 1950s, revived in the early 1960s, and remained vital into the 1970s. Since then, membership and the founding of new associations have eroded precipitously. Some commentators trace this to several reasons, one of which is an overall decline in civil life associated with white flight to the suburbs, a more sedentary lifestyle, and the diversions of popular culture. A second reason involves a shift in politics that places more power and emphasis on lobby and special-interest groups; whereas Americans once sought a greater community, they now seek access to resources for more specialized identity groups. Still another reason may be that fraternal orders never entirely shed their associations with social class. Rotary and chambers of commerce, for example, are largely seen as organizations for the upper crust, whereas the American Legion and 4-H are viewed as friendly to "common" people. Fraternal groups remain an important part of American society, but their immediate future is uncertain.

Suggested Reading

Mary Ann Clawson, *Constructing Brotherhood: Class, Gender, and Fraternalism*, 1989; Robert Putnam, *Bowling Alone: The Collapse and Revival of American Community*, 2000; Theda Skocpol, *Diminished Democracy: From Membership to Management in American Civil Life*, 2003.

FRATERNITIES AND SORORITIES

NEDA MAGHBOULEH

Fraternities and sororities are social organizations formed by college students and established around shared interests, backgrounds, and lifestyles. Generally, sororities are exclusive to women and fraternities exclusive to men, though a small number of fraternities are coed. A uniquely American invention, these groups are known collectively as the "Greek system" because their names traditionally consist of two or three letters from the Greek alphabet.

The modern fraternity or sorority consists of members ("brothers" and "sisters") who typically live in a house located on or near a college campus. Not merely a matter of convenience, group-living situations actively facilitate bonds and familial attachments that survive long after graduation. Members of a fraternity or sorority are collectively dubbed "the house," and they proudly display the Greek letters representing their name near the front door. An unwavering allegiance to one's house and a defense of its most clandestine secrets is crucial for members of Greek society. Similarly, the lifelong influence a house has on the lives of its individual members presents a fascinating example of the power of **social networks** throughout U.S. history.

The first modern "social" fraternity in the United States is widely acknowledged to be Kappa Alpha, formed in 1825 at Union College in Schenectady, New York. Though fraternity-like organizations were founded earlier at the College of William and Mary and Princeton University, Union's Kappa Alpha was the first to thrive as a purely social fellowship rather than an academic one. Many fraternities and sororities have developed into national organizations with "chapters" at individual schools; all adhere to a strict code of laws and rituals binding the chapters together. A major advantage to national membership is the access individual chapters have to resources such as capital (for house loans or renovations) or nationwide "gratis" housing at fellow chapters. Non-national fraternities are considered "local": they do not pay dues to a national office and have the freedom to create their own constitution and bylaws. They do not, however, benefit from the umbrella of resources and legal representation national fraternities and sororities provide.

After the **Civil War** wreaked financial havoc at many colleges, fraternities and sororities evolved to accommodate an assortment of student needs. Family-style meals, housekeeping, recreation, friendship, and supervision (in the form of "house mothers") were extended to Greeks, usually in palatial neighborhood homes. After World War II, the relative democratization of higher education, facilitated by the GI Bill and other expansions of the public university system, irrevocably altered the social makeup of the national student body. By the postwar era, the exclusive nature of Greek life was ever more important in differentiating campus "blue-bloods" from the **nouveau riche** and other neophytes now sitting beside them in the classroom. Prohibitive house dues and a subjective membership-vetting system (the "rush") ensured that only candidates they deemed appropriate found their way into the fraternity or sorority house. The system also provided a convenient way to ensure the development of deepening social, romantic, and eventually professional relationships between members of the privileged class. Thus, as greater numbers of young Americans pursued undergraduate degrees, fraternities and sororities flourished.

By the 1960s and 1970s, membership had dropped off significantly—the secret rituals, formal dances, and general frivolity of Greek life were simply unfashionable on the average campus. To justify their existence during the social justice movements of the era, fraternities and sororities especially emphasized their service-oriented and philanthropic works. Similarly, "rush" was now encouraged among formerly excluded members of the student body. Most notably, particular students of color were singled out to join exclusively "white" houses, and some men-only fraternities actively recruited female classmates to join.

The traditional idea of a fraternity or sorority as a bastion of privilege is perhaps better defined in our times by the "finals clubs" of Harvard, "eating clubs" of Princeton, and "secret societies" of Yale. It remains customary in many schools for some fraternal and sororal groups to cater to **upper-class** students or for existing groups to have secret subgroups that do so, such as the Skull and Bones group at Yale, which several members of the **Bush** family have joined. Although membership in a general fraternity or sorority continues to confer privilege, social contacts, and distinction to some, many Americans think of them as incubators for unhealthy, disruptive behavior in the college community. The Greek system is nowadays notorious for encouraging binge drinking among underage students, facilitating coercive hazing rituals, and encouraging a culture of violence and chauvinism. College administrators and representatives from national organizations face pressure to disband chapters after serious incidents that bring lawsuits or unwanted publicity to the school or house. Some campuses have gone so far as to outlaw the existence of all fraternities and sororities.

Perhaps because media coverage of these incidents has become so commonplace, nearly all of the contemporary academic work on Greek life is concerned with the salacious and dangerous social practices just mentioned. The noticeable lack of inquiry into more nuanced issues, such as class status, might reflect real changes in the composition of fraternities and sororities. Yet to truly understand the impact fraternities and sororities have on American culture, we must turn our attention to the experiences and life outcomes of members and non-members.

Suggested Reading

Hank Nuwer, *Wrongs of Passage: Fraternities, Sororities, Hazing, and Binge Drinking*, 2002; Alexandra Robbins, *Pledged: The Secret Life of Sororities*, 2005; Robbins, *Secrets of the Tomb: Skull and Bones, the Ivy League, and the Hidden Paths of Power*, 2002.

FREE TRADE

ROBERT E. WEIR

Free trade is an economic term that refers to the movement of goods, services, capital, and labor between cooperating nations without encumbering tariffs, taxes, and trade barriers. Supporters of free trade tout the savings to consumers and the promotion of international stability associated with free trade, but detractors charge that free trade enriches investors and stockholders at the expense of the **working class**.

Free trade was a central tenant of early **capitalism**, especially among theorists such as Adam Smith and David Ricardo. Smith believed that all economic decisions would be left to the laws of supply and demand, unencumbered by government interference. He and other advocates argued that free trade promoted efficiency, ensured quality, and created opportunities for investors and workers alike; in theory, one's skill could be bargained across borders like any other commodity. Early capitalist theories conflicted with mercantilist ideals, which attached more importance to national **wealth** than to the wealth of private individuals or companies.

By the mid-nineteenth century, free trade was attacked by isolationists and **communists**, but was also controversial among capitalists themselves. As the **Industrial Revolution** began to unfold, nascent American manufacturers sought government tariff protection to protect their enterprises from better-established, deep-pocketed competitors. They were aided to some degree by the **labor movement** and by farmers. Most unions argued that free trade fostered ruinous conditions that destabilized the economy and endangered jobs, and farmers feared that imported agricultural commodities would further suppress farm prices. Groups such as the **Knights of Labor** paid lobbyists to persuade politicians to support protectionist legislation. Even the working-class icon **Henry George** found his speeches on free trade questioned by disbelieving workers. George argued that free trade would allow an already peripatetic workforce to bargain for higher wages, but most workers sided with small-scale employers in the belief that free trade destroyed rather than promoted competition.

As industry matured in the United States, large corporations and their stockholders grew enamored of free trade and argued for laissez-faire government policy in economics matters that would allow the free movement of capital, raw materials, services, and finished goods. By the end of the nineteenth century, the boundaries of the free trade debate were mostly in place; large corporations, finance capitalists, commodity traders, consumer groups, and investors tended to favor it, whereas labor unions, small businesses, and independent farmers opposed it.

Since the 1870s, the federal government has tended toward free trade, but its impact was blunted by America's rise to global industrial dominance. Even unions such as the **American Federation of Labor** did not forcefully push their opposition to free trade because it did not seem a major threat. Moreover, periodic crises such as World War I, the **Great Depression**, and World War II led the government to enact economic controls that mediated against pure free-trade principles. Free trade became a controversial issue again after World War II. In 1957 six western European nations established the European Economic Community (EEC), or "Common Market," effectively making much of the continent a vast free-trade zone. By the late 1960s America was beginning to lose global market shares to other nations, especially Germany, Japan, and South Korea. Suddenly, foreign imports enjoyed competitive price advantages over American products; by the 1980s vast sectors of manufacturing—including electronics, rubber, steel, and consumer appliances—experienced **deindustrialization**. Expansion of the EEC—which reached twenty-five member states in 2005—has put further pressure on American business.

Free trade was also bolstered by rising conservative political tides. For **Ronald Reagan**'s administration, free trade was an article of faith. Many of Reagan's advisors were enamored of **Chicago School** economic theorists, especially Milton Friedman, who saw free trade as a better way to stimulate the economy than government spending programs advocated by economists such as **John Maynard Keynes**. Stagflation during the 1970s gave Reagan license to advance many conservative economic ideas, of which free trade was one. Reagan also envisioned a western hemisphere equivalent to the EEC. This came to pass in 1994, when the North American Free Trade Agreement (NAFTA) removed trade barriers between the United States, Canada, and Mexico to create a common market just slightly smaller than the EEC. Discussions have ensued to expand NAFTA to other nations, especially Chile and Peru.

Free trade is currently a centerpiece of the economic phenomenon known as **globalization**, and the level of debate surrounding its virtues and demerits rage with intensity not seen since the nineteenth century. Free trade is not entirely "free" on a global basis. Trade agreements are made between nations, and these often contain numerous exceptions to pure free trade. Loopholes in NAFTA have led to an export of jobs out of the United States and Canada to Mexico, where wages are much lower and environmental standards looser, a set of circumstances that seems to confirm the fears of nineteenth-century critics. Moreover, the government is often reluctant to impose economic sanctions on nations whose imports are unfairly propped up by government subsidies or protectionist policies that keep out American imports. Groups such as the **American Federation of Labor–Congress of Industrial Organizations** (AFL–CIO) charge that both Japan and China have flooded the U.S. market with unfairly traded goods. Still other critics point to rising foreign debt and trade deficits as indications that free trade idealism has overwhelmed sound economic planning. There can be little doubt that free trade has hurt the working class; entire categories of **blue-collar** labor have essentially disappeared. Some reformers hold that the concept of free trade should be supplanted by that of "fair trade," which would interject ethics into trade decisions.

Defenders of free trade argue that consumers benefit from low-cost imports and that many of the jobs lost in the United States were undesirable ones. They also argue that international security is enhanced by free trade, with economic self-interest trumping political differences within interconnected economic networks. They also bank on hopes that lost jobs in one economic sector will be replaced by new opportunities in others, an optimism not shared by analysts such as **Jeremy Rifkin**.

The immediate future appears to trend in favor of expanded free trade. Conservative **think tanks** such as the American Enterprise Institute, the Cato Institute, and the Heritage Foundation currently have more political clout than liberal free-trade opponents such as the AFL–CIO, the Friends of the Earth, and the Green Party. There have, however, been worldwide protests against the World Trade Organization, and American free traders ironically face some of their stiffest opposition from ultra-conservatives such as **Pat Buchanan** and H. Ross Perot.

Suggested Reading

Christine Ahn, ed., *Shafted: Free Trade and America's Working Poor*, 2003; Jagdish Bhagwati, *In Defense of Globalization*, 2005; Douglas Irwin, *Against the Tide: An Intellectual History of Free Trade*, 1997; Irwin, *Free Trade Under Fire*, 2005.

FRIEDMAN, MILTON

See Chicago School of Economics.

FUNCTIONAL ELITE THEORY

ROBERT E. WEIR

Functional elite theory is an analytical frame in sociology, economics, and political science whose adherents argue that social inequality is not entirely negative, especially in modern **capitalist** societies. From this perspective, elites possess the skills, training, morality, and access to material **wealth** that are necessary for society to operate smoothly. In fact, according to this theory, they are better able to serve mass society and create opportunities for the **lower classes** than any other group. Functional elite theorists often see themselves as occupying a middle position between supporters of absolute power and those who advocate what they see as romantic grassroots **democracy**.

Ideas akin to modern functional elite theory have an ancient pedigree and show up in such classic works as Plato's *The Republic*, but most modern studies derive from the articulation of sociology as a discipline in the late nineteenth and early twentieth centuries. Emile Durkheim (1858–1917) laid the foundations for functionalism, a school that argues that society is held together through a generalized consensus over norms and values. He tended to view society as akin to a living organism in which all parts are necessary for the body, or society, to function well. By extension, this implied that each part should play its assigned role. Elites are seen as imbuing society with the very character that prevents it from degenerating into either autocracy or **anarchy**.

Functionalism was challenged by **conflict theorists**, but it held powerful sway and influenced **stratification** studies even of scholars who were not strict functionalists, such as **W. Lloyd Warner** and **Robert** and **Helen Lynd**. Other scholars have openly embraced the idea that elites are necessary for society to function well, among them **E. Digby Baltzell**, **Talcott Parsons**, Robert Michels, and Suzanne Keller. All four were skeptical of the ability of the masses to direct themselves, operate the economy efficiently, or operate without strong leadership. Both Baltzell and Keller even posited the **upper classes** with superior ability and intellect. Parsons often uncritically accepted the notion that rewards were associated with performance and that American society was characterized by open **social mobility**. A less aggressive defense of elite **power** is embedded in the **Davis-Moore** theory, which takes the view that society is too complex to operate without some sort of leadership.

Not surprisingly, functional elite theory has come under fire. In addition to **Marxists** and other conflict theorists, critical elite theorists such as **C. Wright Mills** and **G. William Domhoff** have called into question the assumed benevolence of elites, and **pluralist** scholars have attacked the alleged superiority of elites vis-à-vis the masses. Responses to functional elite theory often break down along class and political lines. Those who hold **power**, **prestige**, and wealth tend to support the notion that they are entitled to do so because of their hard work, social stewardship, and knowledge, whereas those of lower **socioeconomic status** charge that elites benefit from **social networks** and other advantages that are inherently unfair and undemocratic. Conservatives tend to support the assumption that elites are natural, necessary, productive, and positive, ideas that also have currency with some neo-liberals. Most liberals and members of the political left, however, support one or more of the criticisms of elites and see them as dysfunctional.

Suggested Reading

G. William Domhoff, *Who Rules America? Power and Politics*, 2001; Steve Fraser and Gary Gerstle, eds., *Ruling America: A History of Wealth and Power in a Democracy*, 2005; Suzanne Keller, *Beyond the Ruling Class: Strategic Elites in Modern Society*, 1963.

FUNDAMENTALISM

MATTHEW PEHL

Fundamentalism—generally described as a reaction against such perceived aspects of "modernity" as scientific naturalism, moral relativism, and social pluralism—has played a part in nearly every major world religion since the end of the nineteenth century. In the United States, however, Protestant Christian fundamentalism has produced the most dramatic social and cultural consequences by far. Rejecting the biblical historical-criticism developed in German universities of the 1870s and 1880s, American fundamentalists insisted on the literal inerrancy of the Bible, the divinity of Jesus, and the reality of Jesus' resurrection and physical return to earth. Today, Christian fundamentalists are vocal and influential forces in debates over politics, law, education, cultural "values," and even foreign policy.

Like many Americans, fundamentalists have generally ignored America's class structure. Some have argued that, because of the ease with which people could achieve **social mobility**, class was essentially a European—not American—problem. Many others have insisted that because individual conversion to Christ ranked as the most important human endeavor, a focus on class was irrelevant and even irreligious. However, a closer look at early fundamentalists reveals that fundamentalism, from both an economic and a cultural perspective, reflected many historic and ideological aspects of the American **middle class**. The story of Dwight Lyman

Moody (1837–1899) offers an important example of this connection. After attaining success in the business world, Moody became an active promoter of Sunday schools and the Young Men's Christian Association (YMCA); as many historians have observed, middle-class Protestants such as Moody hoped that the YMCA might "Christianize" the culture of **working-class** youths in tough urban areas. By the mid-1870s Moody had become a talented evangelizer who had mastered the large-scale organizational challenges common to any successful **Gilded Age** manager. In 1889 he founded Moody's Chicago Bible Institute, which became one of the most important fundamentalist institutions and which operated in a manner similar to many major American businesses of the era.

Moody's most famous successor on the evangelizing circuit, the former professional baseball player Billy Sunday, continued to stress middle-class cultural values in the early twentieth century. Indeed, Sunday represents an especially noticeable split between working-class and middle-class cultures. When Sunday joined the Chicago White Stockings in 1883, baseball was still very much a working-class amusement. In 1886 Sunday converted; a few years later, Sunday left baseball to preach, and by 1910 he was a bona fide religious celebrity. Sunday's hostility toward urban degeneracy, **immigration**, and—especially—alcohol illustrates in many ways the rejection of his one-time life with hard-drinking ball players popular among working-class urban dwellers both native and immigrant. Likewise, Sunday's solution to social ills—simple conversion to Christ—obviously differed from such working-class approaches to social problems as unionization and political activism.

In the shadow of World War I and the Russian Revolution of 1917, fundamentalists across the country found a common enemy in Bolshevism. Of course, many Americans succumbed to the **Red Scare** of 1919, but for fundamentalists, the rise of **communism** in Russia came as prophetic proof of the rapid social degeneration that they had been forecasting for decades. The success of a political philosophy rooted in materialism, the "scientific" management of society, and strident atheism served to affirm the apocalyptic worldview that became ever more central to fundamentalist theology. According to the fundamentalist pre-millennial vision, biblical prophecy foretold the inevitable, war-ravaged decline of mankind before Christ would return to institute a thousand-year reign on earth.

The flourishing of the **Cold War**, the founding of the state of Israel, and the looming threat of nuclear war in the 1950s only served to revivify and heighten these beliefs. Fundamentalists' ferocious rejection of **socialism** and communism led them to an equally vigorous embrace of democracy and capitalism (while distrusting such elements of modern democracies as centralized governments and social **pluralism**). Consequently, many hallmarks of working-class life—from trade unions to political parties to racy music and movies—became anathema to fundamentalist leaders. Politically astute fundamentalists such as Billy Graham and Gerald L.K. Smith fused American triumphalism, Cold War paranoia, and Christian theology into a potent and appealing alternative to radical (or even liberal) politics. By the 1980s a new ethos had emerged among fundamentalists. Although they had previously distanced themselves from secular society, the ascension of **Ronald Reagan** to the presidency propelled fundamentalists into coordinated political campaigns on behalf of public programs that reflected their theological understanding of history. In the years since Reagan's election, this trend among fundamentalists has only strengthened, as can be witnessed by their close relationship with the administration of President George W. **Bush**. Modern fundamentalists are distributed across social classes and are most prominent in the South, the Midwest, Colorado, and California.

Suggested Reading

Douglas Carl Abrams, *Selling the Old-Time Religion: American Fundamentalists and Mass Culture, 1920–1940*, 2001; Paul S. Boyer, *When Time Shall Be No More: Prophecy Belief in Modern American Culture*, 1992; George M. Marsden, *Fundamentalism and American Culture: The Shaping of Twentieth-Century Evangelicalism, 1870–1920*, 1980.

G

Galbraith, John Kenneth (October 15, 1908–April 29, 2006)

Peter C. Holloran

John Kenneth Galbraith was an American economist and public official. He was born the son of Scottish immigrants on an Ontario farm on October 15, 1908, and graduated from the Ontario Agricultural College in 1931. After earning a doctorate in economics at the University of California, Berkeley, in 1934, Galbraith worked briefly in Washington, D.C., for the **New Deal** Agricultural Adjustment Administration. He then taught economics at Harvard University (1934–39) and Princeton University (1939–40) before returning to U. S. government service as the price czar for the Office of Price Administration. As an editor at *Fortune* magazine (1943–48), he introduced the work of the British economist **John Maynard Keynes** to the American public. During World War II, Galbraith served in the U.S. Strategic Bombing Survey (1945) and in the postwar U.S. administrations in Germany and Japan. Returning to teaching at Harvard (1949–75), he became one of the most popular, influential, and iconoclastic economists in the nation and the prolific author of thirty-three books and more than 1,100 articles. As a result some academic colleagues dismissed him as America's foremost economist for non-economists, or the economist as social critic.

Galbraith also served in the administrations of President Harry Truman and President Lyndon B. Johnson, and his friend President John F. **Kennedy** named him ambassador to India (1961–63). But he is best remembered as an iconoclastic economist with an astringent wit who adhered to Keynesian theory long after mainstream economists moved on. Despite his nonconformity, Galbraith served as president of the American Economic Association (1972) and received honorary degrees from Harvard University, Oxford University, the University of Paris, the University of Toronto, and over forty other universities around the world. He was a founder of the Americans for Democratic Action in 1947 and

John Kenneth Galbraith. Courtesy of the Library of Congress.

was an advisor in the Adlai Stevenson, John F. Kennedy, Eugene McCarthy, and George McGovern presidential campaigns. The tall, lanky Galbraith also was an early and prominent opponent of the Vietnam War. Some found Galbraith to be arrogant and difficult, but most admired him for candid views that were unsullied by the fashion of the moment.

Known for his persuasive and lucid writing style, Galbraith's book *American **Capitalism**: The Concept of Countervailing Power* (1952) criticized the free market economy and predicted that the U.S. economy would succeed with equal management by big business, big labor, and big government. His best-selling book *The **Affluent Society*** (1958) argued that the United States was rich in goods but poor in social services. He foresaw major government investment in the infrastructure, especially highways and schools, and introduced the phrase "conventional wisdom." In his most important book, *The New Industrial State* (1967), he critiqued the corporate state and argued that few American industries were truly competitive. These controversial ideas, persuasive to his fellow Democratic Party liberals, outraged Republicans and both liberal and conservative economists. His third major opus, *Economics and the Public Purpose* (1973), criticized the unrecognized role of women in ever-increasing consumption and the new consumer market economy.

Other Galbraith publications that have earned an international audience include *The Great Crash* (1955), *The Nature of Mass Poverty* (1979), three novels— *The McLandress Dimension* (1963), *The Triumph* (1968), and *A Tenured Professor* (1990)—and popular articles in *The New York Review of Books*, *The New Yorker*, and *The New York Times Magazine*. In 1977 Galbraith hosted a popular BBC television series, *The Age of Uncertainty*. Rejecting the mathematical models that many of his peers preferred, Galbraith was an old-fashioned political economist, public intellectual, and aphorist who challenged economic theories that overlook the reality of **working-class** and **middle-class** life. Galbraith retired from Harvard in 1975 and was a frequent commentator on public issues in the media. President Bill Clinton awarded him the Medal of Freedom in 2000, and Galbraith remained an active commentator on economic and political issues until his death.

Suggested Reading

John Kenneth Galbraith, *A Life in Our Times: Memoirs*, 1981; Galbraith, *Name-Dropping: From FDR On*, 1999; Peggy Lamson, *Speaking of Galbraith: A Personal Portrait*, 1991; Richard Parker, *John Kenneth Galbraith: His Life, His Politics, His Economics*, 2005.

GAMBLING

SAMANTHA MAZIARZ

Gambling, or "gaming," is the act of taking a risk or placing a bet on an uncertain outcome in the hopes of winning an advantage. It usually involves a game of chance played for stakes, such as a wager of money, property, or control. Gambling comes in many forms, both legal and illegal, the definitions of which are mandated on a state-by-state basis. Most states allow gambling in the forms of bingo, lottery, **sports** betting at licensed outlets like an OTB (off-track betting) facility, and **casino** gambling. Also variable by state are illegal forms of gambling, which include private card and dice games, unlicensed sports gambling, Internet gambling, under-age gambling, and animal fighting.

The most common types of lottery are instant scratch-off games, daily numbers games (in which a player chooses a set of numbers and hopes they will match numbers drawn by the lottery commission), lotto (in which a player picks a set of non-repeating numbers, usually for a large jackpot), and instant terminal games like keno and quick draw (in which gamblers pick numbers or draws that are held every few minutes on an electronic screen, usually at bars and convenience stores).

Because lottery games are officially sanctioned, government enjoys a gambling monopoly. Early American colonists conducted lotteries in order to fund occasional public improvement projects, such as road paving. In the 1800s, however, lotteries were outlawed because of government corruption. Lottery gambling persisted illegally; in fact, many contemporary lotteries are closely patterned after "numbers" running games in black communities, wherein an agent would collect bets on three and four digit numbers from players in the community and would then pay out money to those people whose numbers matched whatever numbers "hit." In **Harlem** in the 1920s, for instance, whatever numbers matched the last three numbers of that day's stock exchange were a "hit" and paid out. Governments in the 1960s revived lotteries, though with a less clear idea of public benefit than in colonial society.

In 1999 a study commissioned by Congress found that state-sanctioned lotteries prey upon the poor and the uneducated and create compulsive gamblers. States spend considerable amounts of money to advertise games and promote the idea that gambling is an easy way to make money and that the odds are beatable. In fact, New York State was reprimanded for its "Dollar and a Dream" campaign and was forced to alter its slogan so as not to convey unrealistic ideas about the ease of winning large jackpots. (By standard odds, a lottery player is seven times more likely to be struck by lightning than to hit a lottery jackpot.)

Government studies also found that state lotteries carefully create the image that they are beneficial to communities and governments. They often tout themselves as means to generate revenue for **education**, when in actuality lottery states actually spend less of their budgets on education than non-lottery states do.

Casinos have historically operated by circumventing state laws. Riverboat casinos—giant boats equipped with slot machines and table games—board passengers in places in which gambling is illegal, and transport them to bodies of water outside a state's jurisdiction so that the gambling may take place unhindered. **Native American** casinos operate in a similar fashion, in that Indian reservations are considered sovereign land, and therefore the casinos erected on them cannot be regulated by the U.S. government.

Many state governments currently work with Indian casinos, striking profitable deals to place casinos outside of reservations in and around struggling cities. This has raised great controversy between those who believe that casinos are a great source of government revenue and a boon to local economies, and those who believe that they exploit the poor and foster compulsive gambling and crime. Until recently, only Nevada had state-regulated casinos, but the lure of potential revenue for state and local government has led other states to legalize casino gambling.

Studies have shown that most gambling disproportionately targets low-income and minority citizens by preying on their hope for a better life and portraying games of chance as a viable way of attaining a higher quality of living. For example, Ohio's lottery constructed the timing of their marketing efforts to correspond to poor citizens' receipt of **welfare**, **social security**, and payroll checks.

To offset social problems created by legalized gambling, several groups have pushed for education about its dangers. Governments have responded by creating support groups, information packets, and toll-free help hotlines for compulsive gamblers, and many governments have made it illegal to gamble using funds from credit cards.

Suggested Reading

Jeff Benedict, *Without Reservation: How a Controversial Indian Tribe Rose to Power and Built the World's Largest Casino*, 2001; Gail Dines and Jean M. McMahon, eds. *Gender, Race and Class in Media: A Text Reader*, 2003; E. Franklin Frasier, *Black Bourgeoisie: The Book That Brought the Shock of Self-Revelation to Middle-Class Blacks in America*, 1997; Steve Fischer, *When the Mob Ran Vegas*, 2005; Lillian Rubin, *Worlds of Pain: Life in the Working-class Family*, 1976.

GANGS

ROBERT E. WEIR

In the popular imagination a gang is a loosely structured group organized around antisocial, often illegal, activities. Social scientists, however, associate gangs with subcultures, and hence, any organized group with distinctive values and identity that exists in opposition to the hegemonic mainstream could be considered a gang. Normally gangs are marked by a recognizable hierarchy, are organized territorially, and adopt a style and set of practices that dominant groups find distasteful (or define as illegal). Their organized nature differentiates them from mobs. Likewise, an open defiance of social norms defines a gang, as opposed to a cult or so-called alternative lifestyles. Gangs exist throughout America but are generally more of an urban than a rural phenomenon.

The popular view of gangs as collections of marginal and lawless individuals is not new; the association of street gangs with urban violence dates to colonial times, and laws were drafted to regulate the movements and activities of groups viewed as dangerous. Urban society contained numerous gangs on the eve of the **American Revolution**, and one could apply gang definitions to groups that precipitated acts now deemed patriotic, such as protests against the Stamp Act or the Boston Tea Party. For the most part, however, gangs are defined negatively. For example, bands of Irish youths roaming New York's notorious Five Points region in the 1830s were deemed "gangs," even though their levels of violence were often surpassed by those associated with the **labor movement** and by paramilitary groups hired by employers to break **strikes**.

Unlawful and antisocial gangs often proliferate in areas marked by **poverty** and increase in number during periods of social stress. During the nineteenth and twentieth centuries some criminal gangs were ethnic in makeup, appealing especially to unassimilated **immigrants** and their offspring. By the early twentieth century cities such as New York, Chicago, and Philadelphia were home to scores of gangs. The corruption of many urban political machines also proved breeding grounds for gangs. Present-day gangs such as the Jamaican Posse, the International Posse, the Sureños, and the Norteños are heirs to Euro-American gangs, such the Dead Rabbits and the Bowery Boys. Gangs also grow in response to the gap between law and social desire; the drug-running gangs of contemporary society parallel those providing illegal alcohol during Prohibition.

Frederic Thrasher's 1927 work *The Gang* is often viewed as the first important sociological treatise on gangs, the rise of which he linked to the stresses of social change. In 1931 E. Franklin Frazier issued the first of his pioneering works that connected **racism**, poverty, **ghettos**, and social exclusion with the rise of gangs, particularly among African American youth. Despite earlier research and the long history of gang activity in America, however, much of how gangs are viewed today is an offshoot of concerns over juvenile delinquency, which emerged in the 1950s. During the **Cold War** and the economic boom of the 1950s juvenile delinquency was viewed (naïvely) as one of the few social problems that America had not yet conquered.

Edwin Sutherland's (1893–1950) earlier work on differential association was resurrected to explain how growing up in high-crime neighborhoods, where they had extensive contact with norm-breakers, increased the likelihood that youths would become delinquent. This was a key component of the work of Albert Cohen (1955), who argued that gang behavior and delinquency were a response to a perceived lack of legitimate opportunity. Walter Miller (1959) also linked delinquency to **lower-class** and **working-class** lifestyles that emerged in areas in which **middle-class** respectability was absent or frustrated. In such a world street gangs and peer groups are often more important than family or educational ties. **Richard Cloward** followed some of the same lines of reasoning and used Robert K. Merton's work on anomie (norm breakdown) in studies with Lloyd Ohlin in which they argued that social strain often prompted lower-class youths to bypass approved paths to legitimate social goals. The desire for money, for example, is a basic American value, though one might obtain it illegally. The **conspicuous consumption** patterns of contemporary gangs shows the **American dream** remains vital and challenges the idea that gangs are inherently antisocial.

Perceptions of modern gang activity are often filtered through the notoriety heaped upon violent urban groups such as the Crips, the Bloods, the Latin Kings, People Nation, the Black Gangster Disciples, and the Vice-Lords. The violence, robbery, prostitution rings, and drug sales of these groups—and motorcycle gangs such as the Hell's Angels and The Bandidos—have induced middle-class fear and have contributed to white flight to **suburbia**, though studies reveal that gang members are more likely to victimize each other or those within their territory than the general public.

Nonetheless, gangs are a legitimate social concern. At least 120,000 gang members are active in greater Los Angeles, and another 100,000 are in **prison**, where gangs also proliferate. Small cities such as Omaha, Nebraska, have joined larger ones such as Baltimore and Boston in seeing increases in homicide rates spurred by gang violence. Tom Hayden estimates that 25,000 youths have been killed in gang violence since 1980. Scholars continue to seek explanations for rising gang affiliation and the crime associated with it, but in many respects, the economic, social strain, social marginalization, and denied opportunity theories of earlier scholars remain valid. Most studies indicate that gang activity is associated with youth, with just 14 percent of gang members in a 1998 survey being over the age of twenty-four. Studies also reveal that the common reasons for joining gangs include a sense of belonging, the desire for money, the need for protection in high-crime neighborhoods, thrill seeking, peer pressure, and a need for structure in areas with high rates of family and institutional stress. A 2000 study by the National Youth Gang Survey revealed that 50 percent of gang members come from the lower class and another 35 percent from the working class. Given that just 3 percent of gang members come from the upper middle class, one finds high correlation between lower **socioeconomic status** and the likelihood of gang membership.

Suggested Reading

Herbert Asbury, *The Gangs of New York*, 1928; Tom Hayden, *Street Wars: Gangs and the Future of Violence*, 2006; National Youth Gang Center (http://www.iir.com/nygc/default.htm); Sanyika Shakur, *Monster: Autobiography of an L.A. Gang Member*, 2004; James Diego Vigil, *Rainbow of Gangs: Street Cultures in the Mega-City*, 2002.

GATED COMMUNITIES

ROBERT E. WEIR

Gated communities are restricted-access neighborhoods located in American cities and their suburbs. They are usually guarded, and one must have permission to enter them. Gated communities range in size from modest condominium complexes to sprawling independent cities of over 20,000. Many feature amenities such as golf courses, swimming pools, supervised playgrounds, and community centers. All blur the line between public and private space; frequently the relationship between them and the greater municipality of which they are a part is ambiguous.

Most gated enclaves cater to the **middle class** and upper middle class and have gained in popularity because of public safety concerns over crime and urban blight. Critics charge they are forms of self-segregation that are also racial and ethnic in nature, though it should be noted that some gated communities are retirement homes with age covenants rather than racial or ethnic ones. That said, whites of Anglo heritage dominate most gated communities, and custom often segregates by religion as well.

Gated communities are not a new idea, nor are they exclusive to any one area of the country. The Los Angeles neighborhoods of Rolling Hills (1935) and Bradbury (1938) are often cited as the first gated communities in the United States in that they were the first to feature around-the-clock surveillance and restricted entry. In practice, however, suburbs have often functioned as de facto gated communities, and many towns and cities have spawned exclusive neighborhoods to which the general public had limited or no access, such as the Eastern Point region of Gloucester, Massachusetts, or the celebrity homes of Hollywood, California.

There can be little doubt, however, that increased perceptions (not always accurate) of urban crime and racial upheaval in the 1960s led to an expansion of the gated community concept. Many who work in urban areas turned to gated communities rather than move to more distant suburbs. Some constitute veritable compounds, sylvan enclaves whose walls shield them from urban problems. There are usually homeowner associations that develop community rules and set fees that go into escrow accounts to maintain the private roads, parks, and facilities inside the compounds. They do, however, routinely rely upon the outside city for such services as water, sewage, and police and fire protection. The private/public relationship can and has led to disputes over issues such as tax rates and building regulations.

Defenders of gated communities cite that they stem the tide of suburban flight, add to the tax base, and provide services that taxpayers must subsidize elsewhere. They also argue that it is facile to pretend that urban areas are doing a good job of providing security and services; hence gated communities are logical and necessary.

Critics see these enclaves as pretentious at best, if not outright attempts to shirk civic responsibility, justify racism, and perpetuate inequality. Some view them in near apocalyptic terms; gated communities have been compared with the South African townships (in reverse) during the apartheid era and have been the subject of movie and book parodies. Social critics also see them as disturbing reminders of the atomization of American society, while some social planning detractors have labeled them forms of "urban pathology." In recent years, living in a gated community has become a **status symbol**, and they have emerged even in towns like Wailea, Maui, Hawaii, which have never had serious crime problems.

Whatever view one takes, few would argue that gated communities are socially diverse. Nor would they argue that they are insignificant. About 10 percent of all new homes are being built in gated communities; in urban areas they make up 30 percent of all new homes. Currently the West (11 percent) and South (6.8 percent) have higher concentrations of gated communities, but the concept is expanding.

Examples of gated communities include Superstition Mountain near Phoenix; Canyon Lake, California; Colonial Heritage in Williamsburg, Virginia; and numerous enclaves in and around West Palm Beach, Florida.

Suggested Reading

Edward Blakely and Mary G. Snyder, *Fortress America: Gated Communities in the United States*, 1997; Mike Davis, *City of Quartz: Excavating the Future of Los Angeles*, 1990; Renaud Le Goix, "Fulbright Scholar Examines Gated Communities in Southern California" (http://www.isop.ucla.edu/print.asp?parentid=4664).

GATES, BILL (October 28, 1955–)

MELISSA A. T. KOTULSKI

William Henry "Bill" Gates III is among the word's most successful entrepreneurs and **philanthropists** in the late twentieth and early twenty-first centuries. His public persona is that of multibillionaire who contributes greatly to the local and global community and of a businessman who uses varied and shrewd tactics to capitalize on multiple domains. This computer mogul and human rights advocate is thought by many to be the wealthiest man in the world.

Bill Gates's biography is not evocative of the **Horatio Alger** myth because he was born into a wealthy Seattle family. His father, William H. Gates Sr. was a prominent lawyer who was married to Mary Maxwell Gates. His maternal grandfather, the vice-president of a national bank, set up a **trust fund** for his grandson purported to be at $1 million. Young Gates excelled in mathematics in high school and entered Harvard University in 1973, where he joined the computer science program. At Harvard he met several future business partners, including Paul Allen and Steve Ballmer. Gates dropped out of Harvard after two years, when he and Allen developed a way for the computer language BASIC to communicate with other programs. He married Melinda French of Dallas, Texas, on January 1, 1994, and the couple has three children.

Gates amassed his fortune by creating Microsoft Corporation at a time when microprocessors and home computers were not yet widespread. Microsoft's DOS operating system was integrated into the IBM PCs (personal computers) that launched the early computer revolution. The appearance of IBM-compatible PCs was a boon to Gates, who amassed a fortune in licensing fees for DOS. Gates plowed much of his money into software development and product improvements. With the introduction of Windows 3.0 in 1990, Microsoft's dominance of the software world was solidified. In fact, Microsoft was so big that other firms could not compete; some detractors claimed it hampered innovation and made it difficult for superior products to gain a foothold. Others claim that Microsoft simply pirated ideas from others, which was the basis of a 1988 copyright infringement lawsuit filed by Apple Computer. (Apple lost that case in 1992 and the appeal in 1994.)

Microsoft has also been prosecuted for violation of antitrust laws. In 1998, in the *United States v. Microsoft* case, the company was charged with deliberately setting up a **monopoly** in the computer software industry. Since Gates was the **CEO** and owned the bulk of the company's patents, he bore the brunt of the deposition examination. In court Gates gave evasive, but evocative, testimony. Microsoft was ordered to relax some of its hold on the computer software market, especially "bundling" practices that made it hard to disable Microsoft programs or to run non-Microsoft programs from a Windows platform. In spite of court-ordered rollbacks in 1998, Windows continues to be the largest computer operating system in the world. Gates served as CEO of the Microsoft until 2000, at which time he shifted to philanthropic pursuits.

While still working with Microsoft, Gates and his wife established the Bill and Melinda Gates Foundation in 2000. The foundation's grants provide funds for education, disease prevention and eradication, and other causes. Gates gave over $28.4 billion to charities between 2000 and 2006, including $900 million dollars to support the eradication of tuberculosis in developing nations plagued by the disease. A $31 billion pledge by investor Warren Buffett made the Gates Foundation by far the nation's largest philanthropic foundation.

Gates has made the cover of *Time Magazine* on eight occasions, including 2005, when he shared Person of the Year honors with his wife Melinda and Bono, lead singer of the rock band U2, for their humanitarian efforts. Some Gates critics are skeptical of his altruism and note that the Bill and Melinda Gates Foundation was established on the heels of the Microsoft antitrust decision. Some suggest that Gates uses the Foundation to reallocate funds and side-step treaties such as the Agreement on Trade-Related Aspects of Intellectual Property Rights (TRIPS). Criticism of his motives aside, Gates's immense fortune contributes to the development of computer **literacy**, technology in education, and the eradication of disease.

As of early 2006, Gates's net worth was estimated at $50 billion dollars. The Gates family has many of the perquisites one would associate with the **nouveau riche**. Gates owns a $113 million earth-sheltered house in Medina, Washington, with an annual property tax of the same amount as his original trust fund, about $1 million. His also owns the *Codex Leicester*, a collection of writings by Leonardo da Vinci, which Gates bought for $30.8 million in 1994, and a rare Gutenberg Bible. For the most part, though, his patterns of **conspicuous consumption** are more modest than many within the American **upper class**.

Gates has received numerous recognitions, including two honorary doctorates, a ceremonial British knighthood, and a flower named for him. Bill Gates is one of the world's most influential people and is routinely found on high-**status** lists. In 2006 he announced his intention to step down as Microsoft head in 2008.

Suggested Reading

Bill Gates, *The Road Ahead*, 1996; Gates, *Business @ the Speed of Thought*, 1999; John Heilemann, *Pride before the Fall: The Trials of Bill Gates and the End of the Microsoft Era*, 2001; Mark Leibovich, "Bill Gates: The Alpha Nerd and His Alter Egos," *The New Imperialists*, 2002, pp. 139–182; Jeanne M. Lesinski, *Bill Gates*, 2000; James Wallace and Jim Erickson, *Hard Drive: Bill Gates and the Making of the Microsoft Empire*, 1992.

GENDER STRATIFICATION

CHRISTINE W. HEILMAN

Gender stratification is a type of social stratification that refers to social inequalities grounded in biological differences: within American society males often enjoy privileges that are harder for women to obtain.

Social stratification is a hierarchical system that generates inequalities in resources, creates and reinforces rules of allocation for distributing resources across positions or occupations, and creates and reinforces unequal **social mobility** mechanisms. Social stratification theory focuses on economic inequalities resting on the basis of class. Ascriptive processes attribute the social standing of an individual to traits present at birth, such as gender. Inequality is produced by matching social roles to rewards of unequal value and allocating members of society to the positions related to the unequal rewards. The social role of women, for example, is related to an unequal reward for childbearing and childrearing. Mother-work carries heavy responsibilities but lacks the material rewards of employment. In addition, working mothers must fit motherhood into their lives while maintaining their ambitions in the workplace.

Categories of valued goods and assets within the social system of stratification include those that are economic (ownership of property, businesses, professional practices, factories, farms, liquid assets, and labor power); political (household, workplace, and societal **authority**); cultural (high-status consumption practices, good manners, and privileged lifestyle); social (access to high-status **social networks**, social ties, associations and clubs, and union memberships); honorific (**prestige**, reputation, fame, deference and derogation, and ethic and religious purity); civil (**property rights**, legal rights, and civil rights); and human (skills, expertise, on-the-job training, experience, formal **education**, and knowledge).

In relation to the economic category, poor and **working-class** women are less likely to own their own homes, businesses, or professional practices because they do not have the lump sum of money needed to purchase them. They are also less likely to be brought into the family businesses by male family members, who prefer sons and nephews as apprentices. Also, making a living on the family farm has become impossible with the rise of agribusiness, as individual farms cannot compete with the factory farm in production of crops or animal husbandry. Women's domestic labor was more valued on the family farm when feeding the workers was an important job. In addition, liquid assets are less likely to be passed down through generations of poor and working-class women, since cash is consumed in meeting basic needs such as shelter and food. Also, women are less likely to belong to a union or to have control over their labor.

In relation to the political category poor and working-class women have little workplace authority over their time or type of work. They may head a household, but their economic responsibility for family members outweighs any authority. They work both outside the home and inside the home with little help from men with domestic chores like cooking and laundry.

Cultural goods and assets that are valued include some that are secured through birth or childhood socialization, like good manners, and these not necessarily provided to poor and working-class women. A privileged lifestyle includes the ability to travel extensively and spend time and money on higher education. Poor and working-class women are less likely to take time off work to travel, and they often must borrow large sums to afford higher education and will have to pay it back while working in a chosen occupation. Women are less likely to work in more lucrative occupations like engineering than in helping professions like nursing.

Social networks are a valued asset that can result in obtaining a high-paying job for the privileged, but poor and working-class women know only members of their own class, who have little access to high-paying jobs.

Civil assets, such as being a member of a legislative assembly, are unlikely for poor and working-class women, who would need social networks to raise the money needed for a run for public office and time off from working and childrearing to participate. Even freedom of association and speech can be curtailed by the need of poor and working-class women to keep their jobs and housing. Unions like the Service Employees International Union have been organizing service and clerical workers, but the risk of losing a job often keeps poor and working-class women from joining.

Skills, training, and education require time out of the workforce, which poor and working-class women cannot afford. Poor and working-class women are more likely to have children early in their lives before beginning an occupation. In addition, the occupations in which working-class women find themselves are less rewarded economically, so their relative economic success may depend on finding and keeping a partner of equal or higher economic status. If they do work, women must pay the cost of day care for their children, which becomes prohibitive when they have more than one or two children. Often, poor and working-class women work in the restaurant industry or in low-paying **pink-collar** jobs. If they have children and must work to support them, they are denied access to training and higher education, which would allow them to enter higher-paying occupations.

A rigid stratification system can predict the wealth, power, or prestige of individuals based on their prior statuses or those of their parents. For example, few poor or working-class women are able to "jump class" through training or education; they replicate the lives of their mothers in childbearing and childrearing. First-generation female college students are more likely to delay enrollment in postsecondary institutions, which is a barrier to degree completion; only 29 percent of first-generation students enroll immediately after high school graduation compared with 73 percent of students whose parents have college experience. Also, first-generation students are less likely to complete the steps to enroll: only 45 percent take the SAT or ACT and only 26 percent apply to a four-year institution. (Comparatively, among students of parents with a bachelor's degree, 82 percent take the ACT or SAT and 71 percent apply to a four-year institution.) First-generation students are more likely to take remedial courses, have trouble deciding on a major, earn fewer academic credits, and have lower grades.

According to Wendy Bottero gender divisions are both social and economic; class and gender overlap. **Capitalism** and patriarchy have worked together to create gender stratification. Indeed the effects of the social markers of class and gender are not experienced separately. Gender theorists have used the concept of **social closure** to explain why women cluster in lower paying jobs and argue that gender often seals potential avenues of success. It is in the interest of capitalists to recruit cheap female labor, while men control women's domestic labor and exclude them from skilled work. Patriarchy rests on the material base of men's control over women's labor power and their exclusion from essential productive resources. Monogamous heterosexual marriage provides men with control of both jobs that pay living wages and women's sexuality. Women perform domestic labor that men can avoid performing or for which they can avoid providing payment. Childbearing and childrearing consume women's labor and define them socially in relation to men. Children learn their places in the gender hierarchy. In this respect, gender stratification is also a form of **social reproduction**.

Suggested Reading
Wendy Bottero, "Clinging to the Wreckage? Gender and the Legacy of Class," *Sociology*, 32.3 (August 1998), pp. 469–490; David B. Grusky, ed., *Social Stratification: Class, Race, and Gender in Sociological Perspective*, 2001; Heidi Hartmann, "The Unhappy Marriage of Marxism and Feminism: Towards a More Progressive Union" in *Social Stratification: Class, Race, and Gender in Sociological Perspective*, pp. 570–576.

GENERAL STRIKE

ROBERT E. WEIR

A general strike is a tactic used by organized labor in which workers from numerous industries and enterprises withdraw their labor simultaneously. Properly understood a general strike requires that workers place social class above personal interest or the concerns of their particular occupation. The term is sometimes misused to refer to an industry-wide strike, but a true general strike differs markedly from a conventional strike in which workers from a single business or industry walk off their jobs. The general strike is designed to bring such severe economic pressure to an entire region that employers will be compelled to settle their grievances with employees.

The general strike is usually associated with radical labor movements, especially those that espouse general working-**class consciousness**, as opposed to more cautious organizations such as the **American Federation of Labor**, whose constituent unions were more focused on securing rights for individual crafts. Within the United States the general strike has been associated with **anarchists** and left-wing unions such as the **Industrial Workers of the World** (IWW). Groups such as these saw the general strike as part of a larger plan to disrupt and dethrone **capitalism**. The IWW saw little purpose in securing concessions from employers per se as capitalism by its nature exploited labor. It hoped to paralyze society economically, socially, and politically via the general strike.

In U.S. history, a handful of strikes tangentially classify as general strikes. During June and July of 1877, railroad workers across North America struck to protest deep wage cuts and harsh job conditions. These strikes were mostly spontaneous and uncoordinated, but at their height more than 100,000 workers from various industries were off the job. Federal troops were activated to crush the strike, and more than a hundred lives were lost.

The strike of 1877 proved an anomaly in that so many workers from other industries took part across the nation. Most U.S. general strikes seldom spread beyond their immediate environs. May 1, 1886, was supposed to be a nationwide general strike designed to force employers to grant an eight-hour workday, but Chicago was one of the few places where a genuine general strike actually occurred, and it ended in the tragic events of Haymarket Square, where a thrown bomb led to a dozen deaths and a crackdown on radical and labor movements that left the **working class** in a weaker position.

In the twentieth century, the city of Seattle experienced a general strike in 1919, as did Minneapolis, San Francisco, and Toledo in 1934. Although each of these was traumatic and workers won concessions in some cases, none resulted in the revolutionary upheaval of which radicals dreamed. In many respects, talk of general strikes has been more utopian than realistic. In all but a few cases workers have been loath to quit their jobs in solidarity with other workers, and at least in the twentieth and twenty-first centuries, anarchist, communist, and **socialist** groups have been unable to attract a critical mass from which to launch a movement to overturn capitalism. This has especially been the case since World War II, when a postwar crackdown on radicals decimated their ranks and pushed them to the margins of American society. Some scholars see the relative paucity of general strikes vis-à-vis Europe and Australasia and the weakness of socialism as barometers of **American exceptionalism**.

Since the 1980s, **strikes** of any sort have proved difficult, though some argue that renewed interest in general strikes would afford better protection for workers who now find themselves isolated in battles against more powerful employers.

Suggested Reading
Jeremy Brecher, *Strike!*, 1997; Rosa Luxemburg, *The Mass Strike, the Political Party and the Trade Unions*, 1906; Robert Tyler, *Rebels in the Woods: The IWW in the Pacific Northwest*, 1967.

GENTRIFICATION

KAREN BETTEZ HALNON

Gentrification is a controversial and multifaceted process involving strategic invasion of and investment in **lower-class** neighborhoods; transforming them into **middle-class** ones; and ultimately displacing the preexisting inhabitants.

British sociologist Ruth Glass first coined the term *gentrification* in 1964 to describe how **working-class** quarters of London were invaded by the middle classes; how shabby, modest mews and cottages were transformed into elegant, expensive residences; and how this process continued rapidly until all or most of the original working-class occupiers were displaced and the whole social character of the district was changed. The process of middle-class takeover of economically vulnerable neighborhoods is typically accomplished with the aid of city planners, bankers, and real estate companies. In a typical scenario, a relatively large financial interest purchases numerous properties in a working-class neighborhood proximate to the city, makes modest investments in the properties (e.g., installs new heating, electrical systems, or new doors, or applies new paint inside and out) and sells the properties to individual **white-collar** owners or investors. These individuals (who are residents or business people aiming to turn a profit via more extensive remodeling and subsequent resale) make more significant and detailed improvements through restoration and refurbishment, often returning the property to its original historical "purity" but also typically with a "thumbprint" of lower-class dereliction. The process of restoration and refurbishment of what was previously a "dilapidated" community continues until the whole social character of the neighborhood is transformed. Integral to the community transformation is the establishment of new cultural and financial investments in the area, such as upscale boutiques, specialty coffee shops, and aesthetically pleasing restaurants with expensive ethnic cuisines. Property values go up, taxes go up, and soon most of the original community inhabitants have been enticed to sell their properties, can no longer afford to live there, or feel they no longer belong (or that their neighborhood no longer belongs to them). Classic examples of gentrification are Washington, D.C.'s Dupont Circle, Chicago's Lincoln Park, New York's SoHo and Greenwich Village, Boston's South End, Philadelphia's Society Hill, and South London's Wandsworth Common.

Gentrifiers seldom, if ever, label themselves as such. To do so would be to self-criticize, since the term itself suggests snobbery. To self-label as a gentrifier would be to examine critically collective consequences. However, while gentrifiers invest, invade, transform, and ultimately displace members of lower-class neighborhoods (via push out and price out), consequences are typically minimized, ignored, or neutralized as incidental to pursuing individualistic needs and desires. For example, gentrifiers are often motivated by the demand for inexpensive inner city housing close to urban centers; the opportunity for a good investment; pursuing or expressing difference, diversity, and distinction; or escaping routine, resisting the dominant ideals of **suburbia**, or pursuing practices that constitute new conditions for experience. In general, gentrification is a means by which the middle classes, lacking adequate resources to mimic the consumption habits of the upper classes, attempt to establish middle-class distinction.

A central yet relatively under-theorized aspect of the gentrification process pertains to its aesthetic dimensions, or how the gentrification process is one of "cultural consecration." This is what French sociologist **Pierre Bourdieu** called the "transubstantiating" application of "**cultural capital**," involving such things as denial of the profane, consecration of the common, expression of cultural competence, upgrading the culturally tenuous, and historicization.

While gentrification proper has declined in recent years, it is reemerging in a "new frontier," the "symbolic neighborhoods" of the lower classes in popular culture. For example, signature tattoos, custom choppers, expensive health club fitness programs, and the like represent a new form of gentrification, or middle-class takeover of lower-class communities. These and related activities have transformed what was once lower-class distinction into middle-class distinction through activities such as discussing the practices in esoteric language; locating the practices deep in history; treating the practices as optional and autonomous indulgences; gaining the sponsorship of elite institutions; and establishing professional skills and knowledge that provide social distance from the lower classes.

Suggested Reading
Ruth Lazarus Glass, *London; Aspects of Change*, 1964; Karen Bettez Halnon and Saundra Cohen, "Muscles, Motorcycles and Tattoos: Gentrification in a New Frontier," *Journal of Consumer Culture*, 6 (2006), pp. 33–56; Neil Smith, ed., *Gentrification of the City*, 1986; Sharon Zukin, "Gentrification: Culture and Capital in the Urban Core," *Annual Review of Sociology*, 13 (1987), pp. 129–147.

GEORGE, HENRY (September 2, 1839–October 20, 1897)

ROBERT E. WEIR

Henry George was a journalist, economist, labor activist, and Irish nationalist. Very few individuals were as popular among the late nineteenth-century **working class** as George.

George was born in Philadelphia, one of ten children born to a fiercely Protestant Irish family. George left school at the age of fourteen, signed on as a cabin boy, and made two around-the-world voyages punctuated by a brief stint as a typesetter. He married the former Annie Fox in 1861 and settled in San Francisco. A failed publishing venture left him deeply in debt. Although he soon secured other labor, George's first-hand experiences with **poverty** left a deep impression.

George worked as a gas inspector while writing his magnum opus, *Progress and Poverty*, whose first run was self-published in 1879 and consisted of just 500 copies. It appeared amidst the speculative fever, economic upheaval, and labor unrest of the **Gilded Age** and captured its zeitgeist. George already enjoyed minor renown for his various newspaper articles and pamphlets, but *Progress and Poverty* made him internationally famous. It went through numerous printings in the 1880s and 1890s; in the United States it received more attention than the writings of Karl Marx and Friedrich Engels.

Progress and Poverty emerged as the American **Industrial Revolution** was entering its take-off stage of development. Great fortunes were made, but at the expense of workers. The period predated personal and corporate **income taxes**. This meant that rapid urbanization and high levels of **immigration** soon stretched city infrastructures to the breaking point, thereby fostering **ghettos**, overcrowding, and unsanitary conditions. *Progress and Poverty* was stimulated, in part, by George's observations of deplorable human conditions in New York City. The book offered a solution for dealing with social problems.

Progress and Poverty is a treatise on economic theory whose central idea, the single tax, captured the imagination of late-nineteenth-century workers, most of whom never read George's dry and didactic text. George tackled David Ricardo's theory on

Henry George. Courtesy of the Library of Congress.

rents and argued that, in his day, rents violated the "law of diminishing returns." He radically proposed that society do away with all taxes save one, his single tax on the unearned value associated with land. George directly attacked the notion of land speculation, which was rampant in the Gilded Age. To George, unimproved land that increased in value through no action of those who held it should be taxed at 100 percent of its unearned increment. Land values rose, he argued, through one of two means: improvements made by their owners or advances made by society. For example, a person's land might increase in value because he cleared it, fertilized it, and built upon it. For George, that individual was entitled to all of the fruits on his investment and labor. If, however, land increased in value because society provided railroad links, roads, and other infrastructure improvements, an individual was entitled to *none* of the increased value.

George believed that his single tax on unimproved land would create surplus revenue that would eliminate the need for other taxes, fund city services, underwrite infrastructure costs, and provide for humanitarian causes. Economists have debated the soundness of George's reasoning, but his attacks on **upper-** and **middle-class** privilege and their callous disregard for workers and the poor made him a hero among society's lower orders. His open embrace of the **labor movement**, including his membership in the **Knights of Labor** (KOL), also endeared him to workers. He was a capable speaker, a factor that popularized his complex economic theories. The single-tax movement became worldwide and burned with special passion in Australia, Ireland, and New Zealand. Although **Marxism** receives more attention from scholars, the single tax was just as influential, if not more so, for much of the late nineteenth century.

George also traveled to Ireland and, like many **Irish Americans**, became an ardent advocate of home rule for Ireland, which was then controlled by Great Britain. This too enhanced his popularity among the working class. In 1884 George published *Social Problems*, a book whose very title was radical. The prevailing **Social Darwinian** notion among the upper and middle classes was that there was no such thing as a "social" problem: poverty and ill fortune resulted from individual character flaws, not systemic conditions.

Henry George also advocated **free trade**, one of the few positions that engendered debate among workers, many of whom were ardent **protectionists**. In 1886 Henry George ran for mayor of New York City on an independent ticket, finishing a close second to the Democratic victor and far ahead of the Republican candidate,

Theodore Roosevelt. There were widespread allegations that George was robbed of victory by Tammany Hall vote tampering, but across the United States other third parties inspired by George or the KOL did very well in the 1886 elections. For a time it looked as if third parties might seriously challenge the Democrats and Republicans.

In 1897 George published *The Science of Political Economy*, a distillation of his economic theories including a defense of attacks on *Progress and Poverty*. That same year he made a quixotic run for New York City mayor, but died a week before election day. Although the single tax was never implemented, George's ideas formed the basis for land taxes in general and were evoked to argue for income taxes. More than a century after his death, George's theories continue to be debated. New York City sports a Henry George Institute that analyzes current economic policy and argues for the applicability of George's theories in contemporary society.

Suggested Reading
Steven Cord, *Henry George: Dreamer or Realist?* 1965; Henry George, *Progress and Poverty*, 2005; Elbert Hubbard, *Henry George*, 2005; "The Henry George Institute" (http://www.henrygeorge.org/hgi.htm).

GHETTO

CARMELITA N. PICKETT

Ghetto is a term first used in Italy during the sixteenth century to describe a quarter in the city to which Jews were restricted. In modern usage, however, it often refers to dilapidated sections of **inner cities** that are marked by **poverty** and heavy concentrations of ethnic and racial minority groups.

The word was originally used in Italian port cities like Venice, where large populations of Jews were confined to intentionally segregated areas because of their non-Christian beliefs. Ghettos were abolished when Italy unified in 1870, but some remained in Muslim countries and in Russia. When fascists rose to power, more ghettos appeared in Europe during the mid-1930s. Nazis built ghettos in Czechoslovakia, the Baltic states, Hungary, and the Soviet Union. These ghettos often served as holding areas for Jews before they were transported to concentration camps; they were heavily guarded and often separated from other parts of the city by brick or stone walls. Jews lived in deplorable conditions in Nazi ghettos because of severe overcrowding and disease.

The meaning of ghetto has undergone many changes, but in the United States the term is synonymous with low-income neighborhoods that are racially homogenous. American ghettos represent patterns of racial discrimination. Ghettos began appearing in large Northern cities after the Great Migration of African Americans from the South. This migration lasted from 1910 to 1930 and relocated over 1 million African Americans to Northern and Western cities in search of employment opportunities.

The Great Migration often fueled race riots between blacks and whites. Whites felt that the rural black laborers would destabilize their current wages and cause property values to decline. In 1919 a Chicago race riot erupted when a seventeen-year-old African American, Eugene Williams, drowned after being stoned by a white man. Although his white assailant was identified, police refused to arrest him. News of this incident spread rapidly, and more violence ensued. At least fifteen whites and thirty-eight blacks were killed, over 500 more were injured, and approximately 1,000 African Americans were left homeless from bombings and arson. Race riots occurred in other cities such as Atlanta (1906), East St. Louis (1917), Tulsa (1921), and Detroit (1943).

After World War II the term *ghetto* was popularized in the United States to describe overpopulated poor sections of cities typically lived in by African Americans or other minorities. African Americans continued to leave the rural South throughout the twentieth century in pursuit of industrial manufacturing jobs in such cities as Detroit, New York, and Chicago. Rural African Americans also sought to escape **sharecropping** and terrorist tactics such as lynching, a common practice in the South used to terrorize African Americans while maintaining white dominance.

Although most Americans associate ghettos with poor housing and poor people, prior to the 1970s black ghettos were viewed by some African Americans as communities of prosperous businesses and black institutions. **Segregation** forced African Americans to create their own churches, fraternal organizations, social clubs, and businesses. Black ghettos supported the economic and cultural needs of African Americans. This view is supported by some Harlem Renaissance and African American writers such as Langston Hughes (*Negro Ghetto*, 1931) and August Wilson (*Fences*, 1987). These writers often provided fond and vivid descriptions of the ghetto. To some African Americans the ghetto was simply "home."

In contemporary society, however, housing and economic studies reveal that ghettos tend to support the ongoing **disenfranchisement** of citizens, limiting their access to jobs, health care, and quality **education**. Until American ghettos are abolished, these citizens will continue to face high crime, **poverty**, poor housing, drugs, and joblessness.

Suggested Reading

Robert Bonifil, *Jewish Life in Renaissance Italy*, 1994; David M. Cutler, "The Rise and Decline of the American Ghetto," *Journal of Political Economy*, 107.3 (June 1999), pp. 455–506; Sudhir Alladi Venkatesh, *American Project: The Rise and Fall of a Modern Ghetto*, 2000.

GIDDENS, ANTHONY (1938–)

ROBERT E. WEIR

Anthony Baron Giddens is a British social scientist whose theory of structuration is an important part of contemporary debates over social class. He is the former director of the London School of Economics and Political Science and, since 2003, has been an advisor to British Prime Minister Tony Blair. His views on class and politics are sometimes deemed a "third way" between polarized debates between **functionalists** and **Marxists**, as well as between conservatives and liberals.

Structuration purports to describe social systems as they are rather than as theoretical models would have them be. Giddens criticizes what he calls "closed systems," like the functionalism of Emile Durkheim or the evolutionary theories of **Social Darwinists**. Social systems, he argues, tend toward closed patterns, but they can and do change over time. Giddens claims that individuals are seldom subject to such repressive social structures as to necessitate revolution; in the main they tend to replicate the social structure. Giddens argues, however, that if individuals are not autonomous neither are they helpless; faceless and overwhelming social forces do not prevent individuals from changing society. Giddens sees society as a blend between individual action and social structure, one in which the individual both shapes and is shaped by social structures, although the very nature of the latter derives from repeated acts of individuals in concert with others.

Following Durkheim, Giddens agrees that the reality of social classes based on a division of labor does not ipso facto demand the existence of class conflict. Both agreed that class conflict results from either incomplete economic development or from some social "pathology" (to use Durkheim's term). The rules governing social order, Giddens argues, are ubiquitous and operate on individuals even when they are not conscious of them. This is why traditions, morality, social values, and social institutions are often replicated across generations. Those who benefit from these patterns, such as **white-collar workers**, may view social structure in ways akin to Durkheim's emphasis on social consensus. (Giddens argues that white-collar workers are hard to unionize because their work is neither routine nor homogeneous.)

But Giddens also agrees with Marx's assertion that division of labor can result in a system that favors some classes over others and encases have-nots in a structure of dominance and submission. There is a tendency, often exacerbated by the **mass media**, toward **social reproduction** of existing class relations, but there is no imperative. Individuals have the power to ignore certain social conventions, alter social practices, and reform social institutions. Giddens points to feminism, the **labor movement**, and other social reform movements as examples of how structures can be changed.

Giddens's work has been criticized by the political left as insufficiently attentive to how power permeates social structures, though to be fair, he does not ignore that factor. Another line of criticism takes Giddens to task for making commonsense statements overly complex and obtuse. Nonetheless, Giddens's work is useful in the ways that it puts human agency back into the discussion of class. He sees individuals as neither helpless in the face of social forces nor as romantic revolutionaries. Giddens's construction of social structures is also useful in explaining why **class formation** is difficult, and his insistence on looking as society as it is rather than as an ideal type restores corrective balance to debates over the nature of **authority**, class, class conflict, and social change.

Suggested Reading

Anthony Giddens, *The Constitution of Society: Outline of the Theory of Structuration*, 1984; Giddens, *The Third Way and Its Critics*, 2000; theory.org.uk, "Anthony Giddens" (http://www.theory.org.uk/giddens/).

GILDED AGE

PAT REEVE

The Gilded Age generally refers to the last three decades of the nineteenth century. Historians differ over the exact dates of the Gilded Age, but it is customarily viewed as the intermediary period between the decline of **Reconstruction** in the early 1870s and the rise of the **Progressive Era** (circa 1901). As such it also corresponds with what is also called the late Victorian period.

The term came into common usage by 1840, but it derives from the title of a novel written by Mark Twain and Charles Dudley Warner in 1873. The two friends sought to create a novel that would trump the sentimental literature then so popular with Americans. Together they wrote an uncompromising satire of America's economic and political fallibilities. By dubbing the era a "gilded age," Twain and Warner implied that the seeming prosperity of their age was a thin veneer that failed to mask underlying social problems.

Contemporary historians debate whether "gilded age" accurately reflects the complexity of an epoch in which the United States shed its rural past and established itself as a global power. To be sure, this was an age of political venality, unrivaled capital accumulation, and **conspicuous consumption** on the part of the **nouveau riche**. Yet as Walt Whitman declared in 1871, it was also a time when a "new spirit" of **democracy** reinvigorated the rights to freedom and self-sufficiency.

Americans seeking to reconstruct a war-torn democracy reaffirmed its core principles. Movements led by suffragists, farmers, the **working class**, and others mobilized to narrow the gap between democratic theory and practice. Similarly, anti-lynching activist Ida B. Wells called for an end to violence against African Americans, while advocates of the **Social Gospel** and social critics such as **Jacob Riis** and **Jane Addams** spurred Americans to ameliorate the era's inequalities. Yet it was Reconstruction (1865–77), a program of national reunification, that highlighted Gilded Age struggles for the extension of liberty and equality, as well as its failure to achieve such lofty goals.

From 1865 to 1877 Congress debated full citizenship for emancipated African Americans and passed the Fourteenth and Fifteenth Amendments, guaranteeing the rights of citizenship for free blacks. Enactment of the Civil Rights Act of 1875 afforded all citizens "full and equal" access to employment, public facilities, and transportation. Protected by law, African Americans rebuilt their families, founded civic institutions, started their own farms and businesses, and created the nation's first interracial governments. For a brief period, black Americans realized their aspirations for self-rule and self-sufficiency.

Ex-Confederates, angered by their loss of control over African Americans, sought to re-segregate the South. In 1865 Southern lawmakers restricted every aspect of African American life by enacting the Black Codes. Vitriolic white supremacists formed secret societies such as the **Ku Klux Klan** to counter Reconstruction and terrorize black Americans into submissiveness. Arguably, the imposition of Jim Crow policies buttressing racial **segregation** was the single biggest blow to the right of Southern blacks. In 1893 the Supreme Court upheld segregation by overturning the Civil Rights Act of 1875 and again in 1896 by ruling in

Plessy v. Ferguson that "separate" but "equal" facilities were legal. Once again living in a system of racial apartheid, southern African Americans endured by fostering racial solidarity and **self-reliance** and by resisting **racism** when and where they could.

Against the backdrop of Reconstruction, ordinary Americans tacked between optimism and fear as they negotiated the major questions of the day. For example, how legitimate were the claims advanced by aggrieved farmers and workers and their political strategies of choice? Could national unity be reconciled with the influx of **Catholic** and **Jewish** immigrants flowing from Russia and central and southern Europe to U.S. cities? Equally compelling were questions posed by federal **Native American** policy and the nation's experimentation with colonialism. Were these actions congruent with the nation's commitment to democracy? Or were they evidence of institutional racism and the republic's insatiable appetite for the land of indigenous peoples? At stake in these debates were the political values that would guide the United States into modernity.

Meanwhile, innovations in government transformed the political landscape. Wartime expansion of federal administrative capacities alarmed defenders of small government and the separation of state powers. After the war, the federal government again flexed its muscles by intervening in commerce and labor. The Interstate Commerce Act (1887) created an Interstate Commerce Commission overseeing the operations of the railroad industry. With this act, the railroads became the first industry subject to federal regulation. Next Congress passed the Sherman Antitrust Act (1890), which prohibited "every contract, combination in the form of trust or otherwise, or conspiracy, in restraint of trade." The law's first target, however, was not the railroad industry but the American Railway Union (ARU), led by **Eugene V. Debs**. ARU members employed by George Pullman, a manufacturer of sleeping cars, struck in May 1894 in response to decreased wages and increased rents in their Illinois company town. In June the ARU successfully mobilized railway workers nationwide to boycott Pullman cars. In an unprecedented act, President Grover Cleveland mustered federal troops to quash the **strike** and run the trains. He then jailed Debs after charging him with violation of the Sherman Antitrust Act. Relations between the citizenry and federal government were changed fundamentally during the Gilded Age.

Municipal and state political machines also extended their reach after 1865. Machines—unofficial political organization based on patronage and the spoils system—exerted control in electoral politics. Low-wage workers and **immigrants** looked to the machine "boss" for jobs, housing, and other services. Conversely, advocates of good government ("goo-goos") demanded greater transparency and accountability in the political arena. By 1900 most Americas had endorsed calls to professionalize government and dismantle machines such as Boss William Marcy Tweed's infamous Tammany Hall in New York City.

Technological innovations in agriculture and industry also transformed the landscape in which Gilded Age Americans lived. During the **Civil War** demand for foodstuffs and durable goods accelerated the mechanization of agriculture and the intensification of industrial production. These developments spurred, in turn, improvements in communications and railway transportation. Business enterprises seeking greater economies of scale integrated technological innovations with the restructuring of operations, producing corporations of unparalleled scale and productivity. Writing in 1901, the author **Frank Norris** likened Gilded Age commercial enterprises to an octopus that entangled Americans in vast networks of production and consumption.

The consequences for ordinary Americans during the **Industrial Revolution** were mixed. On the one hand, increasing mechanization of production created new jobs for unskilled workers, many of them immigrants. Moreover, the increased availability of food and commodities contributed to a rising standard of living. Furthermore, leaps in productivity greased America's entry into global markets. On the other hand, the mechanization of agriculture contributed to decreasing crop prices, over-cultivation of the land, and irrevocable changes in the patterns of rural life. Likewise, growing mechanization of industry resulted in the deskilling of work, **wage** cuts, and a marked increase in occupational accidents. Aggrieved producers advanced their claims through strikes, boycotts, and campaigns for legal reforms.

Class conflict was a hallmark of the Gilded Age. The permanence of **capitalism** remained contested in the minds of many Americans. The period's extremes of wealth and **poverty** were apparent to all and were celebrated as "natural" by **Social Darwinists** and vehemently opposed by workers, farmers, and reformers. The material wealth generated by industry also produced **robber barons**, who treated workers as interchangeable machine parts. Even some members of the rising **middle class** grew alarmed at excesses within their own ranks. Many more, however, were alarmed by the rising tensions inherent in society and were frightened by **anarchist** and **Marxist** groups calling for the destruction of capitalism. Resurgent labor unions had to contend with both the opposition of employers and (often unfair) associations with radicalism.

After 1865, the **labor movement** achieved unprecedented levels of economic and political organization with the support of the National Labor Union (1866–72), the first national labor federation. Succeeding it was the Noble Order of the **Knights of Labor** (1869–1919). Led by **Terrence Powderly**, the organization organized all workers across lines of skill, race, gender, and occupation. Its demands included the eight-hour work day and employers' liability reform. After a series of stunningly successful railway strikes in the 1880s, the Knights declined because of armed resistance by employers and defection by its constituencies to the **American Federation of Labor** (AFL; 1886–). Federation leader **Samuel Gompers**, a Jewish immigrant and cigar maker, disparaged the Knights' reform unionism and instead promoted organization based on skilled crafts. Neither the Knights nor the AFL was blameless when it came to inclusionary unionism. Both organizations opposed the immigration of Chinese laborers, and the AFL barred African Americans and women from membership in white male locals. Thus organized labor, like other Gilded Age institutions, simultaneously embraced the least and most expansive conceptions of democracy.

Farmers also established networks of social organizations, called granges, to protect their interests and build community. **Agrarianism** remained both the dominant occupation and a romantic ideal in the late nineteenth century, though farming was clearly imperiled. Granges began as social clubs but soon evolved into political organizations targeting the business practices of merchants and railways. In 1892 farmers calling themselves **Populists** formed a national People's Party. Its platform included linking the value of the dollar to silver rather than gold—a means of easing farmers' debt—and state ownership of railways. The Populists enjoyed great success early on, but by century's end the party was in decline, and many of its less radical ideas were co-opted by the Democratic Party.

As the above suggests, the nation's best and worst impulses shaped Gilded Age society, much as they have in other historical periods. Yet the extremes of this epoch number among its defining characteristics. Walt Whitman celebrated the idealism of the age, in contrast to Twain and Warner, who fictionalized its excesses and blind spots. Progressive Era Americans would find inspiration in the former while contending with the latter.

Suggested Reading

Charles Calhoun, ed., *The Gilded Age: Essays in the Origins of Modern America*, 1996; Rebecca Edwards, *Americans in the Gilded Age, 1865–1905*, 2005; Nell Irvin Painter, *Standing at Armageddon: The United States, 1877–1919*, 1987; Thomas Schlereth, *Victorian America: Transformations in Everyday Life 1876–1915*, 1992.

GILMAN, CHARLOTTE PERKINS (July 1, 1860–August 17, 1935)

STACEY INGRUM RANDALL

Charlotte Perkins Gilman was a feminist and author best known for her short story "The Yellow Wall-Paper." Gilman wrote thousands of works, including journalism, books discussing the social realities of women's lives, and poetry. Gilman's major concern during her lifetime was feminism—women's suffrage as well as women's economic independence. She also self-published a magazine titled *The Forerunner* for seven years.

Gilman was born Charlotte Anne Perkins in Hartford, Connecticut. She had a strong lineage; her mother was Mary Fitch Westcott and her father was Frederic Beecher Perkins. This made Gilman the great-granddaughter of the Rev. Lyman Beecher and the great-niece of **Gilded Age** minister the Rev. Henry Ward Beecher and author Harriet Beecher Stowe. Gilman's first marriage, to Charles Walter Stetson, was a difficult one that eventually ended in divorce. They had one daughter, Katherine Beecher Stetson, born March 23, 1885. After the divorce, Gilman moved to California, where she wrote her first books in the 1890s, starting with *In This Our World*, a collection of satiric poems with feminist themes. Gilman became active in Nationalism, a reform movement inspired by **Edward Bellamy**'s utopian socialist romance *Looking Backward*. This work influenced her own utopian novel *Herland*, originally serialized in 1915.

Gilman had three main goals for her writing: reconciling family responsibilities with professional ambitions, being a responsive mother while teaching and writing, and satisfying human needs of love and work. Gilman wanted to explore the value of the ideal woman as one who could experience meaningful

Charlotte Perkins Gilman. Courtesy of the Library of Congress.

work, economic independence, and equal human love in a male-dominated society. These beliefs are very strongly reflected in her writing. Gilman was an extremely intelligent woman who in many ways was far ahead of her time and place. The ideas that she represented were alien to most women during the **Progressive Era**. Her works continue to be studied today, and their importance and value has, if anything, increased.

After the birth of her daughter, Katharine, Gilman was beset by depression and began treatment with Dr. Silas Weir Mitchell in 1886. His recommendations, "live as domestic a life as possible" and "never touch a pen, brush or pencil as long as you live" were later satirized in her autobiography and used the discussions in her most renowned short story, "The Yellow Wall-Paper," which first appeared in *New England Magazine* in 1892. Gilman refused to call herself a "feminist"; her goal as a humanist was to campaign for the cause of women's suffrage. Gilman saw that the domestic environment had become an institution that oppressed women. "The Yellow Wall-Paper" depicts a depressed woman who slowly descends into madness in her room while her well-meaning husband is often away due to his work at a hospital.

At the time of Gilman's death in 1935, she had lectured both nationally and internationally and had published over twenty volumes of work. Gilman learned in 1932 that she had incurable breast cancer. As an advocate for the right to die, Gilman committed suicide on August 17, 1935, by taking an overdose of chloroform. She "chose chloroform over cancer" as her autobiography and suicide note stated. In 1993 Gilman was named the sixth most influential woman of the twentieth century in a poll commissioned by the Siena Research Institute. In 1994 she was inducted into the National Women's Hall of Fame in Seneca Falls, New York. Her work continues to be evoked by feminists and scholars of **gender stratification**.

Suggested Reading

M. Hill, *Charlotte Perkins Gilman*, 1980; J. Kaprinski, ed., *Critical Essays on Charlotte Perkins Gilman*, 1992; Ann J. Lane, *To Herland and Beyond*, 1990; G. Scharnhorst, *Charlotte Perkins Gilman*, 1985; Elaine Showalter, ed., *The New Feminist Criticism*, 1985.

GLASS CEILING

ROBERT E. WEIR

Glass ceiling is a term that refers to restrictions placed on a person's ability to rise in business and society. It is used to describe the experiences of those who struggle to overcome social obstacles and achieve at a high level but encounter conventions and prejudices that block further **social mobility**. Such high-functioning individuals are aware of opportunities above their current station, hence a "glass" ceiling. The term has been appropriated by many minority groups but is generally used in discussing **gender stratification**.

The term originated in mathematics but was first applied to women in a 1984 *Newsweek* article. By that time the successes of the feminist movement of the past decade and a half had slowed, in part because of a backlash against social movements inherent in the administration of President **Ronald Reagan**. Women helped maintain American industry during World War II and entered the workforce in large numbers, just as they had done during World War I. When World War II ended, women were displaced from many higher paying positions and supplanted by returning male veterans. Despite popular stereotypes of the post-war "Baby Boom," a real-enough demographic surge, all women did not placidly retreat to **suburbia** to become mothers and housewives. Women from white **working-class** families, as well as African American, Latino, and other minority women, often lacked the economic wherewithal to remove themselves from the labor market. Although the number of working women dropped from its wartime peak, it did not retreat to prewar levels. By the 1950s, more women were entering the workforce each year. Even **middle-class** families began to realize that a sole wage earner was insufficient for a family to attain material comforts associated with the **American dream**.

As more women entered the workforce, they could not help but notice their lower wages vis-à-vis men and a general inequality in their treatment. The 1963 Equal Pay Act stipulated that the same job had to be compensated equally for all, but this was easily circumvented by manipulating job classifications. Title VII of the 1964 Civil Rights Act theoretically safeguarded women's treatment in the workplace and gave them access to the same jobs and promotions as men, but this too was widely sidestepped, as were affirmative action programs designed to increase representation of women and people of color in the workforce.

Small gains and losses in the workplace coincided with the rebirth of a strong feminist movement in the 1960s, spurred on in part by the publication of Betty Friedan's pathbreaking *The Feminine Mystique* (1963). Much as in the case of the civil rights movement, women's groups also tackled **institutional discrimination**. Laws proved easier to change than entrenched practices, however. Women soon complained of "tokenism," that is, the tendency of companies to put enough women into traditionally male-held jobs to give the appearance of gender sensitivity but not enough to achieve gender equity. This was especially pronounced at the highest levels. Smith College, for example, an **elite** women's college, did not appoint its first female president until 1975, when Jill Ker Conway assumed the post. There was no female president of an **Ivy League** college until 1994, when

Judith Rodin assumed leadership at the University of Pennsylvania. A 1986 study of *Fortune* magazine's top 1,000 industrial and 500 leading service industry firms, appearing two years after *Newsweek* popularized the term "glass ceiling," revealed that 95 percent of all senior managerial positions were held by white males.

Despite more awareness of glass ceiling discrimination, the 1980s backlash has been slow to dissipate. In 2004 just 1.4 percent of *Fortune*'s top firms had female CEOs, a mere 2.7 percent of their top salaries went to women, and only 11.2 percent of corporate officers were women, the latter figure smaller than the percentage (14 percent) of those firms that had no women in senior management positions at all. These numbers are even lower for black and Latino women. This would seem to confirm allegations of a glass ceiling as approximately 50 percent of all professional and lower level management positions are held by women.

The track record is marginally better for **small business**, where women entrepreneurs controlled about 38 percent of all enterprises by 2004. At first glance that statistic looks encouraging, but when one considers that about 30 percent of all business is female-owned, the remaining 70 percent have promoted women at rates only slightly better than the corporate giants. Glass ceiling inequities are also obvious when one considers that about 45 percent of the current workforce is female and just one-third consists of white males.

Suggested Reading

Carole Adair, *Cracking the Glass Ceiling: Factors Influencing Women's Attainment of Senior Executive Positions*, 1999; "Break the Glass Ceiling: Equal Opportunity for Women and Minorities" (http://www.breaktheglassceiling.com/statistics-women. htm); Miriam David and Diana Woodward, *Negotiating the Glass Ceiling: Careers of Senior Women in the Academic World*, 1998.

GLOBALIZATION

ROBERT E. WEIR

Globalization is a catchall term that refers to aspects of modern society in which economic decisions, trade, culture, and politics are considered in a worldwide context. It is an outgrowth of the post-World War II expansion of multinational corporations and represents the ascendancy of **free trade** policies over those of **protectionism**. Champions of globalization see the world as a vast open market for capital investment opportunities, the procurement of labor and resources, efficient manufacturing, and sales. Critics of globalization see it as a threat to national sovereignty, a blow to American workers, and a license for amoral investors to pursue higher profits without regard to human costs.

Globalization has long been an aspect of economic life. Before **capitalism** fully articulated itself in the nineteenth century, mercantilist nations exploited colonies for raw materials and cheap labor. Indeed, **slavery** could be viewed as a perverse type of globalization; imported Africans mined Spanish silver in South America, planted French sugar cane in the Caribbean, and harvested English tobacco in

North America, these raw materials becoming items of global trade. In Colonial America, one manifestation of this was the infamous triangle trade in which slave-produced sugar in the Caribbean was made into molasses, then shipped to New England and made into rum, which was, in turn, traded in West Africa for more slaves to be sold in the Caribbean. After the **American Revolution**, slavery continued to support global trade. Slave-tended cotton left the South for New England textile mills, much of whose cloth was sold abroad and enriched American investors.

The **Industrial Revolution** brought the United States into a broader global market of raw materials and markets. Nineteenth-century economists such as Jean-Baptiste Say and David Ricardo argued the global economy would be self-correcting and that nations would naturally develop relations to their mutual advantage. In practice, though, global competition was prone to be cutthroat and ruinous, and many within the American **labor movement** argued for protectionist policies to ensure the survival of American businesses and stabilize jobs for workers. Nonetheless, stable **gold** specie exchange encouraged expanding globalization.

Competing imperialist claims, World War I, the **Great Depression**, and the decline of gold as an international standard of exchange slowed the growth of globalization in the early twentieth century. The worldwide depression led many nations to look inward and rekindled protectionist sentiment. Globalization was further disrupted by the military conquests of Germany, Italy, and Japan in the 1930s; indeed, the United States restricted the trade of commodities such as scrap iron and oil to Japan, a decision that may have factored into Japan's decision to bomb Pearl Harbor.

Globalization began anew after World War II. In 1947 the General Agreement on Tariffs and Trade (GATT) reduced trade barriers among twenty-three nations. The number of GATT-compliant nations expanded many times before GATT was disbanded in 1994 and replaced by the World Trade Organization (WTO), which had grown to 150 member nations by 2005. Both GATT and the WTO removed many tariffs and other barriers to free trade. The development of the International Monetary Fund in 1947, the emergence of the European Economic Union in 1951, and the passage of the North American Free Trade Agreement (NAFTA) in 1994 also facilitated the spread of globalization. The United Nations and the World Court promote globalization in social and political matters.

Globalization was not widely discussed in the United States when it reemerged after World War II, partly because new global arrangements benefited the United States and its **working class**. As the world's dominant economic power, the United States flooded the global market with goods, services, and technology. American factories operated at near capacity, unemployment was low, and retail shelves were stocked with American-made consumer goods. By the 1960s, however, Europe and Asia had recovered from the ravages of war, sported state-of-the-art manufacturing facilities, and aggressively competed with the United States in the global market. U.S. dominance slipped at precisely the time that energy prices soared and the domestic economy soured. By the mid-1970s, American factories producing steel, rubber, textiles, electronics, and consumer appliances began to fail, unemployment soared, and inflation ran rampant. The latter made U.S. goods even less competitive and encouraged foreign importers. Treaties such as GATT precluded protective tariffs; hence many **blue-collar** jobs simply disappeared.

A resurgent conservative movement, buoyed by the election of **Ronald Reagan** in 1980, also advanced free trade and globalization. Tax credits allowed U.S. firms to set up operations abroad, which supporters claimed made U.S. firms more competitive but which cost untold thousands of jobs. "Capital flight" became the byword of the 1980s, with corporations taking full advantage of Reagan-era tax cuts to relocate operations outside the country, usually in low-wage countries. Tax code changes also made it easier for foreign firms to open U.S. subsidiaries. Since the 1980s, **competitiveness** has been the guiding principle governing the U.S. economy.

Competitiveness is more attractive to entrepreneurs than to workers. There has been a marked increase in fortunes among the **upper class**, but at the expense of others. NAFTA, for example, resulted in a loss of over 200,000 American jobs in its first decade of existence. Globalization has been a disaster for the **labor movement**, which has seen its strength among industrial workers evaporate in the wake of **deindustrialization**. Promised shifts in the economy to replace lost high-wage jobs have not materialized; instead, economic growth has occurred in service industries. It also appears that the **middle class** is shrinking. In addition, the United States faces a massive balance-of-trade deficit as it is now so reliant on imported goods; in 2005, the deficit reached nearly $726 billion.

There have been worldwide protests at WTO meetings. American anti-globalization activists assert that globalization is simply a rush to exploit labor in the developing world, evade environmental standards, avoid taxes, and evade U.S. laws. They have been joined by protestors elsewhere, some of whom oppose the globalization of culture, which they see as dominated by the debased standards of Western nations.

Globalization is likely to remain contested for many years to come. At this juncture, promises made by globalization supporters of rising global economic conditions, greater stability, international justice standards, and the promotion of international understanding have not materialized. Suspicion remains that globalization is little more than the exploitation of the poor on a worldwide basis.

Suggested Reading

Andy Crump and Wayne Ellwood, *The A to Z of World Development*, 1999; Thomas Friedman, *The World Is Flat: A Brief History of the Twenty-First Century*, 2005; Joseph E. Stiglitz, *Globalization and Its Discontents*, 2003; Martin Wolf, *Why Globalization Works*, 2005.

GOLD

ROBERT E. WEIR

Gold is a precious and rare metal upon which major monetary decisions have been based, affecting Americans of all social classes.

Because gold and, to a lesser degree, silver are valued globally, they have been a basis of exchange for much of recorded human history. Coins have long been the basis of domestic exchange within regions and states. Gold and silver came into even greater focus during the eighteenth and nineteenth centuries when mercantilism, imperialism, and the **Industrial Revolution** stimulated worldwide networks that were, in many ways, setting up the structure for contemporary **globalization**. The rise of **capitalism** also stimulated interest in precious metals, as it placed private **wealth** on par with that of the nation as a whole.

Prior to World War II it was customary for Western nations to back their circulating currencies with gold, silver, or a combination of the two. This presented certain social problems, especially if a nation failed to exercise fiscal restraint and issued more currency in the form of notes than it could support. This happened during the **American Revolution**, when Congress issued currency ("Continentals") that proved irredeemable. The phrase "not worth a Continental damn" entered the vernacular, but many of the **Founding Fathers** found little amusing about the nation's shaky finances.

In 1785 the United States pegged its currency to silver, an act reinforced in 1792. Since the silver was itself valued according to a set ratio, the United States had a de facto bimetallic system. This too proved irksome, as the set ratio tended to make silver more valuable internally than it was internationally; hence foreign traders and international currency speculators demanded gold for silver, leading to a drain on gold reserves. The need for new supplies was a major factor precipitating the California Gold Rush. The government also tried to stop currency devaluation by reducing the weight of coins and taking foreign currency out of circulation.

The price of money was and is more than a bankers' dilemma. The amount of money in circulation has a profound effect on interest rates, prices, and wages. Those who loan money, usually members of the **upper class** and upper **middle class**, favor "hard" money, in which the overall supply is tight; hence interest rates are higher and prices lower. Farmers and others who borrow prefer "soft" money, an increase in the money supply that leads to inflation and drives interest rates down and commodity prices up. Members of the nineteenth-century **petite bourgeoisie** often also preferred soft money as many were retailers and shopkeepers. The **working class** was trapped in the middle; soft money made wages go up, but prices and rents increased as well.

The overall instability of the money system hurt all classes, with economic downswings like the Panic of 1837 closing banks, businesses, and shops alike. Another depression in 1857 led to a silver panic in the United States, the full ramifications of which had not been resolved by the time of the **Civil War**. As in the Revolutionary War eight decades earlier, inherently inflationary currency was printed by both the Union and the Confederacy, and all gold and silver trading was suspended. Confederate bills were deemed worthless at the war's end, but the overall currency system was unstable, and attempts to reassert bimetallism proved difficult, in part because organized soft money groups pressed to expand the greenbacks (paper money) introduced during the war. Greenbackers insisted that it was not necessary to back paper bills with gold and that inflationary policies benefited the **masses**.

The last third of the nineteenth century saw a huge expansion of American corporations, a factor in the rejection of appeals from the Greenback movement. Another depression in 1873 led the nation to a gold standard, which was bitterly opposed by the **labor movement** and farmer groups, but which President Grover

Cleveland formalized in 1879. Farmers were especially hard hit by hard money policies, and they swelled the ranks of a growing "Free Silver" movement in the late nineteenth century. These groups demanded a restoration of the old 16:1 ratio between silver and gold, a plan that would increase the money supply. Silver advocates were briefly buoyed by the Sherman Silver Purchase Act of 1890, but Congress repealed it three years later. The **Populist Party** made free silver and abandonment of the gold standard a central feature of its campaign, but in 1900 the United States officially abandoned bimetallism, despite the fact that much of the Democratic Party had converted to free silver.

The gold standard probably did reduce strain on reserves, but World War I put pressure on the idea of a global gold standard, and Britain abandoned it in 1914. Moreover, the passage of the 1913 Federal Reserve Act at long last centralized U.S. banking practices and put into place other mechanisms through which deflation and inflation could be regulated. The United States reestablished the gold standard after the war, but it became a victim of the **Great Depression** and was abandoned in 1933. At the same time, President **Franklin Roosevelt** signed a bill making private ownership of gold illegal in most cases. Historians assert that Roosevelt wished to restore the gold standard, but a worsening of the Depression in 1937 deterred him. In addition, many aspects of the **New Deal** were rooted in the economic theories of **John Maynard Keynes**, who was an ardent opponent of the gold standard.

Shortly before World War II ended, the United Nations Monetary and Financial Conference was held in Bretton Woods, New Hampshire, in which Keynes took a leading role. The forty-four gathered nations decided against an international gold standard and set up the International Monetary Fund (IMF) to facilitate currency exchanges. Although currencies were still, in theory, backed in part by gold, conservative supply-side economists have never been happy with the IMF. (The United States backs about 25 percent of circulating currency in gold.)

Within the United States, bullion remained illegal until 1975. The repeal of the gold ban did lead to speculation, especially since stagflation during the late 1970s made currency less attractive. Texas oil billionaire Nelson Bunker Hunt and his brother William attempted to corner the silver market, but sinking prices bankrupted them, and Nelson was convicted of fraud. This incident aside, trade in gold and silver bullion and coins remains a major activity among rich Americans and is a large source of private **wealth**. By early 2006 gold was being traded for about $540 per troy ounce and silver about $9.40 per ounce. Although few Americans think much about it, the daily international market in gold, silver, and other precious metals continues to impact the economy as U.S. reserves help determine the value of the U.S. dollar vis-à-vis other currencies. That, in turn, influences investment decisions and places pressure on hiring decisions, prices, and wages. Although the U.S. economy is no longer on a gold or silver standard, these metals continue to impact everyone from rich investors to **blue-collar** workers.

Suggested Reading

Peter Bernstein, *Power of Gold: The History of an Obsession*, 2001; Michael Bordo, Forrest Capie, and Angela Redish, eds., *The Gold Standard and Related Regimes: Collected Essays*, 1999; Barry Eichengreen and Marc Flandereau, eds., *The Gold*

Standard in Theory and History, 1997; Lawrence Goodwyn, *The Populist Moment: A Short History of Agrarian Revolt in America*, 1978.

GOLD, MIKE (April 12, 1893–May 14, 1967)

HOLLY M. ALLEN

Mike Gold is perhaps the most important figure associated with the literary left in the 1930s.

Gold was born Itzok Granich but changed his name to Michael Gold. In his remarkably successful autobiographical novel, *Jews without Money*, Gold describes what it was like to grow up in New York's Jewish Lower East Side **ghetto** in the early 1900s. The characters in Gold's novel confront crime, filth, disease, **poverty**, and death, just as Gold did after his **immigrant** father's business failed in 1905.

Forced to leave school at the age of twelve, Gold nevertheless harbored literary and political ambitions. He initially found an outlet for those ambitions in New York's bohemian radical community in the 1910s. In 1914 he published his first poem in *The Masses*, a radical literary magazine edited by Floyd Dell and Max Eastman. Throughout the 1910s Gold sampled and contributed to a range of radical and **working-class** causes. In 1921, after *The Masses* was suppressed during **Red Scare** raids, Gold joined the editorial staff of *The Liberator*, a literary magazine affiliated with the **Communist Party**. Throughout the 1920s, in addition to his editorial work, Gold wrote plays and helped to establish several radical theater groups. In 1926 he helped to found the *New Masses*, a communist literary journal committed to publishing the writings of workers themselves. Gold ascended to the editorship of the *New Masses* in 1928, a post that he held until 1934.

During his editorship, the *New Masses* regularly published letters, poems, and fiction written by ordinary workers from across the country. The publication of *Jews without Money* in 1930 cemented Gold's status as one of the foremost writers and critics of the emergent proletarian literary movement. Beginning in 1933, he published a daily column in the communist newspaper *The Daily Worker*. Gold saw **proletarian literature** as a powerful weapon of a workers' movement but also as something quintessentially American. In his view, the proletarian literature of the 1930s represented a "second American Renaissance." While the proletarian movement suffered ideological fractures later in the decade, Gold remained a Communist Party stalwart throughout the **Great Depression** years.

Although *Jews without Money* features a female protagonist, Gold reinforced masculine conventions in his role as editor and foremost critic of proletarian literature. He praised works that celebrated the manly worker and the male-dominated industrial arena, while doubting literature that focused on women's domestic labor and other nontraditional proletarian themes. Both his enthusiasm for authentic working-class writers and his masculine bias are evident in his call for contributors to the *New Masses*: "Send us a man of art who can stand up to the purposeful deeds of Henry Ford. Send us a joker in overalls," he wrote. He concluded, "Send an artist. Send a scientist. Send a Bolshevik. Send a man."

Never wavering in his commitment to working-class radicalism, Gold was one of the few Depression-era figures who was not cowed by the post–World War II Red Scare. He remained a vital contributor to the American left until his death in 1967.

Suggested Reading

Michael Folson, ed., *Mike Gold: A Literary Anthology*, 1972; Michael Gold, *Jews without Money*, 1930; Joseph North, ed., *The New Masses: An Anthology of the Rebel Thirties*, 1969.

GOLDMAN, EMMA (June 27, 1869–May 14, 1940)

ROBERT E. WEIR

Emma Goldman was an anarchist, feminist, and birth-control advocate.

Goldman was born in Kaunas, a city now in Latvia but then part of Russia. Her Jewish parents, Abraham and Tuave, were members of the **petite bourgeoisie**. Abraham moved his family to St. Petersburg in 1881, at which time Goldman left school to work in a factory. Goldman's teen years were shaped by Russian **anti-Semitism**, harsh working conditions, an incident of sexual abuse, and radical politics. In 1885 she immigrated to the United States to join an older sister in New York City.

Goldman's experiences in America did not live up to her high expectations. She moved into what was essentially a Jewish **ghetto** in New York and was appalled by the widespread **poverty** that plagued the American **working class**. Although already a radical, Goldman cited the injustices associated with the 1886 Haymarket bombing as the reason she converted to anarchism. Eight men were convicted of a Chicago bombing that killed a dozen people, including eight police officers. Most scholars now assert that the eight were convicted because of their beliefs, not the evidence, and radicals of the day certainly believed so. Although Goldman probably embellished the tale, she claimed to have become an anarchist on November 2, 1886, when four of the Haymarket men were hanged.

Goldman placed herself in an informal apprenticeship position with Johann Most, a prominent anarchist immigrant who published the radical German-language journal *Die Freiheit*. By 1889, though, Goldman was caught up in a debate over anarchist principles between those who espoused advancing anarchism through propaganda and those who favored the direct action approach known as "anarchism of the deed." Goldman associated with the latter and split with Most. She also abandoned her earlier work in attempting to establish an eight-hour work-day and instead called upon workers to overthrow **capitalism**.

Goldman's conversion to revolutionary anarchism also entailed shifts in her personal life. She grew increasingly enamored of the theories of Peter Kropotkin, who emphasized a radical **individualism** unfettered by most social constraints. Goldman became fiercely devoted to free speech, birth control, equality for women, and the free love movement. Goldman's name was associated with numerous lovers, including possible lesbian relationships, and her shocking behavior was anathema to the **middle class**.

Among Goldman's lovers was fellow anarchist Alexander Berkman. In the days following the collapse of the 1892 Homestead Steel **strike**, Berkman attempted to assassinate industrial magnate Henry Clay Frick, a man many saw as a **robber baron**. Goldman was rumored to have plotted to shoot Frick, but this was never proven. She was, however, sentenced to a year in jail in 1893 for inciting New York City rioters to steal bread. Innuendo also associated her with Leon Csolgosz, the man who assassinated President William McKinley in 1901. Again, no solid evidence linked Goldman to the deed, though some biographers find it feasible that she was involved.

Goldman was briefly a member of the **Industrial Workers of the World** and was marginally involved in its free speech battles that inspired Roger Baldwin, the founder of the American Civil Liberties Union. In 1906 Goldman established the anarchist journal *Mother Earth*, a publication that gained notoriety for its bold support for birth control, even abortion, and Goldman supported the efforts of **Margaret Sanger**. This led to an arrest for illegal distribution of birth-control literature in 1916.

Emma Goldman on a street car, ca. 1917. Courtesy of the Library of Congress.

In 1917 the United States entered World War I, a conflict bitterly opposed by Goldman and Berkman, who was now out of jail. Many within the radical community, including **Eugene V. Debs**, expressed the opinion that it was a capitalists' war in which workers should take no part. In 1917 Goldman set up several "No Conscription" leagues to oppose the implementation of a military draft. When it was, nonetheless, put into effect, Goldman urged workers to dodge the draft, an act that led to her arrest and a two-year prison sentence. In 1919 Goldman and Berkman were among a large group of radicals deported from the United States during the first **Red Scare**. During her deportation hearing future F.B.I. director J. Edgar Hoover dubbed Goldman "one of the most dangerous women in America."

At first Goldman welcomed her exile, returning to Russia less than two years after its **communist** revolution, but she quickly came to see the Bolshevik government as repressive and intolerant of personal freedom. She was also appalled at the use of the army to repress strikes. She left the Soviet Union in 1921 and penned two books, *My Disillusionment in Russia* and *My Further Disillusionment in Russia*, which recounted her many disagreements with life in the USSR. These books also expressed an emerging rejection of violence as a legitimate tool for social change.

Goldman lived in Berlin briefly before moving to Britain, where she married a Welsh miner. This was clearly a marriage of convenience so she could stay in England, and Berkman remained the great love of her life. While in Britain she wrote an autobiography, *Red Emma Speaks*, which remains widely read. She also obtained a British passport and was allowed a brief visit to the United States in 1934, but she was denied permission to stay in the country. She was in Spain during the Spanish Civil War, perhaps driven equally by the need to busy herself after Berkman's suicide on June 28, 1936, and her enthusiasm for the Republicans battling Francisco Franco. Further attempts to return to the United States failed, and Goldman relocated to Toronto, where she died in 1940. Only upon death did she re-enter the United States; she is buried in Waldheim Cemetery in Chicago, also the resting place of the four men hanged for the Haymarket bombing.

Goldman's politics were too radical to be embraced by the mainstream **labor movement**, but some within the reborn feminist movement during the 1960s and 1970s found inspiration in her no-holds-barred defense of women's equality and her insistence that all aspects of **gender stratification** be eliminated.

Suggested Reading

Candace Falk, *Love, Anarchy, and Emma Goldman*, 1990; Emma Goldman, *Living My Life*, 1931; Theresa Moritz, *The World's Most Dangerous Woman: A New Biography of Emma Goldman*, 2001.

GOLDTHORPE, JOHN (1935–)

ROBERT E. WEIR

John H. Goldthorpe is an emeritus sociologist who spent much of his career at Oxford after stints at the University of Leicester and at Cambridge. Although much of his work mined Western European data, Goldthorpe's studies of **social mobility** and his stratification theories have had profound influence on scholars studying the American class system.

Goldthorpe has been among the foremost critics of affluent worker/embourgeoisement theses that gained currency after World War II. Goldthorpe found very little evidence that members of the **working class** were becoming **middle class** in great numbers. He attacked three prevailing assumptions about advanced industrial societies and **capitalist** economies. First, he found little evidence of common mobility patterns between nations. In a comparative framework, for example, social mobility in the United States seldom matched the rhetoric of its ubiquity. Second, Goldthorpe refuted the idea that social mobility was increasing. The tendency instead has been more toward stasis, and for women, there has been significant downward mobility in occupational terms. Finally, Goldthorpe was highly critical of the conservative view that the economy alone dictates mobility. He argued that factors such as politics and institutionalized class privileges have a profound effect on mobility.

Goldthorpe's mobility studies were integral to how he fashioned stratification. Following the lead of **Max Weber**, Goldthorpe sought to identify class with clusters that Weber dubbed "class situations" and "status situations," which shaped **life chances** more than one's relationship to the **means of production**, as **Marxists** insist. Working with Robert Erickson and others, Goldthorpe situated class in how work itself is organized and the relationship between **authority** and labor markets. In essence, one can be an employer, an employee, or self-employed, with differing implications for authority, control, and labor market bargaining. In addition, one must consider property owners and agricultural production (though Goldthorpe's work has been criticized for undervaluing the importance of the latter). As John Scott notes, if one looks at the various permutations, at least eleven economic classes exist: large property owners, small employers, farmers, the self-employed, a top echelon of service workers, lower service workers, routine non-manual workers, supervisors of manual laborers, skilled manual laborers, **unskilled labor**, and agricultural workers.

In a 1987 work Goldthorpe argued that much of the activity of modern society takes place in seven class categories (usually rendered simply as Roman numerals I through VII): two top levels of salaried professional and managerial "service" workers; three "intermediate" categories of clerical and supervisory workers whose contractual relations are neither salaries nor wages in the strictest sense; and two levels of the **working class**. Goldthorpe's schema is often shorthanded as a division between the service, intermediate, and working-class sectors, and Goldthorpe has been criticized for his uneven use of categories three, seven, and eleven. However, his conclusion that demographic social classes form over time and that movement in and out of those classes is less common than conventional wisdom holds has become a cornerstone interpretation of social mobility.

His work has been critiqued on other levels as well. Marxists often view his take on authority as incomplete and his definition of property owners as imprecise. The latter point has merit as his definition of property owners encompasses everyone from those holding land to those whose "property" lies in controlling corporations or commerce. Still others have criticized Goldthorpe's economic determinism and charge that he underplays cultural and social determiners of class. Still, Goldthorpe's work has been influential in adding sophistication to how class is defined, and his mobility studies have helped puncture unverifiable myths.

Suggested Reading

John Goldthorpe, *The Constant Flux: A Study of Class Mobility in Industrial Societies*, 1992; Goldthorpe, *The Economic Basis for Social Class*, 2004; John Scott, "Social Class and Stratification," *Acta Sociologica* 45.1 (2002) (online version, http://privatewww.essex.ac.uk/~scottj/socscot10.htm).

GOMPERS, SAMUEL (January 27, 1850–December 13, 1924)

PETER C. HOLLORAN

Samuel Gompers was an American labor leader who cofounded the **American Federation of Labor**.

Samuel Gompers. Courtesy of the Library of Congress.

He was born in London on January 27, 1850, the son of poor Jewish immigrants from Holland. He immigrated to New York City with his parents in 1863. Gompers worked as a cigar maker and joined a local union in 1864, winning election as its president and serving in that position from 1874 to 1881. He founded the Federation of Organized Trades and Labor Unions in 1881, which he reorganized as the American Federation of Labor (AFL) in 1886, and he served as AFL president from 1886 to 1895, and again from 1896 to 1924.

He is best remembered for his opposition to **socialism**, cooperatives, and radical causes and politics, and for competing successfully with the **Knights of Labor** (KOL), a union that disappeared in the early twentieth century. Gompers, who learned cigar-making and union principles from his father, was influenced by the **Marxist** idea that the effective economic organization of workers and the emergence of their social class interests required strong central trade union institutions. Unlike the KOL, the AFL under Gompers saw **strikes** as a primary weapon for labor unions, not actions to be avoided at all costs. Nonetheless, his exclusionary brand of craft unionism prompted **Bill Haywood** and **Eugene Debs** to found the **Industrial Workers of the World** for unskilled workers in 1905.

As the leading spokesman for the American **labor movement**, Gompers focused on higher wages, shorter hours, better working conditions, and more freedom for workers and their unions. By the dawn of the twentieth century he had traveled widely to organize nearly 2 million workers and to develop labor's economic power. During World War I he used his personal prestige to keep organized labor loyal to President Woodrow Wilson. Gompers supported Wilson's wartime aims as leader of the War Committee on Labor and as a member of the Advisory Commission to the Council of National Defense. He attended the Paris Peace Conference in 1919 as Wilson's advisor on labor issues. As a result, the AFL maintained strong membership and prestige despite the nationwide anti-union campaign in the 1920s. Although Gompers developed better relations with the government and big business as a leader of the National Civic Federation, the AFL could do little to defend workers in the 1919 steel strike and the 1922 machinists' strike.

The nation's foremost champion of the working class, Gompers made organized workers respected member of their communities. He died on December 13, 1924, in a San Antonio hospital and was buried at Sleepy Hollow Cemetery in Tarrytown, New York. His autobiography, *Seventy Years of Life and Labor*, was published in 1925. In 1937 the Navy named its new destroyer the *USS Samuel Gompers* in his honor.

To his many defenders Gompers was the "father" of the modern labor movement. Gompers did much to disassociate labor unions from radical movements and to advance a pragmatic agenda over idealism. His brand of "pure and simple unionism," a focus on wages, hours, and conditions, was pathbreaking in that Gompers and the AFL were among the first to accept the very legitimacy of **capitalism**. In 1989 Gompers was inducted (posthumously) into the U.S. Department of Labor Hall of Fame.

Gompers also had many critics who decried his cautious views. Historians note that the American **working class** never developed an independent labor party, as was done by workers in numerous European industrial democracies, and they place part of the blame on the AFL's cooperation with the government and with its exclusionary membership policies. Still others accuse Gompers of harboring **middle-class** pretensions and of lacking a sense of solidarity with workers outside of the AFL.

Suggested Reading

Stuart B. Kaufman, *Samuel Gompers and the Origins of the American Federation of Labor, 1848–1896*, 1973; Harold C. Livesay, *Samuel Gompers and Organized Labor in America*, 1993; Florence C. Thorne, *Samuel Gompers, American Statesman*, 1969.

GRAMSCI, ANTONIO

See Althusser, Louis.

GRANT, MADISON

See Eugenics.

GRAPES OF WRATH, THE

VERONICA C. HENDRICK

The Grapes of Wrath is the name of John Steinbeck's famed novel dealing with the plight of Dust Bowl refugees during the **Great Depression**. Some critics have hailed this book as a masterpiece of **proletarian literature**.

John Ernst Steinbeck Jr. was born in California on February 27, 1902, and died on December 20, 1968. Although he was raised in a wealthy farming community, he had the opportunity to interact with poor laborers. These experiences influenced the body of his work, which focuses on the lives of those living in **poverty** in America. Steinbeck also wrote academic studies and newspaper articles discussing the situation of the lower strata of the **working class,** but it is fiction for which Steinbeck is most famous: *Tortilla Flat* (1935), *Of Mice and Men* (1937), and the short stories "The Red Pony" and "The Pearl" were extremely successful. Many of his works were produced as films. Steinbeck was awarded the Nobel Prize for literature in 1962.

Steinbeck won both the Pulitzer Prize and the National Book Award for *The Grapes of Wrath* (1939). This novel, like his other works, makes large social commentary

Film set during the making of *The Grapes of Wrath*, with part of the cast and crew in front of a small, dilapidated house. Courtesy of the Library of Congress.

through the tales of his characters. The setting is the time of the Great Depression, a period when over 25 percent of all Americans were unemployed. This affected the poor more than the **middle-** and **upper-class** Americans. In the United States the Depression lasted through the 1930s, coming to a close only with America's involvement in World War II. Steinbeck focused on the lives of farmers during this difficult period. Not only were farms failing because of economic hardship, but massive areas of the South and Midwest were stressed by over-farming and drought. A region of approximately 150,000 square miles became completely unusable. In some parts of Arkansas, Oklahoma, and Texas as much as 60 percent of the population moved to different parts of the country. The protagonists in *The Grapes of Wrath*, the Joads, are representative of these dispossessed people. The Joad family lost their Oklahoma farm because of economic hardship and was forced to make their way to California in search of migrant farm labor. Because so many people were looking for employment, the Joads find money increasingly hard to earn. Everywhere workers were exploited by employers taking advantage of their desperation.

The exploitation of the **underclass** is a major focus in the novel. The novel emphasizes the need for the lower-class workers to unionize and engage in collective action. The political agenda is clear throughout the novel: Steinbeck argues against the power of big business and its ill-treatment of human beings. The novel also exposes the lack of governmental aid to the struggling poor. Steinbeck keys in on the lack of social welfare programs and the cold-hearted approach employers take toward the poor; in his account, profit trumps humanity. His is a portrait of migrant workers literally starving to death while toiling to sate their employers' greed. The desperate poor are forced to sell their meager belongings to profiteers at less than half their value in a vain attempt to survive. Advertisements promise work in California, but those able to purchase cars and travel west are swindled first by the salesmen and then by the growers. The advertisements prove to be a trick to glut the labor market and drive down pay rates. Steinbeck details the horrible situation in California's immigrant camps, where the Joads briefly stayed, and the brutal treatment the Joad and Wilson families receive from the police. He even made connections between the treatment of the migrant poor and that of **slaves**.

As the novel moves forward, the Joad family slowly unravels; death and jail take two members of the family and another runs off to try his own luck, leaving behind a pregnant wife. The remaining family members move to a government camp, which is a relief for the weary family, but they must eventually move on in search or work. They spend time on a farm where everyone, even the pregnant Rose of Sharon, picks peaches. Here Steinbeck returns to the political agenda of unionization. The Joads realize that their high wages are payment for being strikebreakers. They learn more about the union organizers and discover that one of their friends, Preacher Casey, is the leader. In a dramatic argument, Casey is killed, and Tom Joad takes murderous revenge upon the killer. Tom, who is already on parole, must flee from the police, and his family leaves with him. Ultimately, Tom leaves the family to protect it. He plans to continue Casey's unionizing efforts.

By having the Joads move from one horrific situation to another, Steinbeck emphasizes the difficulties of life during the Depression as well as the day-to-day struggles of migrant farm workers during all time periods. Because of the corruption of the upper-class employers and their unrelenting exploitation of the lower classes, Steinbeck's political commentary focuses on the government's need to provide for the **welfare** of its citizens. The novel concludes with the Joads once again in jeopardy, this time because of a natural disaster. When Rose of Sharon goes into labor, the family is unable to flee. Instead, they huddle on top of the family car, where Rose of Sharon delivers a stillborn child. Although they are completely destitute and the loss of yet another family member has devastated them, Steinbeck ends the novel with an incredible act of kindness. The Joads stumble upon an old man and his grandson. The aged man is starving to death, and Rose of Sharon gives him her breast milk to bring him back to health. Steinbeck uses the humanity of this family to accentuate the contrast with the unfeeling world of those who have financial control over the lives of the poor.

The Grapes of Wrath is considered one of the great works of American fiction, even though its detractors denounced it as **socialist** propaganda. The saga of the Joads was first made into a film just one year after its publication. Director John Ford's eponymous film won two Oscars. It has also inspired songwriters as diverse as **Woody Guthrie**, **Bruce Springsteen**, and Rage Against the Machine.

Suggested Reading
Kevin Hearle and Peter Lisca, eds., The Grapes of Wrath: *Text and Criticism*, 1997; Barbara Heavilin, ed., *The Critical Response to John Steinbeck's* The Grapes of Wrath, 2000; David Wyatt, ed., *New Essays on* The Grapes of Wrath, 1990.

GREAT DEPRESSION

HOLLY ALLEN

The Great Depression was the most serious economic crisis that the United States has ever encountered. It began with the stock market crash of October 1929, which ended a decade of remarkable corporate hegemony, and ended in 1941 when World War II revived the U.S. economy. The intervening years were characterized by watershed developments in the U.S. economy, society, and politics. With the advent of **Franklin Delano Roosevelt's New Deal**, the federal government assumed a much more activist role in U.S. economic and social affairs. Legislation to protect the right to collective bargaining, combined with increasing labor militancy, led to a fundamental shift in U.S. business-labor relations. New Deal social and welfare policies transformed American civic life, creating direct bonds between ordinary citizens and a formerly remote federal government. Such economic and political changes were implemented, in part, to alleviate the widespread turbulence and episodic class conflict that marked the Depression years. Protests ranging from relatively spontaneous anti-eviction demonstrations and food looting to more carefully planned industrial union drives, **strikes**, and boycotts exemplified the heightened social unrest of the decade. Some Americans sought answers to the nation's plight by searching for a usable past, documenting its popular traditions and folk heritage. Many new definitions of Americanism emerged from the Great Depression, influencing national culture for many years to come.

During the Great Depression, the role of the federal government was transformed, as was the nature of the presidency. While Herbert Hoover remained steadfastly committed to longstanding American ideals of rugged **individualism**, community self-help, and a hands-off approach to private enterprise, Franklin Delano Roosevelt responded to the nation's worsening economic crisis in his 1932 campaign by promising "a New Deal for the American people." In the first 100 days of his administration, Franklin Roosevelt introduced an "alphabet soup" of relief and recovery measures, which included programs like the Federal Emergency Relief Administration (FERA), the Agricultural Adjustment Administration (AAA), and the National Recovery Administration (NRA). Such measures, as well as later ones like the Works Progress Administration (WPA), reflected Roosevelt's belief that the federal government had an obligation to assure the well being of its citizens. While some of Roosevelt's initial New Deal measures were later declared unconstitutional and even its most successful programs were arguably ineffective in stimulating economic recovery, his expansion of the role of the federal government and his implementation of a permanent social security system under the **Social Security Act** of 1935 signaled the advent of the U.S. **welfare** state. As a public figure, Roosevelt exemplified the same assertiveness and strategy of direct engagement that characterized his New Deal Administration. Often called "the first modern president," Roosevelt developed a close relationship with the press and with the American people. Always media savvy, he spoke directly and personally to the American people through a range of media outlets, including his weekly series of fireside chats on the radio. The people responded by rallying behind President Roosevelt and supporting his New Deal policies.

If civic life changed dramatically during the Great Depression, so too did the structure of class relationships. Whereas the nation's social and business **elite** had enjoyed remarkable economic and cultural authority in the 1920s, the Depression decade witnessed unprecedented **working-class** militancy as well as populist and radical cultural influences. Indeed, the Great Depression was the most important period for the twentieth-century **labor movement**. In 1935 the relatively moribund craft unionism of the **American Federation of Labor** (AFL) encountered a new rival in the vital industrial unionism of the **Congress of Industrial Organizations** (CIO). The 1930s witnessed the organization of mass-production industries like auto, steel, and electrical products, as well as vital services like the teamsters and bus drivers. Because many of the new unions enrolled all workers in a plant regardless of their job or skill, their ranks expanded to include many workers whom the AFL had excluded, including Eastern European immigrants, African Americans, **Latinos**, and women in unskilled occupations. Another feature of unionism in the 1930s was its radical edge, as **communists** and **socialists** played a key role in organizing some workers. Two strike waves exemplify the militancy and vitality of the industrial union movement in the 1930s. In 1934 San Francisco longshoremen, Minneapolis Teamsters, Auto-Lite workers in Toledo, Ohio, and textile workers all along the Eastern seaboard launched epoch labor demonstrations. Three years later, in the winter and spring of 1937, workers launched hundreds of sit-down strikes, prompting *Time* to note that "sitting down has replaced baseball as the national pastime." Among the highlights of the 1937 strike wave was the sit-down of auto workers in Flint, Michigan, in which the United Auto Workers prevailed over General Motors. Likewise, a contest between steel workers and U.S. Steel resulted in victory for the Steel Workers Organizing Committee. Workers who participated in union organizing drives had new weapons in their arsenal because of the passage of the Wagner Act in 1935, which outlawed yellow-dog contracts (that is, signed promises by workers that they would not join labor unions), summary dismissals of union members, and blacklisting, and which created the National Labor Relations Board (NLRB) to supervise union elections and enforce the guarantee of the right of collective bargaining. The momentum that began in the depths of the Great Depression continued into the war years. By 1945 unions enrolled almost 15 million workers, and about a third of all nonagricultural workers had joined trade unions.

While workers agitated for their rights in labor unions, the broader culture sought for a usable past, which often idealized the "folk" or the "people." Representations of American ideals ranged from communist writings of **Mike Gold** and Meridel LeSueur, to the left-leaning public art of Ben Shahn and Diego Rivera, to the populist novels of **John Steinbeck** and **films** of Frank Capra. Employees on the Public Arts projects and folklorists and photographers working for the Resettlement Administration sought to depict and discover long-standing American ideals of small-town life, folk culture, and traditional gender and family arrangements. While sometimes controversial, particularly when publicly sponsored art or literature expressed subversive themes, this flourishing of an American documentary tradition is one of the greatest legacies of the Great Depression, suggesting how much the nation's cultural landscape, like its politics and economy, was fundamentally altered because of the Great Depression.

Suggested Reading

Eileen Boris and Nelson Lichtenstein, "Industrial Unionism during the Great Depression," in *Major Problems in the History of American Workers* 1991, pp. 361–407; William E. Leuchtenburg, *The F.D.R. Years: On Roosevelt and His Legacy*, 1995; Robert McElvaine, *The Great Depression: America, 1929–1941*, 1984.

GREAT GATSBY, THE

Veronica C. Hendrick

The Great Gatsby is considered the masterpiece of novelist F. Scott Fitzgerald and is a penetrating look at the inner life of the **upper class** during the 1920s.

Francis Scott Fitzgerald was born on September 24, 1896, and died on December 21, 1940. Although he was raised in Saint Paul, Minnesota, he moved to the East Coast of the United States to attend prep school and college. He entered Princeton but failed to graduate. Nonetheless, his writing captures and comments upon the class privilege of such environments.

Fitzgerald's work was especially insightful concerning the "Roaring Twenties" following World War I. It was a period in which great fortunes were made and the mood of the country was optimistic. The **American dream**—the belief that with hard work and a bit of luck any person was capable of rising in social class—was a driving social force. The American public believed that each successive generation would be better off than the previous one and that upward **social mobility** was guaranteed. Fitzgerald worked with this theme and its reverse.

Fitzgerald also focused on the complications of romantic relationships, his own marriage inspiring much of his wiring. Both Fitzgerald and his wife, Zelda Sayre, led wild lives filled with parties and intrigue. The drama in their lives ended badly: Fitzgerald became an alcoholic and suffered mental collapses, while Zelda spent much of her life in and out of mental institutions trying to manage her schizophrenia. Ultimately, Zelda perished in a hospital fire, and Fitzgerald died at the age of forty-four. Their lifestyles were the topic of newspaper stories and gossip mills. They were also reflected in Fitzgerald's second novel, *The Beautiful and Damned* (1922), and can be seen in *The Great Gatsby*.

The Great Gatsby was published in 1925. It is a short novel focusing on life in Long Island, New York, during the 1920s, the halcyon period before the **stock market** crash, the **Great Depression**, and World War II. Underneath the story runs a social commentary about the elitism of the American upper class. The narrator is Nick Carraway, who has just arrived in New York from the Midwest. He is young and naïve. Although it is clear that he has the means and connections to become successful, Nick is just starting to make his way. Nick's naïveté is challenged when his well-established cousin, Daisy Buchanan, invites him to visit her posh home and wealthy community.

Daisy and Nick live near one another, but each town has a different flavor. Daisy lives amid "old money," and her husband, Tom, is representative of this social circle. The Buchanans are not merely wealthy; they have all the required pedigrees for social acceptance: the right family background, listings in the *Social Register*, the proper college degrees, and membership in exclusive **country clubs**. Nonetheless, Daisy and Tom's marriage has many flaws. The open affair between Tom and Myrtle Wilson is one of the many indicators that their lives are empty and corrupt. Tom's brutishness and Daisy's drinking are other signs. Nick, by contrast, lives in a different town, which he jokingly calls West Egg, in contrast to Daisy's East Egg. In West Egg live families with "new money," many of whom had become **social climbers**. Many tried to purchase their entrée into society, but most lacked the breeding to be taken seriously by the old money **elite** of East Egg. Nick lives here because of his youth and his uncertain economic situation. Jay Gatsby, the title character, lives here as well and is the quintessential representative of new money. It is at first unclear where he, or his money, comes from, but something underhanded is clearly part of his economic success. Gatsby does everything to claim refinement and **style**, creating a fictional back story complete with university and military careers. Gatsby has an enormous house with a classical structure and throws lavish parties every weekend. His money is sloshed around like water, but he lacks things that money cannot buy, the main thing being Daisy, his lost love.

The story interweaves the fates of Daisy, Jay, and Nick, each representing a different rung on the social ladder. Nick acts as an intermediary between Gatsby and Daisy, arranging a reunion between the ex-lovers. The affair that begins between the two is short-lived. Even though their affair is obvious to Tom, Daisy does not reject her marriage in the end. However, Daisy is instrumental in causing Gatsby's murder. While driving home after a confrontation between Tom and Gatsby, Daisy has an accident in which she kills the driver of the other car: Myrtle, Tom's mistress. Tom wishes to protect his wife and exact revenge, so he tells Myrtle's husband, Wilson, that Gatsby was the driver. Wilson also believes that Gatsby was Myrtle's lover and, in a fit of rage, murders Gatsby before shooting himself. Gatsby's desire to face his problems is a sharp contrast to Tom's trickery, which emphasizes the falsity of social labels.

Fitzgerald continues his social commentary on the corruption and emptiness of upper-class life at Gatsby's funeral. Although hundreds turned out for his parties, few come to his funeral. One notable exception is a racketeer who helped Gatsby become wealthy; he is one of the few who mourn Gatsby's passing. The funeral highlights the false behavior of the upper class presented in the novel and implies that even mobsters have more heart than the upper crust.

Shaken by what he has witnessed, Nick returns to the Midwest, a metaphor for virtue and pragmatic values. He not only rejects the social elitism and false morality of Daisy's world; he also declines the promise of vast wealth that fueled Gatsby's lifestyle. That is not to say that Nick rejected Gatsby in entirety. Nick was captivated by Gatsby's charm, though he ultimately concludes that Gatsby's greatness came from living out the American dream. Nick believes that Gatsby is the last of his kind because materialism and decay have corrupted that dream.

Suggested Reading

Stanley Cooperman, *F. Scott Fitzgerald's* The Great Gatsby: *A Critical Commentary*, 1965; Katie De Koster, ed. *Readings on* The Great Gatsby, 1998; Dalton Gross, *Understanding* The Great Gatsby: *A Student Casebook to Issues, Sources, and Historical Documents*, 1998.

GREAT SOCIETY

MELISSA A. T. KOTULSKI

The Great Society describes a series of legislative acts passed between 1964 and 1968 and signed into law by President Lyndon Johnson. This flurry of liberal reforms attempted to tackle issues of **poverty**, civil rights, **education**, health, city revitalization, and consumer protection. These acts were enacted in a time when Johnson inherited ideals from the Kennedy administration and civil rights and other social movements were in active phase. The programs resulted from of a series of studies, committees, and congressional acts. The Great Society has had a lasting impact, particularly on education and medical care for poverty-stricken people of the United States because, unlike the **New Deal**, it addressed the underlying causes of poverty. Its central principles of amelioration and opportunity continue to under gird anti-poverty programs.

On March 16, 1964, Johnson declared a **War on Poverty** in a message to Congress in which he submitted the **Economic Opportunity Act** of 1964. The bill passed largely intact and was amended in 1965 with funding to implement programs that worked to educate and train poor children, youths, and adults in cities and rural areas. Of the $962 million in the bill, $727 million was earmarked to support Titles I and II, which created **Job Corps**, Community Action and adult education programs, and voluntary assistance programs for needy children. The bill also created the **Head Start** program, which delivered direct medical, psychological, and educational benefits to poor children.

Federal legislation on poverty during the Great Society was in response to reports and studies that came out in the early 1960s, such as *The Other America* by **Michael Harrington** and the Council of Economic Advisers' report. Harrington showed that 11 million American adults had less than a sixth grade education, while the Council uncovered that one in five Americans were poor, 78 percent of them white. The War on Poverty presented major solutions that ameliorated and exacerbated the conditions of poverty.

Great Society health and education reforms highlighted the socioeconomic and racial disparities of the United States. By 1964, the federal government had no formal **medical care** program, yet still spent $8 billion for health and medical services for the poor. Up through World War II, the American Medical Association (AMA) was a fierce opponent of federal medical programs. Since President Harry Truman's failed health care proposal of 1949, the Kerr-Mills bill was the first limited measure attempting to provide care for the medically needy. Great acceptance of federally funded medical care evolved with health services for Cuban refugees and migrant farm workers in 1962, and Head Start participants and **Appalachian** residents received medical care in 1965. When Democrats won control of Congress in 1964, Johnson contracted a blue-ribbon panel of experts to counter the AMA's resistance to centralized medical care. Chaired by a Houston heart surgeon, the panel reported on the limited access to first-rate medical care in the United States. By 1965, Congress and Johnson passed the bill that enacted Medicare and Medicaid.

The Elementary and Secondary Education Act of 1965 signaled the elevation of education to the status of a right by establishing a statutory federal commitment to equal educational opportunity, and it created a number of new national educational programs to promote school improvement.

Two major pieces of legislation and one report were pivotal in addressing civil rights under the Great Society. The 1964 Civil Rights Act's Titles I, II, VI, and VII were the most important because they dealt with access to public accommodations without regard to race, creed religion, or national origin. They also banned discrimination in federally funded programs, created the Equal Employment Opportunity Commission (EEOC), and expanded voting rights. The 1965 Voting Rights Act supplemented the 1964 act to ensure that African Americans were no longer barred from exercising their fundamental American suffrage freedoms. The 1965 Moynihan Report built on the studies of lower-class life of the 1930s by reporting on the breakdown of the African American family. The mood of the nation shifted in the middle 1960s, and the 1968 Civil Rights Act addressed fair housing but also included strong language against urban rioting. Beginning with the Watts riot in 1965, the mid and late 60s were marred by violence in the **inner cities**. Many of these riots involved African Americans who had grown weary of the slow pace by which **racism** was being addressed.

President Johnson's Model Cities program responded to the flight of whites, white ethnics, and the black **middle class** to the **suburbs**, which Kenneth Jackson dubbed the "crabgrass frontier." This redistribution of **wealth** led to gross disparities in resources for the cities, and the Kerner Commission warned that the United States was "moving toward two societies, one black, one white—separate and unequal." The Housing and Urban Development (HUD) Act planned for federally funded urban development and created the Department of HUD. Declaring that improvements on the quality of city life were the most critical domestic program in the United States, the Demonstration Cities and Metropolitan Development Act programs addressed changes to the urban and metropolitan environment and broadened home loan mortgage and urban sectors insurance, programs for veterans, and flexibility in what was defined as urban.

Consumer protection, environmentalism, eradication of crime, and national culture were also addressed by the Great Society. Most notably, in 1965 **Ralph Nader** began his lifelong stance as a consumer advocate lawyer. His advocacy and book *Unsafe at Any Speed* led up to the passage of the National Traffic and Motor Vehicle Safety Act and Highway Safety Act of 1966.

The Great Society attempted to tap into the idealism of the 1960s by creating programs and legislation to correct the pressing issues of the day. By 1968, riots in U.S. cities, assassinations of key political leaders, the budgetary demands of the Vietnam War, and the election of Richard Nixon shifted the outlook of many Americans. Programs of the Great Society ended with mixed success, in part because of inefficient distribution of funding and the impatience of Americans awaiting fulfillment of Great Society promises.

Since Johnson left office in 1968, scholars and politicians alike have debated the meaning of the Great Society. For conservatives, the Great Society surpassed even the New Deal in its excesses. They charge that it was wasteful, expensive, and antithetical to the American spirit of **self-reliance**; created inefficient federal bureaucracies; and allowed the government to usurp roles best left to the private sector. Liberal critics of the Great Society charge that many programs excluded those being served from the decision-making process, that they were often paternalistic, and that most programs were grossly under-funded and doomed to fail. A few see the Great Society as cruel in that it created rising expectations that it could not fulfill. Liberals also tend to cite expenditures on the Vietnam War as the major reason why the War on Poverty was also abandoned. Nonetheless, between 1965 and 1970, 8 million were raised out of poverty as a result of the Great Society's programs. Many of the programs implemented by the Great Society are still in effect, and its overall legacy continues to have an impact on contemporary social and political discourse.

Suggested Reading

John A. Andrews III, *Lyndon Johnson and the Great Society*, 1998; Lawson Bowling, *Shapers of The Great Debate on the Great Society: A Biographical Dictionary*, 2004; Sidney M. Milkis and Jerome M. Mileur, eds., *The Great Society and the High Tide of Liberalism*, 2005.

GRUNGE AND PUNK CULTURE

See Punk and Grunge Culture.

GUARANTEED ANNUAL INCOME

ROBERT E. WEIR

Guaranteed annual income is a plan that would provide families and individuals with a minimum amount of money irrespective of whether they earned it. Its advocates contain surprising numbers of those on both the political left and the right, with the former seeing it a form of income redistribution rooted in social justice and the latter as a better alternative to **welfare** and as inducing more incentives than the current income tax policy. Its supporters have included Richard Nixon, George McGovern, and the **Rev. Martin Luther King Jr.** There are numerous proposals for instituting a guaranteed annual income, but the three major ones are a guaranteed annual wage, the negative income tax, and the universal demogrant.

A guaranteed annual **wage** (GAW) is generally part of an employment contract that is generally negotiated by a labor union. Under such a contract employees are assured of either a certain number of hours per year or of a compensatory payment to make up the gap between that minimum number and the actual hours worked. Such an arrangement has been used in industries that are subject to seasonal **unemployment** or whose labor needs tend to fluctuate depending on orders, contract bids, or general economic conditions. Labor within food processing plants, for example, is dependent on the harvest, while employment within industries that rely on federal contracts can wax and wane according to the contract cycle. Employers sometimes agree to provide a guaranteed annual wage because it stabilizes the workforce and relieves them of the necessity of training new employees during peak production periods. It also ensures that highly skilled workers will not sell their labor to competitors. The GAW first became widespread after World War II, and a contract negotiated between the United Auto Workers and Ford in 1955 served as a model for subsequent arrangements. Despite widespread **deindustrialization** from the 1970s on, approximately 15 percent of union contracts still contain GAW clauses.

The negative income tax (NIT) is another way of securing a guaranteed annual income. It was first proposed by the economist George Stigler in 1946 and, in a form with built-in incentives, has enjoyed the support of conservative economists such as Milton Friedman. A negative income tax reverses the logic of the current income tax system, which taxes income above a certain level. A NIT would set a floor income for families and individuals and those earning below that level would receive a check from the government. Incentives could be built into the system by also establishing reduction rates and lower income tax rates for those who receive no NIT benefits. If, for example, a $20,000 floor was established for a family of four, a dollar-for-dollar reduction of income up to that level would provide recipients little incentive to work. However, a multiplier reduction rate could be implemented that allows employees to keep a percentage of all that they earn up to the floor while paying the remainder in taxes. A 10 percent tax on even a very low wage, thus, increases a family's income dramatically. For example, $5,000 of earned wages effectively raises family income to $24,500 per year. A negative income tax might also adopt a middle **progressive taxation** level in which a ceiling is established beyond which no NIT tax benefits are received. The government could, for example, declare that $75,000 was the maximum level at which one could get any benefit and create a sliding income scale for what can be written off between $20,000 and $75,000.

For its advocates the beauty of the NIT is that it would eliminate many current programs, some of which are costly and others of which have built-in limits. With the NIT there would no need for unemployment compensation, **Social Security**, or most welfare direct subsidies. Some economists also link NIT proposals to the idea of a **flat tax** that would eliminate most (if not all) deductions, simplify the tax code, and provide greater incentive for high achievers. Some see the current progressive taxation system as unfairly taxing those who obtain high incomes. The NIT would drastically reduce taxes on the wealthy.

The flat tax also figures prominently into the universal demogrant (UD) scheme, which is simpler than the NIT. Under a UD program every citizen (or family) would, simply, be given a tax-free check in the amount the government determines is adequate for survival. All other income would then be taxed at a flat rate.

The guaranteed annual income has many detractors. One objection is that it is regressive in that the tax burden is far greater for those with low to moderate income than for those with fortunes. Others see it as simplistic and level some of the same charges as are targeted at the way the **poverty line** is currently calculated. Any chosen floor is likely to be arbitrary and ignore mitigating circumstances such as regional standards of living, employment opportunities, local **transportation** costs, specialized medical needs, and regional energy costs. Still others simply doubt that complex social problems can be reduced to one-size-fits-all formulas and suspect that schemes for a guaranteed annual income are back-door attempts to dismantle programs for the needy.

There is also great disagreement over how any program would be funded. Proposals run the gamut from income and **sales taxes** to funding through **lotteries** or pollution credits. A pilot program in Dauphin, Manitoba, is being monitored, as are modified plans in Portugal and Alaska.

Suggested Reading

Milton Friedman, *Capitalism and Freedom*, 1962; Harry Katz and Thomas Kochan, *An Introduction to Industrial Relations*, 2000; Martin Luther King Jr. *Where Do We Go From Here: Chaos or Community*, 1967; Robert Theobald, *Free Men and Free Markets*, 1965.

GUTHRIE, WOODY (July 14, 1912?–October 3, 1967)

RON BRILEY

Woodrow Wilson Guthrie was a prolific folk singer and writer from Oklahoma whose music celebrated the common men and women of America during the **Great Depression**. While Guthrie's "This Land Is Your Land" is often proclaimed as a patriotic anthem, the song's verses denouncing social and economic injustice in the United States are often ignored.

Guthrie was born in Okemah, Oklahoma. His perception of humanity and political ideas were grounded in an agrarian tradition of protest in Oklahoma, where a strong **Socialist Party** operated before World War I. He was equally shaped by a radical Christian tradition that viewed Jesus as the champion of the poor and meek, who would inherit the earth and drive the moneychangers out of the temple. He also endured a tragic family history and the experience of his generation with the Depression and Dust Bowl of the 1930s.

Guthrie's father, Charlie, was an entrepreneur whose real estate schemes were unsuccessful. The family was also beset by a series of fires, which led to the death of Guthrie's sister, Clara, and serious injury to his father. The fires were blamed on Guthrie's mother, Nora, who was institutionalized, suffering from Huntington's chorea, a degenerative disease of the central nervous system that eventually claimed Woody as well.

Guthrie's father moved the family to Pampa, Texas, in 1927, and Guthrie joined them three years later. Guthrie married and attempted to support a young family on his meager earnings as a musician and sign painter. Responding to the impact of the Depression and Dust Bowl on the residents of the Texas panhandle, Guthrie penned such songs as "Dusty Old Dust," with its chorus of "So Long, It's Been Good to Know You."

In 1936 Guthrie, like many Dust Bowl refugees, journeyed to California, where he found work on Los Angeles radio station KFVD, teaming with Maxine Crossman for the popular show "Here Comes Woody and Lefty Lou." While working at

KFVD, Guthrie came into contact with Ed Robbins, an organizer for the **Communist Party** (CPUSA). Guthrie began to perform at party functions and wrote a column called "Woody Sez" for *The People's Daily World*, denouncing the **capitalist** system and the injustices of Depression-era America.

Guthrie's politics were becoming too radical for the progressive Fred Burke who owned KFVD, and Guthrie departed for New York City in 1939. In February 1940 Guthrie wrote "This Land Is Your Land" in response to what he considered the shallow patriotism of Irving Berlin's "God Bless America." After performing at a concert to benefit John Steinbeck's Committee for Agricultural Workers, Guthrie was discovered by folklorist Alan Lomax, who helped Guthrie record his first commercial effort, *Dust Bowl Ballads*. The Oklahoman

Woody Guthrie playing a guitar that has a sticker attached reading "This Machine Kills Fascists," ca. 1943. Courtesy of the Library of Congress.

also hosted two radio shows for CBS, but when sponsors pressured Guthrie to abandon his "Woody Sez" column for the communist *Daily Worker*, Guthrie left New York City and secured employment with the Bonneville Power Administration, a series of dams on the Columbia River. Inspired by the potential for public power, Guthrie penned such classic songs as "Roll On, Columbia" and "Pastures of Plenty." In 1966 Washington state honored Guthrie by giving his name to one of the Bonneville power substations.

In 1941 Guthrie accepted an invitation from **Pete Seeger** to return to New York City and join the Almanac Singers, who supported the organizing efforts of the **Congress of Industrial Organizations** and opposed American entrance into World War II. Following Hitler's invasion of the Soviet Union in June 1941, the Almanac Singers reversed course and adopted an antifascist interventionist position exemplified by such songs as "The Reuben James." In 1943 Guthrie wrote his autobiography *Bound for Glory*, extolling the virtues of the common people and detailing Guthrie's early struggles. During World War II, Guthrie served in the Merchant Marine with his singing partner Cisco Houston. Near the war's conclusion, Guthrie was drafted into the Army for a year's service, but the discipline of military life did not set well with Guthrie.

During the post–World War II period, Guthrie's opposition to the **Cold War** was apparent in his support of the Progressive Party candidacy of former Vice President Henry Wallace. Guthrie, however, was spared the inquisition of the second **Red Scare** and **McCarthyism**, as he was diagnosed with Huntington's chorea and was institutionalized from 1954 until his death in 1967. Guthrie never denounced his radical views. It is unclear whether Guthrie actually joined the CPUSA, but he dismissed the question by quipping, "I ain't a communist necessarily, but I been in the red all my life." Guthrie's legacy remains a collection of over 1,000 songs celebrating the struggles of **working-class** men and women.

Suggested Reading

Ed Craig, *Ramblin' Man: The Life and Times of Woody Guthrie*, 2004; Bryan K. Garman, *A Race of Singers: Whitman's Working Class Hero from Guthrie to Springsteen*, 2000; Joe Klein, *Woody Guthrie: A Life*, 1980; Robert Santelli and Emily Davidson, eds., *Hard Travelin': The Life and Legacy of Woody Guthrie*, 1999.